W9-BPS-356

Reading and Writing
Teaching for the Connections

Reading and Writing
Teaching for the Connections

Bill Harp
Northern Arizona University

Jo Ann Brewer
Northern Arizona University

Harcourt Brace Jovanovich, Publishers

San Diego   New York   Chicago   Austin   Washington, D.C.
London   Sydney   Tokyo   Toronto

To Cassi and Hillary.

May their continuing acquisition of literacy be nurtured by knowledgeable and caring teachers.

ISBN: 0-15-575491-2
Library of Congress Catalog Card Number: 90-82257
Printed in the United States of America

Photograph credits
Cover: © Stephen Frisch/Stock, Boston
Page 1: © Stock, Boston
Page 95: © Harriet Gans/The Image Works
Page 173: © Michael Hagan
Page 285: © Spencer Grant/Monkmeyer Press Photo Service
Page 415: © The Picture Cube

Preface

The title of this book, *Reading and Writing: Teaching for the Connections,* is indicative of its contents. Because reading and writing are based on knowledge of language, there are sound arguments for connecting reading instruction with writing instruction. We take a broad view of instruction that considers simultaneously a child's growth in language, reading, and writing. We believe that there are connections among all these areas and that teachers should honor those connections and use each area of learning to support growth in the other areas.

We have learned much about literacy in the past fifteen years—that children develop the abilities to read and write in much the same ways they learn to speak. We know that literacy develops best when children have compelling reasons to read and write—to communicate important ideas to others. This textbook was conceived to help preservice teachers make the leap from reading instruction focused on skill mastery, the dominant mode of instruction in many classrooms, to a more holistic view of literacy development. To accomplish this goal we present a sound theoretical base for approaching reading instruction developmentally and tie that knowledge to informed instructional practice. Instructional practice is described here in enough detail so that beginning teachers can either follow it or adapt it to fit their classrooms.

The reality in American schools is that many reading programs are based on learning both a sub-skill and a skill, and on eventually putting these together in order to comprehend writing. This book builds bridges between the holistic view of literacy development and more traditional practices in reading instruction. Teachers need to know how to help children learn most effectively and how to incorporate the skills of reading into a program based on a much broader view of reading and writing instruction rather than on skills programs alone. Because many schools use a commercial reading program, teachers must make professional decisions about reading selections and activities assigned to the children to increase their reading abilities. We offer many examples of ways in which teachers can progress from traditional bases to writing, to thematic units, and to the use of children's literature.

This book is made up of five parts. The first describes how language and reading and writing develop and how they are integrally connected in a child's life. The second part deals with decisions teachers make and suggests that certain choices will enhance instruction. The third part presents three approaches to reading instruction: basal readers, language experience, and literature. The fourth part presents information about literacy skills that will help children grow in literacy abilities. The final part ties literacy instruction firmly to other subject areas—the arts, social studies, and science. Finally, an epilogue describes in detail how four practicing elementary teachers apply the theories in this book in their classrooms. Each has a unique approach, yet each thinks carefully about learners and about bringing them to literacy.

Literacy experiences are rewarding for children and for the teachers who instruct them. Teachers experience the joy of watching literacy develop—they watch children grow, listen to them as they struggle with the processes, and learn from them. Teachers can help children learn to love reading and writing. In a nation where many adults do not read books at all and where *TV Guide* is the best-selling weekly periodical, instructional changes are imperative. Teaching children *how* to read and write is not enough; we must also teach them to *want* to read and write.

Two features of this book that will be especially useful to both instructors and students are the discussion questions and the suggestions for applications. The discussion questions focus on important, sometimes controversial, issues in literacy. The suggestions for applications invite students to put the things they have learned into practice.

Reading and Writing: Teaching for the Connections is intended primarily for undergraduate classes in the teaching of reading. And most of the references are for readers new to the literature on the development of literacy. However, teachers revisiting the ideas involved in helping children learn to read and write can also find material to challenge their thinking. This will be particularly true of teachers who wish to move from traditional reading instruction to more holistic literacy instruction. This book is also appropriate for courses in which reading and language arts methods are integrated.

We wish to thank Julia Berrisford and the other staff members at Harcourt Brace Jovanovich for their support and assistance. We also recognize the invaluable work of Meredy Amyx and Cece Munson, whose work in the production of this book was outstanding. We express our sincere appreciation to the administration of the Center for Excellence in Education at Northern Arizona University for their support.

Our dreams for the quality of this book would never have come true without the assistance of some other very talented persons. We are indebted to Kathy Koch for her diligence in editing the original manuscript and for giving us both support and helpful suggestions. The reviewers were extremely helpful in both challenging our thinking and in confirming many of our views. They are Tom Barrett, University of Wisconsin; Jack Bagford, University of Iowa; Bernice Cullinan, New York University; Mary Gates, Meadowwood Reading Clinic (Pickerington, Ohio); Lee Galda, University of Georgia; Janie Knight, Memphis State University; Kathryn Koch, University of Wisconsin-Green Bay; and Helen Newcastle, California State University, Long Beach.

We want our readers to know that the teaching strategies we advocate are working for real, practicing teachers. And so to those very talented teachers who wrote pieces for the epilogue we are sincerely grateful. Kay Stritzel, Tom Wrightman, Cheri McLain, and Hilary Sumner were generous in inviting our readers into their classrooms to see how they plan integrated curriculum activities for their children.

And finally, we thank Kati Field who shared with us a piece of her writing about herself as a writer. Kati fulfills our belief that literacy experiences can be joyful for children.

Bill Harp
Jo Ann Brewer

About the Authors

Bill Harp

Bill Harp's elementary school teaching experience ranges from Head Start through sixth grade. After completing a doctorate at the University of Oregon, he taught at the University of Delaware and Oregon State University. He left OSU to be an elementary school principal, but returned to OSU to coordinate the elementary education program. He is now the Coordinator of Graduate Studies at the Center for Excellence in Education at Northern Arizona University in Flagstaff.

Dr. Harp's publications include the popular "When the Principal Asks" column that ran in *The Reading Teacher* during 1988 and 1989. More recently he has edited a volume on assessment and evaluation in whole language classrooms. He has also been active in the International Reading Association, holding offices in local council and state organizations, and he is a frequent IRA conference speaker.

Jo Ann Brewer

Jo Ann Brewer has many years of teaching experience in kindergarten and primary classrooms and has been an Assistant Superintendent for Instruction. Her experience includes teaching in culturally diverse settings and in open schools. She earned a doctorate in early childhood education at Texas Tech University and currently teaches early childhood and elementary education courses at Northern Arizona University. She is especially interested in language development and children's literature.

Dr. Brewer is active in the National Association for the Education of Young Children and the International Reading Association and is frequently on the conference programs of both organizations. She is completing an introductory textbook in early childhood education.

Contents

Chapter 5
Supporting the Reading/Writing Program   144

Chapter 8
When Children Write Their Own Reading Material   255

Part IV

Developing Reading/Writing Abilities   285

Chapter 9
Using Cueing Systems   287

Chapter 10
Assisting Children with Comprehension   321

Chapter 11
Assisting Children with Content-Area Reading   378

Part V
Building Reading/Writing Connections   415

Chapter 12
Teaching Reading and Writing through Social Studies and the Sciences   417

Chapter 13
Teaching Reading and Writing through the Arts   436

Part I

Reading and Writing as Communication

The first part of this book explores the development of language, writing, and reading as parallel processes used in communication. We believe that literacy processes (writing and reading) are learned in much the same way that oral language is learned—through natural, authentic practice in real communicative contexts. Instead of first teaching the subskills of reading and writing, teachers should create situations in which children use oral language, writing, and reading for real communication and problem solving.

How you view reading and writing will profoundly affect the way you teach. Chapters 1 through 3 provide background knowledge about the process of developing oral and written language. This knowledge is valuable as you begin to observe children and draw conclusions about the appropriateness of various classroom activities and experiences.

Chapter 1

The Development of Language

Chapter Overview

- Language is a system of communication on which members of social groups agree. Reading and writing are language-based processes. All languages have universal characteristics: they are arbitrary, rule governed, and changing.

- Language systems—phonology, morphology, semantics, syntax, and pragmatics—help to describe the language and its uses in a given context.

- Learning language is a complex process. Children learn meaning, form, and functions of language all at once, and it is impossible to describe any of the processes accurately in isolation.

- Learning to use oral language and learning to read and write are closely related processes.

- Classroom teachers can help children increase their competence in the use of language.

In the author's note at the beginning of her book *Flossie and the Fox*, Patricia McKissack (1986) observes that long before she was a writer, she was a listener. She listened to family stories and to the language used around her. McKissack is not alone. Each reader and writer is also a "listener" and a participator in the language around him or her. Each person who comes to be literate learns about language in its oral and written forms by becoming a part of his or her speaking, reading, and writing community.

This book is about literacy, the ability to read and write our language. It is about helping children achieve literacy so they can manage easily the functional uses of written language—things like applying for a job, filling out forms, getting a driver's license—and so they can also appreciate the power and beauty of words and take pleasure in the human ability to share thoughts and ideas through the medium of written language.

Literacy is best conceptualized as a continuum on which anyone's degree of skill could be plotted but on which there is no point labeled *"enough* literacy." Even the most well-read person you know becomes more literate in the course of reading new material or employing a new structure in writing. The beginning point of the continuum is the development of language. Once past that first phase, children are engaged in learning about oral language and printed language at the same time. For example, a child may be using two- or three-word sentences, be writing in scribbles, and be beginning to recognize the difference between the Cheerios and the Froot Loops boxes. As individuals move along the continuum, they are able to use speaking, writing, and reading to meet their needs. Since language learning is integral to the process of becoming literate, we will begin by discussing language, what we know about children learning language, and how that knowledge will help us in aiding children as they become literate.

What Is Language?

Characteristics

Language can be defined rather narrowly to include only spoken or sign language or much more broadly to include any system of communication used by a social community. For our purposes, language is defined as a system of communication used by human beings that is produced either orally or by signs. Since this is a book about reading and writing, we are also focusing on language that can be extended to its written form.

Language has some characteristics that help to define it. First, it is rule governed. For example, all languages have rules that determine how words are ordered in sentences. These rules are learned intuitively by native speakers of the language, and only those speakers who make a scientific study of the language are likely to be able to verbalize the rules. To illustrate such rules, hold up four new yellow pencils and ask a group to describe what you have in your hand. If they say "pencils," ask for more detail. They might say "long pencils." If asked again, they might say "long yellow pencils." Finally, they would say "four long yellow pencils." The placement of number words in the series of modifiers is governed by a rule. Native English speakers would never say "yellow four pencils."

A second characteristic of language is that it is arbitrary. There are no logical connections between the sounds that we use to label a certain object and the object itself. It is merely by common social agreement that we use a particular combination of sounds to represent that object.

Third, language is dynamic, always changing. New words are constantly entering our lexicon and others are being discarded. Meanings are also changing. With a little thought, you can probably list thirty or forty

The animated expression of this student of sign language shows that communication is taking place.
© Laimute E. Druskis/Stock, Boston

words that have been added within the last five years and ten or so that have changed meanings. *Longhair* is a good example of a changed expression: before the 1960s, when it began to refer to the personal appearance of youths of the counterculture, it meant a lover of classical music.

■ Systems

Language is composed of several systems: phonology, morphology, syntax, semantics, and pragmatics.

Phonology is the sound system. It includes the sounds that we use to make words, rules for combining the sounds, and patterns of stress and intonation. Different languages use different sounds and allow different combinations of sounds in words. Some languages, for example, make use

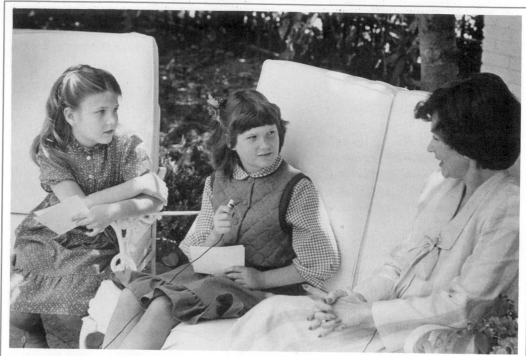

Young interviewers for cable television record their conversation with Texas First Lady
Linda Gale White.
© Bob Daemmrich/Stock, Boston

of clicks that are absent from English. In some, differences in pitch indicate different meanings for the same combination of sounds. The task of the child is to learn to distinguish differences in phonemes—the smallest units of sound in a language—and intonational patterns that signal different meanings.

The morphological system of language deals in the smallest units of meaning—morphemes—rather than units of sound. Some words are morphemes, some are combinations of morphemes. *Cow* is an example of a word that is a morpheme. *Cows* is a combination of the free morpheme *cow* and the bound morpheme *s*. The *s* is bound because it signals meaning but cannot stand alone. Other morphemes signal changes of tense, person, or number rather than changing the meaning of the word. Mastering English morphology includes learning how to form possessives, plurals, and verb tenses. Children learning to read and write have to attend to meaning as conveyed by various morphological forms.

The syntactical system of a language contains the rules for combining words into phrases and sentences and for transforming sentences into other sentences. The syntactical system provides us with information about word meanings because of their place in a sentence. For example, if you heard

The cribbet zooked the lattle.

you would know that the event took place in the past and that *zooked* was something done to the *lattle*. Children mastering the syntactical system learn how to construct negatives, questions, compound sentences, passives, imperatives, and eventually complex sentences that employ embedded forms.

As children read, they often rely on syntactical cues when attempting to decipher an unknown word. In a sentence such as

The boy ran down the _____.

the blank can contain only a limited number of words. You might be able to think of twenty or thirty choices, such as *hill, road, path, fence, sidewalk, highway,* and *hall,* but, out of all the words we might know, only a small number will fit into the sentence pattern. Of course, the *the* preceding the blank is a noun marker and provides some meaning cues to the reader.

The semantic system governs meaning at the word and sentence level. Learning semantics means acquiring vocabulary and meanings associated with words. Children commonly use words that are part of adult language, but assign their own meanings. A child may use a word such as *horsie* to stand for all large four-legged animals. Mastering the semantic system means that a child must learn word meanings and relationships between and among words. Children learning to read and write use the semantic system in order to obtain meaning from sentences and passages. There is not a one-to-one correspondence between a word and its referent. For example, when readers encounter *cat* in print, each may picture a different cat according to individual experience, but they also share enough meaning to understand the author's use of the term.

Finally, the child learning language must internalize the rules for using language in social interactions. Speakers must learn to adapt their language to achieve their communicative goals in various situations. Pragmatics is the use of language to express intentions and to get things done. Social uses of language include pragmatics and the rules of politeness. For example, some cultures have rules about younger people initiating conversations with older people, and all have rules for appropriate language for use in church, on the playground, and at the dinner table. A speaker of any language would not be considered competent in that language before mastering the basic rules for language use in various social contexts. Hymes (1974) described the ability to use language and to use it correctly in various interactions as "communicative competence."

A child who understands the pragmatic applications of language will be able to draw on that knowledge as an aid in comprehension. For example, in reading a passage of a story that described interactions between children and grandparents, readers would probably expect more polite language than children would use among themselves. One third-grader, writing a story about baby dinosaurs, made up some words that he identified as "dinosaur baby talk," obviously understanding that what constitutes acceptable language varies in different contexts.

Early Development of Language

Language development follows a fairly predictable sequence, individual variations notwithstanding. Most children move from differentiated crying (crying that varies in sound, depending on stimulus—hunger, wetness, tiredness, and so on) through cooing, babbling, and one-word sentences. Soon they will deliver longer utterances and learn to produce negatives and questions. At the same time, children's comprehension of spoken language is developing rapidly. By the time they begin school, children will have mastered most of the basic forms in their native language. The chart in Figure 1.1 summarizes typical language development for the first four years of life.

Theories of Language Development

As teachers of reading and writing, we all operate with theories of how language and reading and writing are developed. These theories are important because they influence our choice of materials, strategies, and evaluation systems. For instance, teachers who believe that language learning occurs in small, logical steps, shaped by a system of rewards and punishments, will favor a reading program that emphasizes skill mastery of small steps. Those who believe that language (and therefore reading and writing) is learned more holistically will see the learning of reading as a process best supported by experiences that emphasize the wholeness of language. It is important, then, to become aware of the theoretical explanations for the process of learning language and to begin to consider ways of putting your beliefs into practice in a classroom.

Theorists of language development fall into three basic groups: the behaviorists, the linguistic theorists, and the interactionists. All of them attempt to answer the questions of (1) the role of other speakers, (2) the influence of the environment, and (3) the importance of individual response in developing language. From our observations of children and our view of learning in general, the interactionist view best reflects how children learn language.

Stage	Age range	Mean length of utterance (average number of words per sentence)	Characteristics	Typical sentences
I	12–26 months	1.00–2.00	Vocabulary consists mainly of nouns and verbs with a few adjectives and adverbs; word order preserved	Mommy bye-bye. Big doggie. Baby bath.
II	27–30 months	2.00–2.50	Use of inflections; correct use of plurals; use of past tense, use of *be*, definite and nondefinite articles, some prepositions	Dolly in bed. Them pretty. Milk's all gone. Cars go fast.
III	31–34 months	2.50–3.00	Use of yes-no questions, *wh-* questions (who, what, where); use of negatives and imperatives	Daddy come home? Susie no want milk. Put the baby down.
IV	35–40 months	3.00–3.75	Embedding one sentence within another	I think it's red. Know what I saw? That's the truck Mommy buyed me.
V	41–46 months	3.75–4.50	Coordination of simple sentences and propositional relations	I went to Bob's and I had ice cream. I like bunnies 'cause they're cute. Jenny and Cindy are sisters.

Figure 1.1 Stages of linguistic development, according to Brown (1973).
SOURCE: Joyce Ury Dumtschin, "Recognize Language Development and Delay in Early Childhood," *Young Children* 43 (March 1988): 19. Copyright © 1973 by National Association for the Education of Young Children (Washington, D.C.). Reprinted by permission.

Behaviorist View

The behaviorist view of language learning describes the acquisition of language as being dependent on contingencies and regards imitation as highly valuable in the process of learning. Behaviorists see imitation as a shortcut to behavior without the laborious process of shaping each and every verbal response. According to the behaviorists, the imitation does not have to be an exact copy of the original in order to qualify as imitation, nor does it have to occur immediately. They note that children often parrot words or phrases they have heard. The behaviorist view does not offer a good explanation for regressions in children's language and resistance of children's language to modification (Gleason, 1985). Behaviorists focus primarily on reinforcement rather than on the intent of the child or the child's knowledge of rules.

A reading program that reflected the behaviorist view of language development would consist of practicing the elements of reading and combining the elements in a predetermined sequence. For example, children might learn to respond to a presentation of the letter *m* by saying "mmmm." Teachers would control the reward system, perhaps passing out tokens for correct responses and withholding them for incorrect ones.

Linguistic View

Some theorists look at language acquisition from a linguistic point of view. They explain the rapid acquisition of language in young children by concluding that language is basically inherent in the human brain and only needs social triggering to begin its rapid development. Chomsky (1965) described a Language Acquisition Device (a structure in the brain) that is vital in acquiring language. This device allows the child to process language input and generate language that reflects a knowledge of language structures. Proponents of the linguistic view believe that the child's linguistic environment does not suffice to explain how the child discovers adult grammar. Arguments in support of the linguistic view are that only man has the biological equipment for producing speech, that it is almost impossible to suppress language in humans, and that the sequence for language learning is basically the same for all human beings.

Interactionist View

Interactionists are theorists who look at language as being learned through interaction. Interactionists "assume that many factors (e.g., social, linguistic, maturational/biological, and cognitive) affect the course of development and that these factors are mutually dependent upon, interact with and modify one another" (Gleason, 1985, p. 188). The cognitive interactionists rely heavily on the work of Piaget and the idea of constructivism in explaining language acquisition. To the interactionists, children's language reflects cognitive development, and language learning is governed by the same basic processes that underlie other learning. Social interactionists recognize that human beings possess the specialized physiological equipment for producing speech and that cognitive development is tied to language development, but they focus on the use of language as a tool for interaction.

Interactionists regard intentionality as critical in language development and stress the importance of the linguistic environment for the child learning language. Children are constantly producing hypotheses and testing them in social situations. Evidence to support the interactionist theory includes the early learning of social words such as *mama, dada,* and *bye-bye.* Interactionists also point to the errors children make (such as *goed* and *runned*) as reflecting the generalizations that children have made about language. They explain regressions in language in terms of the child's application of new knowledge or interactions in new social situations.

Teachers who believe that children are the principal agents in their own language development will allow children to choose much of their reading material and will provide instruction when an individual displays a need for it, rather than on a predetermined schedule. The reward system will be primarily intrinsic: a feeling of success at each step in reading and writing spurs the child on to the next achievement.

■ Principles of Language Development

Most of us have little experience, if any, with children who have not learned to communicate through either oral or sign language. We sometimes forget that the process is not a magical one; children do have to learn to use language, and it does take time and effort. Observers of young children learning language have derived some principles of language acquisition: language learning is self-generated, informal, active, holistic, and variable (Jaggar, 1985; Butler and Turbill, 1984; Halliday, 1982). These principles represent an interactionist point of view in explaining language development.

Language Learning Is Self-Generated
To say that language learning is a self-generated, creative process is to say that the learning is controlled by the learner and does not require external motivation. Most parents think they reward their children for language production, and in fact they do, at least for the first few words. But consider the typical weekday morning at home, when Johnny can't find his lunch money, Susan can't find her shoes, the washing machine is running over, the dog is chewing up Mom's new contract, the telephone is ringing, and the toast is burning. Baby, sitting in the high chair and studiously experimenting with the effects of gravity on oatmeal, says "down" for the first time. Who attends to and rewards that language?

  This illustration does not imply that language learning does not require other people. To learn language does require social contact; no child learns language in a vacuum. It just means that children in situations of language use will learn to speak without reward for each word learned. Communication with significant others is enough to keep the child learning. The best motivation for gaining literacy is the example of significant others. When teachers and others share the excitement they find in written words, they provide children with a powerful incentive to learn to read and write.

Language Learning Is Informal
Learning of language occurs without formal instruction. Parents do not give language lessons to their children. With the exception of such rituals as "peek-a-boo" and "this little piggy," parents rarely teach language directly. They play with children, sing with them, make cookies with them, show them the world, and supply words to label the environment, but they do not focus on teaching the child to speak. Participating with the child in

daily living is the focus, and language comes as one result. Language is learned through use in meaningful contexts, not through talking about it or analyzing it.

The other day we observed a child of about four watching his father prune a tree in their yard. Although we could not hear their conversation, we could imagine that the child was asking all kinds of questions: "Why are you doing that? What will happen to the tree next? What will happen to the limbs? What are you going to do with the pieces that you cut off?" and on and on. The father, in answering the child's questions, was helping the child learn language. The child probably learned the names of the tools that the father was using and some vocabulary related to the process of pruning a tree. In contrast, consider the absurdity of telling a child, "Today we are going to learn the vocabulary for tree pruning. This is a limb. This is a shear." No parent does such a foolish thing. Children learn language in the process of living in a social situation and participating in activities with others.

We are not suggesting that children learning to read and write will never have instruction. Rather, we are suggesting that instruction take place in a context that is meaningful to the learner and that the instruction be focused on accomplishing communication rather than on isolating the forms of language.

Language Learning Is Active

Learning the labels that we use to name a cat and a dog is a good illustration of the active nature of language learning. Suppose that a child is approached by a cat. The child may know the word *cat* and call the animal "cat." The nearest adult will probably respond, "Yes, that is a cat." If the child had said "dog," the adult would probably have answered, "No, that's not a dog. It's a cat." Rarely would anyone point out to the child the salient characteristics that distinguish a cat from a dog (partly because it is almost impossible to do so). The child must take the label *cat* and decide what it is about this particular animal that makes it not a dog.

Children are continually engaging in such active learning processes in learning to communicate. They need to have opportunities for active involvement in learning to read and write. For example, children who need more materials for an art project can be encouraged to write a list of supplies needed. Some will be able to use only scribbles or symbols at first, but experience will teach them that they must use particular symbols in order to make the message useful. They will apply problem-solving skills by copying the word *glue* from the glue bottle or discovering other strategies that get them what they need. Active learning also occurs when a class has memorized a poem by rote. The teacher displays the words on a chart for the first time and allows the children to try to read the poem on their

Everyday settings are the language laboratories for children, and social interactions are the exercises.
© Mimi Forsyth/Monkmeyer Press Photo Service

own before supplying the words for them. The moment of triumphant success brings joy to children and teacher alike.

Language Learning Is Holistic

The process is holistic in that children learn about the forms and functions of language all at once. Phonetics (sounds), semantics (meanings), syntax (word order), and pragmatics (rules for using language) all work together simultaneously. A child attempting to ask for a cookie learns to approximate the phonemes in *cookie*, at the same time learns what to expect when the approximation is close enough, and learns that it is of no value to ask her infant brother for a cookie. No one would suggest that language be broken into artificial, discrete units to make it easier to learn.

Language development and the development of literacy are closely related. For years, it has been generally accepted that knowledge of language was required before children could extend that knowledge to the written language system. The newer research does not in any way diminish the importance of a child's language in the development of literacy, but it looks at literacy as developing along with language. In other words, several years ago it was popular to believe that children should not have any experience with reading and writing until they had a firm grasp of the spoken language. As observers of young children now know, children are learning about written language systems before they have mastered the oral language system. Young children in a literate society such as ours begin to explore the written language system at a very early age and concurrently with their growing command of oral language.

If we know that language is not learned by practicing its components outside the process of using it, then it follows that learning reading and writing must also be a holistic process that involves children in actual experiences that require reading and writing. Children learning written language begin to label their scribbles, then insist that their writing says something. The focus of their work in written language is communication. No parent would approach teaching a child to talk by saying, "Today you will practice pronouncing all the nouns on this list. Then tomorrow we will practice some verbs." Yet instruction in reading and writing often requires children to practice some part of the process in isolation from the rest. For example, children might be asked to underline the plurals in sentences that have no meaning for them. Instruction that follows what we know about language learning would have children attend to the plurals that are found in their stories about the baby chicks that have just hatched or in the books about baby chicks that are on the table near the incubator.

Language Learning Is Variable

Each individual has a unique set of experiences and a personal environment that differs somewhat from that of others. Even though children acquiring language pass through predictable stages and most children in the world acquire speech on a similar schedule, there are individual differences. Nevertheless, nearly all will achieve competence in communicating and will have mastered most of the skills required for clear communication by the age of five or six.

Children vary in their approach to language. One child may start by learning the names of everything in the immediate environment, whereas another tackles social words such as *hi* and *bye-bye* first. Yet each acquires both kinds of vocabulary, and both become competent speakers of their language. Likewise, children differ in their personal approaches to written language, and all learners in a classroom will certainly not be at the same point in the process of acquiring literacy. Teachers can recognize these differences and help children move forward at their own pace while remaining confident in the children's ability to succeed.

■ Oral Language and the Development of Literacy

Supportive Environment

If you asked the parents of a newborn child whether they expected that their child would learn to use language, they would certainly say yes, probably also giving you a look that reflected some doubt about your sanity. Parents expect their children to become successful speakers. Mistakes or errors in early speech are treated as normal. Many people go through life with funny nicknames that they acquired from an older brother or sister who could not pronounce their names. Almost everyone knows a few "family words," usually someone's baby talk that remains in the family's private vocabulary. Nobody's parents worry that their child, playing tennis at age twenty, will still be saying, "Ball all gone." We all expect that our children's language will mature and in time match the adult model.

Children who have learned to speak in an atmosphere where everyone expects that they will be successful may be confronted with an entirely different attitude when they are attempting to learn to read and write. It is not at all uncommon to find instructional programs and teachers that regard each error as cause for remediation of some kind, rather than as an indication of the child's current thinking. For example, a child who makes an error in reading may not need remediation in a phonic rule; the child may need more background experience in order to comprehend the material. A young writer may spell unconventionally, but the teacher can focus on intended meaning rather than concentrating on the errors. This sort of teacher attends carefully to information about what children do know about written language and does not look for perfection in form before allowing participation in the process.

Just as children learning language need people in their environment who are interested in them and anxious to communicate with them, so they also need support for their developing literacy. Supportive parents will allow children to "write" with safe writing implements as soon as they can hold the instrument and show interest in writing. Parents may also supply written language for the child at early ages. Many parents of even tiny babies read to them so that they can begin to enjoy the rhythm and sound of written language. They also supply the babies with books that are made for babies. After a number of experiences with such books, children begin to associate reading experiences with positive emotional feelings and begin to make hypotheses about the workings of the written language system. Durkin (1961) found that many parents of "natural readers" (children who teach themselves to read without direct instruction) were unaware of the help that they were giving their children in learning to read. The child would come to the parent and ask what a word said, get a response, and go off to figure out the relationships between the squiggles on the page and what they meant. The nurturance of literacy demands the same conditions that learning language requires: time, support, and an expectation of success.

Meaningfulness

The learning of language is most easily accomplished by those children who have meaningful interactions with others who support and value their efforts. Supportive adults respond to a child's intent, not to the form of his or her utterances. For example, when a very young child makes sounds accompanied by gestures that indicate the cookie jar, the adult is likely to respond to the intent of the child rather than to the speech actually produced. Most parents tend to correct the content rather than the form of their children's language. For example, if the child comes racing into the house and says, "He-Man camed on TV on Tuesday," the parent is likely to respond, "No, He-Man will be on on Thursday." The logical extension of this knowledge about language development is that the teaching of reading and writing must always focus on the meaning rather than on the surface structure of the child's responses.

Goodman (1986, p. 8) has summarized these principles succinctly:

What makes language very easy or very hard to learn?

It's easy when:	*It's hard when:*
It's real and natural.	It's artificial.
It's whole.	It's broken into bits and pieces.
It's sensible.	It's nonsense.
It's interesting.	It's dull and uninteresting.
It's relevant.	It's irrelevant to the learner.
It belongs to the learner.	It belongs to somebody else.
It's part of a real event.	It's out of context.
It has social utility.	It has no social value.
It has purpose for the learner.	It has no discernible purpose.
The learner chooses to use it.	It's imposed by someone else.
It's accessible to the learner.	It's inaccessible.
The learner has power to use it.	The learner is powerless.

For the development of language and literacy, the implications of Goodman's statements are clear. Children need to talk about, read about, and write about interesting experiences in their lives. They need to have their language accepted and valued. They need to use language, reading, and writing for purposes of real communication. In many classrooms, activities involve children in using language, reading, and writing in these ways. In one classroom that we observed, children were choosing books to take home from the classroom collection. They had to write the title of the book on the large envelope used for transporting the book. Their writing was not graded or corrected, but the teacher noticed that legibility quickly increased with their desire to perform the task.

In the same classroom, children were learning rhymes. After they had learned the words by rote, the words were placed on a chart and they were allowed to manipulate them (substitute words, move them around) as they read the rhyme and tried to make new versions of it. These children had real reasons for talking, reading, and writing.

Teachers concerned with the development of literacy will want to help children make as many connections as possible with language, reading, and writing. They will treat speaking, reading, and writing as experiences in communication.

Classroom Applications

Here are some classroom activities that help children make connections between spoken and written language ("print" refers to anything written, not just to printed and mechanically reproduced writing).

1. The children listen to and tell stories, then have the chance to write a response or to see the words in print.
2. The children use puppets to tell a story, then write the script for the puppets. They might also put together a book of puppet plays that have been written by the class.
3. The children learn fingerplays or other rhymes by rote and then have the print presented on charts. A chart with clear plastic pockets in which the words on cards can be placed and rearranged by the children is particularly useful for presenting fingerplays or rhymes. Children can be encouraged to match the words or phrases and then to substitute new words in the rhymes.
4. The children learn songs by rote and then have the print presented on charts. Individual song booklets can also be made for each child so that they can all read along as they sing.
5. The children have play experiences that involve communication and that are accompanied by the appropriate print. For example, children playing that they are going on a train ride might want to make signs for the stations and the cars. They

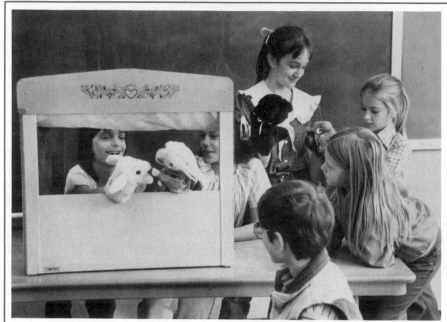

A theatrical event provides a real occasion for language use in this fourth-grade classroom.
© David S. Strickler/The Picture Cube

might also make tickets and schedules. Children playing shoe store might need sale signs, size signs, books for writing sales slips, and a catalog of shoes.

6. The children take field trips to gain the nonprint information they need to make sense of print. These trips can be followed by a written record of their trips and experiences. For example, children visiting a farm will see animals and buildings they may meet later in print. They could also write or dictate a story about their trip, make a booklet of stories about it, or keep a scrapbook of their experiences that included stories and mementos of each trip.

In summary, children need an opportunity to use language about something that is meaningful to them. What they will do tomorrow in class, how long they have had their fish, whose dog had puppies, who has a new baby sister, how much their plant has grown, what they will have to eat later—all these activities of daily living are the content of children's talk, reading, and writing. Teachers can make the most of the numerous connections between spoken and written language in order to help children increase their competence in both.

Language Development in Older Children

Older children offer a challenge to teachers who are interested in language development. Certain changes in language occur as children mature. For example, very young children take every word literally. There are thousands of stories about young children responding in literal terms to expressions that were meant figuratively. One soccer coach told his team of five-year-olds, "We've got to be on our toes for this game." The little players obligingly balanced on their tiptoes. By the time most children are eight or so, they have begun to understand that many words and phrases have multiple meanings; and by about age eleven, they giggle over the double meanings of almost everything they hear. They also begin to participate much more in language play that relies on double meanings for humor. Teachers of older children need to appreciate the growth that these stages represent, just as teachers of very young children must recognize the meaning of errors in verb forms.

Even though most children have mastered the basic forms in their native language by the age of five or six, there is still much for the teacher to do in terms of encouraging language development in school. Many children continue to be confused by such language patterns as "Before you sit down, place your hand on your head." "Before" and "after" statements are often stumbling blocks because the child tends to respond first to the first thing stated. There is also a great need for vocabulary development. Children encounter many new concepts in school, and the value of their exposure to the subject matter areas depends to a great extent on their understanding of the relevant vocabulary.

Children also need to increase their awareness of social rules for language use and gain more flexibility in their employment of speech registers. (*Register* is the linguistic term for the vocabulary and sentence patterns we use, depending on the situation, such as talking informally with our family, making a speech at a banquet, giving an oral report, talking with friends at the yogurt shop.) For example, children in the classroom are frequently admonished, "Use your inside voice." Some children may have no idea what the teacher means by that phrase. They may also need to practice speaking in situations that require the use of various speech registers. Classroom activities for older children may include delivering formal reports to the class and receiving feedback on the appropriateness of their language. Another project might be interviewing a number of adults in the community to learn about the language demands of various occupations.

■ The Classroom Context

School language is often quite different from home language, and the way that children are expected to learn it may differ as well. Zutell (1980) observed, "The predominant modes of learning at home are demonstration and performance; at school, oral instruction and skill practice take their place" (p. 19). In other words, children at home are learning language as they listen to others use it successfully, and they then get feedback on their own competence when they achieve their intentions. At school, the teacher may give instructions about language use that are separate from any use of language by the learner. The teacher may then ask children to practice isolated skills such as selecting the correct verb form to complete a sentence, with no feedback other than the grade on the paper.

Just like the home, the classroom offers a particular context for language learning, defined by its own needs and potentials. Teachers plan activities in accordance with their need to meet certain instructional goals. They must also maintain order and set appropriate limits, such as for noise level. These are all areas for application of language skills.

Teachers who want to encourage language growth will want to know what children can do with language. How can they use it? Are there some functions of language that are more readily observable than others? Is children's playground language very different from their classroom language? How does a child make needs known, settle arguments, pretend, or discuss? Teachers who are interested in fostering the development of literacy in their classrooms will want to become skilled observers of the child's use of language because of the many connections among speaking, listening, reading, and writing.

■ Learners with Special Needs

Teachers must be prepared to deal with the needs of children who speak dialects or whose native language is not English. Teachers can encourage development of literacy by being sensitive to language differences and planning activities that are useful to all children.

Speakers of Dialects

You will be responsible for teaching reading to many children who speak dialects. Many people define "dialect" as speech that differs from their own. The fact is that all of us speak a dialect of some kind. A dialect is rule governed and consistent, and its use does not merely represent errors in grammar. There are regional dialects, social-class dialects, and ethnic dialects. The most important thing for you as a teacher to remember is that children who speak dialects are not using undeveloped language and that they are not less capable as learners than children who speak the "standard English" of the community. Jaggar (1980) says that our judgments of the correctness of children's speech are social judgments, not linguistic ones.

Dialects differ in vocabulary, syntax, and morphology. Instances of vocabulary difference are such terms as those that denote a milk-and-ice-cream drink, a paper container used for carrying objects home from shopping, and parts of a car. They may also include some verb usages, such as "carry" for "take" ("He will carry you to town"). Syntactical differences often involve the deletion of some words. For example, in some dialects the correct form of "He is working today" is "He be working," which indicates that the subject is working at present. Morphological differences include the dropping of some inflectional endings, such as those of the possessive ("that girl shoes"), and the indication of tense and number by different rules ("He go there yesterday"). The differences in dialect are usually minor in nature.

Teachers of children who speak dialects different from the local majority dialect need to be aware of the dialectical differences and to think about their implications for instruction in the classroom. Differences in pronunciation may affect instruction in spelling and phonics. For example, if a child says "dem," the teacher taking dictation will still record "them." Children who speak one of the Bostonian dialects learn to recognize *car* as the word they pronounce "cah." Children who say "ain't" can learn to read "isn't." If the goal of reading instruction is comprehension rather than absolute accuracy, then the teacher of a child who renders "His mother went to town" as "He mama go to town" will not assume that the child cannot read.

The written language of books is quite different from the spoken language of many children, even those who speak a more nearly standard dialect, yet children learn to read it. Being aware of differences and sensitive to them means understanding that children can be successful as readers and writers even when their language does not match standard dialects. Children need many opportunities to use language in a variety of situations that are meaningful, such as storytelling, sharing, dramatic activities, choral readings, story and poetry writing, letter writing, and even writing notes to classmates. "Our job, then, is not to change children's language but to help them expand the language they already have. We must start by accepting the children's dialects and recognizing that, though they are different, they are not deficient. Children can think logically, learn effectively, and talk intelligently in any dialect" (Jaggar, 1980, p. 28).

Bilingual Speakers

Children whose first language is not English may also need extra help in reading. Many schools offer special bilingual programs for students who do not speak English; some provide a tutor whose objective is to help the child learn English; others do nothing at all and expect the classroom teacher to assist the child within the regular classroom context. Even in schools that in theory support bilingual programs, it is often impossible to provide such programs for all the languages that might be represented. Since most teachers will have experience with non–English-speaking children at some time, they need to be aware of some of the research on acquisition of a second language and the classroom implications of that research.

The most successful second-language learning shares some of the same conditions that make learning our mother tongue an easy process. First, the learner needs someone with whom to talk and needs support for attempts at communication. The second-language learner uses the strategies of simplification and overgeneralization that are also common in native-language development. For example, a second-language learner may simplify all verbs to one tense and depend on the context to help communicate the real message: "go" stands in for "went," and an adverbial phrase such as "last week" takes care of the tense. Finally, second-language learners gradually fine-tune their communications for greater effectiveness. For young children, this process may take only a few months; for older children, it may take longer. As in learning a first language, "For a learner to be free to learn another language, the learner must be able to trust others to respond to the messages communicated and not be laughed at or singled out. In addition, a learner must be active in seeking people to talk with" (Urzua, 1980, p. 38). The best school environment for second-language learning includes support, encouragement, meaningful purposes for communication, and a classroom structure that allows for talking with others who speak the second language.

Classroom Applications

Classroom teachers who want to help non–English-speaking children achieve a command of English will give thought to the classroom environment and plan activities that make learning English as much like learning a first language as possible. Take the following suggestions just as a starting point for your own ideas.

1. Plan activities that require children who speak English and children learning English to work together. For example, they could play a board game or build with blocks or Legos. A game situation is informal enough that most children will converse even though they might not communicate in formal situations.

Preschoolers in the bilingual reading corner are absorbed in their literary selections.
© Elizabeth Crews/Stock, Boston

2. Encourage bilingual children to share their first language through bulletin boards, classroom labels, signs, and holiday decorations.
3. Share (or find someone else to share) stories, poetry, or familiar songs in the child's native language and then in English.
4. Use good-quality trade books (nonspecialized, commercially available books) in the child's language and share their contents with the class in both languages.
5. Be careful not to segregate non–English-speaking children or to exclude them from activities that you fear they will not understand. They learn language by listening and watching and following examples as well as from instruction.
6. Base writing and reading activities on the child's growing vocabulary in English. In the beginning, children can create booklets listing and illustrating the new words they learn. After a few weeks, most children are learning too rapidly to continue this technique.
7. Encourage the child's parents to participate by sharing books, songs, rhymes, and other language traditions with the class.

■ Oral-Language Activities

All the children in your classroom—speakers of standard dialect, speakers of other dialects, and children whose first language is not English—need planned activities in language development. Remember that children learn language not to talk or read or write about *language*, but because they want to talk or read or write about the *world* (Cazden, 1981). The most successful oral-language activities offer children a wide variety of speaking situations that require the use of many different speech registers. Activities should provide practice in both formal and informal uses of language. These are some suggestions.

Conversation

Children are encouraged to talk to each other in the process of completing projects, while having meals together, and at other times when talking casually is appropriate. Arrange the room so that children can work in small groups, conducive to conversation. Invite children to participate in setting the rules of the classroom that determine when the children may talk and when they must be quiet. For example, the teacher might list the daily schedule on the board and ask the children to help determine the level of talking that would be most comfortable for the group during each activity. Having something interesting to talk about also stimulates conversation. Some teachers choose to set up a table to display a collection of novel or thought-provoking items, changing the selection frequently to maintain student interest. Older children might enjoy having oral pen pals that communicate by audio tapes.

Sharing

Sharing time in classrooms—formerly known as "show and tell"—can be productive if the teacher is careful to ensure the child's participation in the language process. In some classrooms, sharing times involve so much teacher direction that very little language is actually practiced by the child. Children can share in small groups rather than with the whole class so that the teacher does not have to maintain audience attention for the speaker. Some teachers also help children develop their ability to ask questions during sharing time.

Discussions

Discussions differ from conversations in that generally the talk is confined to a given topic. Teachers can offer opportunities for small-group discussions, such as planning a strategy in problem solving or learning about a topic. Children can participate in more formal whole-class discussions of current events or responses to a speaker or television program. Unable to hold to one topic for very long, younger children have difficulty maintaining a discussion, but they can practice by discussing how they did their artwork or what happened in a story they have just heard. As children mature, they are able to sustain discussions for longer periods.

Role Playing or Creative Dramatics

Role playing can be encouraged by setting up a dress-up area where costumes or pieces of apparel are available for children to use. In costume, children assume various roles and adopt language appropriate to the roles. For example, if the children are interested in hospitals (perhaps after a field trip), costumes for nurses and doctors, stethoscopes, and other medical tools might be added to the dress-up center to encourage role playing. Older children might dramatize experiences they have read about, learning both the context for the language and the remarks and responses appropriate to the situation.

Responses to Literature

Choral readings, storytelling, acting out stories, puppets, and narrating slide shows or filmstrips are some of the means of encouraging oral language as response to literature. Some children's literature is written in beautiful language, and children can make it their own through these activities. Children can learn the language used by the author and learn to express the same thoughts in their own language as they retell or recreate stories, poems, or plays.

Music

Children can dramatize parts of songs, learn the lyrics, and compose new lyrics to fit new situations. Children can listen to carefully selected pieces of music and discuss the feelings evoked by the music. They can also listen to the music in movies or television programs and talk about its effects or the match between the music and the story.

Reporting

Children should have opportunities to share interesting information with their peers in the more formal register of a report. Spend time first in working out how to prepare such reports, beginning with how to do the necessary research and then how to organize the material for presentation. Teachers may arrange for children to report to small groups at the beginning. Reporting to a small group will help children develop the necessary speaking skills and perhaps reduce the initial stress of speaking to the whole group. Children can be encouraged to report to the whole group when the teacher feels that they will be successful.

Practicing the Social Usage of Language

Devise classroom situations that give children the opportunity to learn speech appropriate to such activities as performing introductions, delivering messages, initiating and receiving telephone calls, and requesting information.

■ Major Ideas in This Chapter

- Language is defined as a system of sounds or signs used for communication. All languages are rule governed, arbitrary, and dynamic.

- Languages have systems of phonology, morphology, syntax, semantics, and pragmatics. These systems include the rules for combining sounds, changing meanings, putting words into sentences, and using appropriate language for the social situation.

- How children learn language is best described by the interactionist theory, which explains that the child develops language through interactions. Language development is influenced by biological, cognitive, and environmental factors.

- Language learning is self-generated, relying on interactions with significant others and not on external rewards.

- Language learning is informal, occurring in the context of everyday life.

- Language learning is an active process, developing as the learner explores and manipulates the language environment in order to achieve internal goals for communication.

- Language learning is holistic, involving simultaneous experience with what the learner is learning about sounds, meanings, word combinations, and social contexts.

- Language learning is variable, differing among children in pace and approach even though the stages of mastery are consistent. Favorable environmental factors include expectation of success, discriminating response to errors, and focus on intent.

- Children's knowledge of the systems of spoken language pave the way to learning about written language.

■ Differences between the language of children who speak a dialect and that of children who speak more standard English are minor. Speaking a dialect does not prevent a child from learning to read successfully.

■ Children whose native language is not English can be encouraged by the classroom teacher through a positive environment and opportunities to interact with other children.

■ Language development is an ongoing process. Older children need to increase vocabulary, expand their knowledge of sentence forms, and practice speaking in different situations.

? Discussion Questions
Focusing on the Teacher You Are Becoming

1. Your class is reading some of the stories from *The Tales of Uncle Remus: The Adventures of Brer Rabbit* (Lester, 1987). Although Lester has simplified the dialect in the original Harris version, it remains a prominent feature of the stories. A parent who is observing asks how you know that such stories will not have a negative influence on children's use of language. What will you say?

2. You are given an opportunity to order a language development kit from a school supply catalog. What would you want to know about the kit before you spent money on it?

3. You know that some teachers in your district provide children with worksheets that ask children to select the correct verb form for a given sentence. You do not believe that language is best learned through drill on isolated skills. How do you explain your program for helping children become more skilled users of language?

4. Talk with a small group of your classmates about your own dialects. Which elements of dialects might cause difficulty for children learning to read? How can you plan to help those children?

☑ Field-Based Applications

1. Listen to your students talking. Record some examples of their speech in various situations (classroom discussions, playground, lunchroom, unstructured time with other children) and compare their language with that found in the reading textbooks or social studies and science textbooks. Are the topics, sentence lengths, constructions, and level of

formality similar to children's speech? different from children's speech? Should they be similar or different?

2. Be alert for children's language that is particularly poetic or in some other way unusual and record it to share with others.

3. Set up conversation-stimulating classroom areas such as a dress-up center and for a few days record the types of language used there. Would children have had the same opportunities for language use in other areas of the classroom?

4. Make an exhibit of realia that you think will increase children's knowledge and use of vocabulary. For example, you might display ropes, spurs, chaps, boots, and a saddle to teach the vocabulary of cowboys. Plan a reading/writing experience to follow up on the display.

5. Record on video or audio tape your read-aloud sessions with children. What kinds of language patterns and interactions do you use? For example, you might note the number of questions you ask, the number of questions the children ask, the number of repetitions you use, and perhaps the number of times you encourage children to fill in words as they listen.

6. Record the pattern of language interactions in a classroom discussion. How many are student–student, student–teacher, teacher–student? If you find that the interactions are predominantly teacher–student, plan activities that encourage more language use among students.

7. Read a story that employs dialect appropriately and talk about dialects with your class. What are some common features of your students' local dialect?

▣ References and Suggested Readings

Anastasiow, Nicholas. *Oral Language: Expression of Thought*. Newark, Del.: International Reading Association, 1979.

Berry, Kathleen S. "Talking to Learn Subject Matter/Learning Subject Matter Talk." *Language Arts* 62 (January 1985): 34–42.

Bruner, Jerome. *Child's Talk*. New York: Norton, 1983.

Butler, Andrea, and Turbill, Jan. *Towards a Reading–Writing Classroom*. Rozelle, N.S.W., Australia: Primary English Teaching Association, 1984.

Cazden, Courtney B., ed. *Language in Early Childhood Education*. Rev. ed. Washington, D.C.: National Association for the Education of Young Children, 1981.

Chomsky, Noam. *Aspects of a Theory of Syntax*. Cambridge, Mass.: MIT Press, 1965.

Dale, Philip S. *Language Development: Structure and Function*. 2nd ed. New York: Holt, Rinehart & Winston, 1976.

DeFord, Diane, and Harste, Jerome C. "Child Language Research and Curriculum." *Language Arts* 59 (September 1982): 590–600.

DeStefano, Johanna S. *Language: The Learner and the School*. New York: Wiley, 1978.

Dumtschin, Joyce Ury. "Recognize Language Development and Delay in Early Childhood." *Young Children* 43 (March 1988): 19.

Durkin, Dolores. "Children Who Read before Grade One." *The Reading Teacher* 14 (January 1961): 163–166.

Ellis, Rod. *Classroom Second Language Development*. Elmsford, N.Y.: Pergamon Press, 1984.

Fillion, Bryant. "Let Me See You Learn." *Language Arts* 60 (September 1983): 702–710.

Garvey, Catherine. *Children's Talk*. Cambridge, Mass.: Harvard University Press, 1984.

Gleason, Jean Berko. *The Development of Language*. Columbus, Ohio: Charles E. Merrill, 1985.

Goodman, Kenneth. *What's Whole in Whole Language?* Portsmouth, N.H.: Heinemann Educational Books, 1986.

Halliday, M. A. K. "Three Aspects of Children's Language Development: Learning Language, Learning through Language, Learning about Language." In *Oral and Written Language Development Research: Impact on the Schools*, edited by Y. Goodman, M. Haussler, and D. Strickland. Urbana, Ill.: National Council of Teachers of English, 1982.

Hayes, Curtis W.; Ornstein, Jacob; and Gage, William W. *ABC's of Languages and Linguistics*. Silver Spring, Md.: Institute of Modern Languages, 1977.

Hopper, Robert, and Naremore, Rita. *Children's Speech*. 2nd ed. New York: Harper & Row, 1978.

Hymes, Dell. *Foundations of Sociolinguistics: An Ethnographic Approach*. Philadelphia: University of Pennsylvania Press, 1974.

Jaggar, Angela. "Allowing for Language Differences." In *Discovering Language with Children*, edited by G. S. Pinnell. Urbana, Ill.: National Council of Teachers of English, 1980.

Jaggar, Angela. "On Observing the Language Learner: Introduction and Overview." In *Observing the Language Learner*, edited by A. Jaggar and M. T. Smith-Burke. Newark, Del.: International Reading Association and National Council of Teachers of English, 1985.

Krashen, Stephen D. *Principles and Practice in Second Language Acquisition*. Elmsford, N.Y.: Pergamon Press, 1982.

Lehr, Fran. "Creative Drama and Language Building." *The Reading Teacher* 38 (May 1985): 896–899.

Lester, Julius. *The Tales of Uncle Remus: The Adventures of Brer Rabbit*. New York: Dial Books for Young Readers, 1987.

McCarthy, William G. "Promoting Language Development through Music." *Academic Therapy* 21 (November 1985): 237–242.

McKissack, Patricia C. *Flossie and the Fox*. New York: Dial Books for Young Readers, 1986.

Pflaum-Conner, Susanna. *The Development of Language and Reading in Young Children*. 2nd ed. Columbus, Ohio: Charles E. Merrill, 1978.

Portes, P. R. "The Role of Language in the Development of Intelligence: Vygotsky Revisited." *Journal of Research and Development in Education* 18 (Summer 1985): 1–10.

Shafer, Robert E.; Staab, Claire; and Smith, Karen. *Language Functions and School Success*. Palo Alto, Calif.: Scott, Foresman, 1983.

Urzua, Carole. "Doing What Comes Naturally: Recent Research in Second Language Acquisition." In *Discovering Language with Children*, edited by G. S. Pinnell. Urbana, Ill.: National Council of Teachers of English, 1980.

Waterhouse, Lynn; Fischer, Karen M.; and Ryan, Ellen Bouchard. *Language Awareness and Reading*. Newark, Del.: International Reading Association, 1980.

Wells, Gordon. *Learning through Interactions*. New York: Cambridge University Press, 1981.

Wells, Gordon. *The Meaning Makers: Children Learning Language and Using Language to Learn*. Portsmouth, N.H.: Heinemann Educational Books, 1986.

Zutell, Jerry. "Learning Language at Home and at School." In *Discovering Language with Children*, edited by G. S. Pinnell. Urbana, Ill.: National Council of Teachers of English, 1980.

Chapter 2

The Reading Process

Chapter Overview

- Reading and writing are developmental processes occurring at differing rates in different children.

- Reading and writing are inverse processes. The writer transforms ideas into print, and the reader transforms the print into ideas. A transaction occurs between the ideas of the author and the ideas of the reader.

- Reading combines the reader's knowledge of how language works with the ability to draw on related prior experience.

- Children need to use reading and writing in classrooms that are child centered rather than material centered. Teachers must be aware of the factors contributing to success in gaining literacy so they can plan classroom experiences accordingly.

- Teachers need to understand the observable developmental stages through which children pass en route to becoming proficient readers.

It is a foggy fall morning and you are standing in the back of a first-grade classroom. You need to observe the children in this class in order to complete an assignment for your current course in reading methods. You watch as the children begin to enter the classroom, take off their jackets, and then go to the attendance board. There they move their name tags to the side of the board marked "At School Today." They proceed to the board where lunch information is recorded. You see some children select a slip of paper with their name on it and insert it in a pocket marked "Milk." Others find their names and insert them into pockets marked "Hot Lunch" or "Lunch from Home." You watch carefully as they then move off to various activities available in the classroom. Some children pick out books and sit on a comfortable sofa to read them. Others find paper and markers and begin making drawings. Some children write or draw in their journals. A few decide to play with the blocks or sand, and several more choose the dramatic play area, where they carry on a complicated dialogue about space travel.

You walk around to observe more closely what each is doing. Some of the children who are drawing have begun to label their drawings, others to write stories about their drawings. Children working in their journals have written stories, made lists of words, or drawn pictures. One of the children on the sofa is reading new material very fluently, and another is reciting the words from memory. You notice that some of the children playing with the blocks are even getting paper to make signs for their buildings; the others take no notice. Two who were using the dramatic play area have gone to the library to find information about a particular spacecraft, whereas the rest are content to continue the play without any research. You are impressed by how carefully the teacher is monitoring these activities, aware of what each child is doing. You think, "Will I ever be able to do that?"

What conclusions can you draw about development of literacy from these observations? You notice that these children are at all stages of development in learning to read and write. Some are quite capable readers, some are obviously interested in print and aware of what print does, and some seem indifferent to reading and writing.

You go back to your education class with more questions than answers. What is this process that we label *reading?* What do readers do as they read? How did the children, who are all approximately the same age, come to differ so widely in their reading and writing abilities? What are some of the experiences that foster the development of literacy, both in and out of school? What experiences can the teacher provide in school that will help children continue to grow in their ability to read and write? Your search for the answers to these questions begins with thinking about the process of reading.

Reading: A Complex Process

What is this thing called *reading?* No simple answer to that question exists. In fact, any answer has to be complicated because the process itself is. K. Goodman (1970, p. 5) offered this definition: "Reading is a complex process by which a reader reconstructs, to some degree, a message encoded by a writer in graphic language." Reading and writing are so closely connected that we really need to begin talking about reading by talking about writing.

When we look at the activity of the writer we see that the writer begins with ideas, transforms those ideas into language, and then converts the language into written symbols. Now the reader enters the picture. The reader begins with the written symbols, translates them into language, draws on his or her background of experiences to interpret that language, and then transforms the language into ideas. The goal is that the ideas with which the reader ends will match the ideas with which the writer began. They rarely, if ever, match exactly because of differences in the life experi-

Figure 2.1   Reciprocity of writing and reading.

ences of the two persons, but if the writing/reading process has worked, the match will be close. Figure 2.1 illustrates the inverse nature of the writing and reading processes.

The figure takes special notice of the reader's background experiences and knowledge of how language works. We are coming to a better understanding of the importance of background experiences. At one time, the interpretive aspect would not have been included in the figure. Now we recognize that our background experiences affect how we interpret the world, both in reality and in print. We are continually building theories (inferences, perceptions, assumptions) about the nature of people, our language, and our world based on our experiences. These cognitive structures are called *schemata* (singular: schema). Schemata are simply organized chunks of knowledge and experience, often accompanied by feelings (Weaver, 1988). To understand schemata better, think about family holiday celebrations. Your schema for family celebrations on the Fourth of July may include a trip to the river, a picnic, rides on a boat, water skiing, and fireworks. The person you are dating may have a very different schema for Fourth of July celebrations. It might include watching a parade and listening to patriotic speeches. When you invite your date to your family's celebration, there will be a real difference in expectations and interpretations.

Reading about Fourth of July celebrations would be similarly colored by those differing schemata.

Clearly, the schemata we bring to the printed page very much determine the meaning we give to the print. The reader does not come to the printed page as a "blank slate" on which the ideas of the author will be written. The reader comes to the printed page with a rich cache of meanings to be given to the ideas (as expressed in the words) of the author. The act of reading is thus a very interactive process between the writer and the reader (May, 1986). The continual interaction between the ideas of the author and the schemata of the reader results in the reader's bringing meaning to the printed page. Clearly the degree to which the reader *reconstructs* (to use Kenneth Goodman's term) the message of the writer depends on the orchestration of a great many factors.

A closer look at the components of reading not only helps to define reading but provides some terminology you will need in order to talk about the reading process.

Components of the Reading Process

Reading is so complex that it is difficult to break it apart and talk about the components. When we discuss them, we risk creating the impression that a given component is more important than others. Mature readers use all the components selectively as necessary to create meaning, and probably use them in combination so rapidly that they don't notice discrete steps at all. Our purpose here is to outline the components so that you will have a working knowledge of the terminology used to describe the reading process. Each of the components will be discussed in much greater detail in succeeding chapters.

Word Identification

The step that takes the reader from written symbol to language is called *word identification, word recognition,* or *decoding.* The reader's task is to say the words orally or read them silently. Following is a brief outline of the components of word identification. The process will be described in greater detail in Chapter 9.

I. **Sight vocabulary.** All the words we recognize instantly when we see them in writing. Our sight vocabularies are usually larger than our speaking and writing vocabularies.

II. **Context cues.** All the language cues that exist on the printed page. Effective use of context cues depends not only on our

understanding of how language works but on our background of experiences in creating meaning.

   A. **Syntactic cues.** Cues provided by the structure of the sentence. Your knowledge of how language works lets you
use syntactic cues. For example, the word *the* tells you to
look for a noun.

   B. **Semantic cues.** Cues provided by the meanings of other
words in the same or nearby sentences.

III. **Word-attack cues.** Cues provided by the relationships between letters and sounds. The reader breaks the word down
into parts to get at the whole.

   A. **Structural cues.** Cues provided by root words, prefixes,
and suffixes.

   B. **Syllabic cues.** Cues provided by dividing the unknown
word into syllables based on a set of syllable patterns. The
structure of the syllable sometimes signals the sound of
vowels within the syllable.

   C. **Graphophonic cues.** Cues provided by the fact the letters
represent sounds in our alphabetic language. Problems of
inconsistency aside, our symbols stand for speech rather
than, say, pictures or entire ideas, and consequently they
bear some relation to pronunciation.

■ Comprehension

Once the task of word identification is complete—that is, once we have
moved from printed symbols to language—we can proceed with comprehension. Like word identification, comprehension can occur very rapidly.
The components of comprehension should work smoothly in concert, although discussed individually.

     Frank Smith (1978) and Ken Goodman (1970) have done pioneering
work in helping us understand the reading process and this thing called
"comprehension." They stress the importance of prediction in comprehension. As you read or listen to language, you are continuously predicting
what will be said next. As long as your predictions are confirmed, you continue to read or listen with good comprehension, using the fewest possible
cues provided by the writer or speaker. Comprehension is this process of
predicting the content just ahead, confirming the prediction, and making
the next prediction, a process resulting in the creation of meaning. An interaction occurs between the ideas of the author and the schemata of the
reader. Predictions are based in part on the syntactic and semantic cues on
the printed page or in the speech. But the comprehension process is greatly
facilitated by another cueing system. We said earlier that the ideas you have

about people, your language, and the world are called *schemata*. The cues to understanding provided by your schemata are called *schematic cues*. This cueing system may be the most powerful contributor to comprehension. We have defined *comprehension* in a way that recognizes the importance of schematic cues. Comprehension is the interaction of the ideas of the author and the schemata of the reader that leads to understanding. We will discuss the comprehension process more fully in Chapter 10.

Bearing in mind the components of the reading process, think again about the children whose classroom activities we describe at the beginning of the chapter. Let's examine the development of reading ability that leads to such dramatic variations within a group of children.

Keys to Success in Learning to Read

Children do not enter school with empty minds; they have had many and varied experiences. Some have been taken to the library, read to frequently, and engaged in conversations about books. They live with adults who read and write and who use words for problem solving, self-education and enrichment, and entertainment. Others live in environments where they have never observed an adult reading or writing. Their homes lack books, magazines, and newspapers, and the world outside their homes has offered them limited experiences that involved language or reading or writing. Huey (1908/1961, p. 19) said, "The home is the natural place for learning to read in connection with the child's introduction to literature through storytelling, picture reading, etc. The child will make much use of reading and writing in his plays using both pictures and words."

Ideally all children will have had such a wonderful beginning in the development of literacy, but for most that ideal is far from reality. The responsibility of the teacher, then, is to help every child learn the language, the functions of print, and the pleasures of the written word that will make the development of literacy possible for each one.

We might well have subtitled the first chapter of this book "The Heart of the Matter," for language is at the very heart of the process of learning to read and write, of becoming literate. In addition to receiving strong support in their development of language, children will benefit from several other kinds of experiences in gaining literacy: having opportunities to generate and test hypotheses about print, having opportunities to come to the reading experience with the relevant nonvisual information (and the freedom to use it), and having opportunities to learn the purposes and functions of reading personally. In addition, each child needs to read printed material that is meaningful and predictable and have a teacher or parent who stresses meaning more than mechanics. Understanding these needs will help answer questions about how children have attained such different abilities. Teachers who meet these needs provide the optimal environment for children to learn to read.

■ Forming Hypotheses

Children need opportunities to generate and test hypotheses about print.

Children learning to talk are constantly generating and testing hypotheses about language and how it works. An observer of young children will note that they try out various combinations of sounds when attempting to communicate their needs. The feedback is usually immediate: the child either does or does not get whatever he or she wanted. The child can adjust language, gestures, and other accompanying behaviors accordingly. Children also begin making the same sorts of hypotheses about print in many home situations. For instance, the child observes a truck on the highway bearing a familiar logo and remarks, "That says Pay Less." The adult will usually respond, "Yes, that says Pay Less," if it does, otherwise making the correction: "No, that says Baskin-Robbins." Most adults will not say, "Now, Amanda, pay attention. See, that letter is a *B*, not a *P*. Sound

Reading with a partner turns the process into a three-way interaction.
© *Michael Hagan*

out the letters and you will know what it says." Children learn to recognize commonly seen words such as *exit* and *stop*, as well as commercial logos such as McDonald's and Kraft, through repeated exposure to the print embedded in the context and through repeated feedback.

Y. Goodman (1980, 1986) found that most three-year-olds could read some environmental print when it was presented in context. Children who could not read the exact name of the item could supply a generic label for it. For example, they might say "toothpaste" when shown *Colgate*. Such findings indicate that children respond to print in ways that relate to their experience, rather than just randomly. Goodman found that the ability to read environmental print was not related to ethnic, racial, geographic, or linguistic differences. Goodman also examined the child's understanding of print in discourse. She found that this understanding begins early. Most three-year-olds know how to handle a book, and most five-year-olds know that it is the print that is being read.

Teachers can find ways daily for children to interact meaningfully with print. When teachers transcribe what children say, make charts of song lyrics, and write lists of tasks to be done, they are creating opportunities for children to make their own hypotheses about print and how it works and to test their guesses. A good example of problem solving with print was observed in a local kindergarten. The children were a little upset that not all of them had had a turn to use the new play area. As a group they tried to solve the problem. One child suggested that a list could be made of the children who had had a turn and then all the others would have a turn before those children could play there again. The teacher agreed. The child got a clipboard and some paper and went to the name board to copy down the names of the children to be surveyed. She copied only the geometric shape that was on each child's name card. When she began her survey, she found that the information she had was not enough to be useful, and she was soon back at the board copying the print for each name.

In another class, the children had learned to read a short story about Hallowe'en. The words (and some pictures) had been placed in a pocket chart. Other word cards were available. Some children could read the story only exactly as they had memorized it, but others would substitute words in the sentences and then try to read the new sentences they had made. Freeman and Whitesell (1985, p. 24) recommend that teachers encourage children "to take risks in interpreting all kinds of printed text."

In exploring print, children develop the oral language with which to discuss written language. They begin to learn the concepts and labels of *book, page, word, letter,* and so on. It is important that encounters with the language about print take place in meaningful contexts. In some classrooms, children learn the names of the letters or learn to repeat the letter/sound relationships totally apart from their interactions with print. Therefore, children may believe that these activities are unrelated to reading or writing. As children develop the vocabulary for discussing written language, they are able to talk about what they are doing when they participate in reading and writing experiences. Goodman (1980, 1986) defines the ability to think about and explain the use of language in some overt way as the development of metalinguistic ability. Of course, the child's explanations may not match those of adults for some time. Goodman's research also revealed that many children's metalinguistic knowledge and their level of performance do not match. For example, some children can read and write in the conventional sense without having the ability to think about their knowledge of written language. Others begin thinking about how the language works before they can perform as readers.

Children often demonstrate their knowledge of language in the classroom. For example, in creating sentences that followed the pattern learned in Hoberman's *A House Is a House for Me* (1982), the group had started with "A doghouse is a house for a dog" and were having great difficulty in coming up with a satisfactory second line that would rhyme with *dog*. Finally one child jumped up with a solution: "The sky is the home for the fog." Since the *A* for the next line was already on the chart, he was asked why it had to be changed to *The*. His reply certainly indicated a

Children are constantly engaged in learning language from one another.
© *Michael Hagan*

knowledge of how language worked when he answered, "Everyone knows there is only *one* [sky]." In addition to admiring his poetic language, we can applaud his understanding of the workings of language. Helping children develop the vocabulary of written language and helping them think about their understanding of how language works further the goal of literacy.

■ Applying Experience

Children need opportunities to come to reading experiences with relevant nonvisual information and have the freedom to use it.

Children cannot read material comfortably unless the content is related to their experience. Neither can adults. The following excerpt (Stanley-Samuelson, 1987, p. 105) illustrates the need for background knowledge that relates to the material to be read:

Various eicosanoids appear to be involved in the regulation of a variety of physiological and behavioral areas in representatives of many invertebrate phyla. In some cases (such as mediation of behavioral thermoregulation), the evidence for an eicosanoid function is based on treatment of animals with a single compound and observation of the response. At this level of observation, it remains to be established that eicosanoids are physiologically involved. Given a good base of preliminary observations, important research goals would be to firmly show that, in the case at hand, PGs do mediate thermoregulatory behavior. In still other cases, such as the role of PG in releasing egg-laying behavior in crickets, there is sufficient evidence to accept that certain PGs do release egg-laying, although some details of the physiological mechanism— where in the central nervous system PGs act and how they alter behavior—are not yet understood. Research in this area could usefully be aimed, not at reaffirming the role of the eicosanoid, but at acquiring more details of the action. In study areas where considerable biochemical details are established—as in starfish oocyte maturation—cellular events remain unknown. Again, understanding how eicosanoids act remains a major research goal.

Even if you could pronounce each word correctly, you would find the passage meaningless unless you had enough previous knowledge of biology. For some children, teachers will need to spend instructional time providing experiences that form the background for comprehension. For example, many children have not ridden on an escalator or an elevator, attended a birthday party or a circus, or seen a farm or zoo. If children meet these concepts in print before they have experience with which to connect them, the print may be meaningless.

Having experience is not enough if the child is not allowed to use it. There are some teachers who do not wish children to read and write about their experiences because they are not as "pretty" as the teachers would like. For some children, daily life means relationships marked by violence, fathers or mothers who are absent, and homes without enough food. These children must be allowed to relate print to their own worlds before they can relate to reading traditional stories of middle-class children visiting grandparents on the farm.

■ Discovering Purpose

Children need opportunities to learn the purposes and functions of print personally.

In an ideal world, children would grow up observing the functions of print in a personal way. They would get letters from distant friends and relatives and hear thousands of stories that had been carefully crafted with well-chosen words. They would have followed directions for constructing a toy or model and consulted the encyclopedia to learn more about dogs or dinosaurs. They would have written thank-you notes to their grandpar-

Wanting to telephone a friend is a meaningful incentive to literacy.
© *Michael Hagan*

ents, received invitations to parties, held their own tickets to the *Nutcracker* ballet, and organized their collections of favorite books.

In the real world, not all children have had the chance to learn about print in such ways. Teachers can help children use print to send meaningful messages. For example, children in the morning session of kindergarten may want to tell the afternoon group not to destroy a partially completed block structure. Children who are observing the new crab in the aquarium might be provided with books about crabs, paper on which to record their thoughts or observations, and charts to track whose turn it is to care for the crab. Children may need to see the teacher write a note inviting their parents to visit the class. They may, with the teacher's help, need to compose a message to another child, explaining their feelings about being denied a turn on the swing at recess time. They need to have experience in seeing their own words being recorded and hearing them read at a future time. Without coming to an understanding of the power of print, why would any child want to struggle with the hard work of learning to read and write? A real and personal reason for reading and writing makes the effort worthwhile.

■ Recognizing Meaning

Children need printed material that is meaningful and predictable.

Children learning to read and write need to know that the printed material they are given says something. Adults read for information, pleasure, guidance, and other purposes, but certainly not just to practice the process of reading. Given materials that do not relate at all to their experience or that do not contain language that is real to them, children find reading to be too much effort. They should not be expected to "read" nonsense words. (Playful language used in some books for children is an exception, of course. Such books create a context in which made-up or pretend words mirror the child's own playful experiences with language.)

Predictable materials include pattern books (books with repetitive language patterns, as we explain in Chapter 8) and materials in which the language is predictable in the sense of sounding like real speech. If children are reading materials that describe feeding a hamster, they will be able to predict the word that is omitted from this sentence:

> The hamster, Speedy, ate some of the food pellets and hid
> some in the corner of his _____.

Contrast the task of reading from material that is sensible with that of reading

> The fan was on the _____.

when the missing word is not *floor* or *table* but *van*.

■ Emphasizing Message

Children need a teacher or parent who stresses meaning, not mechanics.

Children learning language have had numerous experiences with adults who have been concentrating on their meaning rather than on the form in which it was expressed. In fact, adults assign intentionality to even very young babies. We act as if they meant to tell us they want food or a toy that they can see or a chance to look out the window long before they can communicate much of that meaning. Children learning to read and write need teachers who respond to their intentions in using written messages, not to the technical precision with which they express themselves.

Young children need to know that teachers will respond to their attempts to read and write with an emphasis on what they mean. Four-year-olds who write random letters expect adults to respond with recognition, not to correct the form. If a child writes "is crem" on the family grocery list, he or she expects to get a treat, not a lesson on spelling. Children who say "Samuel gots three little kittens" when the text reads "Samuel has three little kittens" should receive approval for their ability to understand print rather than correction to achieve an exact match with the text. Even professional readers often make errors when reading aloud. Beginning

Predictable text aids learners in acquiring fluency.
© *Michael Hagan*

readers need support for their attempts and a teacher who trusts that some errors in oral reading—those that do not change the meaning—are best ignored in most situations. When we correct children on every oral reading miscue, we are signaling them that word-by-word "perfect" reading is more important than meaning. This is not to say that perfect reading is never important. There are many situations in which perfect reading is necessary; for instance, in reading recipes, solving math problems, following directions to an unfamiliar place, and carrying out instructions for assembling a model. Initially, however, teachers should be sure to stress meaning rather than mechanics.

Growth in Literacy

Teale and Sulzby (1986, p. xviii) have aptly summarized the current knowledge of how young children develop literacy.

1. Literacy development begins long before children start formal instruction. Children use legitimate reading and writing behaviors in the informal settings of home and community. The search for skills which predict subsequent achievement has been misguided because the onset of literacy has been misconceived.

2. *Literacy* development is the appropriate way to describe what was called *reading* readiness: The child develops as a writer/reader. The notion of reading preceding writing, or vice versa, is a misconception. Listening, speaking, reading, and writing abilities (as aspects of language—both oral and written) develop concurrently and interrelatedly, rather than sequentially.

3. Literacy develops in real-life settings for real-life activities in order to "get things done." Therefore, the functions of literacy are as integral a part of learning about writing and reading during early childhood as are the forms of literacy.

4. Children are doing critical cognitive work in literacy development during the years from birth to six.

5. Children learn written language through active engagement with their world. They interact socially with adults in writing and reading situations; they explore print on their own, and they profit from modeling of literacy by significant adults, particularly their parents.

6. Although children's learning about literacy can be described in terms of generalized stages, children can pass through these stages in a variety of ways and at different ages. Any attempts to "scope and sequence" instruction should take this developmental variation into account.

■ Simultaneous Processes

As young children begin to understand print, they engage themselves with both reading and writing. Consideration of each aspect apart from the rest can be misleading. It is an artificial separation to try to discuss the stages of reading as if the child were not also continuing to grow in language and writing abilities at the same time. The ways in which children process print, in both reading and writing, change as literacy develops. Another problem with describing how children begin to use the reading process is that it is not always linear and sequential. Many children who do not yet read are beginning to understand what it is that people are reading on the page, and at the same time they are becoming aware of the various functions of print in the environment. When thinking about the development of reading, keep in mind that it is not going on in isolation; the child is also growing and maturing in other areas.

Aulls (1985) has described the changes that take place in our use of the various cueing systems as we become more mature readers and writers; Figure 2.2 illustrates them. Note that the knowledge sources listed on the

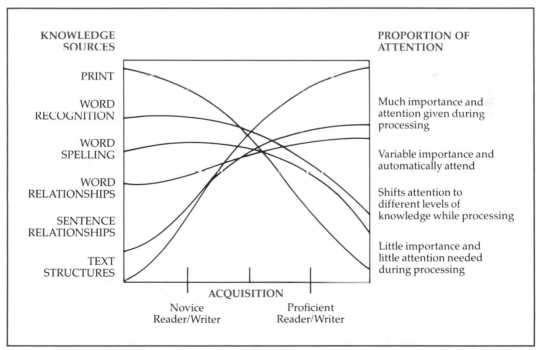

Figure 2.2   Levels of knowledge simultaneously acquired and used in both reading and writing acquisition.
SOURCE: Mark W. Aulls, "Understanding the Relationship between Reading and Writing," *Educational Horizons* 64 (Fall 1985): 39–44.

left range from simple to complex. The scale on the right moves from greater to smaller amount of attention paid to the sources of knowledge by the reader/writer. As reader/writer moves across the bottom of the chart from inexperience to proficiency, the amount of attention he or she pays to each knowledge source changes rather dramatically. For example, the beginning reader/writer pays the most attention to the print; the proficient reader/writer pays the least.

The beginning reader/writer pays little attention to the text structure, but the mature reader pays more attention to the structure (forms of poetry, time sequence, use of flashback, and so on) than to any other aspect of the reading process. If we think about it, we know that when we sit down to read the newspaper we have a clearly defined (although sometimes unconscious) set of expectations for the reading experience. We anticipate that certain kinds of information will be found in certain sections of the paper and that some kinds of information are consistently there, whereas others vary. We know that the material to be read will be presented in newspaper style, which means that the first paragraph of a news article will cover all the major facts. We can read on if we are interested in more detail or skip to another article if we have all the information we want. It also means that a certain vocabulary will be employed and that eloquent prose is not usual.

All our reading experiences as mature readers are colored by our expectations for the structure of the text and by our life experiences. As a textbook reader for at least twelve or thirteen years, you hold certain expectations for textbooks. For example, you expect headings and subheadings that will help you determine which pieces of information are the most important and mark transitions to new topics. You also expect a certain type of language. If your expectations were not met, you would have to spend additional time on the reading task. You have become very sophisticated in the use of the reading process.

The changes that take place in the reader's proficiency have been described as stages in the reading process. Bearing in mind our earlier caveat about falsely segregating the aspects of the process, we will not forget that these stages are also interacting with other aspects.

■ Sequential Stages

In describing the general sequence of beginning reading, authors have looked at different aspects of reading behavior. Cochrane, Cochrane, Scalena, and Buchanan (1984) have taken a global view of reading in their description of reading stages.

1. *Magical stage.* Children seek to understand the purpose of books and begin to think that books are important. They think that books are

magical—they contain stories. Looking at books, holding them, and taking favorite books with them are signs of this stage. Parents or teachers must provide models of the importance of reading by reading to themselves, reading to children, and talking about books.

2. *Self-conception stage*. Children begin to view themselves as readers and begin to engage in reading-like activities. They may pretend to read books, supplying words suggested by the pictures or by previous experiences with the books.

3. *Bridging reader stage*. Children become more and more aware of the actual print in the reading process. They are able to pick out familiar words and notice words that have personal significance. Those who write stories will be able to read them back and can also begin to read familiar print from poems, songs, or nursery rhymes. Some children believe that each word represents a syllable and are confused when they try to match them up. Most children begin to recognize the letters of the alphabet.

4. *Take-off reader stage*. Children begin to use three cueing systems (graphophonic, semantic, and syntactic) together in a process. They are excited about reading and want to read to others. They begin to recognize words even when they are out of context. They become more aware of environmental print and tend to read everything, such as cereal boxes. In this period they may become too attentive to each word or even each letter and overuse the graphic system, the danger being that they may see reading as the decoding of sounds and words rather than the creation of meaning.

5. *Independent reading stage*. Children are able to read unfamiliar books by themselves. They construct meanings using not only the print but also their previous knowledge and experience and the author's cues about meaning. Independent readers are able to predict how the author might express meaning through various syntactic or semantic structures. They are most successful with material that is related directly to their experience, but are able to understand the structure and language of familiar story genres or common expository material, such as the record of a science experiment.

6. *Skilled reader stage*. Children are increasingly able to read material that is further and further removed from their own experiences. They have learned to read and begin reading to learn. They begin to process print that serves specialized purposes, such as in the telephone book or a menu, as well as enjoying stories and poetry. They are able to apply the process of reading to other areas, such as reading music or reading another language.

7. *Advanced skilled stage*. Children at advanced skilled levels use print to fulfill individual needs. They process material at various speeds and with a level of attention to detail that is consistent with the purpose of the reading. They choose to involve themselves with reading on a regular basis.

Why should you be a student of the stages in reading development? Teachers who have a developmental perspective are able to plan instructional activities that are most appropriate for children. The daily activities you plan for students should be selected because of where children are in their development of literacy rather than because they happen to appear next in the textbook and teacher's guide. We hope that an overview of the development of the reading process will help you to be more comfortable with children as they move through the developmental process, knowing that they will continue to grow and develop as readers and writers.

Reading in the Classroom

Now that you have thought about the reading process, how it develops, and the stages in the development of reading, it is time to think about what the teacher can do to foster reading in the classroom.

Traditional Classrooms

The traditional view of reading was that it began with the child's mastering the names of the letters, then mastering the letter–sound relationships, then learning some easy words in isolation, and finally reading simple stories with highly controlled vocabularies.

We know that children learn to use print in steps that are not nearly so linear. Very young children may recognize whole words in context long before they learn the alphabet and may learn about story structure and reading purposes in conjunction with learning some letters or letter–sound relationships. Traditional programs often separated instruction in language, reading, and writing. A typical day might have included a session in which the children could practice language skills. For example, young children might have been asked to match words that rhyme, and older children might have been asked to make sentences using ten new vocabulary words. At another time in the day, they might have had a writing lesson. For many young children, such a lesson involved copying a piece of poetry from the chalkboard; older children might have completed a sentence such as, "On my summer vacation I. . . ." At yet another time in the same day, children would be expected to read, usually from materials that had a rigorously limited vocabulary. These activities were often unrelated and unconnected. In programs that treat language, reading, and writing as parts of the whole of becoming literate, children use all these processes at once. They become more adept at reading as they read stories and poems that they and their classmates have written. They become better readers and writers as they broaden their knowledge of language through exploratory activities and projects that expand their vocabulary and their language usage.

■ Whole-Language Classrooms

There are strong similarities between what readers do and what writers do. For example, both readers and writers begin the process by using previous knowledge about the topic, the way language works, and our alphabetic writing system. Both reader and writer bring certain expectations to the task. These expectations are based on previous reading and writing experiences, knowledge about the purposes of reading and writing, and knowledge about audiences. There are equally powerful similarities between what readers and writers do while fulfilling their respective functions.

Teachers who understand the development of language, reading, and writing provide activities that involve the children in all these processes. They know that the experiences must also be relevant to the children. Taylor, Blum, and Logsdon (1986) describe the characteristics of classrooms that implement a whole-language view of literacy. These characteristics include multiple and varied stimuli for reading, multiple and varied stimuli for writing, accessible and functional display of children's language products, integrative print (print that is integral to classroom activities and routines, such as message boards and storage labels), explicit classroom routines, and child-centered activities and instruction. Such classrooms also have texts that confirm what children know about how language works; they are meaningful and predictable, not artificial and contrived. Children use language in real, communicative contexts.

Whole-language classrooms contain many books, directions, schedules, messages, and other materials for reading. Such classrooms stress functional reasons for writing, such as operating message centers and signing up for activities, and they provide well-stocked writing centers. Materials produced by the children are used in ongoing activities. Teachers make writing a part of typical projects such as hatching eggs so that records can be kept, activities checked off, charts produced, and reference material used. Daily classroom routines provide opportunities for functional uses of print, from taking attendance to rotating responsibility for chores. The print is child centered in that most of it is produced by children and reflects their activities and interests.

The experiences of children in whole-language classrooms are different from those of children in conventional classrooms not only in terms of what they do but in terms of how they feel about themselves as readers and how they perceive reading. The way in which Rasinski (1988) has described the experience of his son Mikey in becoming literate clarifies the importance of interest, purpose, and choice in the literacy-gaining process.

Mikey was involved in a kindergarten program that allowed him to choose to participate in making books and engage in reading and to decide for himself how to accomplish tasks. As a result, Mikey saw himself as a reader and writer. In first grade, Mikey's teacher employed a reading program that depended on worksheets and stories with controlled vocabulary in order to achieve reading goals. Mikey was suddenly confronted with a change in his perception of the reading process: no longer an activity that furthered his personal goals, reading became a task to be performed for someone else.

The teacher's view of literacy and how it is achieved has a profound effect on the way a child views reading and writing. The U.S. Office of Education First Grade studies of the late 1960s (Stauffer, 1969) established that the teacher is one of the most critical factors in the reading process. This is as true today as it was more than twenty years ago. Teachers who choose to treat learning to read as part of the bigger process of becoming literate will provide activities that encourage children to use print to achieve their own goals and to explore how others use it. Your own experience over years of teaching will provide the best answers to some of your questions.

■ Major Ideas in This Chapter

- ■ Reading and writing are inverse processes that begin with the author's ideas and end, if successful, with the reader recreating those ideas as modified by the reader's background experiences. Comprehension is the creation of meaning resulting from this interaction between the ideas of the author and the schemata of the reader.

- ■ Reading is a complex process involving the reader's prior knowledge of the subject, knowledge of the syntactical system, knowledge of word meanings and relationships, knowledge of the graphophonic relationships, and interaction with the printed text.

- ■ Children learning to read need to be able to form hypotheses about print, to acquire and use nonvisual information, to read predictable and meaningful texts, to have teachers who respond to their intentions more than their performance, and to learn the purposes and functions of print personally.

- ■ Reading develops over time in stages that are observable but not always linear and sequential.

- ■ Readers and writers engage in highly similar activities. Classroom activities should be structured to reinforce this similarity in ways that are developmentally appropriate for learners. Teachers should encourage children to use print in ways that have meaning and purpose for them.

Teachers in whole-language classrooms create situations in which children use the processes of literacy in authentic ways.

■ How teachers see the reading/writing processes has a profound effect on how they teach and therefore on how children view these processes.

？ Discussion Questions
Focusing on the Teacher You Are Becoming

1. A first-grade teacher in the building in which you are observing puts a poem on the board for the children to copy each morning and then hands out a packet of dittoed worksheets called "morning work" for them to do. Discuss the appropriateness of these activities in light of the reading/writing connection and the developmental nature of the reading/writing processes. What might be done instead?
2. Interview three young children (age five to seven), asking them, "What is reading?" and, "What do you do when you read?" Interview three older children (age eight to eleven), asking them the same questions and adding, "What do you do when you are reading and you come to a word you don't know?" Share the results of your interviews with your classmates and discuss the views these children have of the reading process.
3. Discuss how your views of the reading process may have changed as a result of studying this chapter. What goals regarding reading instruction do you and your classmates now have for yourselves as teachers?

☑ Field-Based Applications

1. Plan three ways to include reading and writing in daily classroom routines.
2. Observe three teachers conducting reading lessons. Compare and contrast the lessons in terms of what you can infer about the teachers' views of the reading process.
3. Refer to Figure 2.2. Observe a novice reader/writer at work and see if you can verify the chart's ranking of attention to knowledge sources. Do the same with a proficient reader/writer.
4. Help each child write and read his or her own story about a recent classroom experience (or experience outside school). How fluently were the children able to read the story? What does this tell you about the value of background experience in reading and writing?

5. Help children keep their own logs of the reading they are doing. As the children mature, they can record much more extensive information about each book.

▣ References and Suggested Readings

Aulls, Mark W. "Understanding the Relationship between Reading and Writing." *Educational Horizons* 64 (Fall 1985): 39–44.

Bissex, Glenda L. *Gnys at Wrk: A Child Learns to Write and Read.* Cambridge, Mass.: Harvard University Press, 1980.

Cochrane, Orin; Cochrane, Donna; Scalena, Sharen; and Buchanan, Ethel. *Reading Writing and Caring.* Winnipeg: Whole Language Consultants, 1984.

Ferreiro, Emilia, and Teberosky, Ana. *Literacy before Schooling.* Exeter, N.H.: Heinemann Educational Books, 1982.

Fields, Marjorie, and Lee, Doris. *Let's Begin Reading Right.* Columbus, Ohio: Charles E. Merrill, 1987.

Freeman, Yvonne S., and Whitesell, Lynne R. "What Preschoolers Already Know about Print." *Educational Horizons* 64 (Fall 1985): 22–24.

Goodman, Kenneth. *Reading: Process and Program.* Champaign, Ill.: National Council of Teachers of English, 1970.

Goodman, Yetta. "Children Coming to Know Literacy." In *Emergent Literacy: Writing and Reading,* edited by William H. Teale and Elizabeth Sulzby. Norwood, N.J.: Ablex Publishing, 1986.

Goodman, Yetta. "Language, Cognitive Development and Reading Behavior." *Claremont Reading Conference Yearbook,* 1983, pp. 10–16.

Goodman, Yetta. "The Roots of Literacy." *Claremont Reading Conference Yearbook,* 1980, pp. 1–32.

Guthrie, John T. "Preschool Literacy Learning." *The Reading Teacher* 37 (December 1983): 318–320.

Hoberman, Mary Ann. *A House Is a House for Me.* New York: Puffin Books, 1982.

Holdaway, Don. *The Foundations of Literacy.* New York: Ashton Scholastic, 1979.

Holdaway, Don. *Independence in Reading.* 2nd ed. Exeter, N.H.: Heinemann Educational Books, 1980.

Huey, Edmund B. *The Psychology and Pedagogy of Reading.* 1908. Reprint. Cambridge, Mass.: MIT Press, 1961.

Jensen, Mary. "Story Awareness: A Critical Skill for Early Reading." *Young Children* 41 (November 1985): 20–24.

Jensen, Mary A., and Hanson, Bette A. "Helping Young Children Learn to Read: What Research Says to Teachers." *Young Children* 37 (November 1980): 61–71.

Kontos, Susan. "What Preschool Children Know about Reading and How They Learn It." *Young Children* 42 (November 1986): 58–66.

Loban, Walter. "The Absolute Bedrock of Reading." *Claremont Reading Conference Yearbook,* 1981, pp. 21–33.

May, Frank B. *Reading as Communication: An Interactive Approach.* 2nd ed. Columbus, Ohio: Charles E. Merrill, 1986.

McGee, Lea; Charlesworth, Rosalind; Cheek, Martha; and Cheek, Earl. "Metalinguistic Knowledge: Another Look at Beginning Reading." *Childhood Education* 58 (November/December 1982): 123–126.

Rasinski, Timothy V. "The Role of Interest, Purpose, and Choice in Early Literacy." *The Reading Teacher* 41 (January 1988): 396–400.

Schickedanz, Judith. *More Than the ABC's: The Early Stages of Reading and Writing.* Washington, D.C.: National Association for the Education of Young Children, 1986.

Smith, Frank. *Reading without Nonsense.* New York: Teachers College Press, 1978.

Stanley-Samuelson, David W. "Physiological Roles of Prosteglandins and Other Eiocosenoids in Invertebrates." *The Biological Bulletin* 173 (August 1987): 92–109.

Stauffer, Russell G. *Teaching Reading as Thinking Process.* New York: Harper & Row, 1969.

Taylor, Nancy; Blum, Irene H.; and Logsdon, David M. "The Development of Written Language Awareness: Environment Aspects and Program Characteristics." *Reading Research Quarterly* 21 (Spring 1986): 132–149.

Teale, William H., and Sulzby, Elizabeth. "Introduction." In *Emergent Literacy: Writing and Reading,* edited by William H. Teale and Elizabeth Sulzby. Norwood, N.J.: Ablex Publishing, 1986.

Weaver, Constance. *Reading Process and Practice from Socio-psycholinguistics to Whole Language.* Portsmouth, N.H.: Heinemann Educational Books, 1988.

Yaden, David B., and Templeton, Shane, eds. *Metalinguistic Awareness and Beginning Literacy.* Portsmouth, N.H.: Heinemann Educational Books, 1986.

Chapter 3

The Writing Process

Chapter Overview

- Learning to write is very much like learning to speak and to read. It is a developmental process that moves through observable stages. Teachers must have a good understanding of the developmental stages if they are to provide appropriate instruction.

- Reading and writing are closely connected. One reinforces the other. It is appropriate for children to write during the instructional time allocated to reading.

- Classroom environments may be structured to foster writing development. In such classrooms, use of oral language is encouraged and celebrated, children engage in activities that invite thinking, talking, reading, and writing, and literature is shared frequently. Children value each other's work, and the teachers value the work of children.

- Composition is not a single act but a sequence of activities that are described as a process. The process is more important than any one writing product or piece. Working through the process frequently, with positive feedback from others, results in improved writing.

It is a beautiful Tuesday morning. The sun is shining. The kids have been unusually eager to work today. You are feeling really good about the morning. You were even a little surprised when they so eagerly went to work on the books they are writing, but then you know how much they like to write. You have been taking dictation from some children while others were composing on their own. Now you are standing next to the door of the classroom just enjoying the excitement of the activity and feeling good about yourself as a teacher. Your silent celebration is interrupted when you realize that your principal is standing next to you. The principal asks, "Why are your kids writing during reading time?"

What do you say?

1. *Writing and reading are closely connected. Students need to experience and understand the connection.* Children need to understand that both reading and writing involve ideas. Just as they write ideas when they com-

pose, they are also reading ideas when they read. Glance back at Figure 2.1 to be reminded of the reciprocal relationship between writing and reading discussed in Chapter 2. Tierney and Pearson (1983) have described additional similarities between reading and writing. It may be that writers and readers are in fact doing the same things. Writing involves planning, composing, and revising. Good readers do exactly those things. They plan their reading. They compose a tentative meaning as they read, and they revise meaning as they come ever closer to unlocking the message intended by the author. The linkage between reading and writing is very clear. *It is appropriate for children to write during reading time.*

    2. *Children need practice reading material that is truly interesting to them.* Children are typically egocentric. Material they have written about

Writing a message of sympathy to a bereaved classmate, this kindergartner is learning a significant lesson about the expressive power of words.
© *Mimi Forsyth/Monkmeyer Press Photo Service*

their own experiences and thoughts is almost always of great interest to them. They truly enjoy reading their own writing. One teacher reported the joy in the children's voices when she returned stories they had dictated and she had typed. When they saw their writing efforts, they exclaimed, "These are *our* words!" Children of any age enjoy reading the books and stories written by classmates and friends. When we create classroom libraries of the important books written by our students, we are providing a valuable source of interesting reading material for reading practice. *It is appropriate for children to write during reading time.*

3.   *The act of composing reinforces concepts important to reading comprehension.* The concepts of word, sentence, topic sentence, main idea, supporting details, sequence, and plot are all reinforced when children write. Reinforcement also occurs during writing conferences as child and teacher engage in important instructional dialogue about composing. All these concepts (and more) are central to good reading. In this way writing helps to promote reading comprehension. *It is appropriate for children to write during reading time.*

4.   *The act of writing strengthens reading ability.* Any of us who has encouraged disabled readers to write is in a position to know that writing helps children improve their reading skills. Almost as if by magic, children who write enjoy increased success in decoding the printed symbol. The more they write, the better they can read. *It is appropriate for children to write during reading time.*

Your principal smiles and says, "Well, clearly you have good reasons for what you are doing."

As you find yourself standing alone by the classroom door once again, you think of all the other things you could have said. You wish you had added, "Please come back again when you can stay long enough to help us with editing."

As you reflect on the encounter with your principal, you wonder if on another occasion you might have to substantiate your views by citing research. You will be pleased to know there is plenty of support for your position.

The Reading Connection

The words young children use in their own writing stay with them more readily than the words they encounter in reading textbooks, according to Bennett (1971). When children write or dictate as part of the reading program, they are constantly asking for words that are important to them. Bennett concluded that emotionality and meaningfulness account for their superior recall of their own words.

Writing as part of the reading program improves word recognition. In 1971 Oehlkers reported that the early emphasis on creative writing in first grade enhanced achievement in word recognition as much as did early emphasis on reading activities. Harris (1972) found that the reading achievement scores on the Stanford Reading Test for students in first, second, and third grade were significantly higher for those students involved in an "authorship" program.

Stauffer (1980, p. 131) reinforces the relationship between writing and word recognition. "Daily construction [writing] soon has children wanting to use words that are not in their word banks. At first, they turn to the teacher for all needed words, and the semantic efficacy of this spelling and writing of new words results in superior retention."

In their book entitled *Key Words to Reading,* Veatch et al. (1979, pp. 38–39) very strongly state the argument in favor of making writing a part of the reading program: "Writing, by its very nature, is an analytical skill or ability. Therefore, the sooner a child can write independently, the sooner he can read independently. Once the writing ability is acquired, the problem of decoding words in reading is simplified." Veatch also argues (p. 47) that the service words (markers such as *this, it, that, saw,* and *there*), often so difficult to learn, are more readily learned by children who write as part of the reading program.

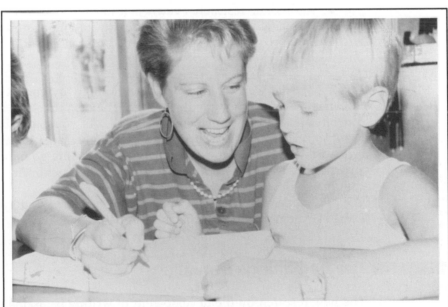

Dictating a story affords the child pride in ownership of the written words.
© *Michael Hagan*

The idea that writing enhances the learning of reading is not new. As long ago as 1943, Grace Fernald believed that a large percentage of children with partial or extreme disability in learning to read needed to approach reading through the kind of analysis that is required for writing language (Clay, 1982).

Perhaps nowhere has the case for writing as a way to learn reading been better presented than in Marie Clay's 1982 edition of *What Did I Write? Beginning Writing Behaviour.* She states:

The theories and experiments . . . suggest many links between early writing activities and the skills needed in learning to read.

Some of the skills and concepts that can be learned are these:

How to attend and orient to printed language.
How to organize one's exploratory investigation of printed forms.
How to tell left from right.
How to visually analyze letters and words.
What to study in a word so as to be able to reproduce it.
How to direct one's behavior in carrying out a sequence of
    movements needed in writing words and sentences.

Additional research evidence (Stotsky, 1983) shows that when teachers combine writing activities with the reading of student texts (such as social studies or science), both reading comprehension and retention are improved.

You did well when asked this morning why you were using reading time to allow your students to write. The next time you are asked, you can offer even more convincing evidence. As you move back into your group of eager authors you think, "I am right. All I have to do is look around this room to know that writing and reading go hand in hand. Instruction in reading is not a substitute for instruction in writing, but I couldn't possibly teach one without the other."

A little voice breaks through your reverie: "How do you spell *transformer?*" And it's back to the business at hand.

The Beginnings of Writing

The new research on the development of writing is fascinating. For years teachers and parents assumed that children would learn to write after they learned to read and that these experiences would take place primarily in a school setting. That view of writing dominated curriculum planning for generations of schoolchildren. Then in 1971 Chomsky departed radically from the prevailing view when she asserted that nonreaders should be writing and that reading instruction should begin with writing. Since that time, there has been a flurry of activity as researchers looked at young children and their writing. The resulting information has greatly expanded our view of what writing is and how it develops.

The more traditional view defined writing in terms that were mostly limited to handwriting. Children were expected to copy letters until they could successfully reproduce a close approximation of the teacher's model. Then they were expected to copy sentences. Copying exercises came from the handwriting text or from a verse or quotation on the board. Children's attempts at writing on their own were basically ignored and certainly not encouraged. Atkins (1984) reports hearing a teacher tell a young child's parents that the child needed to "do something constructive" with her time because she had wasted time writing on the margins of her worksheet.

In light of the research today, writing is generally defined in a much broader sense and includes the child's first efforts at making marks on paper—beginning with scribbles.

■ Developmental Stages

Parents of young children have known for years that children believe they can write. They have cleaned the results off walls and tables. One three-and-a-half-year-old we know wrote all over a hall wall. She tried to convince her parents that her nine-month-old brother had done the writing. What gave her away? The only word spelled correctly was her brother's name! Such interest in writing has typically been ignored or dismissed as scribbling and viewed as unimportant in the scheme of instruction. Goodman and Altwerger (1981) found that when they asked three-year-old children if they could write, the children would answer, "Of course," and make marks on paper that they expected could be interpreted. These same three-year-olds claimed not to be able to read because they had not been taught to do so.

We now recognize that children construct their understanding of written language in a developmental sequence that is distinguishable and very similar for every child. As soon as children begin to make marks with writing instruments, they are beginning to learn about written language and how it works. The first stage in the development of writing is scribbling (Figure 3.1). Just as children babble before they use words, they scribble all kinds of forms before they learn which of those forms are letters and which are not.

By the linear repetitive stage, children have discovered that writing

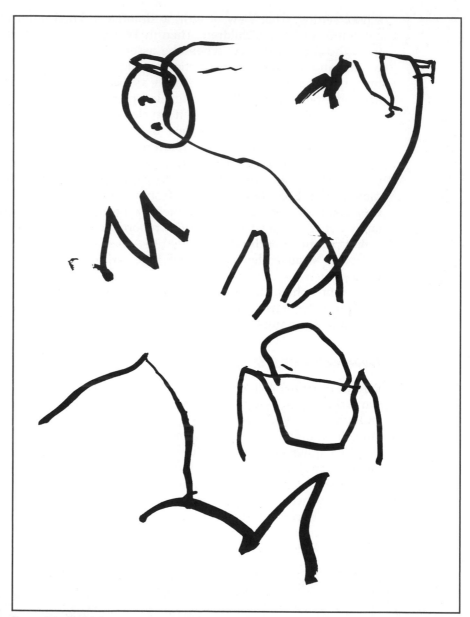

Figure 3.1   Scribbling.

"I love you."

Blaine   4 YRS. 4 MOS.

Figure 3.2   Linear repetitive writing.

is usually horizontal and moves in a string across the page (Figure 3.2).
Schickedanz (1987) found that children in this stage thought that a word
referring to something larger had a longer string of forms than a word referring to something smaller. In other words, children looked for some concrete connection between words and their referents.

Even though there are slight variations in observations, most researchers do agree that the next stage is a random letter stage (Figure 3.3).
Children learn which forms are acceptable as letters and use them in some
random order to record words or sentences. They may produce a string of

Figure 3.3   Random letter stage.

letters that have no relation to the sounds of the words that they are attempting to record. They may also include some forms that are not recognizable as letters because their repertoire of letters is so limited.

In the stage of early phonemic writing (Figure 3.4), children begin to make the connection between letters and sounds. The beginning of this stage is often described as letter name writing because children write the letters whose name and sound are the same. This is when they are likely to write the word *you* with the letter *u*. In time they begin to represent words with graphemes that reflect exactly what they hear. For example, they may use *hz* for *he's*.

As children gain more experience with the written language system, they begin to learn its conventions and to spell some words in conventional ways even though the spelling is not phonetic. A good example is the word *love*. Being exposed to this word so often, children begin very

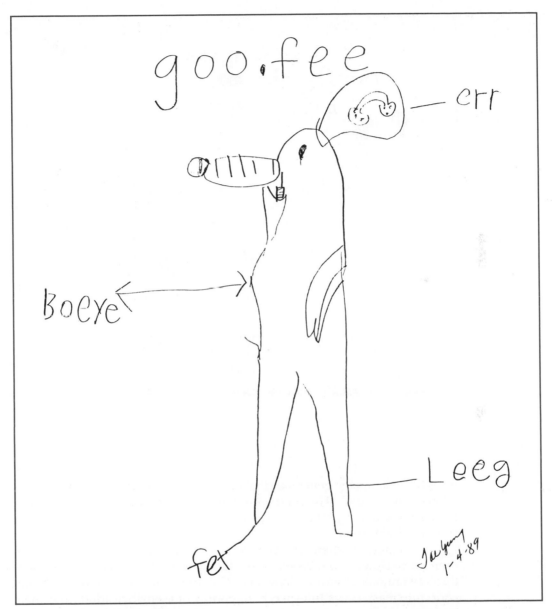

Figure 3.4   Early phonemic writing.

early to spell it in its conventional form. This stage of writing is called *transitional:* children are moving from their phonetic spelling to standard or conventional spelling (Figure 3.5).

Children learning spoken language generalize rules; for example, that adding *ed* produces the past tense of a verb. Similarly, children learn-

Figure 3.5   Transitional stage.

ing written language generalize that adding *e* to the end of a word indicates a long vowel sound. The child who drew this picture added the *e* to *boon*, then marked it out, perhaps reasoning that the two *o*'s produced the correct sound without the *e*.

Finally, children achieve mostly conventional spelling. Just as children move slowly from babbling to adult speech, they need time to adopt the conventions of written language. Children put considerable time and effort into mastering adult speech. Support from sensitive adults aids them in their task. Our hope is that children will have the same support as they proceed from scribbling to mature written language.

■ Discovery of Governing Principles

Clay (1982) describes several concepts and principles that children discover as they learn about written language. The first of these is a concept of signs. When children understand that objects or events can be represented with a sign, they can then move to learning letters as symbols that are arbitrary—not related to their referents. Another concept children develop is that messages can be written down. It is a very important moment when children discover that we can save messages by recording them in writing.

According to Clay, the first units of print must be copied. Children often copy logos and other models found in their environment, such as their names, which are likely to be the model they most frequently see.

Children develop the flexibility principle, which describes "the limits within which each letter form may be varied and still retain its identity" (Clay, 1982, p. 63). The inventory principle refers to the observation that children often take stock of their own learning in a very systematic way, such as making lists of all the letter forms they know or all the words they can write (Figure 3.6). Clay defines the recurring principle as "the tendency to

Figure 3.6   Inventory principle: child displays entire repertoire.

repeat an action" that contributes to the child's ability to form letters quickly and habitually. It becomes very helpful when the child realizes that "the same elements can recur in variable patterns" (Clay, 1982, p. 64).

Finally, the generating principle describes what children do when, knowing some elements and some rules for combining them, they produce new statements—that is, statements that differ in some respect from models they have encountered (Figure 3.7). Such behavior is basic to the development of language because children will not hear someone else speak every sentence they want to produce; they just know the elements and the rules for combining them. It is logical that they would use this same technique when attempting to master written language systems.

Some concepts basic to written language have no relationship to the sounds of words and thus to spoken language. Among them are directionality, space around words, and the use of abbreviations. As children gain more experience, they must also learn to deal with page and book arrangements.

Directionality is the convention that in English, writing begins on the left and moves to the right. Clay (1982) observes that children may temporarily ignore what they know about directionality when presented with the problem of a word that they cannot fit on a line or a page. With experience, they learn to carry words over to the next line or page.

Children develop the concept of *word* itself over time. They first understand phrases such as "It's time for your bath now" as a semantic whole, responding to the meaning of the entire phrase without knowing each individual word. As children gain experience with language, they learn to separate the nouns from the verbs and finally learn to recognize the individual words that compose sentences. As children begin reading and writing, they sometimes believe that each syllable requires a printed word. Gradually their ability to match print with sound improves. Clay (1967, p. 16) describes this behavior:

As [the children] developed skill in matching behavior, fingers were used to point to those parts of the text that were supposed to correspond to the vocal responses. Fluency gave way to word by word reading. At this point the child's reading became staccato as he overemphasized the breaks between words. He could be thought of as "reading the spaces" or "voice pointing" at the words.

Children learning to leave spaces around words must deal with negative space (what is left out)—a difficult concept. Some children attempt to handle the space by placing periods after each word, in an attempt to recognize spaces but to make them positive rather than negative.

Figure 3.7   Generating principle: child produces new statements.

Abbreviations are understood only by children having clear concepts of letter and word and their interrelationships. The use of abbreviations usually signals a child's comprehension that "words are constructed out of letters and that the letters of abbreviations 'stand for' words and could be filled out or expanded into full forms" (Clay, 1975, p. 65).

Children do not make these discoveries about written language and its conventions without considerable experience exploring writing, forming hypotheses about how print works, and then getting feedback that verifies their guesses. A child's exploration of the flexibility principle illustrates this need very well (Figure 3.8). The child writes an *F* and shows it to

Figure 3.8   Experimentation with the flexibility principle.

an adult, who confirms that it is an *F*. Now the child adds two more cross strokes and asks if it is an *F*. The answer is no. Perhaps the child then turns it on its side or backwards. Eventually the child determines exactly how much variation is allowed in the form while still qualifying as an *F*. To make learning as successful as possible, the child needs to write frequently, with understanding adults nearby who praise the child's accomplishments and know that the ability to write with adult conventions is learned over a period of time. No child should be expected to write perfectly at first, any more than a child is expected to speak perfectly at first.

Fostering Writing in the Classroom

Oral Language

Writing begins when children have something to say and they *believe* they can put it on paper. Children are naturally curious about their world, and most are excited about sharing their ideas. The teacher's jobs are to promote their natural curiosity, to provide maximum opportunities for children to talk about their view of the world, and then to let them write their ideas however they can. Children will write willingly only when they have something to communicate. We can expand what children have to say when we promote oral communication in classrooms. Classrooms where children are truly learning must of necessity be somewhat noisy places! People learn by sharing their views of the world with each other. When children express something that they believe, listeners should respond. Feedback from listeners either confirms or challenges their ideas. Talking about new ideas strengthens both those ideas and the quality of communication itself.

As children have new experiences, they must be allowed—in fact, encouraged—to talk about them so that their expanding concepts can be tested, challenged, and reinforced. Children who can discuss new concepts they are learning are acquiring a vocabulary that is meaningful and therefore usable to them as they write. It's simple: the more children know and the more comfortable they are with language, the more they will have to say and the more willing they will be to write. Perhaps Lee and Rubin said it best: "Talk provides the stepping stones between what is thought about and what is written. After a new and interesting experience we 'talk our thoughts' before we write them" (1979, p. 203).

Activities

A classroom that encourages writing must be a place where interesting things are going on that invite children to think, talk, read, and write. The classroom is organized to allow participation in a wide variety of activities, such as going on field trips, interacting with classroom visitors, caring for animals and plants, responding to a wide variety of literature, and conducting scientific research. Children need to have experiences that are novel or, if familiar, at least have a new twist. Children's lively interest in science favors many activities designed to investigate phenomena in the environment.

Children developing new concepts can talk about them, read about them, and write about them. For example, children could participate in an activity such as hatching silkworms, gathering food for the larvae, and observing the metamorphosis of the larvae. They would find that they had to do research about when silkworms can be hatched, what will happen to the silk if the larvae are allowed to mature, and how to preserve some eggs so that another generation of silkworms can be grown. Children involved in such activities are constantly talking about their observations, reading from a variety of sources, listening to the teacher read, and writing about their experiences and feelings. Activities that encourage thinking, talking, reading, and writing should be an ongoing part of every school day.

■ Writing Centers

Teachers who value writing will make sure that the classroom invites writing by providing an area where a wide variety of papers and writing instruments are available at all times. The writing itself need not take place in the writing center, but the materials necessary for helping children achieve their own writing goals should be readily available to all. Some teachers display objects or pictures in writing centers that might stimulate children to write. However, that strategem is not necessary if the classroom is alive with interesting activities and children are experimenting and thinking.

If a computer with word processing software is not available for your writing center, we suggest that you at least include one or more primary (large-print) typewriters. Children enjoy being able to render their final drafts in "real print."

Stock a bin in the writing center with scraps of construction paper (and other interesting kinds of paper) from the art center. For some reason, children are highly motivated by the chance to write on a strangely shaped piece of paper. Adding machine tape is a favorite. Sometimes it really does not matter what the writing is done on, as long as the children are writing!

■ Literature

Children who write need exposure to competent adult models of writing, just as children learning to speak need models of mature speech. The best models of excellent writing are available to children through high-quality children's literature. Teachers are responsible for selecting the best in children's literature and bringing it into classrooms. Children are not likely to be able to write poetry without having heard and read many examples of good poetry. They are not likely to be able to write good descriptive passages without having experience with the writing of authors who are masters at using descriptive language. Teachers can bring the literary models to the child through reading aloud, telling stories, and providing books that children can read for themselves.

Watch for especially beautiful or apt phrases and help children notice and appreciate those finds. Examples of language that delights, touches, transports, or enlightens can be transcribed onto charts as they are discovered. Children must also learn to observe writing techniques they might be able to use as models. For example, they might see facts presented in ways that are unusually interesting. Tomie de Paola's *Popcorn*, *Quicksand*, and *Cloud* books are good examples. Of course, children need to be encouraged to share writing they find especially well done. Only as children begin to read with conscious attention to the writing will they become better writers.

Frank Smith (1983) believes there is too much to learn about writing for children to learn only from instruction. He says, "Children must read like a writer, in order to learn how to write like a writer" (p. 562). Children who are reading like writers learn to appreciate the conventions and style of the authors and actively seek to learn from them. Lucy Calkins (1983, p. 86)* shares her experience with seven-year-old Greg as he comes to understand how the writer and the product are related:

"Before I ever wrote a book [said Greg], I used to think there was a big machine, and they typed a title and then the machine went until the book was done. Now I look at a book and I know a guy wrote it and it's been his project for a long time. After the guy writes it, he probably thinks of questions people will ask him and revises it like I do, and copies it to read to about six editors. Then he fixes it up, like how they say."

Greg and I are both learning how reading is made. And we both read differently because we have an insider's view of reading.

Readers do not read like writers every time they read. For example, readers who do not expect to write a newspaper article will read without

---
*From *Lessons from a Child* by Lucy McCormick Calkins. Copyright © 1983 by Heinemann Educational Books, Inc. (Portsmouth, NH). Reprinted by permission.

consciously looking for the elements of style and format that make newspaper writing distinctive. However, readers who do expect to write for a newspaper will read it while observing the writing and structure carefully. Even though we may not always read everything as if we were going to write, literature serves as a storehouse of written language from which we can later draw.

Bill Martin, Jr. (1975, p. 16),* describes how we save what we read for future use:

Each of us has a linguistic storehouse into which we deposit patterns for stories and poems and sentences and words. These patterns enter through the ear (and the eye) and remain available throughout the course of a lifetime for reading and writing and speaking. The good reader is a person who looks at a page of print and begins triggering patterns that have been stored in his linguistic treasury. These patterns range all the way from the plot structure an author has used in the story to the rhyme scheme that hangs a poem together, to the placement of an adjective in front of a noun as part of the shape of the sentence, to the underlying rhythmical structure in a line of prose or poetry, to the "ed" ending as part of the shape of a word.

Exposure to a wide range of literature and other printed material provides the storehouse from which children can draw as they write. We will share many ideas for using children's literature in Chapter 7.

■ Appreciation and Recognition

Teachers Who Value the Child's Work

The classroom environment is often a direct reflection of the teacher's attitude about what is important work for children and what accomplishments are valuable. Teachers who expect children to write well will demonstrate that they value the products of writing efforts. They will, for example, encourage children to publish frequently—to contribute to class books and write their own books. They will display children's writing and find a way to highlight outstanding passages, pointing out a word that carries exactly the right connotation to communicate a feeling, a unique choice of words,

---

*From *Teaching Suggestions for Sounds Jubilee and Sounds Freedom Ringing* by Bill Martin, Jr. Holt, Rinehart and Winston, Inc. Copyright © 1975 by the author. Reprinted by permission.

or an especially evocative line of poetry. Perhaps they will also ask children to explain how they achieved a particularly outstanding line or composition.

Teachers also use children's writing products for instruction. The children read writing produced by their classmates in order to gain skill as writers and readers. They use the work of other children as models for their own stories or poems. David Greenburg (1978) observes that children writing poetry respond best to samples written by other children. Alert teachers will be aware of opportunities to display, to publish, and to share the work of their writers.

Children Who Value Each Other's Work

You may have heard parents or other adults remark, "Children say the meanest things!" It's true that children can be very open—even blunt—with their comments. They need an adult to help them learn tact. However, children can also be very supportive of the writing efforts of their classmates, given the opportunity and some guidance from the teacher with respect to appropriate responses. Visiting classrooms where writing was taught with enthusiasm and respect, we have seen children eagerly reading their work to their peers, with truly positive results. There is something special in children's discovery that their writing pleases their friends.

Libraries of Children's Work

A classroom library is essential to an environment that supports reading and writing. The library corner should be stocked with materials drawn periodically from the school library, the city library, and the teacher's and children's home libraries. Perhaps the most valuable additions to a classroom library are the works of the authors who occupy that classroom. Each publication by an author in the classroom should be honored just as much as the works of professionally published authors.

A nice plus would be the establishment in the school library of a system for cataloging the edited publications of the children and circulating them throughout the school. Two of our former students, teachers at an elementary school, created what their students called the "Do Your Own Thing Library." These teachers' fifth-grade classes obtained permission from the school media teacher to take over a corner of the library. A section of the library was partitioned off by portable bookcases and refrigerator cartons. The children created various kinds of display units. When the physical space was finally ready, all the classes in the school were notified that the "Do Your Own Thing Library" was about to open and was accepting donations of written works and art works by authors and artists in the school. Each donated piece would be cataloged into the "Do Your Own Thing Library" for a three-week period, during which time it could be checked out by anyone in the school. Open before and after school, the library was completely managed by students in the two fifth-grade classrooms. The project was a tremendous success, and certainly communicated the message that the work of children was important.

■ Writing in the Curriculum

Critics of current American education have consistently pointed out our shortcomings in the teaching of writing. Frankly, we believe that today's high school and college students have difficulty in writing because they *were not taught how to write* in elementary and middle school—and possibly not in high school. Secondary schools cannot be expected to make up the deficit in writing skills caused by a lack of prior instruction.

How serious is the problem? The National Assessment of Educational Progress, a Department of Education project mandated by Congress, reported the results of a survey of the writing of 55,000 fourth-, eighth-, and eleventh-graders in 1987. Conclusions drawn from the survey were that most American students cannot write well enough to make themselves understood, that schools are doing a poor job of teaching the subject, and that students perform worse in writing than in any other major subject. The report included recommendations for improvement ("Newsnotes," 1987):

1. Writing should be taught in all subject areas.
2. Teachers should assign writing more frequently (the average student is given only two or three writing assignments in a six-week period).
3. Teachers should not just correct grammar and punctuation on writing assignments but also focus on a student's ideas and organization.

We believe that recommendation number 3 is extremely important. It may well be the pivotal point in improving writing skills in today's and tomorrow's students. In fact, we suspect that too many teachers have made too few writing assignments and then essentially given students no feedback on their writing. Telling a student that a piece of writing is worth a 75 or a B+ *in no way* helps that student improve his or her writing. Students need frequent writing assignments on which they get constructive feedback that can be used in revising and reworking a writing piece. Writing instruction will improve as teachers learn to evaluate ideas and organization as part of viewing writing as a process.

Shaw (1985) noted that curriculum guides and standardized tests may be detrimental to writing instruction. The guides rarely mention the amount of time that children should be involved in writing instruction; therefore, teachers view it as unimportant. Furthermore, teachers tend to emphasize skills that can be measured on standardized tests, and writing is one subject not generally tested that way. Students will become better writers only when the writing is valued.

The Act of Writing

The writing process consists of six steps: prewriting, composing the rough draft, getting response and making revisions, editing, completing the final draft, and sharing or presenting. The following detailed discussion, adapted from McKenzie and Tompkins (1984), treats each step in turn. Like reading, however, writing is not a totally linear process. Writers move recursively through the steps, falling back from rough draft to prewriting, for example, and then going forward again.

Prewriting

Prewriting is the "getting ready" stage. Here the author makes a choice of topic and gathers both ideas and data.

Children will write well only about what they know. Whereas the teacher may sometimes be justified in giving all students a common writing assignment, most of the time each author should be free to select a topic drawn from his or her own unique background of experience. Authors should be encouraged to think, observe, experience, and talk with you and other students about what they *might* write. Our experience has shown that the more children can talk about what they might write, sharing those ideas in a group, the more diverse and detailed is the writing within that group.

During the prewriting stage, you may want to engage children in conducting research, brainstorming, and looking at books, films, or drama to help in the selection of topic and to foster a growing sense of "I know what I want to say" about that topic. We suggest that as you talk with children about what they might write, you engage them in sensory awareness: "How do you think the boy will feel in your story? What words can you use to describe the way the grease felt when the detective touched it? Close your eyes and imagine how the candy shop smelled. What words could you use to help your reader know that smell?" Nurturing a child's sense of command of the subject will build excitement for the writing. You will know you have done an effective job with the prewriting stage if when you say, "Go write!" your students eagerly tackle the job.

■ Rough Draft

Rough-draft writing, the "getting started" stage, will begin easily if you and your young authors have done a good job in the prewriting stage. Now the author switches back and forth between rehearsal (trying the words out mentally) and composition (writing them down). The writing here is often tentative and exploratory: "How do I want to say that? I'll try it like this. No, I don't like the sound of that. Here, let's try it this way." Good writers shift continuously between rehearsal and composition. You should model this process over and over again on the chalkboard so that children see how the shifting works: thinking, writing, crossing out, writing again, thinking, changing. Rough drafts should be double spaced to facilitate changes.

Young authors must learn the difficult lesson (which we have all tried to avoid) that there is no such thing as a "finished" first draft. Rarely, if ever, is a first draft done well enough to be a last draft. Almost any piece of writing can be improved. Knowing that the first draft will seldom be the last draft encourages some children to take risks they otherwise would not take. However, we believe that children should have the choice of whether or not to take a rough draft any further through the writing process. All of us who have ever tried to write know that sometimes we truly dislike a rough draft and do not want to carry on with it. Young authors have an equal right to abandon work they prefer not to complete.

A second important lesson about rough drafts is that it is appropriate for children to use words they may not know how to spell. Limiting children to words they can spell reduces dramatically the quality of their writing. Children who are encouraged to use the words they choose, even if they have to invent the spelling, will produce much more interesting writing. Their improvisations represent their best judgments about spelling, and the research of Gentry (1982) and Hodges (1981) shows that frequent application of spelling knowledge while writing encourages spelling competency.

Conferring with students who are in the rough-draft stage can lead to improved writing, a payoff that many feel warrants the total investment of time. Rough-draft conferences can be very short—one to two minutes. They involve a quick reading of the draft and asking a key question or two to help the author think about content or organization. "Kelly, tell me about how your writing is going." "Josh, do you really want to tell your reader this much about the clues before the detective begins to solve the mystery?" "Amy, you have been writing about the party. What is going to happen next?" "Is there anything I can help with?" The focus of the conference during the rough-draft stage is to help children get their ideas onto the paper. This is not a time for editing mechanics or grammar.

Graves (1983) offers four principles for helping children during conferences.

Writing conferences between student and teacher are integral to the writing process.
© David S. Strickler/The Picture Cube

1. Follow the child. Base what you say on what the child last said.
2. Ask questions you think the child can answer. When you ask questions first that you are sure the child can answer, you can then follow with more challenging questions.
3. Help the child to focus. Children often know so much about a topic that they simply have too much to say, and then they get off the track. Questions that help children narrow and focus are important here.
4. Offer a final reflection. Say something to the child that encourages his or her continued effort to get words on paper.

To further the immediate goal, the teacher puts aside concern for mechanics until a later stage.

■ Revision/Response

Revision/response is the stage of "getting to the heart of it." Now content and organization become the focus, with some attention to mechanics.

There are many ways to handle this stage. The goals are for the author to respond to his or her own writing and to get feedback from others. To the author, the steps in this stage might look like this:

1. Reread the draft to myself. Does it say what I wanted to say? Make revisions as I see the need for them.
2. Share my draft with a friend and/or the teacher. Then check to see if the reader understands what I meant to say. Make revisions as I see the need for them or as suggested.
3. Go back over my draft to see all the ways I can make it better.

■ Editing

The editing stage means "getting help." The draft is prepared for its final revisions, with the focus on mechanics and some attention given to content and organization. The author, one or more peers, and adults may all serve as editors. Children need to be taught how to perform this important step in the writing process.

Learning what to look for in the editing process should be an outgrowth of a series of lessons over the year. Techniques to cover in those lessons include (but are not limited to) capitalization, punctuation, spelling, structural form, sentences, paragraphs, grammar, vocabulary, and composition. At any stage in the editing process, the focus should be on *some* of these points rather than *all* of them. As writing skill improves, you can add more and more editing "checkpoints" and expect children to make corrections. Meanwhile, you may have to act as copy editor much of the time. By this we mean that you simply correct some of the errors as you type the final copy—or ask the school secretary or a parent volunteer to provide this service. The table in Figure 3.9 shows some standard editing marks. We suggest that you make a large chart of these to display in your classroom and teach your students the meaning of each mark. You will be amazed at how well students will be able to use them in time. Check your school district's curriculum guide to see which editing marks should be introduced at each grade level.

Frankly, getting editing done with a group of children is a very difficult task. You can easily feel overwhelmed when a couple dozen children all need your editing attention at one time. To help you in this important task, we offer some suggestions:

1.   Stagger the beginning of writing activities so that the children are at different stages in the writing process at any one time. Some children may be doing art work to illustrate their stories while some are researching ideas; some are creating first drafts while others are editing. Not everyone will need your attention so desperately at the same time.

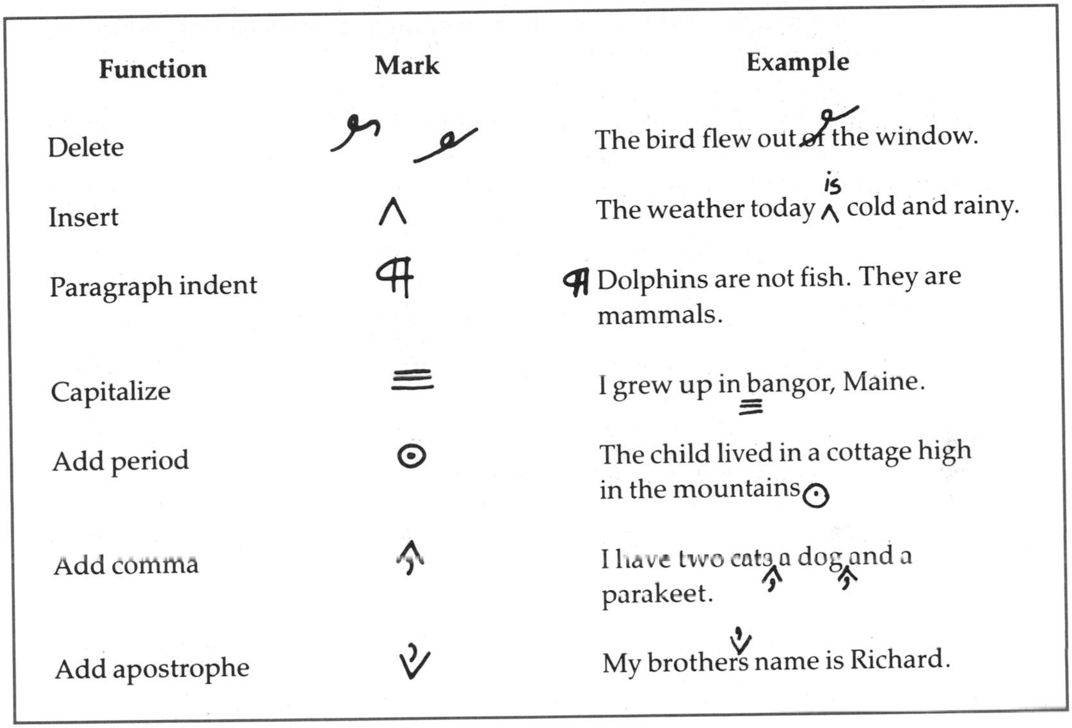

Function	Mark	Example
Delete	ꙮ ꙮ	The bird flew out ~~of~~ the window.
Insert	∧	The weather today ∧ cold and rainy. *is*
Paragraph indent	¶	¶ Dolphins are not fish. They are mammals.
Capitalize	≡	I grew up in bangor, Maine. ≡
Add period	⊙	The child lived in a cottage high in the mountains ⊙
Add comma	⋏	I have two cats a dog and a parakeet. ⋏ ⋏
Add apostrophe	⋎	My brothers name is Richard. ⋎

Figure 3.9   Editing marks.

2.   Do not plan to do all the editing yourself. We suspect that many experienced teachers like ourselves would be ashamed to admit how many student drafts piled up on their desks awaiting their editing attention until the author lost interest in (or forgot about!) the piece. You cannot do the whole job yourself. If you are fortunate, you will have volunteers to help. In some schools, arrangements are made for older students to help younger students; some schools have a publishing house where the students can get help. Parents and other community members volunteer time to work in the publishing house, assisting children in editing and bookbinding.

3.   Use self-editing and peer editing. Encourage students to read their own writing carefully, looking for errors and strengths. After correcting the errors they find, they have a friend read the work aloud to them. Frequently, children will hear mistakes when someone reads their writing aloud that they overlooked when they read it themselves. Have your students engage in one or more of three kinds of peer editing, which we will describe. If children are well trained in the process, peer editing can begin toward the end of first grade. As children move up through the grades, their peer editing strategies become considerably more sophisticated. We

recommend three approaches to peer editing: partner editing, editing committees, and editing groups.

Deciding what to correct and what to ignore for the present is certainly one example of the art rather than the science of teaching. Much depends on the child's age and previous experience with writing. Too much editing may discourage the budding writer, and too little may not challenge the writer as learner of conventions. One rule of thumb says for the very youngest writers, do not attempt corrections; for experienced kindergarteners, one correction per project is enough, and so on. For beginning writers, corrections should be made with the child's permission. One might say, "Juan, we usually spell 'there' t-h-e-r-e. So that no one will be confused by this word, do you want to change the spelling here in your story?" As children learn about various conventions, they can be marked for correction in their writing. By the time children leave elementary school they should correct spelling, sentence structure, agreement, and paragraphing errors. With only a few exceptions, they should be able to write a final draft that is correct by adult standards.

To the student, the stages between prewriting and final draft look like this:

Steps in editing

1. Finish my rough draft.
2. Read my writing to correct the errors I can find.
3. Find a partner for partner editing.
4. Follow all the steps on the partner editing chart.
5. Make all the corrections I can make.
6. Take my draft to an editing committee.
7. Take my draft to my editing group.
8. Make final corrections.

Partner Editing

We have found that these procedures work in partner editing:

1. Find a partner.

2. Exchange papers.

3. Read your partner's paper silently.

4. At the bottom or on the back of the paper, write
   A. something you liked about the paper (not handwriting);
   B. something that could be improved (not neatness or crossing t's);
   C. a list of misspelled words spelled correctly.

5. Show punctuation corrections in the margins.

6. After you have done steps 4 and 5, read the paper aloud to the author and then read your A, B, and C. Discuss with the author why you made the comments you did. If the writer and you cannot agree on what needs improvement, then ask a third person. If there is still no agreement, then take it to the teacher.

7. Return the paper to the owner.

8. The author makes the suggested revisions and corrections and then prepares to write the final draft.

The success of a partner-editing procedure depends on the amount of preparation your students have before they try it. It is important to post the list of steps prominently in the classroom. Go over the steps with the whole class several times so that everyone understands the meaning and importance of each step. The first few times, you may find it helpful to walk the class through the procedure step by step.

Editing Committees

Editing committees are small groups of from three to five students who are charged with a single editing task. The task might be to read rough drafts to check for complete sentences. The task might be to read for proper ending punctuation. Perhaps, thinking of Billy in the cartoon (Figure 3.10), the task would be to check for commas. Billy belongs on the Comma Committee because he is really interested in commas. He likes using commas. He needs a little fine tuning of his understanding of the use of commas, but we suspect that he can learn very quickly to use commas properly. You will find other children who are using commas properly or need only a little reinforcement to do so. These children should be on the Comma Committee.

We suggest the following steps in using editing committees:

1. Select the writing (composition or mechanical) skill or skills you wish to highlight next in your year-long writing plan.
2. Teach a lesson on the selected skill to the whole group or to those children who you know need the instruction.
3. Check writing samples following the lesson to identify those children who are correctly using the highlighted skill or, with a little attention from you, soon will be.
4. Identify from three to five children who will serve on the editing committee. You might want to have them spend some time sitting at an "editors' table" during part of the writing period.

Figure 3.10   Candidate for membership on the Comma Committee.

Let them create hats or badges that name their committee, or
hang a sign above the table.

5. Instruct authors in your class to submit their rough drafts to
   the editing committee after they have done partner editing or
   worked with an editing group. You might have more than one
   editing committee at work at any given time.

Editing committees involve many children in the editing process
and elevate the concern for correctness to an appropriate level. During the
year, each child should have the opportunity to serve on one or more editing committees.

Editing Groups

Editing groups are similar to editing committees, but there are some important differences. Ideally the class is divided into editing groups of six chil-

dren each who remain together throughout the school year. Every child who is able to function in a group is placed in one, and others are permitted to join (or rejoin) when ready. The stability of the editing group is important so that the group may evolve a sense of itself and develop a high level of trust. The task of the editing group is to look at both content and mechanics. Editing groups can be very effective in giving young authors good feedback on their writing. However, the success of the editing group is totally dependent on the care you take in preparing them for the task and in monitoring their work on an ongoing basis. We believe that children in third grade and above can learn to function effectively in editing groups.

These are the procedures for the editing group:

1. Each member reads his or her composition aloud to the group.
2. After a piece is read, each member names at least one thing he or she especially liked about the composition and suggests one or more things to the author as an improvement. Children should be encouraged to make comments of this sort: "I like the way you got your reader's attention early in the story. The dialogue sounds just like the way the characters would really speak, I think. I think you gave too many hints about the solution of the mystery too early in the story. Can you tell us more about how the graveyard looked in the dark?"
3. The author records the comments on the back of the last page of the composition or within the composition at appropriate places.
4. The author asks the group if anyone has further comments or suggestions.
5. Two members of the group exchange papers and read very carefully for mechanics.

In practice, the editing group need not operate in the lockstep fashion this list suggests. You and your students can modify the steps to your liking. As the level of trust grows within the group and as the group gains experience in conducting the editing sessions, you will see tremendous improvement in the comments and suggestions and, in turn, in the writing products of the group.

To a very large extent, the success of an editing group depends on the guidance it gets from you in conducting Step 2. You must carefully teach them the kinds of things to listen for and to say. At first, they will need frequent reminders and reinforcement. You can help by hanging a chart on the wall with suggestions of things to look for and to comment on during editing group time. Marjorie Frank (1979, p. 110)* has suggested these emphases in editing with little children or new writers:

substituting stronger words (more colorful, specific)
rearranging words within a sentence
expanding sentences
cutting apart a short paragraph to reshuffle sentences for a different sound or meaning
making up better titles
changing endings
adding one detail to the ad or article or story.

Frank suggests (p. 111) that older children or more experienced writers in editing groups should work toward these aims:

revising whole pieces
coordinating ideas within paragraphs
varying sentence length and structure
examining word use, using specific and/or vivid words
eliminating overused words and expressions
making effective transitions
appealing to specific audiences
adapting form and style to a particular purpose
inventing exciting beginnings and strong conclusions
creating moods
incorporating dialogue into the writing
arranging details in logical order
supporting statements with specific details
eliminating unimportant words or phrases.

With the completion of the editing group's work, the author is ready to proceed to the next step in the writing process—the final draft.

■ Final Draft

The final draft stage is the "getting it perfect" stage. Taking into consideration all editorial suggestions, the author prepares the final, polished draft. The author makes final decisions about how the work will appear on the

---

*From *If You're Trying to Teach Kids to Write, You've Gotta Have This Book!* by Marjorie Frank. Copyright © 1979 by Incentive Publications, Inc. Reprinted by permission.

page, then carefully copies the work and proofreads the copy. This draft represents the author's very best work.

We strongly recommend that if children are doing the work by hand, they make only one final copy. Permit children to use erasable pens and/or correction fluid, to glue paper over an error, or even to draw a single line through an error. Although we refer to this stage as the "getting it perfect" stage, we all need to recognize that young hands are going to make mistakes. We have too often seen interest in writing destroyed by making children copy a final draft over and over until it is perfect.

Many teachers and students like the ease of doing the final draft with a word processing program on a microcomputer. In fact, in many classrooms students write the original rough draft on the computer and do all revising and editing using the word processing program. However, use of word processing in the classroom requires careful consideration.

First, what level of keyboarding skill do your students possess? The typical fifth-grader hand-writes from ten to twelve words per minute. Children who lack the keyboarding skill to type as fast as they can write manually will soon lose interest in using the computer. Some school districts have found that instruction in the proper techniques of keyboarding, finger reaches, and eye movement enables most students to match their writing speed when word processing; in fact, 75 percent of students can double their writing speed with the word processor. Clearly, children need to learn keyboarding skills before they can employ word processors in the writing program.

Second, what instructional objectives are to be met with word processing? Word processing programs are available in two basic formats. One format provides instruction in writing through a variety of activities and may include supplementary print materials. The other is simply a word processing program. Do you want your classroom computer to assist with writing instruction or simply to be a tool for word processing?

Regardless of how the act of writing is carried out, seeing a work through from rough to final draft is a big commitment. How often should children take a piece of writing through the entire process to publication or presentation? Graves (1983) suggests that children in first and second grade can reasonably publish one book (a polished piece) every ten days, on the average. He says that the norm for children above third grade who are writing daily is one published book within an eight-week period. Our experience and observations in classrooms suggest that many intermediate-grade children can produce more than one book in eight weeks. The choice to publish or not is a very individual one and varies considerably among children. We entirely agree with Graves that publication is important for *all* children.

■ Sharing/Presenting

At last the student reaches the "getting published" stage: the polished writing effort is shared with the intended audience in some way. Publication can take many forms, ranging from bound books to bulletin board displays, reports, letters, newspaper articles, dramatic presentation, and oral reading. We urge you to engage children in deciding on the best way to share a given piece of writing, and to encourge children to vary their presentation formats over time. For example, a child might choose to share a poem by mounting it on construction paper and displaying it on the bulletin board. Another time the child might send the poem to a neighboring classroom or submit it to the school newspaper. One of the most popular ways of sharing writing is to publish books. Individual students may author books, or a class may collaborate on a book. Books may be written independently or in conjunction with a science or social studies theme. Anyone who has witnessed a child's glow of pride in a book he or she has published can never doubt the worth of the activity.

Children need to write *daily*. Recall that it is only through constructive feedback and revision that a child's writing skill grows. In some

Student-authored writing models set an attainable standard for youngsters to emulate.
© Michael Hagan

classrooms the editing and sharing/presenting processes are so protracted that children publish only two pieces in a school year. Wise teachers are cautious in ensuring that no one publishing effort take too much time. Donald Graves (1983) warns that publishing two pieces in one year does not constitute a writing program for a child. When we allow a child to write only two pieces in a grading period, we have robbed that child of chances to grow in writing as surely as if we had allowed the child to "fill in the blanks" all the time and called that our writing program!

Portfolio

How is the decision made regarding which of a child's efforts should be published? We believe in making it a collaborative decision between the child and the teacher, weighted in the child's favor. Although it is rare that a child should be permitted to decide *not* to write, it should be commonplace for the child to decide *what* to write—and what to publish. Each child should have a writing portfolio in which to place each rough draft and in which to keep work in progress. The portfolio can be as simple as a manila folder kept in a cardboard box or as fancy as you wish to have children make them. Children should be permitted (taught and encouraged) to select from the rough drafts in the portfolio those that should be taken through the entire writing process.

If writing samples from throughout the year are kept in the portfolio, you will have a record of children's writing development. It is great fun on the last day of school to have children look at the writing they did at the start of the school year. While taking delight in their growth in writing, the children will protest loudly that they didn't write "that baby stuff!" Similar use may be made of a daily log or journal. On a recent school visit, a first-grader proudly showed us his journal, rejoicing in the strides he had taken in his writing since the beginning of the year. We took great pleasure in hearing him read two of his most recently published books.

A chronology of writing growth is only one of the uses of the writing portfolio. Other uses serve you, the student, and the parents:

1.   The portfolio is a diagnostic tool for you. By quickly glancing through the portfolios, you can determine which writing skills to focus on next. You can also determine candidates for small skill groups or editing committees.

2.   After third grade, children can be guided to examine recent writing samples in the portfolio and set some personal writing goals. The goals can be listed on the inside cover of the portfolio and checked off as they are reached.

3.   The portfolio is a tool for you to use in parent conferences. Your selection of pieces from the portfolio can demonstrate a child's devel-

opment in the writing process. Include an explanation of the writing port-folio in your "back to school" presentation of your writing program to parents. They will see the importance of the portfolio and understand why their children will not be bringing home everything they write.

Publication

Having decided to publish a final draft, a child needs ready access to the materials and tools of publication. Many teachers set up a publishing corner in the classroom. More and more schools are creating "publishing houses" staffed by volunteers who assist children in doing bookbinding and preparing other forms of presentation. Figure 3.11 shows how a school's publishing house might look. Made from refrigerator cartons, held together with large pop rivets, the publishing house could be set up in the school library or a classroom. The publishing house contains all the things children need to publish or otherwise present their work; for example,

> computers and word processing programs
> typewriters
> art supplies for bookbinding and illustration
> pens, pencils, marking pens, scissors, crayons
> paper cutter.

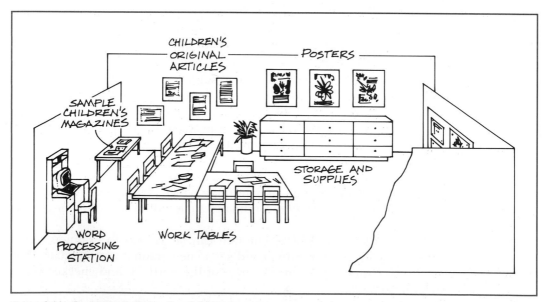

Figure 3.11   Features of a school's publishing house.

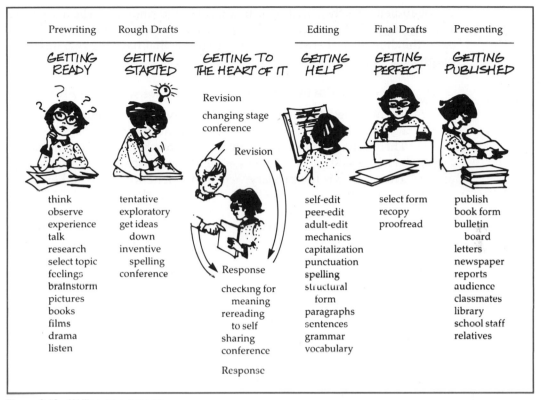

Prewriting	Rough Drafts		Editing	Final Drafts	Presenting
GETTING READY	GETTING STARTED	GETTING TO THE HEART OF IT	GETTING HELP	GETTING PERFECT	GETTING PUBLISHED
		Revision changing stage conference Revision			
think observe experience talk research select topic feelings brainstorm pictures books films drama listen	tentative exploratory get ideas down inventive spelling conference	Response checking for meaning rereading to self sharing conference Response	self-edit peer-edit adult-edit mechanics capitalization punctuation spelling structural form paragraphs sentences grammar vocabulary	select form recopy proofread	publish book form bulletin board letters newspaper reports audience classmates library school staff relatives

Figure 3.12   Writing as a process.

Bookbinding is becoming more and more popular as a way of publishing a child's writing. Instructions for bookbinding are presented in Appendix A.

As we have described it, the writing process is not a simple one. But neither is it so complex as to be beyond the reach of children. Figure 3.12 summarizes the important aspects of the process.

Process versus Product

In this chapter we have underscored the need for writing to be a part of the reading program. Further, we have insisted that writing be seen as a process—an ongoing, recursive process—in which children have many opportunities to select what they write and then polish and publish that writing. Children need frequent constructive feedback on their writing from a variety of audiences if their writing is to improve. We sincerely believe that the writing program must focus on the *process* rather than on the *product*. Consider the differences between writing programs that have the two different emphases:

When we write for a product	When we write as a process
The writing is teacher centered.	The writing is student centered.
The teacher's role is to assign and grade.	The teacher's role is to model and coach.
The teacher is the primary audience.	We write for many audiences.
The product is graded.	The process is evaluated.
The teacher is the primary responder.	The editing group or editing committee is the primary responder.
We write one linear draft.	We write many ever-improving drafts.
A draft is done in class.	The entire process of thinking, writing, revising, editing, and publishing is done in class.

■ Major Ideas in This Chapter

■ Writing is a developmental process that can be observed and encouraged. It takes time for children to achieve competence as they move through characteristic stages from scribbling to conventional spelling.

■ Children explore written language much as they explore the spoken language. By observation and experimentation they discover the principles and conventions that govern writing.

■ Writing success is achieved through a process that moves from prewriting through rough draft, revision/responding, editing, and final draft to publication. Writing daily, and working recursively through the stages of writing, will increase children's skills as writers and as readers.

■ Selection of writing to be carried through the writing process to publication and sharing should be a joint decision. There is a wide choice of forms for presentation.

■ Instruction in writing and editing skills requires careful organization and planning by the teacher.

? Discussion Questions
Focusing on the Teacher You Are Becoming

1. A parent complains that her child talks all the time about the writing she is doing in reading class. The parent is concerned that her child isn't learning to read. What responses can you make?
2. The father of the six-year-old who wrote "wusr apon a time. Ther was a robot thet dint aint have a oonere."* expresses concern at open house that his son is not learning to spell properly. How will you explain the concept of invented or developmental spelling, and what will you say to make the father feel better about his son's progress?
3. Having children read and write as much as we have suggested will take up a lot of the time usually spent filling in blanks in workbooks. What are the issues involved here, and how will you resolve them?
4. If you have thirty-five children in a small classroom, you may not have room for all the centers we have suggested. What are ways to achieve the goals of the centers in limited space?
5. Who should serve on editing committees? Should only the most talented writers have such positions, or are there ways for virtually all children to have a turn?

☑ Field-Based Applications

1. Ask the children to select one of their favorite authors and write a letter to him or her asking how he or she wrote a particular story or section of a story. Encourage them to ask specific questions about revisions and rewriting.
2. Write something yourself and share it with your students. Elicit their feedback for revisions or changes that would make the writing better.
3. Collect wonderful phrases or words from the literature that you and the children are sharing. Discuss how the author might have decided to use that phrase or word.
4. Make a bulletin board from the children's writings on a particular topic or theme, and bind them into a book when the display is taken down.
5. Set aside a time each week for children to share the writing they have done during that week. Give children the option of reading their own work or having you read it for them. Not every child will have something to share every week.

---

*Once upon a time there was a robot that didn't ain't have a owner.

6. Ask children to submit some of their work to the local newspaper.
7. Survey children's writing portfolios and make a list of skills that you could teach over the next few weeks.

⊡ References and Suggested Readings

Atkins, Cammie. "Writing: Doing Something Constructive." *Young Children* (November 1984): 3–7.

Bennett, Stanley W. "The Key Vocabulary in Organic Reading: An Evaluation of Some of Ashton-Warner's Assumptions of Beginning Reading." Ph.D. dissertation, University of Michigan, 1971.

Calkins, Lucy. *The Art of Teaching Writing*. Portsmouth, N.H.: Heinemann Educational Books, 1986.

Calkins, Lucy. "Making the Reading–Writing Connection." *Learning* 12 (September 1983): 82–86.

Chomsky, Carol. "Write First, Read Later." *Childhood Education* 47 (March 1971): 296–299.

Clay, Marie. "The Reading Behavior of Five Year Old Children: A Research Project." *New Zealand Journal of Educational Studies* 2 (1967): 11–31.

Clay, Marie. *What Did I Write? Beginning Writing Behaviour*. Exeter, N.H.: Heinemann Educational Books, 1982.

de Paola, Tomie. *The Cloud Book*. New York: Holiday House, 1975.

de Paola, Tomie. *The Quicksand Book*. New York: Holiday House, 1977.

de Paola, Tomie. *The Popcorn Book*. New York: Scholastic Book Services, 1978.

Frank, Marjorie. *If You're Trying to Teach Kids How to Write, You've Gotta Have This Book*. Nashville: Incentive Publications, 1979.

Ferreiro, Emilia, and Teberoksy, Ana. *Literacy before Schooling*. Exeter, N.H.: Heinemann Educational Books, 1982.

Gentry, J. Richard. "An Analysis of Developmental Spelling in GNYS AT WRK." *The Reading Teacher* 36 (November 1982): 192–200.

Goodman, Yetta, and Altwerger, Bess. "Print Awareness and Pre-School Children: A Working Paper." Occasional Papers, Arizona Center for Research and Development, College of Education, University of Arizona, 1981.

Graves, Donald. *Writing: Teachers and Children at Work*. Portsmouth, N.H.: Heinemann Educational Books, 1983.

Graves, Donald, and Stuart, Virginia. *Write from the Start*. New York: New American Library, 1985.

Greenburg, David. *Teaching Poetry to Children*. Portland, Ore.: Continuing Education Publications, 1978.

Hannan, Elizabeth, and Hamilton, Gord. "Writing: What to Look For, What to Do." *Language Arts* 61 (April 1984): 364–366.

Harris, Gary R. "The Effects of Communication Skills through Authorship: A Language Experience Supplement on the Development of Reading Skills with Primary Students." Ph.D. dissertation, University of Idaho, 1972.

Hodges, Richard. *Learning to Spell*. Urbana, Ill.: ERIC Clearinghouse on Reading and Communication Skills and National Council of Teachers of English, 1981. (ERIC Document Reproduction Service No. ED 202 016)

Lee, Doris, and Rubin, Joseph. *Children and Language: Reading and Writing, Talking and Listening*. Belmont, Calif.: Wadsworth, 1979.

McKenzie, Dan L., and Tompkins, Gail E. "Evaluating Students' Writing: A Process Approach." *Journal of Teaching Writing* (1984): 201–212.

Martin, Bill, Jr., and Brogan, Peggy. *Sounds Freedom Ringing Teacher's Edition*. New York: Holt, Rinehart & Winston: 1975a.

Martin, Bill, Jr., and Brogan, Peggy. *Sounds Jubilee Teacher's Edition*. New York: Holt, Rinehart & Winston, 1975b.

Newman, Judith. "Language Learning and Computers." *Language Arts* 61 (September 1984): 414–417.

"Newsnotes." *Phi Delta Kappan* 68 (February 1987): 484–485.

Oehlkers, William John. "The Contribution of Creative Writing to Reading Achievements in the Language Experience Approach." Ph.D. dissertation, University of Delaware, 1971.

Schickedanz, Judith. "Views of Literacy Development, Then and Now." Paper presented at annual conference of the National Association for the Education of Young Children, Anaheim, Calif., 1987.

Shaw, Robert. "Growing Support for Elementary School Writing Instruction." *Educational Leadership* 42 (February 1985): 16–18.

Smith, Frank. "Reading Like a Writer." *Language Arts* 60 (May 1983): 558–567.

Stauffer, Russell. *The Language Experience Approach to the Teaching of Reading*. 2nd ed. New York: Harper & Row, 1980.

Stotsky, Sandra. "Research on Reading/Writing Relationships: A Synthesis and Suggested Directions." *Language Arts* 60 (May 1983): 627–642.

Temple, Charles; Nathan, Ruth G.; and Burris, Nancy. *The Beginnings of Writing*. Boston: Allyn & Bacon, 1982.

Tierney, Robert, and Pearson, P. David. "Toward a Composing Model of Reading." *Language Arts* 60 (May 1983): 568–580.

Veatch, Jeannette, et al. *Key Words to Reading: The Language Experience Approach Begins*. 2nd ed. Columbus, Ohio: Charles E. Merrill, 1979.

Part II

Planning for Instruction in the Reading/ Writing Program

In the first three chapters you learned about how language develops and forms the basis for the reading and writing program. You examined the processes by which children become literate. You now understand something of how the reading process looks, how the writing process looks, and how they work together.

In Part Two you will learn how to make instructional decisions and implement those decisions in the "basic" areas of the reading/writing program. We will look at the kinds of decisions teachers make, the tools used in making those decisions, and the specifics of decision making. You will be asked to think about decisions in the use of the basal reader, in teaching word recognition and comprehension skills, in the writing process, and in the teaching of study skills.

Chapter 4

Instructional Decision Making

Chapter Overview

■ Because decision making is one of the teacher's greatest responsibilities, the concept of a teacher as decision maker captures most of what you will do in a day.

■ Teachers make critical decisions of six kinds: (1) What will I teach? (2) How will I reach individual children? (3) What are the best ways to teach each concept? (4) How can I keep my students working productively? (5) How can I arrange and decorate my classroom for the most effective learning? and (6) How can I best communicate with children, parents, colleagues, and administrators?

■ As sources of data for instructional decision making, teachers use intuition, observations, and tests. Criterion-referenced tests, often made by the teacher, have direct correlation to the curriculum. Norm-referenced tests are standardized and must be judged in terms of curriculum match.

■ Teachers gain insight into children's understanding of the reading process by analyzing oral reading errors and asking children to retell everything they can remember about a selection. Creating meaning is worth more than correctly decoding graphophonic cues; knowing how a child processes reading is more helpful than knowing the grade level at which a child reads.

■ Evaluating a child's writing using specific models and making suggestions for improvement teaches children more about writing than does assigning a grade.

■ When we administer tests of children's knowledge or skill, we are measuring the product of teaching and learning. When we observe their use of reading and writing, we are assessing the process of teaching and learning, which is more important than the product.

■ Children with special needs should be referred for help arranged collaboratively by teachers, administrators, specialists, and parents. A classroom teacher is not a failure when he or she alone cannot meet the special needs of children.

Teacher as Decision Maker

One of the most comprehensive descriptions of the role of the teacher is as decision maker. Because teachers make hundreds of decisions in a day, the concept of teacher as decision maker captures much of what you will be doing. Some decisions are trivial, such as whether Jorge can sit with Pete or when Sara may leave to go to the media center. Many decisions are very significant in terms of the education of children. Teachers make ten instructionally significant decisions per hour (Berliner, 1984): decisions such as whether to give a child an additional assignment or more guided practice and whether to encourage a child to edit a story for the class book or to move a child to a more difficult reading selection. The many different kinds of decisions teachers make within a day can be grouped into six categories.

Decisions on Scope and Sequence

Decisions about scope and sequence involve looking at what your school district expects you to teach and then deciding which instructional objectives to focus on at a given time. The scope (amount of material to be taught) and sequence (order in which the material is to be presented) of the curriculum are printed in what are usually called *curriculum guides*. Curriculum guides list the instructional objectives within a given curriculum area (usually by grade level).

Most teachers would agree that their job is to help children meet a given grade level's instructional objectives rather than to "get through the material" at a certain grade level. In other words, your job is not to push children through a given set of instructional materials but rather to help children learn whatever it takes to meet the specified objectives. Materials and teaching strategies are then selected to meet those objectives with your students. Mapping out the scope and sequence for your grade level and deciding how to calendar those objectives over a school year involve many significant instructional decisions.

A scope and sequence decision that will profoundly alter the way you teach is whether you will integrate curriculum, by which we mean combining instructional objectives from two or more curriculum areas into one lesson or one unit. We believe that teachers face an impossible task when they view each piece of the curriculum as a single building block and teaching as stacking those blocks one on top of the other. There are too many curriculum blocks to build a tower successfully. In making scope and sequence decisions you need to search for ways to integrate curriculum. Obviously, we believe that reading and writing should be taught together. Other possible combinations are music and reading, reading and art, social studies and writing and reading, and science and physical education.

The combinations are limited only by our imaginations. For example, we could teach the musical concept of melody while using folk songs to teach reading. We could practice reading while studying about line in art. Reading, writing, and social studies objectives could all be met during a unit on community in which children read about the history of their community and write visitor guides for the city information center.

■ Decisions on Individual Differences

You must determine how you will respond to the individual differences among children within your class. Some schools regroup children, moving them from one classroom to another for instruction in the language arts and math in order to create homogeneous groups. In doing so, they assert that they are creating groups with negligible differences—that the children within a given group are, in effect, all alike. We believe that homogeneity in groups of children is a myth. Within any given group of children you will still have to recognize individual differences. It is not possible to put together a group in which every child needs exactly the same instruction as every other child. We must become sensitive to individual differences in learning styles, cultural backgrounds, and abilities in order to see each of our students as an individual with special needs, desires, fears, and challenges.

■ Decisions on Mode of Instruction

Decisions regarding the kind of instructional stance you take at a given moment or in a given lesson hold for only a short while and thus must be made frequently. Perhaps for a rote learning (memorization) objective you will select a drill-and-practice mode. At another time you will decide to create an environment in which children may explore and experiment with little direct instruction from you. For example, learning a graphophonic skill such as decoding initial consonant digraph /ch/* may require repeated experiences in reading such words. When the children had dictated a story to you about chickens, you would then have them find all the words in the story that began as *chicken* does. You would structure the activity so that children made multiple responses to the /ch/ digraph in print. On the other hand, you may want students to experiment independently with sentence structures. You might write the words *Sammy, like, our, doesn't, skukie* (a nonsense word), and *doughnuts* on the board and ask children to make up as many sentences as they can that sound like American English. By ex-

---

*The slashed notation is a convention for referring to a *sound*.

ploring all the ways they used *skukie*, you could lead them to discover the functions of words in slots in sentences.

Sometimes you will pose questions that children should answer; other times you may invite them to pose the questions they seek to answer. You may give them questions to answer as they read, or you may have them make predictions about what they will read. You may choose to begin a unit of study by asking, "What are all the things you would like to know about travel in a space shuttle?" One time you will decide to have children working in learning centers, and another time you will decide that individual work at their desks is most appropriate. You may teach one lesson to small groups based on known learning needs, whereas for another lesson you will require the whole group's attention. No one mode of instruction is universally appropriate. You will constantly be making and adjusting decisions about instructional mode.

■ Decisions on Management and Discipline

Keeping a classroom full of children working productively in a warm, supportive atmosphere takes many carefully made decisions. You have probably known teachers—only a few, we hope—who scared you. But you have also known teachers who made you feel good about yourself, made you feel happy, and motivated you to work. We hope they have been many in number.

How do you account for the difference in the ways these two kinds of teachers approach children? The primary factors are the management and discipline decisions those teachers make. We have often fantasized about installing at the entrance to the college of education a device much like the metal detecting devices through which you walk in airports. Our device would be especially designed to detect motive in those persons who are entering the teaching profession because of the power wielded by teachers. Alarms would ring, lights would flash, and a stern, disembodied voice would tell those people to change their major. We do not need teachers who are looking for ways to be powerful. The very nature of the teaching act lends power to the position. We need teachers who are first and foremost sensitive to the self-concepts of children. These teachers make management and discipline decisions that do not harm the self-concepts of children.

William Purkey (1970) has defined the self-concept as a complex and dynamic system of beliefs one holds true about one's self. The self-concept is certainly complex. We do not have a unitary concept of self, but rather a multifaceted aggregate of self-concepts: concepts of self as learner of math, learner of reading, and learner of writing; concepts of self as teacher, parent, and community member; and so on. Each of these various

The teacher's decisions on classroom management and discipline affect the character of learning in the reading program.
© Elizabeth Hamlin/Stock, Boston

concepts contributes to the whole self-concept. Children must feel good about themselves—and good about themselves as learners—in order for learning to take place. The decisions you make regarding management and discipline must never harm the self-concepts of your students.

Classrooms managed in ways that foster positive self-concepts have certain characteristics. In order for children to feel good about themselves, they must know the limits and expectations for their behavior, and those limits and expectations must be reasonable. In fact, we recommend that you involve children in the decisions of what the classroom "rules" may be. You may find that your role is to moderate their suggestions.

To feel good about themselves as learners and self-managers, children need the freedom to make choices. We cannot always tell children what to do and then expect that at some future point they will make wise decisions in solving problems. They need to be able to make choices and test limits themselves. Ask yourself frequently why you do the things you do as a teacher. If your answer is that you do things because that is how *your* third-grade teacher did them, carefully examine your decisions. If your answer is based on solid educational and psychological information, you may have greater confidence in your decisions.

Some classrooms restrict freedom of choice in even the simplest matters. Take, for example, the rule that you can sharpen your pencil only before school starts. If the purpose of this rule is to reduce classroom disruptions, there must be better solutions to the problem. Involving children in finding a solution is often productive. They might suggest putting the sharpener out of the working area, finding a quieter sharpener, allowing only one person at a time at the sharpener, or other good solutions to the problem.

We need to examine carefully the reasons we restrict freedom of choice. Freedom of choice should extend beyond simple behavioral matters. Children should be allowed to make choices frequently about what they are going to learn, how they are going to learn, or how they are going to use a given block of time. Why insist that all children write stories about what they did on the weekend when the purpose of the activity is to get children to write? Perhaps that topic will interest some children, but others may be much more motivated to write about more pressing topics. At least some of the time, children should have choices in what they wish to read. Chapters 7 and 8 include many tips for organizing reading instruction that provide choices for students. We should allow children freedom to make choices as often as we possibly can.

There is a tight relationship between the decisions that you do make about scope and sequence and instructional mode and the decisions that you must make about management and discipline. When the former decisions result in meaningless or boring activities for children, stress increases and disruptions increase. We once heard prominent reading researcher Ken Goodman say that the most difficult thing for a child to do is nothing and not get into trouble while doing it. The more meaningful, purposeful, and interesting activities we create for children, the fewer management and discipline decisions we have to make.

■ Decisions on Classroom Organization

Visualize several classrooms you have seen recently. Consider these questions in relation to each: What is the visual impact of the classroom? What creates that visual impact? Is it furniture arrangement, bulletin board decoration, learning centers, the arrangement of desks, plants, and displays of children's work? Does it look like a place that was created *for* children? Each of these impressions you have is the result of the teacher's decisions about classroom organization. Classroom organization decisions are those that govern organization and decoration of furniture and spaces. Other environmental decisions include the use of special equipment such as bathtubs or forts for reading nooks. We suggest that you consider the following questions when deciding on classroom organization:

Do the classroom organization decisions I make

1. facilitate learning?
2. create an atmosphere in which children feel safe and comfortable?
3. create an atmosphere that encourages meaningful use of language for cooperation and communication?
4. make me comfortable as a teacher?
5. coordinate with the management decisions I have made?
6. coordinate with the scope and sequence decisions I have made?
7. facilitate the decisions I have made about mode of instruction and individual differences?

The environmental organization decisions you make should, as you can see, be based on far more significant issues than the aesthetics of a classroom. The decisions you make about how to organize your room must

Creating an inviting atmosphere for learning is one goal of decisions about classroom environment.
© Carol Palmer/The Picture Cube

be related to all the other important decisions you make. Rarely can we make one instructional decision in isolation from other instructional decisions.

■ Decisions on Communications

Your success as a teacher may be based as much on the quality of the communication decisions you make as on the quality of all the other instructional decisions combined. Teachers more often lose jobs because they do not get along well with others than because they cannot teach. In effect, they make poor communication decisions, or they fail to recognize the importance of making good communication decisions.

There are four lines of communication that you must maintain daily: communication with students, parents, colleagues, and the building administrator. To a lesser degree you will need to communicate with school district personnel and members of the school board. We offer the following guidelines for you to consider as you communicate with your various audiences:

1.   With children, always be open, honest, and more ready to listen than to talk. Recognize that you are a terribly significant other in the eyes of your students. A glance, a motion, a subtle tone of voice can communicate far more than you might intend. Your communication with students requires sensitivity on your part to the mystery and excitement of the child's world.

2.   Recognize that some parents are going to be afraid, shy, or reticent about talking with you. If their experiences with teachers were not positive, you may pose a threat, or at least a challenge. Some parents will assume you are a very important influence in their child's life and will want to share that influence with you. They will want to volunteer to work in your classroom. Others will simply want you to tell them how their child is doing, how they may help at home, and what they may expect in the future. Some parents will seem not to care much about their child's progress in school. In the eyes of most parents, there is nothing more precious than their child. All communication you have with parents must be based on your understanding of that point of view.

3.   Colleagues are the teachers with whom you work. They, like you, will want to be friends, exchange teaching ideas, and share war stories. You will have to decide how much you want to talk about children with other teachers in your building. We urge you to consider that children respond differently to different adults. The way Jenny acts in Mrs. Smith's room may not at all be the way Jenny will respond to you. Therefore, you need to decide to what extent you want your perceptions of a child to be

colored by the perceptions of a colleague. We know some teachers who never go to the staff room because they don't want to hear talk about children. An alternative to that approach is to develop the skill of being able to say, "I want to discover Jenny for myself, so please don't tell me about her." Many staffs have chosen to limit conversations about children only to positive stories. You will find that your communication with colleagues will be a source of great support, encouragement, and friendship for you.

4.   The building principal should be viewed as the person who has the ultimate responsibility for what happens in your school. He or she is accountable to the district administration and the school board for everything that occurs in your school. Your principal, who may have made the decision to hire you, has a vision of how your school is or should be. Learn what that vision is and how you can help make it become reality. Recognize that the principal is there to help you become the best teacher you can be.

We have often heard teachers say they cannot do something they would like to do in the classroom because "they won't let me." "They" usually refers to the building administration. Our experience has been that when a teacher has an exciting new idea he or she wants to try out, it is possible to get permission to try the new idea. Obtaining permission will depend on your clearly laying out your plan, explaining the rationale, working out the details, and defining how you will demonstrate that student learning has taken place.

Using Data for Decision Making

Teachers do not make decisions haphazardly or at random. They make careful instructional decisions by using a variety of data available to them. In this section we will examine the various sources of decision making data used by teachers.

■ Intuition

One of the most important decision making data sources you have is your intuition as a teacher. The things you know intuitively are things you just know, without rational, logical explanation of how you know them. It is acceptable to know things intuitively. We do not always have to explain *how* and *why* we know everything we know. How does this apply to teaching?

We live in an age of accountability in education. Our critics insist that we must be held accountable for student learning. They demand that we document student learning gain in a variety of ways, virtually all of them involving testing. We agree that teachers must be accountable for student learning. But we disagree that accountability invariably requires testing. If you are sure that a student knows certain things or possesses certain skills, the intuitive basis of that information is sufficient. You do not need to test that student to prove what you know about him or her.

Some principals have been known to advise teachers to record the date on which they intuitively knew a child had mastered a skill or grasped a concept, rather than testing for that skill or concept. Such advice will shock some teachers who have been encouraged to believe that the *only* way they can know that a child possesses a skill, trait, or knowledge is to test. To deny teacher intuition is to ignore half of the teacher's brain. The left hemisphere of the cerebral cortex knows things in logical, linear, rational ways. The right hemisphere is intuitive, divergent, and holistic. We want teachers to use their whole brains in the teaching/learning act. Not only is it acceptable for teachers to be intuitive but in fact the longer you teach, the more intuitive you will become as a teacher.

■ Observation

Like intuition, observation is one of the most important and helpful sources of data available to you in making important instructional decisions. You may have heard that teachers have eyes in the backs of their heads. It would be wonderful, though unsettling to our hair stylists, if that were true. But experienced teachers behave as if they did have eyes in the backs of their heads. Developing your observational skills is one of the most helpful things you can do as a beginning teacher. Every encounter you have with children should, in a sense, be diagnostic. For example, you may observe that a child never chooses to go to the library corner, so you introduce the child to a new book. You note that a child usually writes very short sentences, so you propose sentence-expansion activities.

You need to search continuously for signs that point to what the child knows and needs to learn next, how the child learns and feels, what challenges the child and what fails to capture the child's interest. Much of the time the observations will become the basis for your instructional decisions.

Some teachers who respect their own observations and thoughts record them in notebooks. Called *anecdotal records,* these notes can then be referred to later during planning time or during parent conferences.

■ Criterion-Referenced Tests

Criterion-referenced tests are so named because the criterion for passing them is determined in advance and the student's performance is measured against it. The examinations you take in a college course may be criterion

Learning is enhanced by supplementing print with the use of other media.
© *Michael Hagan*

referenced. If so, the professor establishes in advance that in order to get an A you must earn 92 percent of the possible points on the exam. Teachers are commonly the designers of criterion-referenced tests. They may accompany basal reader materials or other textbooks, or they may be purchased separately as additional instructional supplies. There are many criterion-referenced tests available for your use. Here we will review four: Piagetian task tests, informal reading inventories, holistic writing analysis, and basal reader tests.

Piagetian Tasks

All teachers should deal with the question of readiness for learning. Teachers in kindergarten and first grade face the issue of reading readiness. Parents and some teachers ask, "Is this child ready to read?" Though frequently asked, this is not a very helpful question. If the answer were no, what kind of instructional decision could the teacher make? One cannot decide that a child is not ready to learn to read and simply send the child home.

A much more realistic question is, "For what kind of reading program is this child ready?" In order to determine a child's readiness for a given reading program we must look at the child's current capacities in relation to the demands of the program (Ausubel, 1959). For example, if a child has limited auditory discrimination skill (limited ability to hear differences in letter sounds), would we put that child in a reading program that stresses learning sound–symbol relationships from the beginning? We would hope not. We have to examine a particular reading program and ask ourselves what capacities a child must have in order to be successful in that program. Typically when dealing with reading readiness we test such things as auditory discrimination, visual discrimination, and the knowledge of color, shape, and numeral. Harp (1987) has asserted that the most important readiness question typically goes unasked. That question is, "Where is this child in terms of cognitive development?"

In a first- or second-grade classroom, the chances are *very good* that many students are preoperational and that many others are in transition between preoperational and concrete operational thinking. Brewer (1987) has said that asking a preoperational child to perform an inappropriate learning task can be both difficult and discouraging. Although in general little attention has been paid to Piagetian theory in research on reading, the one area attracting some notice is the relationship between performance on Piagetian conservation tasks, achievement test scores, and reading skills (Lange, 1982). Haupt and Herman-Sissons (1980) found that conservation task scores and IQ were often predictive of reading success, with conservation scores most closely related to decoding skill. There is a clear relationship between cognitive development and reading success in some reading programs.

In addition to the other important questions we ask before beginning reading instruction, we must determine where a child is in terms of cognitive development if we are going to make sound instructional decisions about the nature of the beginning reading program. Preoperational readers need a different kind of program from that of their classmates who are more cognitively advanced.

Several characteristics that typify the thinking of children who are preoperational are described by Wadsworth (1984):*

1.   Preoperational children are fooled by their perceptions. They do not conserve mass, length, volume, or area after objects have been manipulated. You can pour equal amounts of unpopped corn into two plastic glasses and have the preoperational child agree with you that the glasses contain equal amounts of corn. Ask the child to watch as you pour the corn from one glass into a pie dish, and then ask whether the pie dish or the

---

*From *Piaget's Theory of Cognitive and Affective Development* by Barry J. Wadsworth. Copyright © 1984 by Longman Publishing Group. Reprinted by permission of the publisher.

other glass now contains more corn or they are the same. The preoperational child will tell you there is now more corn in the pie dish. If something *appears* to be more, then it *is* more, as far as they are concerned. They do not conserve.

2.   Preoperational children tend to focus on one aspect of a situation and fail to consider other aspects. Lay two groups of ten plastic poker chips out in front of the child, ten of the chips blue and ten red. Arrange the blue chips so that they extend over a longer distance than the red chips. Ask the child whether there are more blue chips than red chips or they are the same. The preoperational child will tell you there are more blue chips. If you then ask whether there are more blue chips or more plastic chips, the child will answer that there are more blue chips. Preoperational children cannot do multiplicative classifications.

3.   Preoperational thinkers often lack the ability to reverse actions and follow them back to their beginning. For example, a child may not be able to take down a structure in the reverse order of its construction.

4.   Preoperational thinkers are not able to follow transformations. They tend to see static beginnings and endings, but are not able to track the dynamic changes of matter. For example, when a pencil falls from a table, the child can see it on the table and on the floor, but cannot mentally reconstruct its passage from one place to another.

When we consider that preoperational children lack ability in reversibility and transformations, we must then wonder what undue challenge we may be offering in asking them to deal with parts to wholes to parts in working with sounds in words, sounds in isolation, and the meanings of words to boot. Preoperational children may have difficulty holding onto the meaning of a word while engaging in graphophonic analysis (relating sounds and symbols). In fact, graphophonic analysis may be reduced to meaningless, isolated learning tasks for the preoperational thinker.

Elkind (1979) argued that preoperational children believe that an object has one and only one function. Similarly, they believe that every letter can have only one sound and that every word can have only one meaning. Therefore, learning phonics is quite difficult for preoperational children. Only as concrete operational thinkers can children know that an object, letter, and word can have more than one function. In reviewing studies of the relationship between learning to read and cognitive development, Waller (1977) concluded that movement from preoperational thought into concrete operations correlated most highly with reading success in traditional reading programs.

Once you have determined which of your students are preoperational thinkers, what might be the implications for their reading program? You will have to consider these realities:

■ Preoperational children cannot memorize a "rule" and then decide which words follow the rule and which words do not. They are not able to generalize from one situation to another.

■ Preoperational children have trouble with multiplicative classifications. The multiple sounds represented by one letter are often confusing. What are we asking of the children who cannot do this cognitive manipulation when we ask them to recognize that the symbols in Figure 4.1 all represent the sound of *a* as in *apple,* but then sometimes they represent the sound of *a* as in *ate* and still other times (many other times) they represent neither of these sounds? And *a* is only the beginning!

■ Preoperational children have difficulty in converting graphemes to phonemes and then back to graphemes if they lack reversibility in their thinking.

When you think of the characteristics of preoperational thinkers and then consider how many children in a classroom may be preoperational, you are likely to conclude that you had better begin planning a strategy for a whole-language program for these children, carefully controlling the amount of graphophonic analysis instruction. Some researchers (Kirkland, 1978, and Ribovich, 1978) have argued that those concerned about cognitive development and reading should design reading programs for preoperational children that would expose children to a variety of reading experiences with a wide variety of reading materials (bulletin boards, school mail, notes, student-authored material). Children in those programs would draw their own conclusions about print rather than always being told how print works. Potter (1986) asserts that we must pay greater attention to the cognitive style of young children and modify the curriculum

Figure 4.1   Variations on a theme.

along developmental lines. Wouldn't it be wonderful to find out what would happen if we delayed phonics instruction until we knew children were concrete operational thinkers?

The tasks to help assess cognitive development are easy to administer. Complete descriptions of several of the tasks are found in Appendix B.

Informal Reading Inventories

In an informal reading inventory (IRI), the child is asked to read a set of sequentially graded reading selections. The teacher, aide, or volunteer follows along on another copy of the selection and codes the oral reading errors, called *miscues*. A word recognition score is determined by counting the number of words read correctly. Next the child is given a selection to read silently and then asked comprehension questions. A percentage of comprehension is calculated. The percentages of words correctly read and comprehension questions correctly answered are then used to determine the child's functional reading level.

Functional Reading Level

The informal reading inventory identifies three functional reading levels: independent, instructional, and frustration. The independent reading level is that grade level of material that the student can read easily with good understanding. Criteria for the functional reading levels have not been standardized, but typically the independent level is defined by a word recognition score of approximately 98 percent to 100 percent and a comprehension score of approximately 90 percent to 100 percent.

The independent level defines the reading material we would give the child for recreational reading. The instructional level is that grade level of material that the child can read with understanding but that provides some challenge to the child's reading ability. The instructional level defines the material we would give children for reading instruction. Typically, the instructional level is defined as a word recognition score of 91 percent to 97 percent and a comprehension score of 70 percent to 89 percent.

The frustration level is that grade level of material that is too difficult for a child to read with understanding. Word recognition is less than 90 percent and comprehension is less than 70 percent. We would avoid using material at this level for instructional purposes. However, a child may choose to read frustration-level material recreationally and gain some information from it. We recommend never telling a child that he or she cannot read a book because it is at his or her frustration level. We have seen children with keen interest and high motivation read material that we would have thought much too difficult.

Please recognize that the functional reading levels are determined using an informal reading inventory taken on a very small sampling of reading behavior. Your observations of the child's reading may yield far more valid results. When there is conflict between the results of IRI testing and your own observations, trust your observations and become even more observant.

A note of caution, too, is in order about the concept of grade level. Grade level is an artificial segmentation of the curriculum. When the term is applied to reading material, it is determined by the publisher through applying readability formulas to the text. Readability formulas assume that small words and short sentences are easier to read than longer words and longer sentences. We doubt the validity of this assumption. Nevertheless, grade-level designations are typically used to identify functional reading levels. Typical criteria for the three functional reading levels are summarized in the table in Figure 4.2.

Miscue Analysis

A second, and perhaps more important, use of the informal reading inventory is a careful analysis of the child's oral reading miscues. By analyzing the miscues a child makes, we can draw some valuable inferences about the cueing systems upon which the child relies as a reader. For example, if the text word is *house* and the child reads "horse" without noticing the loss of meaning, we can infer that this reader relies much more heavily on graphophonic cues than on semantic cues. If, on the other hand, the miscue makes sense because the word *home* was substituted for *house*, we can infer that the reader relies most heavily on semantic and syntactic cues and places less reliance on graphophonic cues. Miscue analysis helps us understand whether a reader is attempting to construct meaning when reading or simply decoding letter–sound relationships. This information will help us build on the reader's strengths while improving reading weaknesses. We can learn a great deal about how a reader views the reading process through miscue analysis.

Classification	Score	
	Word recognition	Comprehension
Independent level	98%–100%	90%–100%
Instructional level	91%–97%	70%–89%
Frustration level	90% or less	70% or less

Figure 4.2   Functional reading level classification scores.

A teacher unobtrusively records a child's miscues for later analysis.
© *Michael Hagan*

Yetta Goodman introduced the concept of miscue analysis in 1970. Since that time, the *Reading Miscue Inventory* (RMI) has become a powerful tool in helping teachers to understand the reading process and the reading behavior of students. About the *Reading Miscue Inventory* Yetta Goodman says (Goodman, Watson, and Burke, 1987, p. x):*

Little did we realize when we introduced the ideas behind the RMI to 25 teachers in a school district near San Diego in 1970 that two decades later we would be part of a movement of professional educators and researchers who are committed to understanding why readers do what they do, to understanding that what students do when they read reflects their knowledge about language and the world, and to realizing that the more they understand about the processes of reading and learning to read the more they are able to facilitate and support the growth of literacy.

The scoring of the RMI is dramatically different from the traditional scoring of an informal inventory. Traditionally, teachers counted each error with equal weight in determining the word recognition score. The only analysis of errors made may have been to look for patterns of errors that suggested weaknesses in word-attack skills. The traditional scoring was a quantitative analysis of oral reading errors. The RMI scoring is a *qualitative* analysis of miscues, asking why the miscue was made and what its impact, if any, was on the reading process. Analysis of miscues involves asking questions such as these (Goodman, Watson, and Burke, 1987, p. 5):

1. Do miscues result in sentences that are semantically and syntactically acceptable?
2. Do miscues cause grammatical transformations?
3. To what degree do miscues retain the grammatical function of text items?
4. To what degree do miscues retain a semantic relationship to the text item?
5. To what degree do miscues retain graphic and phonological similarity to text items?
6. In what ways do readers use strategies such as self-correcting and predicting?

To help you understand the importance of miscue analysis, let's examine the scoring of an informal reading inventory in the traditional way

---

*From *Reading Miscue Inventory: Alternative Procedures* by Yetta Goodman *et al.*
Copyright © 1987 by Richard C. Owen Publishers, Inc. Reprinted by permission.

and then look at the changes in our interpretation as we apply miscue analysis. Figure 4.3 illustrates the kinds of miscues that are typically counted as errors in the traditional scoring of an IRI and shows how they are marked.

Traditional IRI Scoring versus Miscue Analysis

Figure 4.4 shows the miscues made by a child reading a first-grade selection entitled "Store Doors." Notice that according to the marking system shown in Figure 4.3, there are two omissions, three substitutions, and three insertions, for a total of eight miscues. The child scored 100 percent on comprehension. In the traditional scoring of an IRI, each of these miscues would be counted with equal weight. Eight errors in ninety-nine words yields a word recognition score of 92 percent. According to Figure 4.2, we would say this first-grade material is at this child's instructional level in terms of word recognition.

When, using Goodman's miscue analysis questions, we examine the miscues marked in Figure 4.4, we conclude that the only miscue that truly resulted in a loss of meaning was the last one. The reader read "Is it" for "It's." "Is it magic?" has a different meaning from "It's magic!"—a question rather than an exclamation. If we count that as two errors, an insertion and an omission, we get a word recognition percentage of 98. According to Figure 4.2, we would say this first-grade material is at this child's *independent level* in terms of word recognition. The comprehension score substantiates the fact that the child does indeed function at this level. *If we had given equal weight to each miscue, we would have misinterpreted this child's functional reading level.* The use of the Goodman miscue inventory questions results in

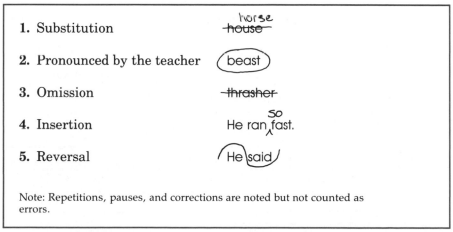

Figure 4.3   Miscues marked and counted as errors in the traditional scoring of an IRI.

"Store Doors"

Rick's mom asked him to go
to the ~~big~~ store up the street.
His little sister Susan said,
"I want to go, too! I want to go, too!
I'*will*~~ll~~ be good."
So Rick took his little sister
to the big store.
There were two big doors.
One door has the word IN on it.
The other door had the *other* word OUT.
Rick and Susan went
to the IN door.
~~Whish!~~ *Swish!*
The doors opened all by ~~itself!~~ *themselves!*
Susan said, "Look. The doors
opened!
Is It'~~s~~ magic!"
"You are silly!" said Rick.
"It isn't magic.
The electric doors work by motors."

Comprehension Questions

1. Who went somewhere? (Rick and Susan)
2. Why did they go? (mother asked them) *to buy something*
3. Where did they go? (store up the street) *to the store*
4. What was written on the doors? (IN, OUT)
5. What seemed like magic? (door opening by itself) *the doors*
6. What was the magic really? (electricity)

Results

Word Recognition __8__ errors in 99 words; __92__% recognized correctly

Comprehension __0__ errors in 6 questions; __100__% answered correctly

Tension Symptoms _____

Phrasing _____

Reading Level _____

_____

Figure 4.4 Miscue analysis at first reader level.

a much more accurate and realistic interpretation of functional reading level than the traditional approach allows, as well as giving us rich information about the cueing systems upon which the reader relies.

The Miscue Inventory also gives us a better window on comprehension than does the traditional informal reading inventory. In the RMI the reader is asked to retell as much about the selection as possible. We once heard a child read a selection leaving out a crucial word each time it appeared. When asked to retell the story, the reader rendered it completely, making several references to the omitted word. Clearly, ability to decode the print, the surface structure, is not a good indication of creating meaning—understanding the deep structure.

Word Recognition Score versus Comprehension Score

Frequently in the scoring of an informal reading inventory it happens that the percentages do not work out in neat categories as shown in Figure 4.2. Suppose, as in the example above, that the comprehension score were 100 percent—unarguably at the independent level—but the word recognition score were 92 percent, plainly in the instructional category. How would you classify the reading of the selection?

Your answer to that question tells a great deal about what you believe reading to be. To rank the word recognition score as more important suggests that you attach a very high priority to perfect word identification. Favoring the comprehension score suggests that you value constructing meaning above all else in the reading process. Where you stand will dramatically color your decisions about scope and sequence and modes of instruction. Partisans of comprehension are likely to want to start beginning readers off with meaningful texts, have children read interesting material well modeled by the teacher, and only later deal with the subskills of reading as necessary. Advocates of word recognition are likely to begin reading instruction with graphophonic analysis activities. We place emphasis on comprehension over word recognition every time.

Holistic Writing Analysis

As we move away from a view of literacy development as a compilation of discrete skills building one upon the other until a child can finally read or write, we have increasing need for ways to assess the processes of developing literacy. What the Goodman Reading Miscue Inventory does for our assessment of a child's understanding of the reading process, the Analytical Trait Writing Assessment (ATWA) does for our measurement of a child's understanding of the writing process. The ATWA is an example of what is known as *holistic grading* of writing. When we grade a writing sample holistically, we do not assign a letter grade to the piece; instead, we rate it overall against a model or specified criteria.

The ATWA was developed by the Beaverton School District in Oregon. Using the prescribed set of writing traits or characteristics, the young author is trained to analyze his or her own writing, with the goal of bringing each new piece closer to the criteria or model. The selection is read and an overall rating is assigned to the piece. The manuscript is judged as a whole (hence the term *holistic writing assessment*). It is not dissected. Comments are not written on the paper. Instead, an overall rating is assigned for each of six categories: ideas and content, organization, voice, word choice, sentence structure, and writing conventions. Within each category the paper is assigned a rating of 1, 3, or 5, with 5 representing the best effort.

To understand better how each paper is judged, examine Figure 4.5, which lists the criteria for the "ideas and content" rating. As you read the criteria for each higher level, notice the increase in writing sophistication it demands. The complete Analytical Trait Writing Assessment will be found in Appendix C.

The use of holistic assessment in writing allows you to track the writing growth of your students as well as to involve them in the assessment. Over time you will see the proof of your literacy program as your students' papers earn increasingly higher ratings. The rating system also permits you to see where a student's progress is arrested. When a student seems to be stuck at a certain rating in one or more categories, you can use the scale as a decision-making tool and then focus your instruction in writing on the troublesome traits within those categories.

Perhaps the most compelling argument for using a rating scale in writing is that such scales are meaningful. Not only do they offer specific feedback to the young writer but they provide clear criteria for ways to improve writing. When an author's work is rated 3 in "word choice," one need only look at the scale to see ways to improve (use fewer general or ordinary words, eliminate new words that do not fit, eliminate "big" words that were used to impress, reduce the use of slang). Such assessment of writing is much more to the point for the writer than getting a paper back from the teacher with the notation "B+ Good Job." "B+ Good Job" does not tell the author what was good about the piece or how to improve it.

Basal Reader Tests

Basal readers are sequentially graded pupil texts, workbooks, teacher's guides, and supplementary materials for grades K–8. The tests that accompany the basal readers are undoubtedly some of the most widely used criterion-referenced tests in the educational system. Although there are variations among publishers, essentially the tests that accompany basal readers consist of placement tests, end-of-unit tests, and end-of-book tests.

I. Ideas and Content

5 Paper

The paper is clear and holds the reader's attention all the way through.

- The writer seems to know the topic well, and chooses details that help make the subject clear and interesting.
- The writer is in control of the topic and has focused the topic well.
- Important ideas stand out. The writer uses the right amount of detail (not too much or too little) to make the important ideas clear.

3 Paper

The reader can figure out what the writer is trying to say, but the paper may not hold the reader's attention all the way through.

- The writer has some things to say, but doesn't seem to know quite enough about the main idea(s).
- Some ideas may be clear, while others may be fuzzy or may not seem to fit.
- The writer may spend too much time on minor details and/ or not enough time on main ideas.

1 Paper

The paper is unclear and seems to have no purpose.

- The writer has not thoughtfully explored or presented ideas; he or she may not seem to know the topic very well.
- Ideas seem very limited or seem to go off in several directions. It seems as if the writer wrote just to get something down on paper.
- Ideas are not developed. The paper may just restate the assignment.

Figure 4.5   Analytical trait ratings for ideas and content.

SOURCE: © 1986, Interwest Applied Research. This document may be used and reproduced without permission for instruction and assessment by state and local educational agencies, colleges and universities. However, the document (or portion thereof) may not be sold, included in a document to be sold, used for commercial purposes, nor attributed to another source without written permission. Revised 11/12/86.

Some publishers provide informal reading inventories based on the content of their texts. The testing program that accompanies a basal reader is intended to help you place children in the reading series and to move them through the series as they master various skills.

Basal placement tests are administered to a group of children at one time. They typically test reading comprehension following the reading of short selections from the basal. The intent of the tests is to help you decide which level of difficulty within the reading program is most appropriate for a given child. The greatest limitation of using these tests is that you cannot discover as much about a child's view of the reading process as you can using an informal reading inventory and doing a miscue analysis. Their greatest advantage is that they are quick to administer and interpret.

End-of-unit tests that accompany the basal are administered at points throughout the use of a given book to check mastery of various skills. Basal publishers claim that end-of-unit tests can help prevent reading failures by enabling you to ascertain that "critical skills" are mastered before a child moves on in a book. The assumption is that you will reteach skills that students have not mastered before moving further into the text.

In the same way, end-of-book tests give you information about a child's skill attainment within a book or level of the basal program. The intention is that you will not place a child in a more advanced level until the child has mastered the skills at a given level.

Evaluation may be viewed as part and parcel of literacy events. For example, when discussing a piece of literature shared by a group, children have opportunities to demonstrate that they can draw conclusions, identify main ideas, make judgments, distinguish fact from opinion, use pronoun antecedents, and ask important questions. Such activities are far more genuine indicators of comprehension than dealing with small bits of language on a test (Watson and Weaver, 1988).

We believe that the most serious limitation of basal tests is that they are essentially quantitative rather than qualitative. Like the traditional scoring of an informal reading inventory, they tend to count all errors with equal weight without really examining the *processes* the child uses in reading. No one error in reading is important. Patterns of errors can be important. But how the child views the reading process is of utmost importance. Procedures that allow you to examine the child's view of the reading process and his or her reading behaviors are more useful than the typical basal test.

Process versus Product Assessment in the Basal Reader

Basal tests that measure the mastery of discrete skills are essentially product oriented. They ask the question "Does the child possess this or that skill?" We recommend that you use procedures that are process oriented in making decisions about moving children through a text. Comparing a miscue analysis done at the beginning of a book with another analysis at the end would be helpful in determining the child's progress in use of semantic, syntactic, and schematic cues. As reading skill develops, the child typically shifts from reliance on graphophonic cues to greater and greater use of semantic, syntactic, and schematic cues.

This move toward seeing reading as a meaning-creating process is more important than "mastering" any single set of graphophonic skills. You will be able to document this growth in reading if you periodically administer an informal reading inventory and do a miscue analysis. Although time consuming, periodic analyses can be very informative. You will gain the greatest insight into a child's reading if you yourself do the inventory. However, parent volunteers and teacher assistants can be trained to conduct the informal reading inventory, permitting you to do the analysis later. One teacher we know reports using the reprint of the basal story in the teacher's guide to do a quick miscue analysis. As the child reads, she marks the miscues on the guide copy of the text, with the reader's name in the margin. Afterward, she can do a quick analysis.

Figure 4.6 is an example of a miscue analysis checklist that could be reproduced and used for either a complete miscue analysis or a quick analysis like the one just described. A three-ring binder might hold several for each child. The form is simple to use. You categorize the miscues by type:

> substitution—one or more words substituted for the text word
> omission—one or more words left out
> insertion—word(s) added to the text
> repetition—word(s) repeated
> reversals—words whose spelling was reversed (sounds transposed) during reading.

You make a check mark in the first or second column, depending on whether a particular miscue resulted in loss of meaning or not. Circle the check mark if the reader notices the miscue and attempts to correct it. Over a period of time, the forms would document changes in the child's use of graphophonic, semantic, syntactic, and schematic cues. Corrected miscues that alter meaning would indicate that the child is paying greater attention to creating meaning during the reading process—a major goal of instruction.

Be sure to have the child retell the story after reading it. The retelling is often the best window we have on a child's comprehension. After the child has retold the story without assistance, you may prompt the child's recall and assist in the retelling by asking questions. This procedure will enable you to make a reliable assessment of the child's comprehension. Figure 4.7 is an example of a comprehension checklist to be used during the

MISCUE RECORDING CHECKLIST

Name _Todd_   Date _9/10_

Selection _The Red Balloon_

Put a checkmark in the appropriate column when the child makes a miscue.   ✓
Circle the checkmark if the child notices the miscue and attempts to correct it.   Ø

Type of miscue	Miscues resulting in no loss of meaning ("home" for "house")	Miscues resulting in loss of meaning ("house" for "horse")
Substitution	✓Ⓥ ✓ ✓ ✓ ✓	✓ ✓
Omission	✓ ✓	
Insertion	✓ ✓ ✓ ✓	
Repetition		
Reversal	Ⓥ	

Summary:

Total number of miscues   _16_

Miscues resulting in no loss of meaning   _14_

Miscues resulting in loss of meaning   _2_

Correction attempts   _2_

Comments: _Todd is a fluent reader whose miscues do not alter the meaning of the texts_

Figure 4.6   Miscue recording checklist.

SOURCE: *Impressions: Teacher Resource Book: East of the Sun* by Jack Booth *et al.* Copyright © 1985 by Holt, Rinehart & Winston of Canada. Reprinted by permission. P. 279.

COMPREHENSION CHECKLIST

To be used after oral or silent reading

Name _Todd_

Selection _The Red Balloon_

Date _9/10_

Oral or Silent

Plot	Unassisted retelling	Assisted retelling
The child gives a plot summary. (What was the story about?)	✓	
The child relates the sequence of events. (What happened after _____ ?)	✓	
The child recognizes cause and effect relationships. (Why did _____ happen?)	✓	
The child makes inferences. (Why do you think _____?)	✓	
Characters:		
The child recalls the main characters. (Who was in the story?)	✓	
The child relates what the characters did. (What did _____ do in the story?)	✓	
The child understands the relationship of the characters to one another. (How did _____ feel about _____?)	✓	
The child can describe the characters. (What was _____ like?)	✓	
The child understands the relative importance of the characters. (Who was more important in the story?)	✓	

Summary:

Level of comprehension: Full and detailed ☑

Partial ☐

Fragmentary ☐

Comments: _Todd appears to be an independent reader. The quality of his miscues and retelling demonstrated the development of independent reading strategies._

Figure 4.7   Comprehension checklist.

Source: *Impressions: Teacher Resource Book: East of the Sun* by Jack Booth *et al.* Copyright © 1985 by Holt, Rinehart & Winston of Canada. Reprinted by permission. P. 280.

retelling of the story. The major aspects of understanding the plot and characters are checked during unassisted retelling and then during assisted retelling. This checklist offers a quick examination of comprehension, but we believe that it can be strengthened by asking the reader to relate aspects of plot and character development to his or her own experience. You might ask questions like these: Can you tell me about a time you had such an experience? Who do you know that behaves the way this character did? Can you describe this person's behavior?

Another useful tool is a checklist entitled "Reading: A Guide for Observation" (Figure 4.8). You would keep this checklist for each of your students, updating your observations periodically (one column per date). Reading through the items on the checklist will help you understand what we mean by process evaluation of a child's reading. The checklist will enable you both to document the child's growth in understanding and use of reading as a process and to share your observations with the child's parents.

Figure 4.9 is a checklist that categorizes reading behaviors into three stages of development: beginning reading behaviors, behaviors of the developing reader, and characteristics of the independent reader. Again,

READING: A GUIDE FOR OBSERVATION

Name _____

Knowledge About Books   Date

● Recognizes different kinds of books (stories, anthologies, non-fiction, dictionaries)					
● Has favourite books					
● Is aware of authors (seeks out books by a particular author)					
● Visits the school library					
● Has visited the public library					
● Owns books					
● Can use a table of contents					

Figure 4.8   Checklist for a process evaluation.   (continues)
SOURCE: *Impressions: Teacher Resource Book: East of the Sun* by Jack Booth *et al.* Copyright © 1985 by Holt, Rinehart & Winston of Canada. Reprinted by permission. Pp. 268–269.

Reading Behaviour	Date					
● Voluntarily chooses to read						
● Signs out books from the library						
● Enjoys stories read aloud						
● Is relaxed while reading						
● Participates in choral and shared reading						
● Uses picture and context clues						
● Can retell a story						
● Self-corrects where appropriate (rereads when the sentence doesn't make sense)						
● Makes meaningful substitutions of words while reading orally						
● Chooses to read aloud for a group						
● Can interpret character and mood while reading orally						
● Reads silently						
● Understands the concept of a word						
● Can locate specific words and phrases						

Notes _____

_____

_____

_____

_____

_____

_____

_____

_____

Figure 4.8   (*continued*)

the teacher's observations are recorded at intervals. A checklist of this kind is especially helpful in schools that group children by reading level, across ages—placing, for example, kindergarteners, first-graders, and second-graders in one class. It also recognizes that within any group of children there will be readers at different stages of development. It is much more

READING DEVELOPMENT CHECKLIST

Name _____

STAGE 1—THE BEGINNING READER	Date				
• Enjoys listening to literature					
• Voluntarily chooses to look at books					
• Uses literature as a basis for dramatic play or painting					
• Has favourite stories and wants to hear them repeatedly					
• Can retell past experiences					
• Can relate a sequence of events					
• Understands some environmental print and common words					
• Shows a desire to see his/her words written down					
• Role-plays reading by attempting to match his/her memory of the selection with the actual words on the page					
• Reads back short-experience stories written by the teacher					
• Can follow a line of print in enlarged text					
• Realizes that print has constant or fixed meaning (it always says the same thing)					
• Understands directionality of print (left-to-right, top-to-bottom)					
• Can identify and name most letters					
• Can make meaningful predictions using context and syntax clues					
• Attempts to write using some consonant sounds					

STAGE 2—THE DEVELOPING READER	Date				
• Understands the concept of a word					
• Recognizes some phonic generalizations (rhyming words, words that start or end the same, blends)					
• Sometimes finger points while reading					
• While writing, he/she represents all syllables using invented spelling					
• Uses some conventions of print in writing					
• Reads some things independently					
• Has a store of sight words in reading and writing					
• Uses all the cueing systems					
• Makes meaningful substitutions when reading					
• Comprehends what has been read; can retell a story					

Figure 4.9   Reading development checklist.   (*continues*)
SOURCE: *Impressions: Teacher Resource Book: East of the Sun* by Jack Booth *et al.* Copyright © 1985 by Holt, Rinehart & Winston of Canada. Reprinted by permission. Pp. 273–274.

READING DEVELOPMENT CHECKLIST

Name _____

STAGE 3—THE INDEPENDENT READER	Date				
• Reads silently but sometimes subvocalizes when the text is difficult					
• Makes predictions about a word (is likely to be using all three cueing systems)					
• Self-corrects when reading does not make sense					
• Comprehends at different levels (literal, interpretive, critical)					
• Adjusts silent reading rate to material and purpose					
• Invented spellings are closer to standard spelling					

Notes:

_____

_____

_____

_____

_____

_____

_____

_____

_____

_____

_____

_____

_____

_____

_____

_____

_____

_____

_____

_____

_____

_____

_____

_____

Figure 4.9   (continued)

useful to describe a reader's development in terms of characteristics in the checklist than to say, "Sally is reading at second-grade level."

Each of these checklists provides valuable diagnostic information, as well as offering a clear and complete way to report children's progress in reading. Each of these exemplifies the ideal of looking at the development of the processes of reading rather than looking only at discrete skills.

■ Norm-Referenced Tests

Norm-referenced tests are so named because performance on such tests is judged in comparison with a norm ("normal performance") established in the past. When a norm-referenced test is developed, it is administered to a group representative of the people for whom the test was designed. This group is called the *norming sample*. Their performance on the test becomes the yardstick against which all future performance is judged. The statistics that describe the performance of the norming sample are the norms for the test. For example, if in the norming sample the average score of the fourth-graders was 87 correct responses, the norm becomes 87 as the average fourth-grade standard. When your fourth-graders take the same test, they are then compared with the fourth-graders (and others) in the norming sample. A school district's announcement that its sixth-graders are scoring "above the national average in mathematics" means that its average sixth-grade scores were higher than the average sixth-grade scores in the norming sample.

Achievement Tests

Perhaps the most commonly used norm-referenced tests in elementary schools are achievement tests. Achievement tests span a broad range of curriculum or skill areas, with a limited sampling within each area. In other words, test items may cover a wide array of subjects, but each is tested to no great depth. Norm-referenced achievement tests have essentially two purposes:

1.   They measure overall achievement of students within a school or school district so that district administrators and school board members can make a comparison against a "national norm."

2.   They provide a gross screening assessment to alert you to students who may be having achievement losses in certain areas of the curriculum. When a student scores well below average on an achievement test, that finding should alert you to increase your observation of that child,

to use some criterion-referenced measures to examine performance more carefully, and possibly to confer with the child and the parents. Poor performance on an achievement test may indicate a need to refer a child to specialists within your building or district who can do additional in-depth diagnosis.

Special note: Achievement tests in reading commonly overestimate a child's instructional reading level by one to two years (Spache, 1981). Therefore, you should *never* use scores on achievement tests to determine functional reading levels.

Diagnostic Tests

Norm-referenced diagnostic tests sample a single curriculum or skill area in considerable depth. It is possible to determine a student's strengths and weaknesses in reading comprehension or word recognition, for example, from a diagnostic test. Typically, norm-referenced diagnostic tests are used by specialists in reading or learning disabilities rather than by classroom teachers. These tests are frequently used after you have referred a child in your classroom for further diagnosis.

Validity Issues

Suppose that your professor came into class and said, "I have decided to stop using the quizzes I create in this class to measure your performance. Instead, I will use a new norm-referenced test on the teaching of reading and writing. After I created the test items, I used the doctoral students in reading as the norming sample." How would you feel? Would this norm-referenced test fairly assess your performance in this course?

Probably you would feel very worried. Such a norm-referenced test would not fairly assess your performance in this course. It would not be fair because you and your classmates were not represented in the norming sample. The nature of the norming sample is only one of the questions you should ask about a norm-referenced test. When we ask if a test is valid we are asking whether it is appropriate to use with our students and whether it tests what it purports to test. There are several validity concerns you should address:

1. Are your students represented fairly in the norming sample? If the ethnic, socioeconomic, and geographic characteristics of your students are not represented in the norming sample, the yardstick by which their performance is to be measured is an unfair one.

2.   Do the test items seem to test adequately the curriculum area(s) for which the test is intended? Do the authors of the text define reading as you do? Does there appear to be sufficient breadth in the test items? It is in these respects that norm-referenced tests have a serious limitation, in our view. An examination of test items permits you to infer the test makers' definition of reading—namely, that reading is a process of transforming the print symbols into language, with no interaction between the ideas of the author and the schema of the reader. The typical norm-referenced test is presented in a multiple-choice format. Multiple-choice questions offer the child no opportunity for retelling the story, which is one of the more powerful sources of insight into comprehension.

3.   Is there a match between what the test measures and what you teach? Students cannot be expected to do well on a test if they have not been taught the material the test covers. A test that is valid for your students matches your curriculum. Some states are now writing their own norm-referenced tests, thereby achieving a closer match between the goals of the curriculum and the scope of the test.

Classroom teachers rarely have a choice about whether to use norm-referenced tests or what particular test to use. You are likely to be instructed to administer a certain achievement test to your students (third grade and above) in October and/or again in May. Refusal to do so could be considered insubordination. The fact that you have to give the test does not excuse you from being a careful and thoughtful test consumer. You are the one who will have to interpret the test, both to children and to parents, and you must be able to explain the various scores obtained. You will also have to decide whether to implement any instructional changes on the basis of the results. This responsibility obligates you to raise questions about validity. If the test you use fails to satisfy any one of the conditions of validity, you should deem it invalid for your children. It is professionally sound practice to say so to your building principal and to explain your reasons. You might also communicate your concerns in a letter to the district's testing coordinator or the official or committee that selects the tests.

Scores Used in Norm-Referenced Tests

Raw Score

The first score obtained on a norm-referenced test is a raw score, which represents the number of test items correctly marked. The raw score alone is relatively meaningless, telling you nothing about how the student performed in comparison with the norming sample. Suppose your child came bounding into the house after school and announced that he or she had gotten a score of 48 on a reading achievement test. You wouldn't know whether to offer praise or to worry about your child's achievement! To evaluate performance on an achievement test, you have to know more than the raw score.

Percentile Score

One of the scores most commonly used to interpret normed test performance is the percentile score. The percentile score tells you the proportion of the norming sample that your student outperformed; that is, the percentage of the norming sample that scored below your student's score. A percentile score of 89 means that the student scored as well as or better than 89 percent of the norming sample. Percentile scores should not be confused with percentage scores. Percentage scores tell you the percentage of total test items marked correctly. Percentile scores give you a comparison between your student's performance and that of the norming sample.

Stanine Score

Perhaps the easiest norm-referenced test score to explain is the stanine score. It shows you where your student stands in relation to the norming sample by placing his or her score along the baseline of the bell-shaped curve. Stanine scores range from 1 to 9, each score representing a percentage of the distribution from the lowest to the highest scores along the baseline. For example, a stanine score of 5 places your student in the middle stanine—the one bracketing the mean (average) score in the norming sample. Both percentile and stanine scores permit you to compare a student's performance across subtests and years. They are more stable and reliable than grade scores, which are, in fact, the most confusing and most difficult to explain.

Grade Score

The grade score is intended to tell you how your student performed in comparison to the norming sample. A grade score of 4.3 means that your student performed as well as the average fourth-grader in the third month of fourth grade. That is all the grade score means. Here comes the confusion. People often assume that a grade score is equivalent to an instructional-level score. We have warned that a grade score often overestimates an instructional-level score. The confusion becomes deeper when a grade score is statistically extrapolated. For example, you may have a student who receives a grade score of 10.4 on a norm-referenced reading test. To many, it might suggest that this student can read tenth-grade material. In fact, there may have been no tenth-grade material on the test. Arrived at by statistical calculations, the grade score of 10.4 means only that the student performed as well on the test as the average tenth-grader in the fourth month of tenth grade. The International Reading Association passed a resolution in 1982

Communication with parents is vital to a successful reading program.
© Alan Carey/The Image Works

calling for test publishers to cease using grade scores because of the confusion they create. Many of the publishers have acceded to this request. We suggest that if you are asked to interpret grade scores to parents, you point out the limitations we have discussed here.

State of Assessment in Literacy

For more than forty years, we have thought of assessment in reading (and to some extent in writing) as test based. The proliferation of psychological tests during and after World War II set the stage for educational assessment for years to come. This test-driven view of assessment is now undergoing serious questioning and debate. Two issues central to the debate are the role of the teacher and the assessment of process versus product.

Role of the Teacher

We have shown throughout this chapter that the role of the teacher as observer is crucial to good assessment and decision making. The teacher's elevation to this role assumes truly professional, even expert, behavior on the part of the teacher. A novice at classroom evaluation will look at a sample of writing and see scribbles. The expert sees evidence of a developing writer. The novice listens to a child read and hears miscues. The expert hears a child using increasingly more semantic, syntactic, and schematic cues (Johnston, 1987). The teacher who is an expert observer has little, if any, need for traditional tests as assessment tools. Observations of and interactions with children are far more significant.

In making the same argument, Johnston (1987, p. 747) stated, "This view of evaluation implies the need to liberate teachers and students from the disempowering and isolating burden of centralized, accountability testing. The cost of the liberty is increased responsibility on the part of the classroom teacher, some of which is passed on to the student." In fact, if teachers and students are to be freed of the burden of accountability testing, teachers will have to accept the responsibility for ever more expert observation, analysis, and recording of student behavior. Paradoxically, as teachers trade in the tests born of the "accountability movement" for their own expert observation of children's progress, they are in effect becoming more *accountable* for the learning of their students.

Teachers are responsible for having their students meet the instructional objectives specified in the curriculum. The ultimate objectives of whole-language instruction are the same as objectives in reading instruction have nearly always been: that children read and write effectively with enjoyment. But many of the interim objectives have changed. For example, along the road to proficient literacy we are much more concerned about the child's ability to create meaning in reading and to write a variety of clear sentence structures than we are about drilling on decoding initial consonant *d* or punctuating someone else's sentences on a worksheet. What has changed is not the product of our instruction but the processes for generating that product.

◼ Assessment of Process versus Product

When we give a test to determine what a child knows or can do, we are looking at the product of teaching and learning. When we assess the child's understanding of literacy through observing his or her use of reading and writing, we are looking at the processes of teaching and learning. Products are important, but the processes are more important still. Likewise, an examination of the processes is far more instructive to the teacher than is looking only at the product.

Professional organizations are recognizing the importance of a process-oriented assessment model. The International Reading Association's Early Childhood and Literacy Development Committee has endorsed a process-oriented view and offered six principles of assessment (Teale, Hiebert, and Chittenden, 1987, pp. 772–774):*

With insights from research, we are formulating views of early childhood literacy development, with conclusions like the following: (a) Listening, speaking, reading and writing abilities develop concurrently and inter-relatedly in early childhood, not sequentially. (b) The functions of reading and writing are as much a part of literacy learning as are the formal skills. (c) Children's early behaviors are a legitimate phase of, rather than a precursor to, literacy. (d) These behaviors and conceptualizations develop in predictable ways toward conventional literacy.

. . . The principles presented here are grounded in the perspective just described, which implies the need for a comprehensive assessment program, not a one-shot test of a child's general knowledge of reading and writing. These principles also reflect the new concept of emergent literacy.

In the best beginning literacy programs, assessment facilitates the goals of the curriculum and shows the following characteristics:

(1) Assessment is a part of instruction. Assessment and teaching go hand in hand. Assessment enhances teachers' powers of observation and understanding of learning. . . .

(2) Assessment methods and instruments are varied. Conventional assessment (e.g., standardized readiness tests or screening inventories) is only one approach. Analyses of performance samples (tapes of children's reading, compositions they wrote) and systematic teacher observation of everyday behaviors (looking at or reading books, listening to stories, using environmental print, using print in dramatic play) are integral parts of the assessment program.

(3) Assessment focuses on a broad range of skills and knowledge reflecting the various dimensions of literacy. The cognitive and linguistic resources that children bring to reading and writing tasks are identified. Programs capture a complete view of emerging literacy. . . .

(4) Assessment occurs continuously. The teacher constantly assesses the children's behavior informally in order to arrange appropriate activities. Regular systematic assessments (e.g., analysis of performance samples) are scheduled to ensure that each child's progress is documented over the year. . . .

(5) Literacy is assessed in a variety of contexts. Because reading or writing requires integration of processes, children may perform differently on tasks that presumably measure the same skill (e.g., not recognize

---

a letter on a test sheet but readily identify it in a familiar book). Assessment of a particular skill should assume several forms.

(6) Measures are appropriate for children's development levels and cultural background. Good measurement strategies permit the child some choice in how and when to respond and are appropriate to a variety of cultural backgrounds. . . . Especially important: informal assessments that resemble regular classroom activities.

The National Association for the Education of Young Children (NAEYC) in 1987 adopted a similar statement on standardized testing of young children. The complete text of the NAEYC statement may be found in Appendix D. The statements on assessment presented by these two very large and important professional organizations give clear indication that assessment in literacy is in a state of change. We hope soon to see process assessment as the norm, with far less reliance on test scores derived from fragmenting the processes of literacy.

Making Decisions about Children with Special Needs

Most of our discussion in this chapter has dealt with making decisions about children in the regular classroom. It would be wonderful if we could meet every need of every child in each of our classes. But that would not be a realistic expectation. In fact, you will encounter many children who, because of certain handicapping conditions, cannot progress as you would like in your classroom. What do you do then? Help is usually available, although the amount of help may vary dramatically from school to school.

In most large schools a group of professionals called the Student Services Team is charged with collaborative decision making about children with special needs. This group typically consists of a learning disabilities teacher, a counselor, a reading specialist, the principal, the classroom teacher, and other consultants called into service on special occasions. The Student Services Team is charged with handling referrals, screening, diagnosis, planning, and instruction of children with special needs. You are a vital member of this team. Because you know your students better than anyone else, you are often the person responsible for bringing children with special needs to the attention of the Student Services Team. That point brings us to the important matter of referral.

We have heard beginning teachers say they are reluctant to refer a child for special help because they fear it will make them look like failures. But it is no failure to recognize that a child needs more than you personally can provide. The true failure is the failure to take the steps necessary to get special help for children who need it. Better to refer too many children for assessment for special help than to refer too few!

Under Public Law 94-142, known as the Handicapped Act, the federal government has made funds available to the states to serve the needs of handicapped children. This law requires that children with handicapping conditions be educated in the "least restrictive environment," meaning that they are to be taught in the regular classroom if possible. Now you see why you are such an important part of the Student Services Team. In cooperation with specialists, you will be helping to design and carry out the instruction of the handicapped child. Under the federal law, an individual educational plan (IEP) must be written for each child who is identified as handicapped. You will probably have an important role in creating as well as executing the IEP for your own student.

Getting special help for a child would typically proceed by these steps:

1.   You realize that the child is not learning as well as he or she should. Or the child arouses your concern in some other way, such as having emotional outbursts, appearing to have difficulty hearing, squinting when looking at the board, or being ill a great deal.

2.   You make a decision to refer this child to your building's Student Services Team. If there is none, you refer the child to your principal, who then brings the case to the attention of the appropriate specialists. Figure 4.10 is an example of a referral form.

3.   The Student Services Team examines your referral and may ask you for additional data. The team makes a decision to assess the child, to refer the child to outside specialists, or not to assess at all.

4.   The child's parents are informed by the leader of the Student Services Team of the suspected problems and the plan for assessment. The approval of the parents is granted, or the process stops here. You may be asked to join in the meeting with the parents. At this point the parents are presented with the parents' rights statement. Figure 4.11 is a statement of parental rights under Public Law 94-142.

5.   The necessary assessment is carried out. This may involve testing by specialists in your building, by specialists brought in from the school district or elsewhere as consultants on this referral, or by medical professionals.

6.   Those involved in the assessment process meet to share their data and make recommendations for fulfilling the needs of the handicapped student. The Student Services Team, including the classroom teacher, participates in this meeting. By law, the parents are also included. At this time the IEP (sample in Figure 4.12) is presented and modified as necessary. Once the parties have agreed on the plan and the parents have indicated approval, the plan is put into effect.

REQUEST FOR STUDENT SERVICES

Copy for student's Behavioral File

Student's Full Legal Name _____

last   first   middle   nickname

_____
today's date
(This form must be completed and a copy sent to the
referring party within ten school days of the date of referral)

BIRTHDATE_____ M F

month   day   year   circle

_____
referring person

SCHOOL_____   GRADE _____

_____
phone

parent's name

_____
relationship to student (teacher, parent, etc.)

parent's address   zip code

PHONE _____

home   other

CHECK ALL AREAS OF CONCERN:
____ Academic (Subject:_____)   ____ Clothing   ____ Health   ____ Speech/Language
____ Attendance   ____ Educationally Advance ____ Hearing   ____ Vision
____ Behavior   ____ Family   ____ Motor Skills ____ Other_____

DESCRIBE BEHAVIOR OR PROBLEMS:_____

_____

WHAT EVALUATIONS HAVE ALREADY BEEN DONE?_____

_____

WHAT ACTION WOULD YOU LIKE TAKEN? _____

_____

This form should be given to the
in-building Student Services Team Coordinator

_____
signature of person completing form

FEEDBACK REPORT
(This form is for surveying information already on file, *NOT* for requesting an assessment)

Information to be gathered:	Task assigned to:	Date of informaton	Initialed when task completed
_____	_____	_____	_____
_____	_____	_____	_____
_____	_____	_____	_____

Recommendation: ☐ No action to be taken.
                 ☐ Action plan to be developed.
                 ☐ Assessment plan to be developed (Form SS-2).
                 ☐ Other_____

Explanation: _____

_____

Date referring person given feedback report _____

Signed _____
       Student Services Team Coordinator

**CONFIDENTIAL INFORMATION – REVIEW AND RETURN
TO STUDENT SERVICES TEAM COORDINATOR**

DISTRIBUTION:
  white — Student's Behavioral File
  canary — Special Education Teacher
  pink — Student Services Team Coordinator
  white — Referring Party

Lift page for directions on completing form

Figure 4.10   Referral form.

PARENTS RIGHTS IN IDENTIFICATION, EVALUATION AND PLACEMENT

The following is an explanation of your rights according to federal and state rules and regulations (45CFR 121a.500, ORS 343.163, ORS 343.173 and OAR 581-15-075). The intent of these rules and regulations is to keep you fully informed concerning the decision about your child, as well as your rights should you disagree with the decision.

EVALUATION
Right to refuse consent for preplacement evaluation.
You can deny permission for your child to be tested for intial placement in special education.

Right to obtain an independent evaluation
If you disagree with the identification, evaluation, individualized education plan, placement or the provision of a free appropriate education to your child, you may request that an independent educational evaluation be made pursuant to OAR 581-15-094. **You** can also have the right to request from the school district information about where an independent educational evaluation may be obtained.

PLACEMENT
Right to refuse consent for initial placement of your child in a program providing special education and related services.

RECORDS
Right to request a list of the types and locations of educational records collected, maintained or used by the school district.

Right to inspect and review your child's records
You have the right to inspect and review all educational records with respect to the identification, evaluation, individualized education plan, and educational placement of your child, and the provision of a free appropriate public education to your child. **You** also have a right to a response from the school district to reasonable requests for explanations and interpretations of your child's records. **You** have a right to request that the school district provide copies of records at a reasonable cost unless the fee would effectively prevent you from exercising the right to inspect and review the records in which case the copies shall be provided without cost to you. **You** have the right to have your representative inspect and review your child's records.

Right to request that your child's records be changed.
You have the right to request amendment of your child's educational records if there is reasonable cause to believe that they are inaccurate, misleading, or otherwise in violation of the privacy or other rights of your child. If the school district refuses this request for amendment, it shall notify you within a reasonable time, not to exceed 30 days, and advise you of your right to a hearing to challenge information in the records.

Right to refuse consent for the use of your child's records.
You have the right to refuse consent for the disclosure of personally identifiable information related to your child to anyone other than school officials or persons acting in an official capacity for the school district collecting or using the information. **You** also have the right to refuse consent for the use of personally identifiable information related to your child for any purpose other than the identification, evaluation, individualized education plan or educational placement of your child, or the provision of a free appropriate public education to your child.

Right to request the destruction of your child's records.
You have the right to request the destruction of personally identifiable information collected, maintained, or used by the school district for special education when it is determined by the school district to be no longer needed to provide educational services to your child. However, the required contents of the permanent record must be retained in accordance with the provisions of OAR 581-22-717.

HEARING RIGHTS
Right to ask for an impartial due process hearing.
If you disagree with the schools' actions at any point concerning the identification, evaluation, individualized education plan, or educational placement of your child, or the provision of a free appropriate public education to your child, you have the right to request a hearing. If you desire a hearing, you must notify the school district in writing within 20 days of the date the prior notice was mailed to you. The school district will inform you of any free or low cost legal and other relevant services available in the area if you request it or if either you or the school district initiates a hearing.

Figure 4.11   Statement of parents' rights.

INDIVIDUALIZED EDUCATION PROGRAM

Copy for Student's School File

Student's Full Legal Name _____ last _____ first _____ middle _____ nickname

Birthdate _____ month _____ day _____ year   circle M F

School _____   GRADE _____

Eligible for the following services:

primary _____ code _____ service starting date (month-day-year)

secondary service(s) _____ code _____ service starting date (month-day-year)

Parent/s Name _____

Parent/s Address _____

Parent/s Phone _____ home _____ or _____

Check appropriate box for this IEP:
☐ INITIAL PLACEMENT
☐ REVISED IEP (optional)
☐ ANNUAL REVIEW
☐ 3rd YEAR RE-EVALUATION
☐ CONCLUDING IEP

Anticipated duration of service on this IEP: _____
Percentage of time in regular program: _____

Physical Education: ☐ Special ☐ Regular ☐ unknown
Date of initial placement: _____
Most recent evaluation date: _____ (month) _____ (day) _____ (year)
Due date of 3rd year re-evaluation: _____ (month) _____ (day) _____ (year)

Parents fill out this section:

YES ☐ NO ☐ I have been advised of my Parents' Rights. (Parents' Rights statement on reverse of parent copy.)

YES ☐ NO ☐ I have reviewed _____ of _____ pages.

YES ☐ NO ☐ I agree with the program eligibility and placement.

parent responsibility _____

parent signature _____
date of IEP conference _____ (month-day-year)

Present Performance Levels	Services: Frequency/Time/ Duration/Provider	Initial Objectives, Evaluation Procedures, and Criteria	Long Range Goals (Prioritized)

Signatures of Placement/Review Committee:
Names:
_____ Title: _____
_____ Case Manager _____

Lift page for directions on completing form

Salem School District 24J complies with provisions of the Fair Employment Practices Act and/or Title IX Regulations in employment and educational programs and activities.

Page _____ of _____ pages
Use IEP continuation form if needed.

DISTRIBUTION:
white — Student's File
canary — Special Education Teacher
pink — Parent Copy
green — SS Team Coordinator
white — Student Services Office
other copies

Figure 4.12 Individual educational plan.

■ Major Ideas in This Chapter

■ Teachers make many important instructional decisions. A critically important scope and sequence decision is whether or not to integrate curriculum. The instructional decisions you make in the areas of scope and sequence, individual differences, modes of instruction, management and discipline, environmental organization, and communication are all interdependent.

■ Intuition is a very valuable and legitimate source of data for decision making. As you gain more teaching experience, your intuition should become more powerful. Observation of children at work—a skill that strengthens with time—is an indispensable source of decision-making data.

■ Evaluating a child's readiness for reading involves a comparison between the child's current capacities and the demands for success of a given reading program. Crucial to this question is the child's current level of cognitive development. Children who are preoperational thinkers need a reading program that does not emphasize the learning of discrete skills outside the context of meaningful print.

■ Informal, criterion-referenced measures aid the teacher in observing the *processes* the child uses in reading and writing, rather than focusing on the less important subskills. The product of whole-language instruction is enjoyable, competent reading and writing, with greater emphasis on creating meaning than on subskills.

■ Norm-referenced tests, although regularly used, are not necessarily valid for a given group of students with a given curriculum. The child's abilities to use effectively all four cueing systems in reading and to write clearly and creatively are rarely assessed by norm-referenced measures.

■ Assessment in literacy is in a state of change. The movement from assessing discrete skills to assessing the ways in which children process reading and writing will have profound effects on our view of assessment. The use of checklists that guide the teacher's observations of literacy processes is helpful in decision making and in documenting students' growth to both parents and administrators.

■ Your role as a classroom teacher is central to meeting the special needs of children. You should refer children who may need special services, and you should play an important role in the writing of their individual educational plans.

? Discussion Questions
Focusing on the Teacher You Are Becoming

1. How are your classroom management decisions affected by your choice of reading program emphases? Can you change program emphases without changing assessment systems?
2. Are the miscue analysis and analytical trait evaluations of writing worth the time and effort they require in terms of useful information they give the teacher?
3. Some schools release achievement test scores, sometimes even broken down by classroom, for publication in the local newspaper. How do you think these schools view the processes of reading and writing?
4. What questions will you ask if, as a beginning teacher, you work in a school that chooses to group children by ability groups for reading and mathematics instruction?

✓ Field-Based Applications

1. Interview a teacher who integrates curriculum. Observe his or her classroom if possible. Ask questions that will help you make your own decision about where you stand on this important scope and sequence issue.
2. Visit an elementary school classroom for a day. Using the six categories of decisions identified in this chapter, keep a record of the kinds of decisions you see being made. Try to identify three things: how many significant decisions you see being made per hour, how many decisions you see being made within each of the six categories, and the reasons for making those decisions.
3. Join forces with other students and take an entire first-grade classroom through at least five Piagetian tasks. How many of the children are pre-operational? Brainstorm ways in which their reading program might be modified to accommodate their level of cognitive development.
4. First with a group of second-grade children and then with a group of fifth-grade children, use the Analytic Trait Writing Assessment (Appendix C). What differences do you see in the writing of the two groups? For each child, what writing-improvement goals would you set?
5. Interview five classroom teachers about their feelings toward norm-referenced tests. Ask them what use they have made of norm-referenced test data. Begin to formulate your own position regarding norm-referenced testing in the elementary school.

6. Ask to see an individual educational plan written for a child in the classroom in which you are working. Collect as much information as you can from the classroom teacher about the *process* of writing that IEP. Ask especially about the role of the classroom teacher in the process. If IEPs are confidential in the school district where you work, ask the teacher to tell you how they are written.

7. In the school where you are working, spend time getting to know a child whose native language is not English. Try to find information about the conflicts between English and the child's language (use of gender markers, use of double negatives, and so on). Plan a reading experience that might help the child overcome one of these language differences.

▣ References and Suggested Readings

Ausubel, David P. "Viewpoints from Related Disciplines: Human Growth and Development." *Teachers College Record* 60 (February 1959): 245–254.

Berliner, David C. "Making the Right Changes in Pre-Service Teacher Education." *Phi Delta Kappan* 66 (October 1984): 94–96.

Brewer, JoAnn. "Ready or Not?" *Early Years* 17 (January 1987): 96–99.

Elkind, David. "Beginning Reading: A Stage-Structure Analysis." *Childhood Education* 55 (February/March 1979): 248–252.

Goodman, Yetta M.; Watson, Dorothy J.; and Burke, Carolyn L. *Reading Miscue Inventory Alternative Procedures.* New York: Richard C. Owen, 1987.

Harp, Bill. "When the Principal Asks: Why Are You Doing Piagetian Task Testing When You Have Given Basal Placement Tests?" *The Reading Teacher* 41 (November 1987): 212–214.

Haupt, Edward J., and Herman-Sissons, Therese M. "Conservation as a Supplementary Predictor of Reading Skill." Paper presented at the annual convention of the Eastern Educational Research Association, Norfolk, Va., March 1980. (ERIC Document Reproduction Service No. ED 207 030)

Johnston, Peter. "Teachers as Evaluation Experts." *The Reading Teacher* 40 (April 1987): 744–748.

Keraithe, J. M. "A Framework for Teaching English Reading to Bilingual Students." *44th Claremont Reading Conference Yearbook.* Claremont, Calif.: Claremont Reading Conference, Center for Developmental Studies, Claremont Graduate School, 1980.

Kirkland, Eleanor R. "A Piagetian Interpretation of Beginning Reading Instruction." *The Reading Teacher* 31 (February 1978): 497–503.

Lange, Bob. "ERIC/RCS Report: Piaget and Reading." *Language Arts* 59 (May 1982): 520–523.

Potter, Gill. "Commentary: Early Literacy Development—It's Time to Align the Curriculum with Children's Developmental Stages." *The Reading Teacher* 39 (March 1986): 628–631.

Purkey, William. *Self Concept and School Achievement.* Englewood Cliffs, N.J.: Prentice-Hall, 1970.

Ribovich, Jerilyn K. "Cognitive Development: An Area Worth Studying for Teachers of Beginning Reading." Paper presented at the 23rd annual convention of the International Reading Association, Houston, May 1978. (ERIC Document Reproduction Service No. ED 177 468)

Spache, George D. *Diagnosing and Correcting Reading Disabilities.* 2nd ed. Boston: Allyn & Bacon, 1981.

Teale, William H.; Hiebert, Elfreida H.; and Chittenden, Edward A. "Assessing Young Children's Literacy Development." *The Reading Teacher* 40 (April 1987): 772–777.

Wadsworth, Barry J. *Piaget's Theory of Cognitive and Affective Development.* 3rd ed. New York: Longman, 1984.

Waller, T. Gary. *Think First, Read Later! Piagetian Prerequisites for Reading.* Newark, Del.: International Reading Association, 1977.

Watson, Dorothy, and Weaver, Constance. "Basals: Report on the Reading Commission Study." *Teachers Networking—The Whole Language Newsletter.* New York: Richard C. Owen, 1988.

Chapter 5

Supporting the Reading/Writing Program

Chapter Overview

- Teachers must sometimes place children in groups for instructional purposes. The traditional method, ability grouping, is not as effective as flexible grouping or cooperative learning groups.

- Key elements in the reading/writing program include guided reading activities, enrichment activities, and skill-development activities. Guided reading activities involve interaction with children while they read. Enrichment activities integrate reading and writing with other curricular areas. Skill-development activities focus on specific skills in meaningful contexts based on instructional need. Other key elements are student–teacher conferences and activity centers.

- Learning centers facilitate student self-direction in learning. Centers permit students access to instructional materials without the direct assistance of the teacher.

- Managing the classroom so that children are productive and happy is aided by planning instructional activities that are challenging and meaningful and by following certain guidelines.

- Parents are keenly interested in their children's progress in literacy. Teachers must communicate clearly with parents and help them learn how to assist their children in developing literacy.

- The school principal is an ally with whom teachers must maintain clear communication, following some helpful guidelines.

- The microcomputer facilitates the development of literacy through word processing and telecommunications, which can add an exciting dimension to a whole-language program.

The warmth of a classroom, the amount of freedom and creativity permitted or encouraged, the smoothness with which students go about their work, and the amount of learning happening are all determined by the support system the teacher creates. This chapter will examine in greater detail some of the critical decision points identified in Chapter 4. Areas in which implementation of decisions is crucial are the grouping of children, key elements in the reading/writing program, classroom management, working with parents and administrators, and the use of microcomputers in instruction.

Working with Children in Groups

Ability Grouping

The criteria for placing children in instructional groups have plagued teachers probably since the first classroom was built. In journals and other forums, educators continue to debate the pros and cons of placing children in groups and the criteria by which grouping decisions should be made. At the heart of the controversy is a practice that has come to be known as *ability grouping*. Despite different interpretations in various educational settings, the term consistently implies some means of grouping students by ability or achievement so as to create instructional groups that are as homogeneous as possible (Slavin, 1987a). Underlying the concept of ability grouping is the assumption that if teachers can create groups of children who are alike in learning needs, instruction will proceed more efficiently and effectively. This assumption has been challenged in the educational literature.

What the Research Says

Perhaps the most comprehensive analysis of the data on ability grouping has been done by Robert Slavin (1987a). Slavin revisited old research and examined new research in an effort to define the effects of four kinds of grouping practices. He studied these grouping patterns:

1. Ability-grouped class assignment. Children are assigned to their classrooms on the basis of achievement or ability.
2. Regrouping for reading and mathematics. Children are assigned to relatively heterogeneous classrooms but regrouped across classrooms at a given grade level for instruction in reading and math.
3. The Joplin plan. Children are assigned to heterogeneous classrooms for most of the day but regrouped across grade lines for reading; under this plan, a teacher might have a reading class composed of fourth-, fifth-, and sixth-graders all reading instructionally at the fifth-grade level.

4. Within-class ability grouping. Children are placed in small instructional groups within the class on the basis of ability or achievement.

Slavin's findings offer some direction for the classroom teacher. Ability-grouped class assignment, he concluded, does not enhance student achievement in the elementary school. Regrouping for reading and mathematics across classrooms at the same grade level has few, if any, benefits for student achievement, although it may be beneficial if the teacher is careful to tailor the level and pace of instruction to the abilities of the specific group. The evidence across many studies indicates that the Joplin plan is effective in terms of children's achievement in reading. However, grouping patterns 2 and 3 share one potentially serious limitation: when a teacher has a group of children only for reading instruction, it is very difficult to integrate instruction across curricular areas. Although there is some support for within-class grouping, it is limited to mathematics in upper elementary school.

The work of Sorensen and Hallinan (1986) adds to our understanding of the effects of ability grouping. They concluded that reading-ability grouping provides fewer opportunities for learning because the more groups a teacher has, the fewer contacts there can be between teacher and learner. However, they also concluded that when students are grouped by ability, the instructional time that is available to any one group is better used. High-ability groups have more opportunities for learning than low-ability groups. In fact, students assigned to high groups are taught more than students assigned to low groups. An inequality in instructional outcomes is a result of grouping.

A persistent concern about reading-ability grouping is its effect on the self-concepts of children, especially children placed in less-skilled groups. Although the research results in this area are not consistent enough to yield firm conclusions, there is a tendency to believe that ability grouping has negative effects on the self-concepts of children in low-achieving groups, while at the same time resulting in more positive self-images for high achievers (Borg, 1966; Weinstein, 1976). In fact, Weinstein concluded that the group to which a child is assigned has a significant effect on achievement, regardless of previous record: performance on school tasks often drops right along with self-concept when children are placed in low-achieving groups.

In examining years of research on grouping by reading ability, Hiebert (1983) found interesting differences between teachers' interactions with low-ability and high-ability groups of children. Low-ability groups were directed to spend much more time on decoding tasks than high-ability groups, which focused on unlocking meaning. Low-ability groups spent more time on oral reading; high-ability groups spent more time on silent reading. Teachers interrupted poor readers more often than they interrupted good readers who made the same oral reading miscues. Teachers treated children in low-ability reading groups differently from children in high-ability groups. We wonder if this differential treatment of low-achieving group members may account, in part, for their low achievement.

Implications for Classroom Practice

In the face of the research on ability grouping, the classroom teacher is justifiably confused about grouping practices. Good teachers want to avoid grouping practices that harm children in any way, and yet they are overwhelmed by the prospect of totally individualizing instruction. What directions for the teacher are suggested by the research on grouping? Here are our conclusions:

Implications for Classroom Grouping

1. Children should not be assigned to classrooms on the basis of ability or achievement.
2. Although across-grade grouping (the Joplin plan) has been shown to result in learning gains, the gains must be carefully measured against the limitations imposed by having a group of children *only* for reading instruction, an arrangement that makes curricular integration and thematic teaching virtually impossible.
3. Ability grouping within a grade level does not yield results sufficient to outweigh the possible risks to self-concept and achievement of less skilled children.
4. The differential treatment afforded low groups and high groups by teachers indicates that such grouping should be avoided.
5. Assignment to an instructional group should depend on instructional need at a given point in time.
6. Teachers cannot assume that a group formed for a specific instructional need will all share a future instructional need.
7. Permanent groups based on ability or achievement should not be formed in classrooms.
8. Ability grouping should be avoided because it results in less instructional time and less learning for low-ability groups.

■ Flexible Grouping

Flexible grouping is part of the answer to the teacher's desire to use grouping effectively. In flexible grouping, children are placed in temporary

Flexible grouping arrangements provide children with learning opportunities not possible in traditional whole-class instruction.
© Freda Leinwand/Monkmeyer Press Photo Service

groups on the basis of their *level of independence as learners*; that is, their place on a continuum from highly independent learners to highly dependent learners. Groups are not formed to deal with a given set of instructional materials, as is often the case with ability grouping; rather, groups are formed and reformed to engage in a variety of tasks. Unsworth (1984, p. 300) has identified a set of principles that guide the use of flexible groups:

1. There should be no permanent groups.
2. Groups should be periodically created, modified, or disbanded, to meet new needs as they arise.
3. There are times when whole-group instruction is appropriate.
4. Groups should vary in size from two or three to nine or ten, depending on the group's purpose.
5. Group membership should never be fixed; it varies according to needs and purposes.

6. Students' commitment is enhanced when students know how the work of the group is related to the overall program or task.
7. Children should be able to evaluate and recognize the progress they make and the teacher's assessment of it.
8. There should be a clear strategy for supervising the work of the group.

When a group is to embark on a task, that task must be clear and appropriate to the needs and interests of the students. There must be variety in tasks, and there must be clearly understood follow-up activities when the group's work is completed (Unsworth, 1984).

Flexible learning groups may be formed on the basis of interest, learning styles, social needs such as friendship groups, and short-term needs for skills such as writing dialogue or using a glossary.

■ Cooperative Learning Groups

A more complete answer to the problem of instructional grouping is cooperative learning groups—heterogeneous groups of four or five students who work together to meet assigned team tasks and are rewarded on the basis of the group's overall performance. Over the past eighteen years, more than fifty research projects have studied the effects of cooperative learning and concluded that students in cooperative learning groups consistently achieve more than do students who are in traditionally structured classes (Stevens, Madden, Slavin, and Farnish, 1987).

Operational Features

There are variations in the application of the cooperative learning concept, but most models share the following characteristics (Slavin, 1987b):

1. Teacher instruction. Lessons often begin with a presentation by the teacher.
2. Team practice. Students work in mixed-ability groups of four or five to practice the material and master the lesson presented by the teacher. During this time, student activities may include completing appropriate written assignments, drilling one another on information, teaching a lesson to team members, formulating and discussing common answers, and assessing each other's learning. The goal is to have each member of the group succeed at learning so that the team will be cooperatively successful.
3. Individual assessments. Each student's learning is individually assessed by the teacher.

4. Team recognition. Each individual student's score or performance is averaged with the rest of the team to produce team scores. Special recognition is given to teams that reach a certain predetermined criterion of performance.

The basic idea underlying all cooperative learning models is to motivate each student to do a good job of helping fellow group members learn. Because a team or group can be successful only if each member of the group succeeds at learning, group members take responsibility for their own and each other's learning. Cooperation is emphasized and competition eliminated within the group. Most of us have experienced the feeling that the best way to learn something is to teach it to someone else. In a cooperative-learning environment, children learn as they teach other children, sharing their view of the world with others.

Benefits of Cooperative Learning

The process of developing small groups of learners who function well together produces several benefits (Fehring, 1987):

- Interpersonal and small-group skills. Children need guidance in communicating, listening, sharing, resolving conflicts, making decisions, gaining the ability to work with others, and tolerating differences—skills that are all critical to cooperative learning.
- Positive interdependence. The primary motivation in cooperative learning is to help each member of the group achieve the intended goal. Children's reliance on one another to determine the goal or goals, share the resources, and carry out specific assignments builds positive interdependence.
- Skill in face-to-face interaction. Debating, questioning, and discussing are the tools of cooperative learning.
- Individual accountability. Traditional classrooms typically encourage self-reliance and competition. Cooperative learning requires a new orientation: each person is responsible for the achievement of the group's goals. Each child is therefore accountable for his or her achievement as a contribution to the total effort of the group.

All these skills are difficult to learn and take time and patience on the part of the teacher. But if cooperative learning is to be successful, each must be present in the work of groups. In addition, children have to learn to keep their group's noise down to a level that does not distract others from their work, and they must learn to move about the room without causing disruption.

Cooperative Integrated Reading and Composition

Researchers at Johns Hopkins University conducted a major study on the effects of cooperative learning strategies in elementary reading and writing instruction (Stevens et al., 1987). The project, called Cooperative Integrated Reading and Composition (CIRC), was carried out with third- and fourth-grade students who worked in heterogeneous learning teams for all reading, language arts, and writing activities.

In reading, students read from basal readers and then formed teams of partners to do follow-up activities, including partner reading, decoding, study of story structure, prediction, and story summary. Team practice followed instruction in comprehension.

In writing, students engaged in peer conferences during planning, revising, and editing as they worked through the writing process. Team practice followed lessons on language mechanics and activities in language expression that were related to the students' writing.

The researchers found that the students in the CIRC program scored higher than control-group students on standardized measures of reading comprehension, reading vocabulary, language mechanics, language expression, and spelling. The CIRC students also performed better on writing samples and oral reading assessment. Cooperative learning is demonstrably a powerful way to work with groups in the reading/writing program.

Cooperative learning takes very careful planning. The task of the group must be clearly defined. Group responsibilities and individual responsibilities must be thoroughly understood by each group member. A plan for assessment of the group's work must be known. Figure 5.1 illustrates a cooperative learning lesson that fulfills these requirements.

■ Whole-Class Instruction

In classrooms that make the most of the reading/writing connection, you will see more whole-class instruction than in classrooms that divide the curriculum into discrete parts. You will see teachers who value instruction in literacy doing frequent modeling of the processes of literacy before the whole group. The following list merely suggests appropriate whole-class instructional activities; it is by no means exhaustive.

1. Model the writing process on the board with various types of composition. This demonstration will include the recursive processes of rehearsal and composition. Children need to see you compose, erase, think, compose, approve, compose, think, erase, and so on.

2. Model the process of predicting, reading, confirming your predictions, and reading. As you share a piece of literature with your students, engage them in your thought processes: "What will this story be

Westward Expansion

Task: Each group will produce a serious skit based on some incident in the social studies unit about westward expansion. The teacher will have presented the basic information in advance, and class discussion will enhance each student's current knowledge of the topic.

Group Responsibilities

1. Choosing an incident to illustrate.
2. Involving each group member in activities.
3. Assigning roles and responsibilities.
4. Presenting skit for other class members and invited guests.
5. Conducting assessment activities.

Individual Responsibilities

1. Doing background research employing as many source materials as possible.
2. Writing the script for the skit with other members.
3. Designing costumes or props based on research findings.

Assessment

1. Videotaping skits and critiquing performances.
2. Evaluating group skills in making decisions, achieving goals, and helping each other.
3. Completing a test on facts and concepts about westward expansion.

Figure 5.1   Sample cooperative learning lesson.

about? What will happen next? I thought this would happen, but now I think that will happen."

3. Share a "big book" (an oversize version) with your students, modeling the reading of the story as they follow along. You will show them your approach to print: left to right, top to bottom, predictive, interactive. After you have read the selection, invite them to read it in their books.

4. Use the work of a student who already possesses a skill to model the skill for the rest of the class. Suppose that the curriculum guide specifies the writing of compound sentences as a goal at your grade level. Using a student's writing sample in which compound sentences are well

Fifth-graders collaborate on a letter to the editor of a newspaper.
© Lora E. Askinazi/The Picture Cube

done, conduct a lesson on compound sentences with the whole group. Invite the students to attend to that skill during their writing.

5.   Devise a first-hand experience of a concept before formal presentation. Suppose that you are about to have cooperative learning groups research the effects of discrimination. Beforehand, divide the class into two groups and for one day let one half have all the usual privileges afforded students—free use of the pencil sharpener, free access to learning centers, free access to other areas of the building, and so on. Explain to those in the other half that they must always have a pass to use these facilities, and that the number of passes is limited. You control the issuance of passes and their time of expiration. At the end of the day, engage the whole group in a discussion of how they felt, preparing them for the research they are going to do.

6.   Teach the whole class how to do bookbinding, or share a specific illustrator's art and talk about how the students might use the same technique in their next book.

7.   Let the class as a whole make plans to produce a play based on a book you have read to them or one that a child has shared with the group.

8.   Reconstruct a story on the basis of the children's knowledge of story grammar and meaning. This worthwhile activity is best done with

stories having highly predictable structures—first *a*, then *b*, then *c*, and finally *d*, or *Once upon a time there was*, then *the antagonist did thus*, then *the hero did so*, and finally *thus and so*. The story is cut into sections and given to the group. Children decide which part goes first, second, third, and so on. This exercise invites children to use prior knowledge and prediction and focuses them on the features of the text, allowing them to talk about language and about texts generally. Readers discover that all texts teach them about reading (Watson, 1988).

The use of flexible grouping, grouping for specific instructional needs, cooperative learning, and whole-class instruction will contribute to the effectiveness of the decisions you make about individual differences, as well as to the success of your management decisions. Children learn best when they feel good about what they are doing and when they are challenged in ways that make success attainable. We believe these forms of grouping will help you achieve these important learning goals.

The ways in which you handle grouping are critical. So are the ways in which you make use of the key elements in the reading/writing program.

Sharing children's writing with the whole class conveys the message that their work is valued.
© *Michael Hagan*

Key Elements in the Reading/Writing Program

Certain key elements must be planned into the reading/writing program if the reading and writing processes are to be honored. These key elements need to be present regardless of the nature of the instructional materials used or the patterns of organization adopted (for example, self-contained classroom, team teaching, multiage grouping, and so on). Many of your instructional decisions regarding individual differences, modes of instruction, and scope and sequence are carried out through the use of the key elements.

Guided Reading Activities

Guided or shared reading activities encompass all the things you do in creating shared reading experiences with children. When you sit down with one or more children to guide their reading of a selection, you are using this structural element. Guided reading activities may take a variety of forms. The Directed Reading Activity and the Guided Metacomprehension Strategy are explained in Chapter 10. Much of the important work in comprehension instruction happens as a part of guided reading activities.

Skill-Development Activities

Skill-development activities are the instructional strategies you use when you take the reading or writing process apart and focus on one element. Most classrooms spend too much time in isolated skills instruction; nevertheless, there definitely are times when children need instruction on specific skills. The components of skill lessons are discussed in detail in Chapter 9. It is important to keep skills instruction in proper perspective. Isolated skills instruction is not worthwhile. Skills instruction should be an outgrowth of real reading and writing experiences, based on known needs of the children.

Enrichment Activities

Enrichment activities build bridges between curricular areas. They can be used to enhance either reading or writing experiences. For example, after reading a selection on westward expansion, children might engage in library research, visit a museum, make model Conestoga wagons, or write entries in the diary of a pioneer child. The children might be encouraged to read *Caddie Woodlawn* (Brink, 1935), *The Sign of the Beaver* (Speare, 1983), one of Laura Ingalls Wilder's Little House books, or other books about pioneers. They might create watercolor illustrations, make book jackets for the story, interview a local author, or videotape a dramatic performance of one part of the story. Although the greater share of time should be spent on actually reading and writing, enrichment activities contribute significantly to the reading/writing program.

■ Student–Teacher Conferences

Student–teacher conferences play an important role in the reading/writing program because they allow the teacher to have one-on-one time with each student. Conferences may be used as part of the editing process in writing and as a means of monitoring comprehension activities when children are reading books they have selected individually. They can help the child plan writing efforts and select reading materials, reveal concerns the child may be having about progress or about working with a group, facilitate assessment of the child's progress, and yield decisions about future instructional goals. Amid the crush of demands on your time, conferences are difficult to schedule, but they reward the effort. The conference is a good time to make use of the developmental checklists discussed in Chapter 4. A three-ring binder containing a page for each child is a useful way to keep anecdotal records of other things you learn during conferences. Confer with each child as often as possible. One approach is to allot a given amount of time to conferences each day and ask children to sign up for a conference.

■ Activity Centers

Activity centers are essential to a productive reading and writing classroom. To engage in truly meaningful reading and writing activities, children must be permitted to select many of their own activities and carry them out individually or in groups, without dependence on the teacher's time. It really is as simple as this: while a teacher is working with an individual or a small group of students, there must be things for the rest of the class to do, and those activities should be interesting, meaningful, and productive. Handing out a stack of worksheets as "morning work" does not meet the criteria of interesting, meaningful, and productive! But centers can provide a variety of activities that do.

A word of caution is in order here. Beginning teachers have too many things to do, think about, and manage. Centers are essential, but they should be initiated slowly and carefully. We suggest that you plan one center, perhaps the library center, and then introduce your students to its operation. Make clear to children that their access to the center depends on using it properly, in ways that do not interfere with the work of other children. Once one center is operating smoothly, introduce another. Continue opening one center at a time as the children demonstrate their ability to use them properly and you remain comfortable with the operation of your class.

Library Center

A rotating and permanent stock of books from the school or city library, books published by authors in the classroom, newspapers and magazines, and maybe even old basal readers should make up the collection in the classroom library center. Especially important are the books authored by children in the classroom—or by children who occupied the classroom in previous years. The creation of the library center affords an opportunity to honor the work of class authors. Many teachers partition the classroom library off from the rest of the room by an arrangement of moveable bookcases. Beanbags, carpet samples, rocking chairs, and even towers and forts might complete the furnishings of a classroom library center, making the area inviting and comfortable for children. It is appropriate for children to go to the library center and *read*.

Listening Center

The listening center should be stocked with audio tapes of children's books and stories, accompanied by the printed text for reading along. Classroom authors enjoy recording their own books to put in the listening center, and some parents or grandparents may volunteer to make audio recordings. Tapes are a good way to handle selections that teachers want children to experience but that may be too difficult for them to read. Recordings of songs and illustrated song booklets make enjoyable listening at the center. The heart of the listening center is media equipment, often called a "listening post," that connects eight to ten headsets to a tape recorder or record player.

Art Center

The art center should be located near a cabinet and a sink and should house easels for tempera and watercolor painting. Except for the painting, children can take materials from the art center and use them elsewhere in the room. The art center becomes the "warehouse" for art supplies and equipment that are needed for illustrating books and doing other art work. Materials for binding books should be stored either in the art center or in the writing center.

Writing Center

The writing center is not necessarily a place where children go to write; rather, it is a place where they will find the materials to do writing. Stocked with a variety of pens, pencils, markers, paper, and dictionaries, the writing center becomes an important support for the children's writing efforts.

In the listening center, children gain valuable familiarity with the text of a story.
© *Frank Siteman/The Picture Cube*

Some teachers create displays at the writing center to spark ideas for story or poetry writing tied to a theme or unit currently under study. A system for storing the writing portfolios of the authors in the classroom should be part of the writing center.

Teachers who plan for these key elements in the reading/writing program find that children will learn to work productively, with considerable independence, as they produce important work in writing and as they become increasingly more competent readers. The richer the classroom is in terms of interesting options for children, the easier the class will be to manage.

Classroom Management

As new teachers gain experience in the classroom, their concerns move from their own survival to more student-related, professional concerns. In fact, teachers-in-training who have early field experiences complete their training with much more professional, student-focused concerns than their counterparts who have limited contact with children (Harp, 1971). With experience, teachers' concerns change from "Will the children like me? How can I get them to listen? What will I do if they don't do what I ask?" to "How can I figure out why Tom doesn't want to read? How can I meet the needs of each of my students?" and "How can I improve the status of our profession?"

Managing a classroom in which children behave appropriately, stay on task, and enjoy learning is one of the greatest challenges of teaching, and one of particular concern to the new teacher. These are some management guidelines we have found helpful:

1.   Classrooms in which the learning environment is rich with stimulation are classrooms in which children are productive and happy. When children are engaged in thinking about and doing interesting things, they seldom misbehave. Many of the "management problems" some teachers experience are a result of boredom on the part of the students.

2.   Classroom expectations must be clearly spelled out, and the consequences of failing to follow them must be known. Engaging children in setting the classroom expectations and identifying consequences gives them ownership of the expectations.

3.   When an academic or behavioral problem does occur, the teacher's first thought should be, "What is to be learned here, and why are the kids misbehaving?" Every student problem then becomes an educational challenge. If and when we must punish a child, the punishment should provide a learning experience (Gathercoal, 1987). Whenever possible, the result of misbehavior should be a logical consequence of the behavior.

4.   The overriding expectation should be that students do nothing that prevents other students from learning. Often asking the question "Are you keeping Troy from learning?" is enough to prompt a child's recognition that his or her behavior is inappropriate.

5.   When a child has misbehaved, the first question the teacher should ask the child is, "What did you do?" or, "Why am I unhappy with what you have done?" Almost without fail, children know when they have misbehaved and what they have done. Establishing this fact verbally with the child is a productive first step to rectifying the situation. The second question from the teacher should be, "What are we going to do about it?" This approach gives the child some ownership of the consequence and permits the child to suggest what the consequence or reparation might be.

6.   Never punish the group for the misbehavior of a child, and never ridicule a child. Self-concepts must always be protected in management situations.

7.   Never send students out of your classroom to sit in the hall. If you must remove a student from your classroom, have him or her escorted to the office. The hallway can be a wonderfully entertaining place, and sitting there is rarely, if ever, a natural consequence of misbehavior.

8.   Never lose your temper. Remember that you are the professional in control of the learning setting and that children can be responsive without threat, fear, or intimidation.

Each teacher must develop his or her individual style of classroom management. One teacher's style may be very different from that of another; this is fine, so long as the integrity of the child is maintained. Helping children behave in appropriate ways in school is a partnership effort between the child, the teacher, and the parents.

Working with Parents

Importance of Parental Involvement

There is no doubt that parental involvement has strong effects on the child's developing intelligence and achievement (Becher, 1982; Olmstead and Rubin, 1983), typically measured by standardized tests for research purposes. Involving parents in the reading instruction of their children can yield improved reading scores. Several studies have concluded that teaching parents to help their children at home resulted in gains on standardized reading tests (Garber, 1972; Keele and Harrison, 1971; McKinney, 1977). Grimmett and McCoy (1980) found that improving teachers' communication with parents also led to improving their children's reading performance. These results are not especially difficult to interpret. Parents who are aware of what their children are doing in reading instruction and who feel that the school is interested in keeping them informed and in hearing their opinions are much more likely than others to demonstrate interest in their children's reading performance. Greater interest means more time spent in reading and more involvement with their children's reading instruction. Children who spend more time in reading become better readers. Therefore, parental interest and concern lead to better performance on measures of reading achievement.

It is the rare parent who is not interested in the child's progress in school, and specifically in reading. Parents tend to be more concerned about reading than about other school subjects. They also have a set of expectations about school and about reading instruction, many of which are based on their own experiences in school and on their view of success in reading. To put parental interest to work most effectively for your students, you must be able to communicate with the parents.

The first rule for communicating successfully with parents is to respect their right to information about their child's school experiences and recognize their interest in their children. The second rule is that communication from the school must be sensitive to parents' concerns. For example, in sending out a survey asking parents what they read at home and what they have available for their child to read, the school should include an explanation of why the information is needed and what will be done with it, enabling parents to justify their contribution of time and information. Third, the school has an obligation to explain its programs and practices in language parents can understand; the jargon of education and even the programs themselves are unfamiliar to many parents.

■ How Parents Can Help

The suggestion most frequently given to parents who want to help their children with reading is to read aloud to them. Many parents do not know why reading aloud helps their child to perform better as a reader. Becher (1985) reports that parents are often surprised to learn about the significant benefits of reading aloud: improved listening and speaking vocabularies, longer spoken sentences, gain in comprehension skills, acquisition of general information, heightened interest in books, and attachment of more value to reading as an activity. Reading aloud introduces children to a variety of sentence patterns and provides the child with opportunities to begin to break the code of printed language. Being read to is helpful even to children in intermediate grades.

Parents will ask how much time they should devote to reading aloud to their children. Studies have found that children read to on a regular basis (at least four times a week) for eight to ten minutes express more positive attitudes about reading and show higher levels of achievement in reading than those not read to (Romotowski and Trepanier, 1977). Vukelich (1984) found that a twenty-minute reading interaction time each evening could help children begin a lifelong reading habit.

Parents may also have questions about the strategies that are most productive when reading aloud. Children who had higher performances on reading tasks were those who talked more about the story and who asked more questions during the reading process (Becher, 1985; DeFord and Rasinski, 1986). This information will be useful to those parents who might have believed that being quiet and listening were the most important behaviors during read-aloud sessions.

A second suggestion often made to parents is that reading material should be available in the home. Whether owned or borrowed from the library, a wide range of reading material should be provided for parents and children alike. Parents are also encouraged to model reading behaviors—to

Children know reading is important when their parents take them to the library.
© *Robert V. Eckert, Jr./The Picture Cube*

read when their children can observe them reading for a variety of purposes. In today's world of working parents, even heavy readers might not realize that they do all their own reading after the children are asleep.

An important factor in reading achievement is the parent's expectation for success. "Expectation of success" does not mean exerting undue pressure on the child or punishing the child for not achieving at the level the parent hopes for. It means expression and demonstration of confidence that the child can learn.

Parents whose children achieve well in reading are involved in the process of instruction. They help their children select reading goals and reading materials and they help them employ reading in solving problems. For example, they help their children look up information. They use reading in daily tasks with their child, such as cooking or putting together a model. They also spend time listening to their children read and giving direct instruction on specific reading techniques (Becher, 1985).

■ Teachers Helping Parents

Teachers interested in helping parents assist their children will provide specific guidelines for time and strategies that are most productive. They will plan field trips for parents and children to visit libraries and will help parents understand the importance of modeling reading behavior and having reading material available. They will help parents understand the difference between expectations and pressures and they will supply information to assist parents in giving actual instruction. They will provide information about resource material for choosing books for their children. One example is *The Read-Aloud Handbook* (Trelease, 1986).

Teachers interested in helping parents will plan homework assignments that can be accomplished with the parent's involvement. For example, if a class of older children is reading mystery stories, a homework task might be to watch a mystery program on television with a parent and discuss the plot elements and the use of clues. Teachers can help parents select meaningful activities to do with their children, as opposed to assigning isolated practice of reading subskills. For example, instead of drilling on letter forms from a workbook, parents might help children put together their own alphabet book showing toys or familiar household and neighborhood objects.

Most of the information parents need about reading instruction can be communicated in newsletters, booklets, or brochures. The advantage of these printed materials is that they are available for quick and repeated reference by the parent.

Making parents feel welcome at school is another means of communicating interest in parents and their involvement in their children's education. Casual school visits are not especially useful for conveying information, except insofar as they permit observation and reveal broad goals. Schools and teachers concerned with parental involvement can provide courses or workshops in which materials to be used at home are constructed or techniques such as storytelling are demonstrated. Such hands-on classes for parents have been found effective in helping parents as they help their children (Vukelich, 1984).

■ Tips on Communicating with Parents

- Meetings for groups of parents should be short and present information that parents can use tomorrow. Many parents are reluctant to attend meetings because they feel that they go on and on and are lectures. Get parents involved in making materials, playing reading games they can use with their children, or binding blank books for children to write in.

- Begin conferences with positive information. Share something that you really admire in the child and ask parents to name something that they enjoy about their child.
- Try to deliver any negative message in a face-to-face situation. No parent wants to find pinned to the child a note that says negative things.
- Make sure that you have positive communications with every parent on a regular basis. Keep a class list and call one or two parents every few days or send home a positive note. Some schools have notes printed with a positive message so that it takes only a second to personalize the message and sign it.
- Try to make telephone calls at convenient times, and keep them short.
- Send home a newsletter from your class on a regular basis. Some schools publish a school newspaper, but a class news-letter with information about specific class activities is still appropriate. Include reading-related news about favorite books, times when parents are especially invited to share ac-tivities, topics that the class is studying, and field trips taken or planned.
- Welcome parents to your classroom as visitors or workers. Your attitude about parents will show!
- If parents want to help, let them. Find something parents can do who cannot come to school. They can type children's stories, make materials, make costumes, make tape record-ings, and so on. Acknowledge the contributions of parents frequently and publicly.

Working with Administrators

Many of us learned to spell *principal* by recalling the saying, "The principal is your pal." "Pal" may not be a sufficiently professional descriptor for your principal, but the message is an important one. The building principal is or ought to be one of the classroom teacher's closest sources of support. Most principals see themselves as curriculum leaders whose first job is to sup-port the classroom teacher in every way possible. Although collective bar-gaining has created a labor/management dichotomy in the thinking of many educators, the principal still shares the same concern for the learning and welfare of children that is the basic concern of the teacher. These are some guidelines for teachers to follow in working with the building administrator:

- Recognize that the principal is not just the person in charge but also a professional educator who is very much concerned about your success as a teacher.
- Ultimately, the principal is responsible for everything that happens in the school. This fact makes it imperative that you communicate openly and honestly with the principal about the good and not-so-good things that happen under your supervision.
- View the principal as a resource for teaching strategies and ideas. Let the principal know what your needs are in terms of equipment and other kinds of support.
- Do not assume that "they" won't let you try new things (the *they* in that context usually meaning the building administrator). It has been our experience that the great majority of principals will support a teacher's efforts to innovate so long as that teacher's plan is well thought out and clearly explained and the teacher defines his or her measure of accountability for the learning of students.
- Share information from in-service and professional organization meetings and your own reading that supports your plans or goals.
- Invite the principal to participate in activities with your children. Administrators have many demands—often unscheduled—on their time; nonetheless, they enjoy relaxed contact with children in classrooms. Don't think you are imposing by extending the invitation.

Using Microcomputers in the Reading/Writing Program

When microcomputers first came on the scene, many teachers thought the devices were going to be the answer to all of education's ills, just as the teaching machines and programmed instruction of the 1960s were once thought to be a panacea. Computers have been in elementary school classrooms for years now, but they have not always been used effectively or in ways that are consistent with our understandings of the reading and writing processes. Those who viewed reading as a set of subskills to be mastered and orchestrated into literacy viewed the computer as a glorified workbook (Newman, 1984). Programs were developed to provide drill and practice in the subskills of reading and writing. Most of the software currently available in the language arts is a product of this subskill-oriented view of the reading and writing processes, probably because exercises of this type are relatively easy to program.

However, there are programs emerging that allow the use of the computer in ways that recognize the holistic nature of reading and writing. Computer programs that encourage children to make predictions, confirm those predictions, and draw on their own background knowledge in constructing meaning are much more consistent with our view of the reading process than are the drill-and-practice programs. The new programs lend themselves to cooperative learning experiences because groups of students can work together to make predictions about story events.

Word processing systems have clear linkages to the teacher's reading/writing program. As we implement instruction in writing as a process, the ease with which children can edit work on a word processor greatly enhances the richness of their writing. The word processor makes it easy for children to take control of their writing and rework a piece with little effort, allowing them to concentrate on the message rather than on the medium. Teachers who have observed children painstakingly transcribing each word manually, with great effort, have to appreciate the freedom word processing brings to the act of writing.

The most recent application of the computer in the reading/writing program has occurred in the area of telecommunications. Electronic mail is permitting children in the United States to communicate with children all over the world in a matter of hours. Pen pals in Australia, France, and England, for example, can exchange letters with American students within a twenty-four-hour period.

As the value of telecommunications in educational settings is being realized, schools are making efforts to move the activity beyond simple "pen pal" kinds of communication. A telecommunications service operated by Simon Fraser University in Vancouver, British Columbia, has begun a series of educational forums on a variety of topics. Distant schools can either join a forum in progress or start their own forum and invite other schools to participate.

An effort to put teachers in touch with teachers is under way with a telecommunications system set up by McGraw-Hill Book Company. Called MIX, the system is intended to bring people together to solve problems, develop curriculum, create lesson plans, and take electronic field trips to other classrooms around the globe.

Teachers implementing a telecommunications writing program have found the following steps helpful (Weddle, 1988):

1. Talk with the principal about telecommunications and how it can benefit students.

2. Generate interest among teachers. Having several classes involved will make the project more exciting.

3. Select a teacher—one who is dedicated and flexible—to pilot the initial communications; that is, to venture first into telecommunications with his or her class.

4. Commitment must come from the students. It is difficult, if not impossible, to find a student who is not interested.

5. Arrange to purchase the modem, software, and word processor and to install a phone line dedicated only to this purpose.

6. Determine which telecommunications service to join.

7. Decide who is going to be responsible for the actual transmission of the messages, and train the person. It is possible to practice by sending mail to yourself.

8. Communicate with partner teachers overseas. There must be a firm commitment on both ends that all mail will be answered promptly and that all students who send a letter will get an answer.

9. Have students write a letter of introduction to their prospective pen pals. Develop and mail "welcome packets" of materials about your town and the school: perhaps pictures of the class, posters, postcards, anything the children think will give a good picture of their life in their town.

10. Share your successes with the principal, other teachers, the local newspaper, and the school district administrators.

■ Major Ideas in This Chapter

■ Critical decisions must be made about the grouping of children, key elements in the reading/writing program, classroom management, working with parents and administrators, and the use of computers.

■ The criteria by which children are grouped for instruction are controversial. Ability grouping lowers the self-concepts of low-achieving students and affords them less learning time and less achievement. Flexible grouping patterns and cooperative learning groups work better than ability groups. Cooperative learning groups have proven to be a powerful way to work with groups in the reading/writing program.

■ Key elements that support the reading/writing program are guided reading activities, skill-development activities, enrichment activities, the use of student–teacher conferences, and the use of activity centers.

They contribute to a classroom environment that is stimulating and challenging.

■ Careful adherence to guidelines for classroom management will result in greater comfort for the teacher and appropriate behavior from the students.

■ Parents can and should play a critical role in the education of children. Teachers must maintain good communication with parents.

■ The building principal should be a source of support to the classroom teacher. Effective communication with the principal is crucial.

■ Computer programs that emphasize the processes of reading and writing should be sought over drill-and-practice programs. The use of computers in telecommunications can enhance the reading/writing program.

? Discussion Questions
Focusing on the Teacher You Are Becoming

1. Interview several of your classmates about their experiences working in groups when they were in elementary school. Try to determine what factors made the experience positive or negative.
2. Role-play a teacher–parent conference while other classmates observe your patterns of interaction. Are there ways you can improve your communication skills?
3. In the Gallup polls published every September in the *Kappan* (journal of Phi Delta Kappa, an education honorary society), parents say discipline is a major problem in the schools. Discuss ways that you could help your community feel more positive about the discipline in your school.
4. Discuss some of the communications possibilities available at school as technology advances. What are some of the benefits to children? to teachers?

✓ Field-Based Applications

1. Interview three teachers at different grade levels to find the criteria they use for grouping students. Ascertain their feelings about ability grouping.

2. Arrange to visit a classroom in which cooperative learning groups are used. Plan a series of lessons to do with a group of children. Examine your emerging view of cooperative learning.
3. Set up one or more learning centers and help children learn to use them.
4. Interview a group of children at each of three grade levels to find out what they think classroom rules or expectations should be. How do they view appropriate consequences? Try applying the management guidelines suggested in this chapter and then critique them.
5. Arrange to sit in on a parent–teacher conference. Write a statement of what you learned about communicating with parents.
6. Read *The Complete Handbook of Personal Computer Telecommunications: Everything You Need to Know to Go Online with the World*, by Alfred Glossbrenner (St. Martin's Press, 1985). Visit a classroom that is using a telecommunications service.

◉ References and Suggested Readings

Adams, Phyllis; Kloefkorn, Merrillyn; and Harvey, Steve. "Parents Rate Themselves on Home Factors Supportive of Reading Development." *California Reader* (April/May 1985): 31–37.

Becher, Rhoda. "Parent Education." *Encyclopedia of Educational Research*. 5th ed. New York: Macmillan and Free Press, 1982, pp. 1379–1382.

Becher, Rhoda. "Parent Involvement and Reading Achievement: A Review of Research and Implications for Practice." *Childhood Education* 62 (September/October 1985): 44–50.

Borg, W. R. *Ability Grouping in the Public Schools*. Madison, Wis.: Dembar Educational Research Services, 1966.

Brink, Carol. *Caddie Woodlawn*. New York: Macmillan, 1935.

Butler, Dorothy, and Clay, Marie. *Reading Begins at Home*. Exeter, N.H.: Heinemann Educational Books, 1982.

DeFord, Diane, and Rasinski, Timothy. "A Question of Knowledge and Control in Teaching and Learning." In *The Pursuit of Literacy*, edited by M. Sampson. Dubuque, Iowa: Kendall-Hunt, 1986.

Eder, Donna. "Ability Grouping and Students' Academic Self-Concepts: A Case Study." *The Elementary School Journal* 84 (1983): 149–161.

Fehring, Heather. "Cooperative Learning Strategies Applied in the Language Classroom." *Reading Around Series* (publication of Australian Reading Association), March 1987.

Garber, Malcolm. "The Florida Parent Education Program." ERIC Document Reproduction Service No. ED 058 953, 1972.

Gathercoal, Forrest. *Judicious Discipline*. Ann Arbor: Prakken Publications, 1987.

Grimmett, Sadie, and McCoy, Mae. "Effects of Parental Communication on Reading Performance of Third Grade Children." *The Reading Teacher* 34 (December 1980): 303–308.

Harp, M. William. "Early Field Experiences and Student Concerns: A Potentially Powerful Force." *The Elementary School Journal* 74(6) (March 1971): 369–374.

Hiebert, Elfrieda H. "An Examination of Ability Grouping for Reading Instruction." *Reading Research Quarterly* 18 (Winter 1983): 231–255.

Johnson, David W., and Johnson, Roger T. *Learning Together and Alone: Cooperation, Competition and Individualization.* Englewood Cliffs, N.J.: Prentice-Hall, 1975.

Keele, Reba, and Harrison, Grant. *The Effects of Parents Using Structural Tutoring Techniques in Teaching Their Children to Read.* Chicago: Rand McNally, 1971.

McKinney, John. "The Development and Implementation of a Tutorial Program for Parents to Improve the Reading and Mathematics Achievement of Their Children." ERIC Document Reproduction Service No. ED 113 703, 1977.

Newman, Judith M. "Online: Reading, Writing, and Computers." *Language Arts* 61 (November 1984): 758–763.

Olmstead, P. P., and Rubin, R. I. "Linking Parent Behaviors and Child Achievement: Four Evaluation Studies from the Parent Education Follow Through Program." *Studies in Educational Evaluation* 8 (1983): 317–325.

Rasinski, Timothy, and Fredericks, Anthony. "Sharing Literacy: Guiding Principles and Practices for Parent Involvement." *The Reading Teacher* 41 (February 1988): 508–512.

Romotowski, J. A., and Trepanier, M. L. "Examining and Influencing the Home Reading Behaviors of Young Children." ERIC Document Reproduction Service No. ED 195 938, 1977.

Slavin, Robert E. "Ability Grouping and Student Achievement in Elementary Schools: A Best-Evidence Synthesis." *Review of Educational Research* 57 (Fall 1987a): 293–336.

Slavin, Robert E. *Cooperative Learning: Student Teams. What Research Says to the Teacher.* Washington, D.C.: National Education Association, 1987b.

Smith, Carl, ed. *Parents and Reading.* Newark, Del.: International Reading Association, 1971.

Sorensen, Aage B., and Hallinan, Maureen T. "Effects of Ability Grouping on Growth in Academic Achievement." *American Educational Research Journal* 23 (Winter 1986): 519–542.

Speare, Elizabeth. *The Sign of the Beaver.* Boston: Houghton Mifflin, 1983.

Stevens, Robert J.; Madden, Nancy A.; Slavin, Robert E.; and Farnish, Anna Marie. "Cooperative Integrated Reading and Composition: Two Field Experiments." *Reading Research Quarterly* 22 (Fall 1987): 433–454.

Trelease, Jim. *The Read-Aloud Handbook.* New York: Penguin Books/International Reading Association, 1986.

Unsworth, Len. "Meeting Individual Needs through Flexible Within-Class Grouping of Pupils." *The Reading Teacher* 38 (December 1984): 298–304.

Vukelich, Carol. "Parents' Role in the Reading Process: A Review of Practical Suggestions and Ways to Communicate with Parents." *The Reading Teacher* 37 (February 1984): 472–477.

Watson, Dorothy. "Coming Whole Circle." In *Reading Process and Practice*, edited by Constance Weaver. Portsmouth, N.H.: Heinemann Educational Books, 1988.

Weddle, Mike. Teacher, Waldo Middle School, Salem, Oregon. Personal interview, 1988.

Weinstein, Rhona S. "Reading Group Membership in First Grade: Teacher Behaviours and Pupil Experience Over Time." *Journal of Educational Psychology* 68 (1976): 103–116.

Part III

Implementing Plans in the Reading/Writing Program

You have carefully examined the nature of literacy and ways to develop the reading and writing processes in real communicative situations. Now that you have looked further at the critical decisions to be made in a literacy program, it is time to examine ways to implement those decisions.

In Part 3 you will learn how the decisions you make become realities as you use a basal reader, have children write their own material for reading instruction, and select examples from the wide world of children's literature to use for instruction. You will learn how to integrate writing and literature in a basal program. You will begin to visualize how your own reading program will look—the material you will choose for instruction and how you will help children become literate.

Chapter 6

Basal Readers in the Reading/Writing Program

Chapter Overview

- Basal reading series are sequentially graded student texts, workbooks, teacher's guides, and supplementary materials designed for reading instruction in grades K–8.

- The currently popular basal reading series share some common elements in their approaches to reading instruction: most suggest activities involving sight, phonic analysis, pattern recognition, and writing skills.

- Teachers use the basal readers in various ways: as the primary reading material, as supplementary material, and as the source of materials selected to fit thematic units.

- The teacher's guides that accompany basal reading texts contain suggestions for activities before, during, and after reading. Teacher's guides have become more and more detailed over the years.

- Skillful teachers make adaptations in basal reading programs that help meet the needs of individual children. Teachers choose selections that will meet their reading objectives and choose activities that will help children read the selections successfully.

If you were asked to predict the equipment and supplies one might find in the elementary classrooms of the United States, you would be very safe in guessing there would be a basal reading series of some kind. Most of the reading instruction in today's schools is either conducted directly from a set of basal readers or built around a basal. There are numerous choices to be made when a school or district adopts a basal reading series. Various publishers' basal series differ in philosophy, sequencing of skills taught, and content presented. They may also vary in the amount and type of material that accompany the books the children will use. This chapter will help you recognize the strengths and weaknesses of basal readers and present some suggestions for using the texts in reading instruction.

Introducing Basal Readers

Definition

Basal means forming the base, or fundamental; in an educational context, it refers to something used for teaching beginners. Basal readers are textbooks designed specifically for reading instruction. Most basal reading series begin with readiness material and include graded material that is planned for each of the grades through grade six or grade eight. Readiness material typically consists of tasks that help children learn to recognize letters of the alphabet and perhaps match them with the sounds they represent. First-grade material often comes in several books: pre-primers, primers, and a first reader. Sometimes the material for higher grades is divided into two books, the second more advanced than the first. The students' texts contain stories, poetry, expository material, and perhaps selections or excerpts from literature. Most modern basal reading series include teacher's guides, assessment systems, workbooks, skill practice sheets, and other materials to be used in reading instruction, such as tape recordings and word cards. If you learned to read with Dick and Jane or Tom and Janet, then your teacher used a basal reader for your instruction. Even if you do not remember Dick and Jane, you probably had a basal text if groups of children in your class were all reading the same book.

History

In colonial America, the earliest books used for reading instruction were hornbooks, consisting of a single page mounted on a piece of wood and covered with a translucent piece of horn to protect it from wear. The hornbook contained the alphabet, a syllabarium, and the Lord's Prayer (Goodman, Shannon, Freeman, and Murphy, 1988). At the beginning of the eighteenth century, the *New England Primer* was probably the most popular text for reading instruction. The primer contained religious sayings for each letter of the alphabet. By midcentury, reading was usually introduced from a spelling book. Venezky (1987) reports that Webster's spelling book was the most popular reading text from about 1790 to about 1840.

Around the turn of the nineteenth century, as more children attended school and the school year was extended, some reading books began to appear in a series. Elementary schools were first organized into grades in about the middle of the nineteenth century, and by the end of the century reading books were also graded. The most popular of the instructional books published in the nineteenth century were the *McGuffey Eclectic Readers*. From their first publication in 1836 until 1920, about 120 million copies of the readers were sold. After the Civil War, reading series that resemble today's readers began to appear. Most had a primer and five or six graded readers. In the early part of the twentieth century, a pre-primer was added to help children learn the vocabulary of the primer. After World War II, readiness materials were added; the series then looked very much like modern reading series. Books designed for teaching reading were not commonly labeled *basal* until the early 1960s, although the term was first used by a publisher in the 1930s (Venezky, 1987).

Books used to teach reading changed over the years, and so did the reasons for encouraging reading. For early American settlers, reading was important chiefly for the sake of Bible study. Reading instruction for many years continued to rely heavily on religious or moralistic stories that also taught children how to behave and what to value while they learned to read. The purposes for reading instruction have broadened greatly since the days of the colonists.

Suggested methodologies for reading instruction—that is, techniques that teachers use to help children learn—have also evolved. The reading methodology most popular in colonial times was to teach children to recognize the letters, then to spell words, and finally to read the words, so early reading books were really spelling books. Rote learning of entire texts was common in early schools. Teachers often asked students to recite what they had learned or led children in choral readings of texts. These methods were probably necessary to some extent because of the lack of books and paper. Most schools did not even have chalkboards or slates, so the reading/writing program of today would hardly have been possible. The emphasis in reading instruction gradually moved from the names of the letters to the sounds of the letters to words and finally to meaning.

Among other changes in reading is the treatment of oral reading. The early Americans considered reading to be primarily an oral activity. The reading books published for older students in the nineteenth century were elocution texts, and reading instruction was focused on oral presentation of material. Later in this chapter we will discuss the current instructional purposes of oral and silent reading.

Instructions to teachers included with the reading materials have undergone drastic alterations. One author (Venezky, 1987) noted with some irony that the more knowledgeable teachers become, the more detailed are the teacher's guides they are presented with. Teachers in early schools had little or no training as teachers; many had not even graduated from high school. Yet no instructions to teachers accompanied most early reading materials. In the early 1800s, materials for teaching reading began to include some instructions for teachers. Compared with the teacher's guides of today, these instructions were minimal. For example, a reader copyrighted in 1886 devoted two pages to instructions to the teacher, consisting of vague suggestions like this: "An occasional drill on these sounds, or a part of them, is advised for the sake of clear articulation" (Campbell, 1886, p. iii). The preface to *The New McGuffey Fourth Reader* (1901, pp. 3–4) states:

> While the majority of the selections are new to the series, care has been taken to maintain the same high literary and ethical standard that has hitherto so distinctly characterized these books. Lessons inculcating kindness, courage, obedience, industry, thrift, true manliness, patriotism, and other duties and obligations form no small portion of the contents. . . . The Elocutionary Introduction . . . presents in brief scope the most important rules for oral reading and those principles of the art that are most necessary for the pupils to master. The teacher should, at the very outset, become thoroughly familiar with the subjects here presented, and the pupils should be referred to this discussion of elocutionary principles as often as occasion may require.

Instructions to the teacher became slightly more detailed in the early 1900s. In 1926, Lippincott published *Silent Reading for Beginners* (Watkins, 1926) and included in the teacher's edition "full notes" consisting of about a page of instructions to the teacher for each story: lists of vocabulary words and sections called "How to Teach the Lesson," "Check-Up," and "Follow-Up." The instructions are not very specific. In "How to Teach the Lesson" (p. 18), the notes say, "You can not start too early to train little children in the duties of citizenship, which include the care of school property, buildings, books, sidewalks; their relation to each other and the rights of others." The "Check-Up" section on the same page says, "Can the child read page 30 orally and do it well?" Compare these instructions with those in modern teacher's guides, which typically contain as many as one hundred pages of instructions for a small paperback pre-primer.

Instructional Approaches Incorporated in Basal Readers

Over the years several approaches to reading instruction have emerged. Early reading methodology required children to spell words before reading them. Gradually, spelling was separated from reading, and the word method was introduced. The word method required students to read whole words and then talk about their meaning. The average person on the street, if asked how reading is taught, would probably answer either "by phonics" or "by sight." Both these approaches have grown out of the historical roots of teaching spelling, sounds, or words. Chall (1967) classified approaches to reading as having code emphasis or meaning emphasis. In her scheme, phonics and linguistic (patterns in words) approaches are code-emphasis approaches; sight-word and language-experience approaches are meaning-emphasis approaches.

A more useful way to categorize approaches is to look at what happens when reader and text meet. In the "bottom-up" view, the text is primary; the reader's job is to decode the text, a process that results in meaning. The sight, phonics, and linguistic approaches are all bottom-up approaches. In the "top-down" view, the reader's previous experience and schema determine the meaning brought to the reading; meaning is derived from the interaction of the reader and the text. Language-experience and whole-language approaches belong to the "top-down" classification.

What the authors of basal reading series believe about learning to read usually has to be inferred from statements concerning goals of the program and from the exercises and materials presented for reading instruction. Authors of reading materials rarely state in direct terms their philosophy of how children learn to read. But the basal reader itself reveals the authors' intent to concentrate either on a skills-driven approach or on a more holistic view of the reading process. If the book contains stories in which the vocabulary is highly controlled by phonic regularity, and skills exercises that are drills in letter–sound relationships, then the authors lean in the direction of phonics as the basic tool for unlocking the meaning in print. If, on the other hand, the basal contains selections of literature for children and suggests that children read pieces orally together or that they learn a piece by rote before they are introduced to the words in print, and the "skills" exercises involve comparing the forms of several pieces and thinking about different points of view, then the authors lean more in the direction of whole-language instruction. All the basal readers today have an eclectic approach, which means that they include activities from all the approaches and are not identifiable as being sight, phonics, or linguistic readers.

■ Bottom-Up Approaches

Sight

The sight approach to reading instruction means that students are presented with words to be learned as wholes. Students depend on visual memory to recall the word when it is presented in different contexts. The words are studied by configuration (shape of the word) and by repeated presentations. Critics of the sight approach say that children cannnot learn to generalize what they know about words to new words and therefore lack skill in decoding unfamiliar material. The old Dick and Jane books were based primarily on the sight approach. That is the explanation for the constant repetition in the stories: "See Dick. See Jane. See Spot. See Puff. See Dick run," and so on.

Phonic Analysis

The phonic analysis approach focuses on learning the letter–sound relationships and practicing those sounds. In some phonics approaches, the words are learned as wholes first, then analyzed in terms of their component sounds, and then repeated as wholes. This process is called an *analytic* approach to phonics. In the *synthetic* approach to phonics, the words first are "sounded out" by using the letter–sound relationships, and then the word is pronounced by blending the sounds. Pronouncing the word is supposed to trigger knowledge of the word from the child's oral vocabulary. Vocabulary in readers with a phonic focus is selected on the basis of phonic rules. Sometimes the result of selecting words on such a basis is sentences or stories that are not very meaningful. For example, a story about a coyote was selected for inclusion in one basal reader, but the word *coyote* was changed to *fox* because *fox* followed the phonic rules already learned, whereas *coyote* did not. Of course, the change produced an inaccurate story about foxes.

Most phonic approaches today do not advocate drill on charts of letter–sound relationships. They treat phonics as one tool for helping children decode new or unfamiliar words and present generalizations about the sounds represented by given letters as part of the skill instruction that accompanies each lesson. Even in the most phonic-based approach, some words in English cannot be decoded graphophonically because they are irregular in their sound–symbol representations. *The* is one of the most common of the irregular words.

Linguistics

The linguistic approach groups words together on the basis of their spelling patterns. A few years ago, there were several basal series based on the patterns found in words. Usually the first pattern introduced to beginning readers was the consonant-vowel-consonant (CVC) pattern. Words such as *cat, hat, mat, fat, red,* and *bed* follow the CVC pattern. Next came the consonant-vowel-consonant-silent *e* pattern: *like, home, page, ride,* and so on. The stories produced by selecting words on the basis of their patterns were often nonsensical and bore little resemblance to real language. Most basal readers today include some skill exercises that call for noting the CVC or CVC*e* pattern of words and for producing new words by substituting different consonants for the beginning consonant. Children might be asked to change the *m* of *mat* to *b, c, f, h, p, r, s, t,* and *v* and then to read the words that they have produced.

■ Top-Down Approaches

Language Experience

Because the language-experience approach depends on children's writing their own material for reading instruction (as described in Chapter 8), basal series have not been developed using this approach. Roach Van Allen did develop some teacher's guides with topics and some resources to help teachers organize instruction. These materials were eventually expanded into kits called *Language Experiences in Reading* (Van Allen, 1976), which contained suggestions for activities and resources.

Whole Language

It is difficult to write a short description of whole language. Many people would classify whole language as an approach to reading. We think that whole language is much more than that. We believe it is a philosophical

Language experience involves children with literacy at a more personal level than a prepared text allows.
© *Ray Stott/The Image Works*

approach to teaching, not just to teaching reading. It is a mind-set toward teaching that empowers both the teacher and the learner. Whole-language teachers draw on research in language development, linguistics, psycho-linguistics, sociolinguistics, anthropology, and education in creating their curriculum.

Whole-language instruction is based on the premise that there are always constraints on any written material and that when children are learning to read they need to learn from materials written for a variety of purposes rather than materials written for reading instruction. For example, children would learn to read poetry, narrative stories, nonfiction reports, and descriptive writings. One typical technique would be the teacher's modeling of fluent reading; another would be reading a big book together until the class knows it well and then writing individual stories following the model of the big book. (A "big book" is a large-size version of a book for whole-class instruction, either commercially published or prepared by the teacher.) Writing is an integral part of reading instruction in the whole-language classroom. Skills are taught in context and as children need them.

Whole-language instruction focuses on such ideas as the author's intent, the intended audience for the piece, the point of view of the author, and the knowledge that the author needed before writing. Children learn to recognize conventions used by professional authors so they can employ those conventions in their own writing. The advocates of whole-language instruction view reading as much more than a collection of discrete skills that can be practiced outside the reading experience. Several current basal series label themselves as "whole language" readers. Most of these readers have content selected from the body of children's literature rather than written for that series, and their suggestions to teachers reflect a focus on language and writing conventions.

■ Teacher's Role in Reading Programs

In addition to differing in their approaches to reading, basal series also demand different levels of involvement from teachers. Some programs, such as DISTAR (Englemann and Bereiter, 1983), which are tightly controlled and highly prescribed, specify all the teacher behaviors and responses needed to teach the program. Teachers do not have to decide what to teach, or in what order, or what activities to assign. Language-experience and whole-language approaches, which are heavily teacher dependent, require significant teaching decisions. Teachers must choose the content to be taught, the order in which to teach it, and the activities that will help the children achieve reading goals. Most basal programs fall somewhere in the middle, requiring teachers to make some decisions but prescribing others, such as sequence of presentation.

Teacher's Guide

Before reading this section, please read Appendix E: "Why Rabbits Have Long Ears," from Smiles, *a Level 5 (end of first grade or beginning of second grade) reader published by Harcourt Brace Jovanovich.*

The typical basal reading series is accompanied by a teacher's guide containing several sections. One section, the scope and sequence chart, provides the teacher with an overview of the skills to be covered in the reading program and the order of their introduction. Figure 6.1 shows part of a sample scope and sequence chart. The complete chart includes scope and sequence sections for each of the following topics: decoding phonics, decoding structural analysis, comprehension, language, study skills, literature appreciation, and vocabulary. Note that this program calls for introducing each skill at a certain grade level, continuing instruction after that grade level, and testing the skill within the grade levels marked with a *T*. For example, for the skill of decoding phonics, the program introduces initial consonants in the kindergarten material and tests them in second grade, even though it is expected that children will continue to use the skill of decoding initial consonants throughout the program. In the literature appreciation section, notice that setting is introduced in kindergarten, tested at the end of first grade, and tested again at grade three and grade seven.

The teacher's guide suggests activities for students to carry out before reading a selection. In Figure 6.2, the first suggested activity is to practice decoding the /sh/, /ch/, and /th/ digraphs; next, to learn the vocabulary words that are new in the current story and to practice reading them. The teacher introduces the story by providing any necessary background and asks questions to establish the purpose for reading.

Having completed all the introductory activities, the children read the story independently, a page or a specified number of pages at a time. The teacher's guide nearly always includes a reproduction of the text as given to the students. For each page of the story, the guide suggests questions to be asked or words to be defined (Figure 6.3).

The teacher's guide offers suggestions for follow-up activities after reading the selection: questions to ask, guidelines for rereading the selection, and activities for extending the reading experience. The example in Figure 6.4 includes questions designed to check on story comprehension, a skills activity, and an optional writing experience. There is also a section for helping to guide the oral reading of the selection, followed by several

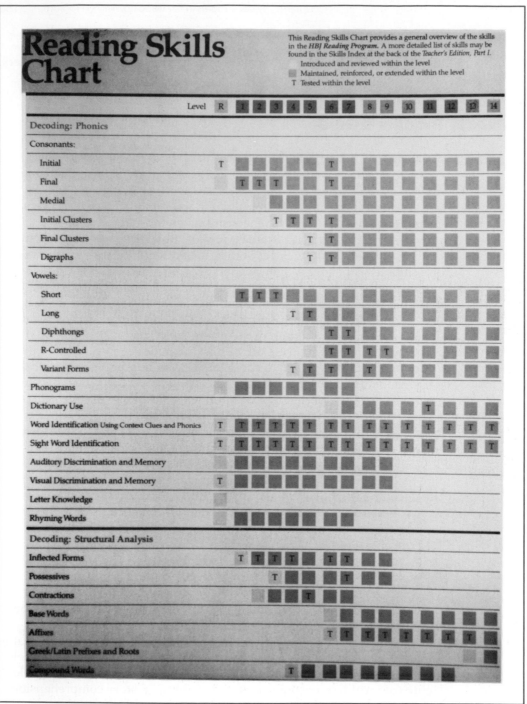

Figure 6.1   A scope and sequence chart. (continues)

SOURCE: *HBJ Reading Program—Smiles, Teacher's Edition, Part I* by Margaret Early *et al.* Copyright © 1987 by Harcourt Brace Jovanovich, Inc. Reprinted by permission of the publisher.

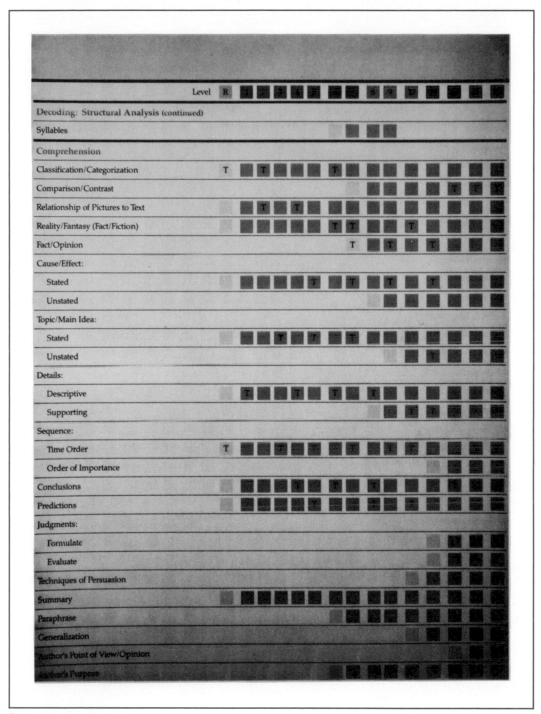

Figure 6.1   *(continues)*

185

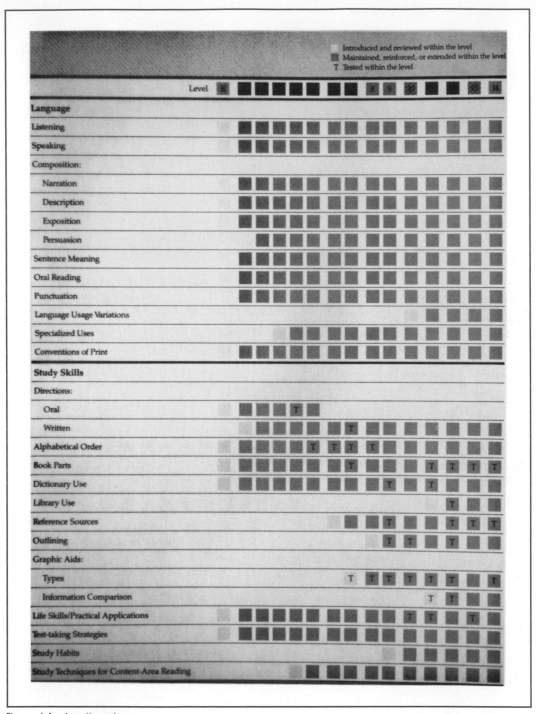

Figure 6.1 *(continues)*

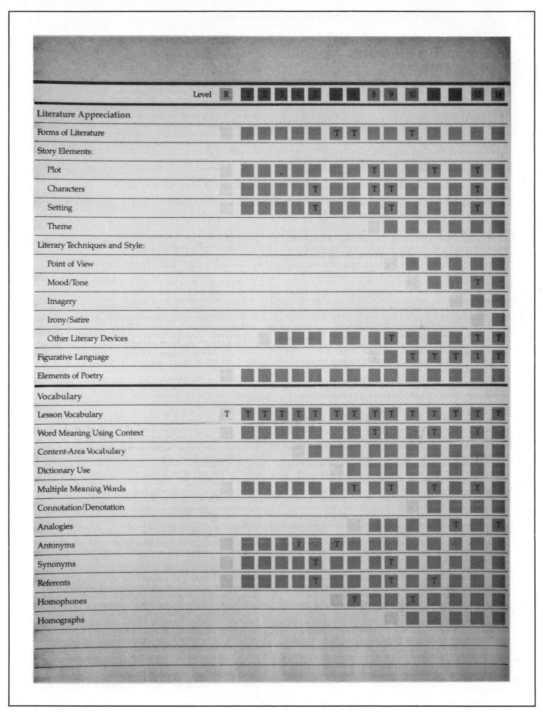

Figure 6.1   *(continued)*

187

1 Preparing to Read

DEVELOPING SKILLS

Decoding

*R,T★ Identify initial and final
correspondences* /ch/ch, /sh/sh, /th/th

CHART
132–133 **TEACH**   On the chalkboard, write:

chair	such
chick	which
chip	much

Read aloud the words in the first list. **What is the same in all the words in this list?** (They all begin with *ch*.) **All these words begin with the sound you hear at the beginning of *chair*. The letters *ch* stand for the sound.** Then read the second list of words. **What is the same in all the words in this list?** (they end with *ch*) **All these words end with the sound you hear at the end of *much*. The letters *ch* stand for the sound. The letters *ch* may come at the beginning of a word or at the end of a word.** Then ask specific students to read the following words:

chill, peach, check, chin, each, inch, chick

Repeat the same procedure for the initial and final correspondences /sh/ *sh* and /th/ *th*. Use the following words:

/sh/*sh*		/th/*th*	
ship	wish	thank	path
short	fresh	thick	with
shoulders	crash	thought	teeth
shine, rush, short,		thin, bath	moth
dish, cash, shape		thumb, thick, cloth	

Remember, the sound of *ch* as in *chair* may be at the beginning or end of a word; the sound of *sh* as in *ship* may be at the beginning or end of a word; and the sound of *th* as in *thank* may be at the beginning or end of a word. Knowing the letters and the sounds they stand for will help you read new words.

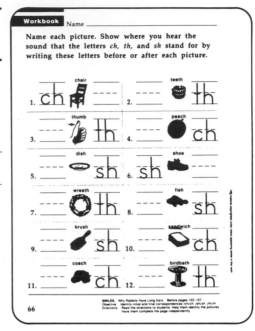

Workbook Name _____

Name each picture. Show where you hear the sound that the letters *ch, th,* and *sh* stand for by writing these letters before or after each picture.

1. ch   2. th
3. th   4. ch
5. sh   6. sh
7. th   8. sh
9. sh   10. ch
11. ch   12. th

66

SMILES. Why Rabbits Have Long Ears. Before pages 122–127
Objective   Identify initial and final correspondences /ch/ch /sh/sh /th/th
Directions Read the directions to students. Help them identify the pictures
Have them complete the page independently

CHART
133 **PRACTICE AND APPLY**   On the chalkboard, write:

1. wi __ __	5. __ __ oulders
2. cra __ __	6. __ __ ick
3. __ __ ort	7. lun __ __
4. whi __ __	8. __ __ in

On separate paper, have students complete the words in the list as you dictate them: 1. *with,* 2. *crash,* 3. *short,* 4. *which,* 5. *shoulders,* 6. *thick,* 7. *lunch,* 8. *chin.* Have students read aloud their words and write the correct answers on the chalkboard. Then ask individual students to identify the words that answer the following questions:

1. Which word means "the opposite of tall"? (short)
2. Which word names a part of the body to which your arms attach? (shoulders)

You will meet the words *shoulders* and *short* in the story that you are about to read.

WB
66 Use *Workbook* page 66 for more practice with the initial and final correspondences /ch/*ch*, /sh/*sh*, /th/*th*.

Figure 6.2   Prereading activities.

SOURCE: Valery Carrick, *HBJ Reading Program—Smiles, Pupil Edition* by Margaret Early *et al.* Copyright © 1987 by Harcourt Brace Jovanovich, Inc. Reprinted by permission of the publisher.

Directing the Reading Process

Checking Up (pages 122–123)

page 122

1. **What have the sheep and rabbit planned to do?** (They've planned to build a house.) *literal: identify details*

2. **When does this story take place?** (It happened long ago.) *literal: identify details*

3. **How do you know that the sheep and rabbit are friends?** (They played together. They did everything together.) *literal: identify details*

Checking Up

page 123

1. **Why did the sheep and rabbit go into the forest?** (They needed to get some logs to build their house.) *literal: identify details*

2. **Read what the sheep says he will do.** (I can push this tree down.) *literal: identify details*

3. **Did the rabbit think that the sheep could push down the tree? Why? Why not?** (No, because the rabbit has never seen the sheep push down a tree.) *inferential: make judgments*

4. **What makes you think that the rabbit and the sheep are speaking to each other in an excited way?** (the exclamation points that follow many of the sentences) *literal: identify details*

Thinking Ahead (page 124)

Do you think the sheep can push down the tree? Why? (Accept reasonable responses: No, because it would be too hard to do; yes, because the sheep has horns.) *inferential: predict outcomes* **Read page 124 to find out.**

Figure 6.3   Directing the reading process.
SOURCE: Valery Carrick, *HBJ Reading Program—Smiles, Pupil Edition* by Margaret Early *et al.* Copyright © 1987 by Harcourt Brace Jovanovich, Inc. Reprinted by permission of the publisher.

EXTENDING COMPREHENSION AND THINKING SKILLS

Summarizing the Selection

Discuss the Selection   Remind students to think carefully before answering the questions. Encourage them to look back to pages of the story if they wish. For question number one, you may wish to refer to the predictions that were made before reading the selection in "Setting Purposes/Predicting."

1. **Do you think this story about why rabbits have long ears is true? Why?** (No, because animals can't talk. It's a made-up story.) *critical: make judgments*

2. **Why did the rabbit's head go down into his shoulders?** (He hit the tree so hard that his head went into his shoulders.) *literal: identify cause-and-effect relationships*

3. **What made you laugh in this story?** (Accept reasonable responses: the rabbit trying to push down a tree; the sheep pulling hard with his mouth) *inferential: identify cause-and-effect relationships*

4. **When was the first time in the story that you knew that the rabbit would have long ears?** (When the sheep put the rabbit's short ears in his mouth and started to pull.) *inferential: draw conclusions*

5. **Which character in the story did you like best? Tell why.** (Accept reasonable responses.) *inferential: recognize comparisons and contrasts*

Apply the Skills (Exclamatory sentences)   When Sheep and Rabbit talk to each other they are very excited. Let's look at page 123 in the story and find all the sentences ending with an exclamation point. Lead students to understand that this mark may indicate strong feeling on the part of the speaker. Discuss the conversation on page 123 by having students read each exclamatory sentence and then tell the feeling that each character expressed in these sentences.

For further practice of this skill, see "Maintained Skills" under "Providing for Individual Differences," page T300.

Think and Write   This is an optional activity that correlates reading and writing. You may elect to use the writing as a homework or an extra-credit assignment. The suggested steps in the activity are designed to help students understand better the writing process.

Prewrite   Guide students through a brainstorming session having them name some animals. Next have them think of questions about the animals such as "Why do pigs have snouts? Why do lions have manes? Why do dogs bark? Why do cats have long tails?" Write students' questions on the chalkboard.

Compose   Have students write one of the questions about an animal on their paper. Then have them write the answer to the question. Encourage students to illustrate their writing.

Revise   Have students use the proofreading checklist for sentences to proofread and revise their work.

Publish   Display illustrations and revised work on a bulletin board entitled "Animal Tales."

Figure 6.4   Follow-up activities.
SOURCE: Valery Carrick, *HBJ Reading Program—Smiles, Pupil Edition* by Margaret Early *et al.* Copyright © 1987 by Harcourt Brace Jovanovich, Inc. Reprinted by permission of the publisher.

more pages of suggestions for maintaining skills that have been introduced in previous lessons and for teaching literature, study skills, and language.

Contrast the directions to the teacher in this more traditional basal reader with the prereading suggestions presented in Figure 6.5. These whole-language-oriented suggestions are from *Impressions* (1986), to accompany a story in *East of the Sun*, a second-grade reader. They focus not on phonic skills but on building schemata that will help the reader use previous knowledge to make sense of the selection. Note also that the teacher may read the selection aloud rather than asking the children to read it. The teacher determines the procedure on the basis of knowledge of the children's developmental reading level. After the selection is read, the children are asked to respond in various ways—discussing, painting, shared reading, making a book.

NO ELEPHANTS ALLOWED *by Deborah Robison*

Pages 136–145

BEFORE THE SELECTION

Reporting

1. Discuss bedrooms:
   —Do you have any posters in your room?
   —Who decided how your room will be decorated?
   —Who tidies your room?
   —What do you like to do alone in your room?

Recalling and sharing information

2. Discuss and list pesky things that bother the children. For example:
   —older children,
   —mosquitoes.
   What are some remedies for these bothersome things?

Recognizing problems and their solutions

3. Have the children brainstorm how to keep:
   —aliens away from earth,
   —clouds away from a picnic,
   —sharks away from a beach.

EXPERIENCING THE SELECTION

1. Read the selection aloud to the children.

EAST OF THE SUN

Page 136

TAPE

2. Have the children work in groups of five to read the selection in parts: narrator, Justin, mother, father, sister.
   Switch parts.
3. Have the children listen to and read along with the listening tape.
4. Have the children read the selection independently.

> 1 is most suitable for beginning readers.
> 2–3 are most suitable for developing readers.
> 2–4 are most suitable for independent readers.
> Some beginning and developing readers may be able to read the selection independently after following some of the other methods.
> All the children should have opportunities to use the listening tape.

RESPONDING TO THE SELECTION

Hypothesizing

1. Discuss Justin's choice of deterrent:
   —Why do you think he chose a gorilla?
   —What would you have chosen?
   —Why do you think the gorilla made Justin feel safer?
   —Did you think it would work?
   —What makes you nervous at night?

Reporting on past experience

   —What do you do when you feel nervous at night?

Figure 6.5   Prereading activities.

SOURCE: *Impressions: Teacher Resource Book: East of the Sun* by Jack Booth *et al.* Copyright © 1985 by Holt, Rinehart & Winston of Canada. Reprinted by permission.

Some News about Basals

Most teachers in the United States use a basal reading series, whether it constitutes their entire reading program or is one of several they use to complement their reading program. Of the teachers who responded to a national survey, 50 percent used a single basal as the basis of their reading program, and 10 percent did not use a basal at all (Turner, 1988). Some teachers used a single basal to complement their reading program, and some used several basals for that purpose. Most of the teachers (60 percent) used workbooks to reinforce skill instruction either all the time or most of the time.

There are many reasons why teachers rely so heavily on basal readers. They believe that they are covering all the skills if they follow a basal, they feel that they do not have time to organize and run individualized reading programs, and they believe that more children will learn to read successfully through a structured program. They may also believe that the district administration expects them to complete the basal program. Some districts do put pressure on teachers to complete the basal work and rely on basal test results to group children within and across classes. Shannon (1982) believes that teachers rely on basal readers because, being excluded from making instructional decisions for reading, they see themselves as technicians whose task is to apply the materials. This view is particularly likely to hold in districts where decisions are made at the district office and teachers are not fully involved in making them.

■ The Good News

Basals are good instructional tools for helping teachers achieve their reading goals. Their content is much improved over the content of just a few years ago. Many basal series now include literature such as the texts of picture books, excerpts from books, adapted versions of popular books, children's poetry, and nonfictional material. Some of the basals have been criticized for changing the language in children's stories when they are included in reading texts, but others are faithful to the original. Vocabulary control has also improved. For many years the content of basals was controlled by readability formulas, which count the number of words in a sentence and the number of syllables in words to yield a grade-level score of difficulty. Cassidy (1987) believes that most publishers now consider the content and writing style as well as the readability scores when making decisions about placing material in a given basal. Cassidy also reports that teacher's guides were criticized for containing instructions to teachers that helped them test comprehension, not teach it. Today's guides are more likely to contain specific suggestions for teaching comprehension. Suggested questioning strategies have also been improved in recent years.

The teacher's guides that accompany basal readers can be valuable aids. Once teachers have determined the objectives to be met in reading, the basal guide can provide much useful information for reading passages and planning activities that will help children meet those objectives. Suppose these were among the objectives defined for your students (*Reading Framework for California Public Schools*, 1980, p. 9):

- Improve their comprehension through the use of writing
- Respond in writing to stories they have read
- Write stories and articles to be shared through reading.

You might look through the basal reader and select a story or stories that would be appropriate for meeting these objectives. For example, you might choose a selection that children could rewrite in their own words to increase comprehension or that children could evaluate while learning to write a critical review.

The skills lists in the basal series can be very helpful to teachers in planning instruction. For example, if contractions are introduced in the basal series at second grade, then second-grade teachers can emphasize contractions in children's writing and call attention to them in reading. If a reading objective is to acquire skills in comparison and evaluation, teachers can use the basal alongside commercial books on the same subject. For instance, "The Old Woman and the Rice Cakes" in *Landmarks* (1987, pp. 298–307) pairs neatly with *The Funny Little Woman* (Mosel, 1972) for purposes of comparison.

Teachers have listed the following as the strengths of basals: (1) the logical sequence of skills presented, (2) easily identifiable storylines, (3) increasing difficulty of stories, (4) controlled vocabulary, (5) convenience of having the same book for every child at a given level, and (6) the comprehension and word analysis strategies that are suggested in the teacher's guides (Russavage, Lorton, and Millham, 1985). But many teachers view some of these same features as weaknesses. A teacher who believes that skills are not best taught in a predetermined sequence does not regard a skills sequence as a positive feature. Many teachers object to the controlled vocabulary, feeling that language in texts should be as much like real language as possible. Real language is a speaker's or writer's attempt to communicate with a listener or reader: "I saw Dick and Jane today." Contrived sentences such as, "I saw Dick. I saw Jane. I saw Dick today. I saw Jane today," do not resemble real language.

■ The Not-So-Good News

Students' perceptions of the reading process are influenced by the kinds of activities that are presented to them as "reading." When teachers rely heavily on basals for instruction, children are likely to believe that reading is mostly a matter of decoding and/or word recognition skills (Cairney, 1988). They also believe that success in reading depends on their behavior, completion of tasks, neatness, and written answers.

Teachers who want children to believe that reading is constructing meaning from print in a variety of forms and for a variety of functions will be careful not to present skill exercises as reading. Whenever schools or districts place too much emphasis on test scores in reading, they run the risk that teachers will spend disproportionate amounts of time on skills instruction rather than on reading. When basal programs are used, only 10 to 15 percent of reading time is spent in silent reading of cohesive texts (Goodman, Shannon, Freeman, and Murphy, 1988). Many children spend as little as two or three minutes a day of their "reading" time actually reading; the rest of the time is spent completing worksheets or practicing skills.

Some basal readers ignore what children already know about print and how it works before they come to school. (Recall the description in Chapter 2 of reading as a developmental process.) Children know about many of the functions of print, may recognize words and logos that are meaningful to them (their names, "love," "the end"), and have a good sense of the alphabetic nature of our language before they come to school. Basals tend to begin reading instruction with studies of letters or letter–sound relationships that are out of context and not connected to children's experiences. Some children beginning school will know the letters and be able to write them, whereas others will have too little experience with print to make sense of the instruction.

Teachers' perceptions of children may also be influenced by the use of a basal program. A very thoughtful teacher recently reported that she had begun to think differently about the children as learners and readers after they were grouped by reading level for instruction in the basal program. She had started the year using whole-language reading activities, primarily with whole-group instruction. After experiencing some pressure to identify individual children's reading levels, she assessed the children with basal tests and placed them in ability groups. Soon she realized that she was beginning to think of children in the lower group as less capable learners and readers. Knowing what teacher perception does to student achievement, she returned to whole-language instruction so the work of each individual could be valued without comparison to the work of others.

Teachers who identified some of the strengths of basal reader programs were asked in the same study to name the weaknesses. They cited (1) quality of story content, (2) lack of opportunities to apply word analysis and comprehension skills, (3) controlled vocabulary, (4) lack of stories on current topics, and (5) inability to meet individual needs (Russavage, Lorton, and Millham, 1985). It is obvious that what is to some teachers a strength is to others a weakness. These differences of opinion occur because teachers have different views on how children learn to read and what activities are most useful in helping them along in the process.

What teachers actually do in the course of instruction may not be very good news either. Durkin (1984) has done several studies of what teachers actually do in reading instruction, in comparison with what teacher's guides suggest that they do. Most teacher's guides recommend about the same sequence for lesson presentation: first some prereading activities, then silent reading of the stories, with questions by the teacher at intervals, next oral reading of parts of the story, and finally skill development. What Durkin found was that, contrary to suggestions in the guides, most teachers introduced the new vocabulary without context. None of the teachers that she observed spent any time in developing background information for the selection to be read, and very little use was made of prereading questions. Most of the silent reading was done at the students' desks, without observation by the teacher.

As they continued the lessons, teachers often asked the suggested comprehension questions *after* the reading, but not during. They often required written answers, justified by the need to see which students could actually answer the questions—a check they said was not possible with oral answers. The teachers' expressed goals in having the children read the selections orally, round-robin fashion (with each child reading a passage in turn), were (1) to check on the child's ability to read the new words (although none made note of which children missed words), (2) to check on comprehension (even though the children had previously demonstrated understanding), and (3) to ascertain that the children were able to read with expression. All the teachers skipped some of the skills lessons but assigned all the worksheets. All the teachers did isolated phonics work, whereas the manuals always recommended phonics instruction within the context of words. None of the teachers told the children why an assignment was being given or how it related to learning to read. The teachers were most concerned with monitoring students' ability to finish the assignments and get the right answers (Durkin, 1984).

If the purpose of basal readers is to help children learn to be competent in reading a wide variety of reading materials, then the news about basals is also disappointing. Flood and Lapp (1987) found that most of the material in basal readers was either narrative writing or poetry. For teaching decoding strategies, the type of material is not very important. But for teaching children to interpret a wide range of expository writing as well as narrative pieces, the basal must include the same range. Flood and Lapp also note that the instructions for teaching narrative and other kinds of materials do not reflect differences in the techniques for reading various materials successfully. Teachers who rely mostly on the basals will have to think about newspapers, magazines, commercial children's books, and informational books on a variety of topics to supplement the narratives presented in the basal.

Some teachers find it difficult to alter their use of the basal even when evidence demonstrates that some adaptation increases their effectiveness. For example, researchers helped a group of teachers to analyze the basal material and reorganize their instruction (Duffy, Roehler, and Putnam, 1987). Their collective analysis of the skills lessons showed that many were not reading lessons but spelling lessons, such as exercises in changing the *y* to *i* and adding *ed,* and that many had no applications in the stories they accompanied. The researchers guided teachers in recasting some of the skills lessons as strategies and helped them place skills with stories to which they could be applied. At the end of the study, the children demonstrated increased knowledge not just of subskills but of strategy usage and achievement. However, the teachers found it difficult to continue making such decisions in the face of pressures to follow the basal recommendations.

The Basal Reader and the Reading/Writing Connection

Helping children become literate does not mean that the teacher cannot use the basal reader. It does mean that, while choosing instructional materials and activities, the teacher must think carefully about the goals of instruction, the outcomes likely to result from various activities, and what is known about the process of becoming literate. The following suggestions for using the basal reader are merely suggestions and nothing more. Professional teachers have to evaluate basal reader activities and assume responsibility for selecting those that best meet the needs of the individual children in their classes.

Selecting Basal Reader Activities

Before Reading

One of the tasks of the reading teacher is to build background information before reading a selection. Please recall the example in Chapter 2 of the passage from a biology journal that was difficult to read without background information about the topic. Children are often presented with stories or expository writing that are made unnecessarily difficult by lack of background information. Approaching a story such as Grahame's "The Reluctant Dragon" (*Landmarks,* 1987, pp. 390–423), a teacher concerned with background information could begin the lesson by asking the children what they know about dragons and listing their characteristics on the chalkboard. The children's background knowledge will almost certainly include fairy tales or fantasy stories involving dragons. For children who are not familiar with them, the teacher might read *Saint George and the Dragon* (Hodges, 1984). Hodges' story has the same characters as Grahame's, but it is definitely not the same story. The teacher could then discuss the structure of fairy tales and help children set their expectations for this story. Finally, the teacher might ask for predictions about the nature of a dragon whom the title describes as "reluctant."

Another strategy for helping children connect what they know with information presented in a reading selection is to use guided imagery, a technique for encouraging children to think about how an incident would feel, how a setting might look, and how characters might respond. Harp (1988) believes that guided imagery improves comprehension because it increases the children's visualization of settings, characters, and actions. They can then relate their previous experience to the new information presented. Children reading "Your Own Best Secret Place" (*Cross the Golden River,* 1986, pp. 246–253) would be asked to visualize their own secret or "best" place for being alone and thinking. They would imagine items they like to keep there. They would think about how they might feel if someone else found their place or if they could not go there anymore. Guided imagery before reading increases comprehension more than do questions after reading.

Reutzel (1985) looked at the sequence of instruction suggested in the teacher's guides and recommended rearranging the elements of instruction to reflect more of what is known about learning to read. For example, he found that many of the enrichment activities following the lesson would make good prereading activities, building background information that could aid comprehension.

During Reading

When children begin to read a selection, the teacher can use the Directed Reading Activity and the Guided Metacomprehension Strategy described in Chapter 10. Making predictions, reading to confirm or deny the accuracy of those predictions, and then making new predictions are techniques that assure active involvement on the part of the reader. Any time readers are thinking about what they are reading, comprehension will increase.

Silent Reading

Most of the children's reading time should be spent in silent reading. For beginning readers, comprehension remains about equal whether the children are reading silently or orally. For children past the beginning stages of reading, comprehension is greater during silent reading. The reason is obvious: oral reading is a performance. When the reader attends to the pronunciation, speed, tone of voice, and other elements of performing a piece, it is difficult to attend to the content of it too (Spache, 1981).

Oral Reading

It is difficult to trace the beginnings of the round-robin method of oral reading (Hoffman, 1987). Teacher education programs do not teach the use of round-robin reading, nor is it suggested by the authors of the teacher's guides for basal readers. It seems to be learned primarily from tradition. Perhaps you may remember sitting in a small group with your own teacher and taking turns reading a selection aloud. What actually happens is that the child due to read next is practicing his or her portion of the text, and the children who have already read are thinking about other things. Even if children really did what their teachers often admonish them to do—"Keep your eyes on the words that Nicole is reading"—they would be developing inappropriate reading habits. An efficient reader (past the very early stages of reading) can read much faster silently than anyone can read orally. Following text as it is read orally can force a reader into the habit of reading too slowly. Comprehension is reduced when attention is directed to following the words being read aloud, rather than to the meaning of the print.

When Durkin (1984) asked teachers why they had children read entire selections aloud in round-robin style, they said it was to check knowledge of new words, monitor comprehension, and check ability to read with expression. Teachers choosing oral reading need to think carefully about the purposes of the experience. For example, children may know the meaning of words that they cannot pronounce. Reading aloud requires that the reader know the pronunciation of each word, but comprehending a selection does not. There are more effective means of demonstrating comprehension than oral reading, such as retelling the story, answering questions, modifying predictions, drawing pictures, performing a skit, and writing a story following the same model.

The reading that most adults do is silent. Very few occupations—such as broadcasting, teaching, and the ministry—require oral reading. Oral reading can certainly contribute to the reading program if the activities are thoughtfully selected and their purposes are clear. Some basic guidelines will help to make oral reading more productive as a means of gaining reading skill. First, children should not read aloud material that they have not had a chance to read silently. Ideally they will also have had a chance to practice reading the material aloud before they are asked to perform it for an audience. One way of organizing this kind of reading experience is to set aside a certain time when children are encouraged to share some material with their classmates through reading orally. Children might select an excerpt from a book they are reading, a poem, a riddle, a newspaper clipping, or some interesting fact that they have discovered in a reference book. They choose their own material, have a chance to practice their presentation, and then share it with an audience. ("Audience" implies that only the performer has the text!)

Another guideline is that children should read material orally that has been modeled by a fluent reader. The teacher should read a passage aloud and after practice time help the child read the same passage. This technique has been particularly helpful with readers who are not achieving as well as they might (Hoffman, 1987).

■ Conducting Skills Instruction

Skills instruction in most basal reader programs is poorly placed, coming after rather than before the stories and depriving children of the chance to apply the skills in real reading. No instruction in skills should take place without letting the children know how those skills will make them more efficient and knowledgeable readers. Skills instruction should also be determined by the needs of the children. Nothing kills interest in reading more quickly than having to sit through unneeded skills instruction. Skills can be approached through many different activities and should not be isolated from the child's real experience with reading.

One way of approaching skills is through writing experiences. Many of the skills listed in the basal are encoding skills that children need for putting together discourse, not interpreting it. For example, for "The Reluctant Dragon" the teacher's guide suggests that children learn to identify figurative language. The teacher could read examples of figurative language. In their own writing over the next few days or weeks, children should focus attention on including more colorful expressions when appropriate. They could also look for figurative language in their other reading. Katherine Paterson, for example, is a master of figurative language, so this would be a good time to introduce one of her books. Children might also compare the basal version of "The Reluctant Dragon" with the original story by Kenneth Grahame, thinking about the language and why it was changed in the basal version.

Another set of skills comes into play in writing a letter as if from one character in a story to another. For example, after having read "The Garden of Abdul Gasazi" (*Cross the Golden River*, 1986, pp. 166–175), the teacher could read *The Jolly Postman* (Ahlberg and Ahlberg, 1986) and talk about the different models of letter writing it includes. Then children could

One of the joys of reading is sharing with an audience.
© *Michael Weisbrot/Stock, Boston*

write a letter from Alan or the magician to another book character or to one of their friends. An observant teacher will notice many skills being applied in such meaningful learning activities. Participating in the letter writing activity just described, children were observed using the following skills:

Reading

List of books
Text of letter
Decoding
Comprehension
Analysis and critique of ideas, order, word choice

Listening

Recalling book titles
Interchange of ideas
Listening to text being read
Recall of text

Oral language

Discussion
Questions
Persuasion
Focusing discussion
Reiteration of ideas
Dictation of letter parts
Brainstorming—letter types, audience, etc.
Word meanings

Writing

Consideration of audience
Letter format
Address and greeting
Handwriting
Spelling and punctuation

In addition, the children learned about social uses of language and group dynamics. Contrast those skills with the lack of real learning taking place when children fill in blanks in workbook exercises.

Teachers who decide to use workbook pages to help children develop control of some skills should make careful selection of the pages. Osborn (1981) has suggested that teachers think about the most important aspects of what is being taught before assigning workbook pages and that only pages that are relevant to the instruction should be used. Workbook tasks should involve reading and writing, he says, and cute, nonfunctional tasks should be avoided. Teachers should make sure there is enough content in workbook tasks to enable children to learn something from completing them. Workbook assignments should be made only when the assignment is the best means of achieving reading objectives.

■ Integrating the Basal with Reading and Writing Experiences

Assume the children have read the story "The Fifth Quimby" (*Landmarks*, 1987, pp. 156–169), which is an excerpt from *Ramona Forever* (Cleary, 1984).

To make connections between the story and both reading and writing, the teacher could encourage children to choose one or more of the following activities:

- Read *Ramona Forever.* Tell why you think the author who selected the material for the textbook chose "The Fifth Quimby" as the part of the original book to include. Why did the author choose to change its title?
- Read one or more of Beverly Cleary's other books. Find other children who have read one of Cleary's books and discuss the character of Ramona. Are her adventures similar in many of the stories? Are there incidents in each of the stories that give the reader new clues about Ramona's personality or thinking?
- Write a letter to a pen pal of Ramona's as if you were Ramona. Would your descriptions of the incidents match Cleary's?
- Write a description of one of Ramona's adventures from the point of view of Ramona's mother or father.
- Find biographical information about Beverly Cleary and write an author profile modeled on the form in the textbook.

Activities like these can help children see that reading in the textbook is not an isolated experience but one that can be connected to "real" reading and writing that interests them.

Another sort of example uses "On the Frontier with Mr. Audubon" (*Landmarks*, 1987, pp. 546–572). This selection is written as a journal kept by Joseph Mason, who accompanied Audubon on his trips. These are some possible reading and writing connections:

- Read other examples of books written in a journal format, such as *A Gathering of Days* (Blos, 1979) and *Dear Mr. Henshaw* (Cleary, 1983). Talk about the style and point of view in journal writing. Compare journal writing with other writing styles, such as newspaper and informational.
- Examine some journal writing that is not fictionalized, such as the journals of Lewis and Clark. Who did they expect would be the audience for their journals? How are their journals different from a journal kept by children in your class?
- Choose a book character or real person and write a journal for a week as if you were that person.
- A journal often reveals feelings and emotions as well as facts. What are some words that are especially useful for describing emotions?

- Imagine that you will someday be famous for your achievements. Write a journal for a week or a month describing how you got started in your chosen area—playing tennis, playing the piano, writing novels, drawing illustrations, or whatever it may be.
- Think about your own journal entries. If someone else were to read them, would that person be excited by your choice of words or the unique way you describe your daily adventures?

Integrating the Basal Into a Thematic Curriculum

Using a basal reader as the core of a reading program does not exclude the possibility of a thematic approach to curriculum. Teachers who have chosen to organize their curriculum around a particular theme or topic can use the basal as a resource or, as in our examples, a beginning point for organizing other curricular experiences. We will also illustrate the use of the basal in planning themes.

In planning a theme, one can choose any of several organizers. One of these could be an author and the works of that author. For example, if the teacher felt that the children were interested, they could choose to organize a theme around the works of Chris Van Allsburg. Children could be encouraged to read one or more of Van Allsburg's books. After becoming acquainted with his work, children could participate in some of the following experiences:

Reading

- Compare one of Van Allsburg's stories with those of another author you enjoy. How do they differ in style? What are the elements of each that make them enjoyable reading?
- Read "The Garden of Abdul Gasazi" in the basal *Cross the Golden River* (1986). Why did the author of the textbook choose this story to include in the collection? Prepare a commercial for this story in oral, written, or videotaped form. How would you persuade someone who had not heard of it to want to read the story?
- Read or ask an adult to help you read the author profile of Chris Van Allsburg in *Language Arts* (Kiefer, 1987). What do you think are the most important influences on his writing?

The need for concentration on the task at hand makes reading and writing serious work for youngsters like this fifth-grader.
© *Rhoda Sidney/Monkmeyer Press Photo Service*

■ Read or ask an adult to help you read Van Allsburg's (1986) speech when he accepted the Caldecott award. Did you learn something new about his writing and/or illustrating?

■ Writing

■ Write a story for one of the illustrations in *The Mysteries of Harris Burdick.*

■ Write a critical review of one of the books for the school newspaper. Be sure to read several book reviews in your local newspaper first so you will know what to include in your review.

■ Write a sequel to *Jumanji.*

- Write your answer to the riddle of the identity of the visitor in *The Stranger.* List your evidence. Seal your answer in an envelope. When all envelopes have been collected, open them and compare the answers. Get your principal to help all of you think about how well you looked for clues.

■ Social Studies

- Find the landmarks that are included in *Ben's Dream.* Locate them on a map. Are there other landmarks that you would have included in the book? Find information about one of the landmarks in a reference book. Be sure that you can tell where it is, when it was built, and why it is important.
- Why is it important to the farmers in *The Stranger* that the seasons change? Compile a list of occupations that depend on the weather for success.

■ Science

- Find information about the animals included in *Jumanji.* Where do they live, and what do they eat?
- In *The Wreck of the Zephyr* a sailboat can sail on air. Find information about how airplanes are able to fly. Tell or write why you think a sailboat can or cannot fly; if not, what adaptations would make flying possible?

■ Art

- Find information about the art techniques that Van Allsburg uses in his illustrations. You may need to visit your local art museum or have an art teacher come in to talk about the various techniques.
- Choose one of the techniques that Van Allsburg uses in his illustrations and try it in illustrating one of your own stories.
- One of the interesting aspects of Van Allsburg's art is his use of perspective. Find other artists who have used perspective in unusual ways.

These are only a few of the many possibilities for building a theme around an author. A pioneer theme could make good use of the selection "You're It! Games Kids Played on the Frontier" (*Landmarks,* 1987, pp. 530–539) in conjunction with "High Elk's Treasure" (pp. 472–485) and "Sioux Artifacts" (pp. 486–491). The works of Laura Ingalls Wilder and Paul Goble could be used, along with other pioneer stories such as *Caddie Woodlawn* (Brink, 1935). There are also many good collections of Native American chants and poetry, such as *In the Trail of the Wind* (Bierhorst, 1971), that could be included. Almost any theme you might choose could include works from basal readers.

Final Comments on the Basal Reader

The basal reader offers many possibilities for good instruction when used thoughtfully by the teacher. A teacher thinking about individual needs of children would never believe that every child should "cover" every page of a given basal and complete every workbook exercise. Neither would most teachers choose to ignore the basal totally, disregarding not just all the selections offered for reading but all the ideas for helping children develop into mature readers. Teachers take advantage of the skills ideas in doing their own planning for instruction, but they do not mindlessly put children through skills exercises without reference to larger goals. Just as in using any other instructional tool, the teacher is responsible for helping children see how learning in school relates to real experience and how reading and writing are invaluable in life—not just exercises to be completed at school.

■ Major Ideas in This Chapter

- ■ Basal readers are used in a majority of elementary classrooms. Teachers use basal readers in various ways, singly or in combination.

- ■ Basal reading series differ in their philosophies and their approaches to skills instruction. A "bottom-up" approach emphasizes decoding text; a "top-down" approach stresses the interaction of the reader and the text is most important for getting meaning. Current basal reading series include activities that reflect a broad range of ideas about reading instruction.

- ■ Basal readers can be used effectively by integrating reading and writing experiences with the basal and by including the selections in thematic planning.

? Discussion Questions
Focusing on the Teacher You Are Becoming

1. What do you personally consider the strengths and weaknesses of basal readers?

2. Discuss reasons for choosing not to order the workbooks that accompany the basal. How might you convince a principal that this action was appropriate?
3. Recall your own experiences in learning to read. How did you feel about reading orally to the class? Do you think most students shared your feelings?

☑ Field-Based Applications

1. Examine several basal reading series. Try to determine their approaches to skills instruction and identify the authors' philosophies.
2. Choose one selection from a basal for a grade that you want to teach and develop two or three ideas for building background information before the children read the story. Check the teacher's guide and compare your ideas with the ones it suggests.
3. Choose one selection from a basal and think about writing activities that would be appropriate to accompany that selection.
4. Choose one selection from a basal and think about how it could be integrated into a thematic approach to curriculum.
5. Plan an oral reading experience using one selection in the basal. Possibilities include having two children read the dialogue in a story and another read the narration, having one child read the story (or an excerpt from it) to the class, and setting up partner reading, in which two children read aloud to each other.
6. Compare the original version of a book with the version printed in a basal reader. What changes, if any, were made in the language? Why do you think they were made?

⊡ References and Suggested Readings

Ahlberg, Janet, and Ahlberg, Allan. *The Jolly Postman.* Boston: Little, Brown, 1986.

Bierhorst, John, ed. *In the Trail of the Wind.* Toronto, Calif.: Collins, 1971.

Blos, Joan W. *A Gathering of Days: A New England Girl's Journal 1830–32.* New York: Macmillan, 1979.

Brink, Carol. *Caddie Woodlawn.* New York: Macmillan, 1935.

Cairney, Trevor H. "The Purpose of Basals: What Children Think." *The Reading Teacher* 41 (January 1988): 420–428.

Campbell, Loomis J. *New Franklin Second Reader.* New York: Sheldon & Co., 1886.

Cassidy, Jack. "Basals Are Better." *Learning* 16 (September 1987): 65–66.

Chall, Jeanne S. *Learning to Read: The Great Debate.* New York: McGraw-Hill, 1967.

Cleary, Beverly. *Dear Mr. Henshaw.* New York: Dell, 1983.

Cleary, Beverly. *Ramona Forever.* New York: Dell, 1984.

Cross the Golden River. Toronto: Holt, Rinehart & Winston of Canada, 1986.

Duffy, Gerald; Roehler, Laura; and Putnam, Joyce. "Putting the Teacher in Control: Basal Reading Textbooks and Instructional Decision Making." *The Elementary School Journal* 87 (January 1987): 357–364.

Durkin, Dolores. "Is There a Match between What Elementary Teachers Do and What Basal Reader Manuals Recommend?" *The Reading Teacher* 37 (April 1984): 734–744.

Englemann, S., and Bereiter, C. *DISTAR Reading*. Chicago: Science Research Associates, 1983.

Flood, James, and Lapp, Diane. "Forms of Discourse in Basal Readers." *The Elementary School Journal* 87 (January 1987): 299–306.

Goodman, Kenneth. "Basal Readers: A Call for Action." *Language Arts* 63 (April 1986): 359–363.

Goodman, Kenneth; Shannon, Patrick; Freeman, Yvonne; and Murphy, Sharon. *Report Card on Basal Readers*. New York: Richard C. Owen, 1988.

Grahame, Kenneth. *The Reluctant Dragon*. New York: Henry Holt and Company, 1983.

Harp, Bill. "When the Principal Asks: 'Why Are You Doing Guided Imagery during Reading Time?'" *The Reading Teacher* 41 (February 1988): 588–590.

Hodges, Margaret. *Saint George and the Dragon*. Boston: Little, Brown, 1984.

Hoffman, James V. "Rethinking the Role of Oral Reading in Basal Instruction." *The Elementary School Journal* 87 (January 1987): 367–373.

Impressions. Elementary Reading Series. Toronto: Holt, Rinehart & Winston of Canada, 1986.

Kiefer, Barbara. "Profile: Chris Van Allsburg in Three Dimensions." *Language Arts* 64 (October 1987): 664–673.

Landmarks. Orlando, Florida: Harcourt Brace Jovanovich, 1987.

Mosel, Arlene. *The Funny Little Woman*. New York: Dutton, 1972.

The New McGuffey Fourth Reader. New York: American Book Company, 1901.

Newman, Judith. *Whole Language: Theory in Use*. Portsmouth, N.H.: Heinemann Educational Books, 1985.

Osborn, J. *The Purposes, Uses and Contents of Workbooks and Some Guidelines for Teachers and Publishers*. Reading Education Report No. 27. Urbana-Champaign: University of Illinois, Center for the Study of Reading, 1981.

Reading Framework for California Public Schools. Sacramento: Bureau of Publications, California State Department of Education, 1980.

Reutzel, D. Ray. "Reconciling Schema Theory and the Basal Reading Lesson." *The Reading Teacher* 39 (November 1985): 194–197.

Russavage, Patricia; Lorton, Larry; and Millham, Rhodessa. "Making Responsible Instructional Decisions about Reading: What Teachers Think and Do about Basals." *The Reading Teacher* 39 (December 1985): 314–317.

Shannon, Patrick. "Some Subjective Reasons for Teachers' Reliance on Commercial Reading Materials." *The Reading Teacher* 35 (May 1982): 884–889.

Spache, George D. *Diagnosing and Correcting Reading Disabilities*. 2d ed. Boston: Allyn & Bacon, 1981.

Turner, Rebecca R. "How the Basals Stack Up." *Learning* 17 (April 1988): 62–64.

Van Allen, Roach. *Language Experiences in Reading*. Chicago: Encyclopedia Britannica Educational Corporation, 1976.

Van Allsburg, Chris. *Ben's Dream*. Boston: Houghton Mifflin, 1982.

Van Allsburg, Chris. "Caldecott Medal Acceptance." *Horn Book* 62 (July/August 1986): 420–424.

Van Allsburg, Chris. *The Garden of Abdul Gasazi*. Boston: Houghton Mifflin, 1979.

Van Allsburg, Chris. *Jumanji*. Boston: Houghton Mifflin, 1981.

Van Allsburg, Chris. *The Mysteries of Harris Burdick*. Boston: Houghton Mifflin, 1984.

Van Allsburg, Chris. *The Polar Express*. Boston: Houghton Mifflin, 1985.

Van Allsburg, Chris. *The Stranger*. Boston: Houghton Mifflin, 1986.

Van Allsburg, Chris. *The Wreck of the Zephyr*. Boston: Houghton Mifflin, 1983.

Van Allsburg, Chris. *The Z Was Zapped*. Boston: Houghton Mifflin, 1987.

Venezky, Richard L. "A History of the American Reading Textbook." *The Elementary School Journal* 87 (January 1987): 247–263.

Watkins, Emma. *Silent Reading for Beginners*. Chicago: Lippincott, 1926.

Chapter 7

Literature in the Reading/Writing Program

Chapter Overview

- Literature can be used as the base for reading and writing instruction in the classroom. Children's literature offers source material for instruction in literacy abilities, including recognizing the structures of various genres, analyzing techniques employed by authors, and analyzing the choices made by the author.

- There are picture books for both younger and older children, and they can serve as models for writing and illustration.

- Reading aloud is an important component of reading instruction. It can contribute to vocabulary development, increase interest in reading, and serve as a model of reading.

- A variety of curricular experiences can be organized around literature, which can enhance activities in social studies, science, art, music, and mathematics.

- Reading and writing instruction based on literature can be organized using specific strategies for individuals and groups.

Learning to read is a wonderful experience only when that learning opens the door to the magic of real books in the real world. Of course, reading serves many functional purposes—finding telephone numbers, following the directions for completing a model airplane, and cooking a gourmet meal—but it is reading real books that excites the reader. Through children's literature, teachers can open that world of real books to children, at the same time motivating them to read and write and to become more skillful.

Real Books

Tomie dePaola shares a story about his beginning reading experiences, recalling his disappointment when the exciting story he had expected to find on opening the book was only "See Dick run." He knew that nobody talked like that. Over the weekend he learned all the words in the book so he could get a library card—his key to real reading. He says, "If I knew that Dick and Jane and Spot and Puff couldn't hold a candle to Jack and the Beanstalk and Red Riding Hood and Pooh and Peter Rabbit, then many, many children must feel very much the same way, even though Dick and Jane have given way to Meg and Billy or any other string of 'current' names. There is no substitute for *real* books. They are rarely boring or sanitized or squeezed into a 'reading system' that children can smell a mile off. So logic says if we want *real* readers we must give them *real* books; give our young people good literature, good art, and, surprisingly, these young people may do the rest" (Cullinan, 1987, p. vi). As teachers help children learn to read, they also need to make sure that children know about the wonderful world of literature waiting out there and give them opportunities to discover at least some of it.

California is one state that has taken a stand on the importance of literature in the reading program. The California Reading Initiative is a comprehensive plan for including the reading of literature in the elementary curriculum. It includes a booklist, a language arts framework based on literature, and a testing program matched to the reading program. State Superintendent Bill Honig stated (Cullinan, 1986, p. 766):

Reading is one of the most effective ways of learning. I want to encourage students to read and I want them to enjoy reading. Good reading skills are critical to success in all academic areas. We are launching the California Reading Initiative to address serious concerns about students' reading abilities and practices. Recent figures indicate that we are experiencing an alarming increase in illiteracy in this nation. Many of our students who can read are having difficulty understanding what they read. Further, many of our students who can read and who can understand what they read simply don't read.

The California Reading Initiative has been developed to address these concerns. An important part of our strategy is to improve reading instruction and to provide students access to good books. A love of reading and books is one of the most important gifts that teachers and parents can give our young people.

The California Reading Initiative is a statewide effort to recognize the importance of literature in the curriculum and the importance of books in achieving the goal of lifelong readership.

Literature—that is, printed material written to inform or entertain—is one source of material for use in reading instruction. Children can be taught to read a variety of materials. Books written specifically for reading instruction often contain sterile stories of the kind that dePaola remembered. Literature offers meaningful texts for reading, which can come from all genres and take the form of fiction, nonfiction, or poetry.

The appeal of literature lies not only in its variety but in its intrinsic interest, which motivates reading. Literature of the very highest quality should be offered to children. It has something for every individual, from those who want to know about asteroids to those who are zoo lovers. Whether a child likes hot rods, motorcycles, or dolls, books and poetry can be found to fit that interest. Very few children actually got personally involved with the tales of Dick and Jane, but many have eagerly read all the books in *The Chronicles of Narnia* (Lewis, 1950). Interest and motivation are critical in any reading program.

Literature can add zest and interest to the classroom. It can enliven topics in the traditional subject matter, motivate further reading and broaden children's reading interests. Helping children analyze their reading in ways meaningful to them will deepen their understanding of literature. Writing experiences can be encouraged through an introduction of

The media center expands children's awareness of the world of literature.
© *David Strickler/The Image Works*

some of the models of writing found in literature. The authors of the best in children's literature use literary techniques that children can learn to apply in their own writing efforts. Noticing the words and phrases chosen by outstanding authors will help children become more knowledgeable and thoughtful about the words and phrases they use.

Selecting and Using Literature

Thousands of books are published each year. Selecting the best of them for use in the classroom is sometimes difficult. Obviously, no teacher can read every book available. Help can come from your school's media specialist and from book reviews in professional journals. Your school library probably subscribes to *Horn Book,* the premier journal in children's literature. Very useful book reviews are also found in *Language Arts, The Reading Teacher, Childhood Education,* and *Young Children.* Each year the October issue of *The Reading Teacher* publishes "Children's Choices," a list of children's favorite books. In addition to book reviews, *Language Arts* features biographical articles on authors and illustrators of children's books. Some newspapers also have book review sections for new children's books. Even though these sources cannot review every new book published, they will certainly help you know the new work in the field of children's literature.

In advertising their books for sale, most publishers list an age level for which each book is appropriate. The age level is usually given as a span of four or five years. The school or district librarian may have publishers' catalogs containing those listings. The librarian will also have insight into books that appeal to the age level for which you are making selections.

When choosing books for the classroom, the teacher must think about intended use: will the book be read aloud to the class or made available for free reading? Will it add interest and depth to particular topics of study, help children solve problems, or aid in reading and writing instruction? In each case, there are some general and specific guidelines to follow when selecting books.

In general, the theme, setting, plot, characterization, and style must be considered when choosing a book of fiction for classroom use. The theme must be one that is worthwhile. For example, many books have themes that help children better understand relationships, perseverance, honesty, or courage. Settings are important if they make the book more or less difficult to understand. A book set in another time or place, such as historical fiction, may require explanations or background knowledge in order to be comprehensible. The plot of the story must be lively. Most children enjoy action and a plot that moves along. The characterization must be such that children can relate to the characters in the book. Children need to be able to relate to the emotions of the characters and feel that their actions are plausible. Style is basically the quality of writing. It means that the author has interesting sentence patterns, chooses words and phrases carefully, paces the story appropriately, and writes so as not to distract the reader. Books should contain a quality of language and writing that will serve as models for children's writing. Good books also serve to increase children's vocabularies and understanding of figures of speech such as similes and metaphors.

The American Library Association annually presents the Newbery Medal for the most distinguished contribution to literature for children. Award winners may not always be children's first choices, but they have qualities that make them appropriate for classroom reading instruction. The books that have won the Newbery Medal represent most of the genres

Our definition of a good book is one that children want to read.
© *Freda Leinwand/Monkmeyer Press Photo Service*

of children's literature, including mysteries, historical fiction, modern fantasy, realistic fiction, and nonfiction.

As children move into the intermediate grades, their individual reading interests vary widely. Many children become avid readers during this time, reading everything they can find on a given subject, such as horses or space travel, some pursuing a particular genre, such as mystery or biography. It is very important that teachers continue to select literature for a broad range of interests and reading abilities.

In this chapter we will discuss read-aloud books, picture books, books with repetitive language, alphabet books, poetry, and books for independent reading. Each section will include some suggestions for using literature in the reading and writing program and some examples of appropriate literature.

■ Read-Aloud Books

A book that is to be read aloud by the teacher should meet several criteria:

1. It should be a book that the teacher enjoys personally. There are too many wonderful books available to choose a book that is not appealing to the reader.
2. It should be suitable for reading aloud: short enough to fit into a reading period or divisible into chapters or segments that can be read separately.
3. Its content and subject matter must be appropriate to the audience.
4. If the book has illustrations, their size and clarity should be considered with respect to visibility at a distance from the reader.
5. The book should contain action or dialogue that makes listening interesting.
6. The book should contain language that is slightly above the reading level of most members of the group. Books that are written to be "easy to read" are not usually good choices for reading aloud because the level of the language is not interesting to the listener and the stories are rarely very interesting to the reader. Children deserve the very best in terms of language use and writing style.

Two resources that can help teachers select books for reading aloud are *The New Read-Aloud Handbook* (Trelease, 1989) and *Adventuring with Books* (Monson, 1985), both of which contain useful annotations. Read-aloud books for young children should include alphabet books, counting books, picture books, concept books, and poetry. Children in the primary grades may continue to like alphabet books and some counting books, picture books, information books, and poetry. They will also enjoy some short novels. Most children remember hearing *Charlotte's Web* (White, 1952) in second or third grade. Older children will enjoy a variety of prose (both fiction and nonfiction), selected picture books, selected ABC books, and poetry. Books that have been popular over the years for reading aloud to older children include the *Little House on the Prairie* series (Wilder, 1953), the trilogy of Madeleine L'Engle books (L'Engle, 1962, 1973, 1978) and such novels as *Sounder* (Armstrong, 1969).

Reading aloud to intermediate-grade children introduces them to many different genres and exposes them to books they might never have chosen on their own. It provides a common reading experience and can be the stimulus for other reading and writing activities. Teachers can provide lead-ins to stories that children might find difficult to read on their own. For example, because the names of many mythological figures are difficult to pronounce, many children find myths overwhelming to read without an introduction by the teacher. Once the teacher has read some myths aloud and given the children a chance to relate them to their own experience (references in other literature, references in advertising, terms used in sports, and so on) then they are much more likely to be successful in reading myths independently. Usually the most popular book in the classroom for individual reading is the book that the teacher has just finished reading aloud.

■ Picture Books

Picture books are books of which the illustrations are an integral part. In fact, the text of a picture book is rarely sufficient to carry the story. Imagine reading Sendak's *Where the Wild Things Are* (Sendak, 1963) without the illustrations. There are only about 300 words in the text, and there wouldn't be much left of the story if the illustrations were missing.

Picture books have changed rather drastically since Comenius published the first picture book—*Orbis Pictus: The World Illustrated*—in 1657. We would describe this book more as an illustrated dictionary than as a picture book. Technological advances in printing have made possible the reproduction of various art techniques and print/picture layouts that would not have been possible a few years ago. Picture books deal with family life, school experiences, friends, animals, and adaptations of folk tales. Today's picture books also treat topics once considered taboo for children, such as death. Another relatively new idea is the wordless picture book, of which Tafuri's *Jungle Walk* (1988) is one example. There has also been renewed interest in pop-up books and books that have moveable parts.

Many picture books invite reading aloud.
© Mimi Forsyth/Monkmeyer Press Photo Service

Picture books appeal to a vast audience; they are certainly not meant to be restricted to the youngest children. For examples of picture books created for older audiences, see the journey books of Anno, such as *Anno's Journey* (1977) and *Anno's U.S.A.* (1983). These books have sophisticated material and require background knowledge that young children would not possess. To truly appreciate the detail of Anno's books, the reader must be able to recognize at least some of their references to works of art, architectural styles, children's games, literary selections, and musicians. *The Geranium on the Window Sill Just Died But Teacher You Went Right On* (Cullum, 1971) is a picture book written for an adult audience. If the media center in your school or public library labels the picture-book section

"Easy," perhaps you could lobby for a change in designation to "Everybody's Books."

The best-known award for picture books is the Caldecott Medal, given annually by the American Library Association for the most distinguished picture book published in the United States. Caldecott winners offer opportunities to introduce various art techniques, as well as being useful for planning extended experiences in the curriculum. For example, 1988 winner *Owl Moon* (Yolen, 1987) is a gentle narrative about a child who goes to look for an owl. It could be the basis for a series of activities such as studying owls, visiting a natural history museum, finding other essays about family adventures, and writing about individual experiences. Children could study the illustrations in *The Snowy Day* (Keats, 1962), the 1963 Caldecott winner, and then make their own pictures using collage. They could also write about their own snow adventures.

In selecting picture books, one must consider the interaction of the illustrations and the text. Do the illustrations accurately reflect the content of the text, as well as the mood and tone of the book? Is there enough detail to make the illustrations interesting? Are there unique and special qualities about the illustrations? Picture books must also meet the criteria for any other literature selected for classroom use, including a worthy theme and carefully chosen language.

Picture books can be used as adjuncts to thematic studies in the classroom, as models for teaching the basics of story structure, as subjects for analysis, and as springboards for writing activities.

Developing Reading and Writing Experiences around a Picture Book

In developing a theme or topic, you can choose to build several activities around one book or to use several books on related topics. To illustrate the possibilities for building curriculum activities around a book, we have chosen *Blueberries for Sal* (McCloskey, 1948). This is a simple story about a mother and daughter picking blueberries for canning while a mother bear and her cub are eating blueberries to store up food for the winter. You might plan curriculum activities like these:

1. Bake blueberry muffins.
2. Visit a blueberry farm and pick blueberries. Write about the experience or a description of the farm.
3. Draw pictures of events in the story and place them on a time line and/or a plot tension line (illustrated later in this section). A plot line would help children discover the parallel structure of the story. Let them write a story of their own that has parallel structure.

4. Read other stories about bears or other animals that must hibernate.
5. Write the story from the little bear cub's perspective, showing how he felt munching blueberries and being frightened by a human.
6. Draw an illustration of what happens in the winter, after the action of the story (family having blueberries for dinner, bears sleeping in their den) and write a narrative to accompany the illustration.
7. Find the words that describe the sounds in the story and then think of other sound words and list them on a chart.
8. Dramatize the story.
9. Write stories about their own family adventures.
10. Read other books by McCloskey and compare the art and stories.

Picture-Book Activities for Developing Literacy

Many picture books are appropriate for use with older children, some as read-aloud books and others as models for their writing. Some can help children learn to analyze plot structures and other literary techniques. For example, the fables collected in *Fables* (Lobel, 1980) could be read aloud over a period of time and compared with fables in other collections, such as Aesop's, the Panchatanra, Arabian fables, or the fables of La Fontaine. Having learned the structure of a fable, children can write their own fables. The teacher might then read *Hey, Al!* (Yorinks, 1986) and help the children recognize that the author used the structure of a fable in writing the story. A list could be started of other books or stories that employ the fable structure, such as the stories of Lionni, which have been collected in a volume entitled *Frederick's Fables* (1985).

A picture book such as *The Mysteries of Harris Burdick* (Van Allsburg, 1984) is excellent for encouraging children's writing. This book has illustrations with titles and captions, but no narrative. Children could select an illustration and write the narrative for it. Another of Van Allsburg's books, *Jumanji* (1981), ends in a way that almost demands a sequel. Vera Williams has written two books that are especially effective in inspiring writing. *Stringbean's Trip to the Shining Sea* (Williams and Williams, 1988) is a postcard record of Stringbean's trip across the country with his older brother. Children could map their journey and use the postcard technique for recording trips of their own. *Cherries and Cherry Pits* (Williams, 1986) has a main character who draws pictures and then writes stories about them. Not only is this book a model of writing about illustrations but it gives the children a chance to observe the switch from descriptive to narrative writing style. Some picture books can show older children how to write stories for a younger audience.

Picture books provide an occasion to analyze plot structure. *Roland the Minstrel Pig* (Steig, 1968) is one good choice. After listening to the story, children could be asked to think about the major events in the story and then plot them on a graph, with tension as the cross axis (see Figure 7.1). As the children think about the amount of tension caused by each event

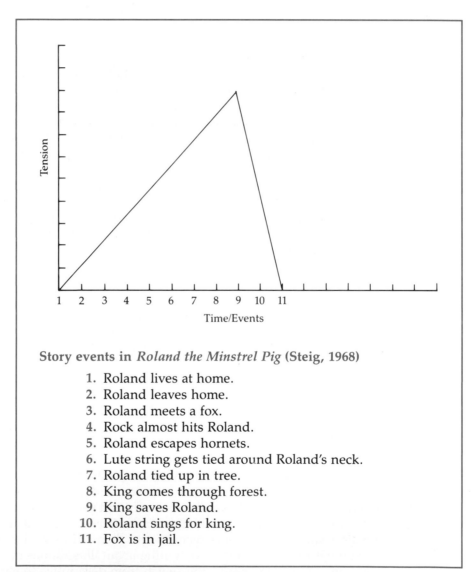

Story events in *Roland the Minstrel Pig* (Steig, 1968)

1. Roland lives at home.
2. Roland leaves home.
3. Roland meets a fox.
4. Rock almost hits Roland.
5. Roland escapes hornets.
6. Lute string gets tied around Roland's neck.
7. Roland tied up in tree.
8. King comes through forest.
9. King saves Roland.
10. Roland sings for king.
11. Fox is in jail.

Figure 7.1   A graph of time and tension.
SOURCE: *Roland the Minstrel Pig* by William Steig. Copyright © 1968 by Simon & Schuster Books for Young Readers. Reprinted by permission of the publisher.

and plot it on the graph, they create a visual representation of the build-up, followed by the relaxation of tension at the solution of the problem. A plot line can help them see how the author has structured the story in terms of heightening and then relieving the tension. They can then use a plot line to check the structure in their own stories.

Folk literature is prime material for helping children compare plot structures and story elements. There are, for example, hundreds of versions of the Cinderella story, among them "The Brocaded Slipper" (Vuong, 1982), *Yeh-Shen* (Louie, 1982), one of the Perrault versions, such as *Cinderella* (Brown, 1954), *Cinderella* (Evans, 1972), and "Cinderella" in *Grimms' Fairy Tales* (Lucas, Crane, and Edwards, 1925). Find as many versions of Cinderella as possible and compare the basic elements and differences of the stories. Figure 7.2 shows a chart that the class might construct to compare the elements of each of these stories. After thinking about these common elements, children could look for some of the same elements in other stories, such as *Moss Gown* (Hooks, 1987) and *Mufaro's Beautiful Daughters* (Steptoe, 1987).

For intermediate-grade children, picture books such as those by Byrd Baylor—*The Way to Start a Day* (1977), *I'm in Charge of Celebrations* (1986), and *If You Are a Hunter of Fossils* (1980)—are excellent for inspiring children's writing and for serving as focus units. Most good picture books will lend themselves to a variety of extended experiences. Teachers must choose books that have enough substance to make additional experiences worthwhile for the class.

	Setting	Characters	Problem	Magic	What happened to stepsisters
"Cinderella" (Perrault)					
"Cinderella" (Grimm)					
"The Brocaded Slipper"					
"Yeh-Shen"					

Figure 7.2 Comparison of elements in Cinderella stories.
SOURCE: Adapted from an idea in Galda, Lee, "Teaching Higher Order Reading Skills with Literature: Intermediate Grades." In *Children's Literature in the Reading Program*, edited by Bernice Cullinan (Newark, Del.: International Reading Association, 1987).

■ Repetitive-Language Books

Books containing words, phrases, or sentence patterns that repeat throughout the story are described as repetitive-language books. The repetition is particularly helpful to young children in recognizing sight words and gaining fluency. Children can also model their own stories after the original story. Several authors (May, 1986; Wuertenburg, 1983; Rhodes, 1981) point out the value of using patterned books in reading instruction. Books that contain predictable patterns or words help children build familiarity with "book" language, an understanding that is especially useful to those children who are not accustomed to having books read to them. Children who have been read to frequently know to expect words and sentence patterns in books that they do not normally hear in spoken language. Here is one strategy for using predictable books (Bond and Dykstra, 1967, p. 124):

---

1. Teacher selects an enjoyable patterned book.
2. Teacher reads book out loud.
3. Teacher reads book again, with the children joining in whenever they can predict what comes next.
4. Children take turns with echo and choral reading.
5. Teacher reads the text from teacher-made charts with no picture clues. Then children read with the teacher.
6. Children place matching sentence strips on charts. (Teacher has made charts so that a sentence strip can be taped under a sentence on the chart.)
7. Children later place matching *word* strips on charts, saying the words as they match it. (Teacher has children match words in correct order the first time this is done; later in random order.)
8. Children and teacher chorally read the entire story.
9. Teacher places word strips in *random order* at the bottom of the chart. Children come up and match the strips to words in the story, saying each word as they match it to one in the story.

Of course, not every patterned book will lend itself to precisely this treatment. Some will need to be read repeatedly, and some may be read by the group from big books. The teacher may not choose to place the text on strips. Some invite imitation and innovation, such as by having the children substitute their words for words in the text. For example, children might listen to the poem "Alligator Pie" (Lee, 1974) and then substitute other words for *pie* or *alligator*. One class wrote "crocodile pie" and another wrote "alligator stew" (without hearing the second verse of Lee's poem).

Children can be encouraged to create their own variation based on the original repetitive book (Lawrence and Harris, 1986; Wuertenburg,

1983), just as they might write new lyrics to songs they have learned. For example, *Brown Bear, Brown Bear* (Martin, 1970) can be used at the beginning of kindergarten as the model for very simple stories. The children might write, "Billy, Billy, what do you see? I see Jennifer looking at me. Jennifer, Jennifer, what do you see? I see Noah looking at me," and so on until all the children in the group have their names in the book. Another class might write a Hallowe'en version following the same pattern: "Witch, witch, what do you see? I see a goblin looking at me. Goblin, goblin, what do you see?" One teacher used the pattern to help students remember the order of the planets when they were studying the solar system: "Flaming Sun, Flaming Sun, What do you see? I see tiny Mercury looking at me. Tiny Mercury, Tiny Mercury, what do you see?"

Research by Bridge, Winograd, and Haley (1983) found that children who were instructed in a sight-word vocabulary in a program that employed predictable books learned significantly more words than children in a pre-primer program. These children also had more flexible strategies for decoding unfamiliar words and more positive feelings about reading aloud. Teaching with predictable books is not only interesting but also effective!

Please refer to Appendix F for a list of books with repetitive language.

■ Alphabet Books

Alphabet books provide an excellent format for children's reading and writing experiences. There are even many alphabet books that are appropriate for use with older children; the alphabet format does not necessarily indicate that the book is simple. Some alphabet books are arranged by theme, with each entry related to the topic, and some are focused on the letters themselves rather than on a topic. *Wild Animals of America ABC* (Ryden, 1988) is a themed ABC book containing beautiful photographs of wild animals. After reading it, a class could investigate wild animals in their region by reading reference material and visiting a local wildlife exhibit. Then they could publish their own ABC book.

Creating an ABC book can be a fine activity to culminate study of various topics. After studying their own state, children could write an ABC book of their state. The project would require careful reading of background material and decision making about the most suitable entry for each letter. *I Unpacked My Grandmother's Trunk* (Hoguet, 1983), based on an old children's game, might prompt children to produce their own game and their own book. *Alligator Arrived with Apples: A Potluck Alphabet Feast* (Dragonwagon, 1987) could help children think about not only animals but foods that begin with each letter. *What's Inside? The Alphabet Book* (Kitamura, 1987) is a guessing-game ABC book that could inspire children to write their own guessing-game book. Another guessing-game book is *Q Is for Duck* (Elting and Folsum, 1980). What fun for kids to make up their own combinations for their friends to guess!

Alphabet books can serve as writing models for older children as well. *Ashanti to Zulu* (Musgrove, 1976) describes African people and traditions; it can serve as a model for putting together information on almost any topic. *A Peaceable Kingdom: The Shaker Abecedarius* (Provensen and Provensen, 1978) not only provides a little insight into the Shaker sect but also names animals in rhythmic pattern that children can learn and duplicate with other words. *As I Was Crossing Boston Common* (Farber, 1973) describes very unusual animals crossing the Common. Children can practice research skills by looking up information about the animals mentioned and seeking out other unusual animal names. *Anno's Magical ABC: An Anamorphic Alphabet* (Anno, 1981) and *Anno's Alphabet: An Adventure in Imagination* (Anno, 1975) both offer children models for looking at the alphabet from a new perspective. *Arlene Alda's ABC Book* (Alda, 1981) can challenge children to find letter forms in natural materials. There are hundreds of good alphabet books on the market and many more being published each year in classrooms across the country.

Many ideas on ways to use alphabet books in the elementary classroom are presented in *Alphabet: A Handbook of ABC Books and Activities for the Elementary Classroom* (Roberts, 1984). A good resource for other writing ideas based on literature is the booklet *Writing Is Reading: 26 Ways to Connect* (Tway, 1985). Did you guess that it is written in an ABC format?

■ Poetry

When selecting poetry for use in the reading and writing program, teachers should be aware of the difference between poetry written about childhood and poetry written for children. Many poems about childhood are sentimental recollections from an adult point of view and rarely appeal to children. Interesting poetry is available for any topic that would be part of an elementary curriculum and any interest that a child might have. Children respond well to a variety of types of poetry. They like humorous poems, narrative poetry, and descriptive poetry.

One of the poets whose writing is very popular with younger children is Jack Prelutsky. He has published several books of poetry, including *It's Valentine's Day* (1983), *My Parents Think I'm Sleeping* (1985), and *The New Kid on the Block* (1984). Dennis Lee has authored *Alligator Pie* (1974) and *Garbage Delight* (1977). These poems depict children's everyday activities in humorous terms. Older children are delighted with the poetry of Shel Silverstein. His books, *Where the Sidewalk Ends* (1974) and *A Light in the Attic* (1981), probably contain the poetry most often quoted by children today.

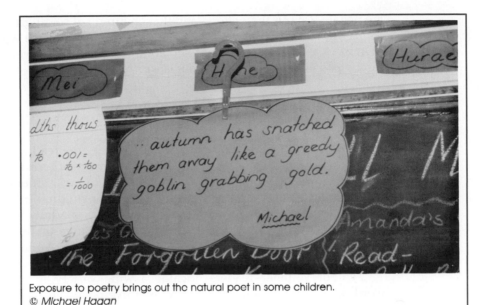

Exposure to poetry brings out the natural poet in some children.
© Michael Hagan

Teachers will also want to include the poetry of Langston Hughes, Karla Kuskin, David McCord, Eve Merriam, Myra Cohn Livingston, and a host of other poets.

Two good anthologies of poetry for children are *The Scott, Foresman Anthology* (Sutherland and Livingston, 1984) and *Poetry and Verse for Urban Children* (Bissett, 1967), which contain poetry ranging from nursery rhymes to sonnets. Poetry can be included as part of a theme (later in this chapter we use a moon theme as an example) or as enrichment for topics of study in the classroom. For example, if the topic of study were colors, then *Hailstones and Halibut Bones: An Adventure in Color* (O'Neill, 1961) would be a good choice for enrichment. Poetry is written to be read aloud, and teachers should do so often. It is also important to encourage children to share poems they like with their classmates.

Writing poetry can encourage children to select words carefully, appreciate the use of figurative language, discover more colorful adjectives, and value the skill of talented poets. Before they begin to write, children should have many, many opportunities to listen to poetry. After sharing many examples, the teacher might lead a class discussion of the techniques used by the poet. Once they understand the form, the class could write a piece as a group and then as individuals. Greenberg (1978) suggests to teachers that they never offer negative criticism of children's efforts and that they not allow children to write rhyming poetry. He believes that children will not continue to attempt to write poetry if teachers are negative about their efforts and that children get so caught up in trying to produce words that rhyme that they lose meaning. He also suggests that, as in any writing, content should always be valued over form. Form can be polished later if the content is worthy of more work.

■ Literature for Independent Reading

Fiction

Literature available for children to choose in their free reading time should cover a wide range of reading levels, treat a variety of topics, and employ various formats. The range of reading abilities in a classroom of younger children can easily span five years; among older children, it may be even wider. Children's interests vary as much as those of adults, and changing themes of study throughout the year also mean changes in the class library. Teachers may choose to provide multiple copies of class favorites, but a single copy of most books is probably adequate.

For younger readers, include a wide variety of picture books, wordless picture books, books with repetitive language, and easy-to-read books. Many beginning readers will want to look at books that they know, so books that the teacher has read aloud and books of familiar stories, such as folk tales, are good choices. As children become concerned with text, they will often choose the beginning reading books. With children's progress in reading ability comes increasing sophistication in the class library. Children will read more books written in chapters and look for a wider variety of genres. By the end of elementary school, class libraries should contain books from all genres, on a broad diversity of topics and covering a wide span of reading difficulty.

Nonfiction

In addition to fiction, teachers will want to provide expository books as choices for independent reading. Books selected to enhance specific subject-matter themes must be evaluated in terms of accuracy of information, format, and style. The author must be careful to signal the inclusion of opinion in a factual format. Teachers will want to choose the most up-to-date books and to help children learn to check the facts with several sources. For example, children studying their state's history could read accounts of the same incidents in more than one textbook or reference book and compare them. Questions of format concern whether the material is organized logically and presented in segments that aid the children's comprehension. Like format, style may vary a great deal. How the author chooses to present facts can determine how palatable the facts are. Tomie dePaola's *The Cloud Book* (1975), *The Quicksand Book* (1977), and *The Popcorn Book* (1978) present the facts in the context of a story.

Books used to enhance social studies topics need to be selected carefully. For example, books of historical fiction add color and help to personalize a particular period of history, but historical fiction often distorts historical fact. Teachers who select such books should take care to help children understand any distortions and the reasons for their inclusion in the books. For example, teachers should explain that a mouse did not really talk to Ben Franklin; some incidents are invented because the author cannot know every detail of a character's life. As much as possible, use primary sources—accounts written by participants in or witnesses to the events chronicled. The books should also have a clearly defined perspective and should avoid superficial or sensationalized versions of historical events.

Libraries in most primary-grade classrooms will need many books about animals, plants, machines, the earth, insects, and space. The topics children study in science and social studies should be complemented by books that are available for free reading. For example, dinosaurs seem to be a very popular topic now, and there are several good books about dinosaurs, such as *The News about Dinosaurs* (Lauber, 1989). Because the interests of older children vary widely, teachers will want to include mystery stories, sports stories, survival stories, and stories about growing up.

It is difficult to draw the line between literature for children and literature for young adults. By the end of elementary school, some children

There's a book to fit every reader.
© Mimi Forsyth/Monkmeyer Press Photo Service

are beginning to read young-adult literature. Classroom libraries should include the works of such authors as Scott O'Dell, Cynthia Voight, Mildred Taylor, Ann Nolan Clark, and Joseph Krumgold. Some classes may be ready for the work of S. E. Hinton or Robert Cormier. The teacher will have to be very knowledgeable about the literature available and the needs of the class.

Children can keep a record of books read in free time by writing personal responses to books in a reading log, by simply writing the titles on a record sheet, or by preparing some sort of book report. Such records help teachers monitor students' interests, provide information about reading ability, and give clues to what to suggest for further reading—for example, another book by the same author or a book that broadens the child's interests. Whatever the teacher chooses to do, one caution is to emphasize the quality of reading rather than the number of books read. When success is measured in quantity, children have reason to favor books that are short and easy to read and have little incentive to reread a book.

Basing Reading and Writing Activities on Literature

Participating in drawing discussion webs that depict characters, plot, themes, and setting as they are discussed will aid children in their reading, as they build their knowledge of story structure, and in their writing, as they pay attention to these elements in their own narratives. Figure 7.3 is an example of a discussion web that might be developed after reading *Cracker Jackson* (Byars, 1985). Reading fairy tales might produce a discussion web built around common elements such as imaginary kingdoms or magical events (see Figure 7.4).

Particular genres offer opportunities for specialized analyses. For example, mystery stories must have a mystery and clues to the solution. Having read a mystery, children could be encouraged to reread and note the clues, including any that are misleading or irrelevant. Analysis of a biography might entail making a time line of major events in the life of the person or of world events that influenced the person's life. It might also involve comparison with other biographies of the same individual or with accounts of events as they appear in reference materials or journals. Realistic fiction requires that the characters, settings, and events be possible in the real world. Children can make charts of words that are descriptive of the characters, construct dioramas or other three-dimensional representations of the settings, and make maps of the action of the story.

Children's literature offers many possibilities for writing experiences: sequels, endings, stories following the same structure, diaries, journals, letters, newspaper articles, headlines, and advertisements. Children who have read *Dear Mr. Henshaw* (Cleary, 1983) could be encouraged to write letters to their favorite authors. *The Jolly Postman* (Ahlberg and Ahlberg, 1986) is excellent for letter writing examples. Children could write friendly letters, business letters, invitations, and postcards from one storybook character to another and share them with their classmates. After reading books of historical fiction, children might produce more serious letters as if from one historical character to another. They might also make up advertisements for products that characters might need. *A Gathering of Days* (Blos, 1979) is an example of journal writing. Children could write a journal

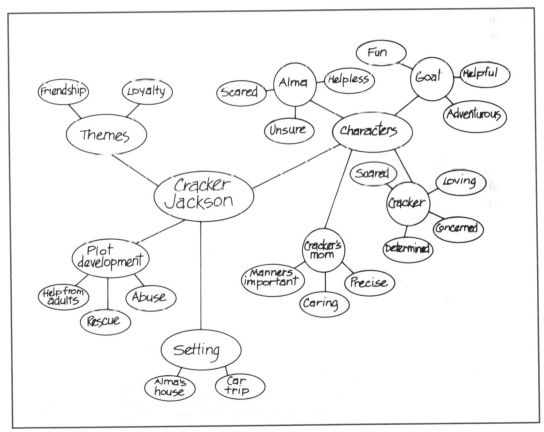

Figure 7.3   Discussion web based on *Cracker Jackson*, by Betsy Byars.
SOURCE: Adapted from Donna Norton, *Through the Eyes of a Child: An Introduction to Children's Literature* (Columbus, Ohio: Charles E. Merrill, 1987).

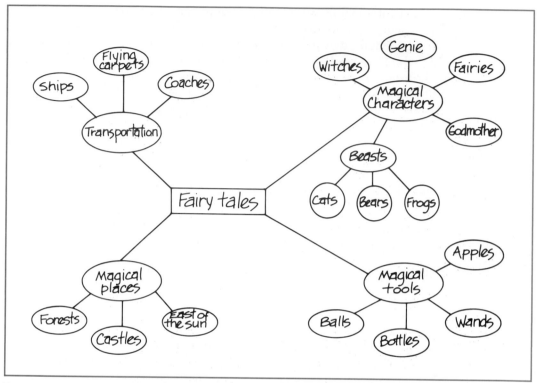

Figure 7.4   Discussion web based on fairy tales.
SOURCE: Adapted from Donna Norton, *Through the Eyes of a Child: An Introduction to Children's Literature* (Columbus, Ohio: Charles E. Merrill, 1987).

as if they were one of the characters in a book they are reading. For example, while reading *The Witch of Blackbird Pond* (Speare, 1958) they could write a journal for two weeks as if they were Kit.

Children can rewrite nursery rhymes or folk stories in various styles. A newspaper report based on "The Three Bears" might read:

Woodville Police Reports: Burglary at the home of the Three Bears, 3618 Woodland Drive. Missing: one bowl of porridge. Theft occurred between 8:30 and 9:30 A.M. on Thursday. The bear family, having left their home to go for a short walk while the porridge cooled, returned to find one bowl of porridge empty. Suspect is a juvenile seen running away from the home. The bears describe suspect as a young female with long blond pigtails. Police are looking for a young person known as Goldilocks for questioning in the case.

Children learning to use a thesaurus could rewrite a nursery rhyme in more complex language. ("A Trio of Sightless Rodents"). They might also enjoy rewriting a nursery rhyme or folk tale in modern language. The Ahlbergs' book *The Clothes Horse* (1987) is a collection of stories whose titles are common phrases. Children could follow its example by writing stories about phrases they hear. They could write newspaper headlines for the stories they read and let their classmates guess which books they go with. For example, they could write "Girl Rescued after Years of Living Alone on an Island."

Organizing for Reading Instruction

Reading instruction based on children's literature can be organized in several different ways. In individualized reading, each child chooses a book and reads it. In some classrooms, children are provided with study guides for the books they choose, and they can complete the activities at their own pace. Another strategy is to divide the class into small groups for reading,

Individual instruction allows this student teacher to concentrate on a first-grader's specific needs.
© Elizabeth Crews/The Image Works

discussing, and doing activities based on their chosen books. Organizing reading instruction around a theme or genre can apply to individual, small-group, or whole-group instruction.

■ Individualized Reading

Individualized reading instruction means that the children are allowed to select their own reading material and read it at their own pace. One advantage of individualized reading is high motivation: the child can read material that matches his or her interests and ability. Other advantages are (1) wide exposure to genres, (2) development of reading ability at an individual rate, and (3) individual attention for the child through a conference with the teacher. Individualized reading programs do not relieve the teacher of responsibility for reading instruction. Keeping good records of the child's progress is necessary for documenting learning. Conferences afford the teacher opportunities both to assess and to encourage the child. Individualized reading requires an accurate record-keeping system, assessment and evaluation by the teacher, and good time management to ensure provision of individual and group instruction. Teachers must also plan time for children to share their reading experiences. Possible disadvantages of individualized reading include (1) the risk of the child's choosing material that is not challenging, (2) the difficulty of monitoring growth when each child is working independently, and (3) the tremendous task of allocating time to individual conferences as well as small- and whole-group instruction. What teachers who choose individualized reading must remember is that individualized reading is not synonymous with sustained silent reading. While the children are reading, the teacher must be involved in holding conferences, assessing progress, and providing skills instruction.

In order to manage individualized programs more easily, some teachers develop study guides or packets of activities to accompany the books. Figure 7.5 is a portion of such a study guide. Figure 7.6 is a portion of a guide that was developed for use with primary-grade children. Some teachers prefer to place the children in groups that stay together to read and discuss each chapter and complete the activities; others permit the children to do the activities at their own pace and hold individual conferences with each child. In either case, children are encouraged to think about story elements, plot structures, and writing techniques and/or styles employed by the authors.

Teachers choosing to use study guides would want to provide a variety of activities to carry out rather than just answering questions about every book. Some guides could suggest activities in art, drama, and small-

Island of the Blue Dolphins

Chapter 1

Vocabulary

Aleut	kelp	ravine
intruders	ornaments	cormorants
mesa	toyon	parley

Questions

1. What does Won-a-pa-lei say that shows you that ships have come before?
2. What kind of trouble do you think occurred with the ships that came before?
3. What did Captain Orlov want?
4. What price was agreed upon?
5. What do you learn about the kind of person Won-a-pa-lei is when she keeps gathering roots even when she is excited and would rather run off with Ramo?
6. How do Won-a-pa-lei's people differ from us in their use of names?
7. When we describe one thing by saying it is *like* something else, we are creating a simile. When we describe something by saying it *is* something else, we are creating a metaphor. Find examples of similes and metaphors in Chapter 1.

Chapter 2

Vocabulary

league   pursued

Questions

1. In what ways did the Indians show their distrust of the Aleuts?
2. Do you think there would have been a difference if the Indians had shared their fish with the Aleuts? Why, or why not?
3. Draw the Island of the Blue Dolphins, using the information given about it in the chapter. Include a compass showing directions. Include land features such as the hills and Coral Cove.
4. Why did the villagers watch the Aleuts and the Aleuts watch the villagers?

Figure 7.5   Study guide for individualized reading.

Write as many words as you can that rhyme with cat.

Name as many words as you can that can be used to describe cats.

Figure 7.6   Study guide for *Hi, Cat!*, by Ezra Jack Keats.

group discussion. Most of us would never reread a novel we studied in a literature course because we analyzed it to death. A balance among types of responses will keep children from feeling that way about their reading. The challenge is to provide interesting activities for as many books as are required in the classroom.

Figure 7.7 is a general outline of the kinds of activities that would be taking place in the classroom while the children are reading. Figure 7.8 outlines a possible format for individual conferences with children about their reading. Teachers will select one or two questions from each category

A plan for individualized reading

I. Teacher–student planning
   A. Book selection
   B. Self-directed activities
   C. Selection of pupils for conference
   D. Selection of pupils for group work

II. Activities

Pupils

A. Read themselves out (i.e., to the point of satiation)
B. Preparation for teacher
C. Self-selected activities
   1. Book center
   2. Writing center
   3. Art center
   4. Science center
   5. Manipulative materials center
   6. Supply center

Teacher

A. Conferences
   1. Questions, etc.
   2. Records
   3. Closure
B. Group work
   1. Special-needs groups
   2. Friendship groups
   3. Interest groups
   4. Novel—creative reading

III. Sharing of individual activities

IV. Clean-up

Figure 7.7   Sample reading plan.

Conference

I. Comprehension skills
   A. Central thought
      1. What kind of story is this?
      2. What is it mainly about?
      3. Does its setting make a difference?
      4. Does its time affect the story?
      5. Does this book remind you of any other book?
      6. Did you think it is a _____ story? (happy, funny, exciting, scary, etc.)
      7. Could you describe this in a couple of words?

Figure 7.8   Sample guide for individual reading conference.

(continues)

B. Inferences and critical reading
   1. Do you think the story is really about _____?
   2. Is there something here that isn't actually said?
   3. Is there a lesson to be learned in this book?
   4. Was there anything in the story that was not the same as you've heard somewhere else?
   5. Do you think you can believe what it said?
   6. What is the problem of the character in the story?

C. Value judgments
   1. Do you agree or disagree with this story?
   2. What is your own opinion about _____ in the story?
   3. Is this something everyone should read?
   4. If only a few people should read it, who would you choose?
   5. Is the story making fun of us all?
   6. If you could pass a law, or have your own wish, would this book influence you?
   7. Do you trust what you read?
   8. Do you believe everything you read?
   9. Can you trust what this author says?

D. Author's purpose
   1. Who is the author?
   2. What do you know about the author's family, etc.?
   3. What other books of this author's do you know about?
   4. What do you feel the author is trying to tell people in his or her stories?
   5. If you could talk to the author, what would you tell him or her?
   6. Do you think the author has children of his or her own?
   7. Does the author like animals?
   8. What ideas are you sure about when you read this author's stories?

E. Necessary plot sequence
   1. Tell me the story.
   2. After _____, what happened next?
   3. Tell me what happened first, then _____.
   4. If such-and-such happened before so-and-so, does it make any difference in the story?
   5. If you could, would you change the story around at all?
   6. What was the best part of the story to you? Beginning, middle, end?

Figure 7.8   *(continues)*

II. Personality adjustment and reading selections
  A. Insight into personal interest in story
    1. Was this a good story?
    2. Why did you choose this book?
    3. Did you ever have an experience like this?
    4. Would you like to be just like the person in the story?
    5. What about this story made you angry?
    6. If you could become one of the characters in this story, which one would suit you?
    7. If you could, would you wave a magic wand and live in this time?
  B. Awareness of group reaction
    1. Who do you know that likes this type of book?
    2. Would they like this one?
    3. Are you going to tell them about it?
  C. Insight into possible personality behavior change
    1. Did you have a problem like this person in the story?
    2. Does this story make you feel like doing something?
    3. Did you see something about yourself after you finished this story that you didn't know before?
    4. Is there something here you didn't like and never would do?

III. The mechanical skills
  A. Word definitions
    1. Here is an unusual word. Can you tell me what it means?
    2. Here is another: _____.
    3. Can you tell me another word that means the same thing?
    4. If I said _____ (homonym or antonym), would you say this word was the same or the opposite of it?
    5. Did you find any words that meant something different when you read them somewhere else?
  B. Study skills
    1. Show me the index.
    2. Find the page where such-and-such is described.
    3. How do you find things in the index?
    4. Did the pictures help you read this book?
    5. Can you find the place on the map where the story was laid?
    6. Can you find the general topic of this story in another book?
  C. Ability to analyze unknown words
    1. Show me a word that you didn't know. How did you figure it out?

Figure 7.8   (continues)

2. What is in this word that you know (digraph, initial letter)?
3. Let me cover up part of it. Now what do you see? Say it. Now here's the whole word. Can you say it?

IV. Ability to hold audience attention
   A. Oral reading of selection
      1. What part of the story did you choose to read to me?
      2. Tell me what happened up to this point.
      3. (After the reading) Now tell me what happened next.
   B. Retelling of long story briefly

Figure 7.8   (continued)

Name			
Date	Book	Problems, concerns	Notes and Interests

Figure 7.9   Sample record-keeping form.

or focus on different categories of questions at each conference. Figure 7.9 suggests a record-keeping format for use in a ring binder, one sheet per child.

■ Literature Sets

Multiple copies of the same book, for children to read in small groups, are called *literature sets*. Grouping for literature sets is determined not by ability but by the children's interest. A group size of six or seven seems to work best. Groups of only two or three are too small to have lively discussions and differences of opinion. Groups that are too large afford too few opportunities for individual members to participate actively. The number of groups is determined by the time available and the teacher's ability to manage the groups, an important consideration because the teacher meets with each group as a member of the group, not as the director or leader.

To begin, the children meet in their groups to discuss the book and determine how far they will read before the next group meeting. They write their responses to their reading in their own individual logs, and the teacher or other children read and respond to their entries. Having finished the book, each group shares its reading with the other members of the class, whether by bulletin board, videotape, song, skit, poem, or other means.

Using literature sets with younger children may begin with shared reading of big books. While reading the print aloud, the teacher moves one hand under the line of print to demonstrate the directionality and return sweep of the lines. As the children become familiar with the story, they are encouraged to join in the reading, and later they may read it chorally with the teacher assisting only as needed. Finally, when the children can all read the story, they are given individual copies of the text and asked to read it to themselves and/or to a partner. The teacher helps the children discuss the author's choices of words or phrases and use of writing techniques. For example, the children may talk about story structure, words that signal the reader about what is to follow, or why they think the author chose one word as opposed to another. They will also discuss the story's meaning to them and their feelings about it.

Older children may be involved in more detailed discussions of writing styles or conventions. They may learn to evaluate their reading strategies (Did they read at an appropriate speed for the material? Did they use the author's organization to help them read more easily?) and the writing of the author. For example, when reading expository material they might want to know if the author is qualified to write about the topic and how to find out. When reading fiction, they might discuss what the author needed to know to write the piece and what information the author might have chosen to omit.

Children respond well to the opportunity to choose their reading material and to discuss with others what they are reading and writing. Teachers must work out ways of using group reading experiences that are comfortable for them—there is no formula that works for everyone. Figure 7.10 suggests some of the possibilities for using literature sets in the classroom with younger and older children. Teachers should draw freely on this outline, improvising as needed, rather than following it as a prescribed program.

The advantages of the literature-set approach include allowing the child to select his or her reading material, enabling children to share reading experiences with others, creating opportunities for small-group instruction, and facilitating the development of speaking, listening, reading, and writing around common interests. Use of literature sets requires that

Literature study groups

Primary grades

Teacher presents a choice of books
Children select book to read
Teacher leads reading
   Reading from a big book (if possible)
   Children and teacher discuss book
Children draw or write a response to book
Children participate in group discussions of reading
Rereading experiences
   Assisted reading
   Echo reading
   Teacher reads, children join in when possible
   Children read in pairs
   Children read individually
Extension activities
   Children write or dictate a story based on model of book
   Children draw/paint illustrations, murals, posters
   Children create puppet plays, mime activities, drama based on book
   Children review other books on same theme, by same author, and so
      on
Evaluation
   Participation in selecting, reading books
   Increasing ability in literacy skills
   Motivation/interest in reading

Older readers

Teacher selects and presents books
Children select book to read
Children read book independently
Children keep a log of reading responses
Children participate in group discussions of reading
Extension activities
   Children create posters, bookmarks, bulletin board based on book
   Children participate in written conversations (serial comments on
      paper, ultimately returned to originator) about book
   Children create songs, dances, drama based on book
   Children share poetry or special passages from book

Figure 7.10   Some uses of literature sets in the classroom.   *(continues)*
Source: Based on Dorothy Watson, Speech, Tucson, Ariz., December 1988.

Evaluation
Evidence of reflective thinking in discussion/writing
Children's evaluation of reading/writing
Children's increasing ability in literacy
    Critical reading
    Writing techniques modeled in individual writing
    Comprehension
    Other reading goals

Figure 7.10   *(continued)*

the teacher make important instructional decisions, including which books to offer and what activities should accompany each book.

■ Reading Based on a Genre or Theme

Some teachers organize their reading instruction around specific genres or themes. Children might be reading different books, but all within one category, such as historical fiction, fantasy, biographies, or science fiction. The teacher can develop a packet of generally applicable activities, some for completion by the class or group and some for each child to do individually, depending on the type of book.

Earlier in the chapter, we suggested extension activities based on reading one book, *Blueberries for Sal* (McCloskey, 1948). Another way to organize curriculum experiences is to use a thematic approach. Suppose the teacher chose the moon as an organizing theme. In addition to studying it scientifically, the class could listen to books and poetry about the moon, write their own stories or books, and use factual and reference books for research projects. The following are but a few of the many literary possibilities for classroom use:

1.   Read *Papa, Please Get the Moon for Me* (Carle, 1986). This very simple story presents the idea of the moon's phases. The book has folded pages; children can make their own books with folded or cut pages.

2.   Read *Many Moons* (Thurber, 1943). Compare the actual distance to the moon with the distances reported by the characters in the story. Highlight the various descriptions of the moon.

3.   Read *The Nightgown of the Sullen Moon* (Willard, 1983). This story has the structure of a myth in that it explains the cycles (disappearance) of the moon. Children could write other explanations for the regular disappearance of the moon. Be sure to note the words for "moon" in several languages.

4.   Read *Moon Song* (Baylor, 1982). This Indian legend explains the close relationship between the moon and coyotes and tells why coyotes howl at the moon. Children could read other Indian legends and write their own explanations of other relationships found in nature.

5.   Read some of the "Moon-Uncle" rhymes from *Moon-Uncle, Moon-Uncle* (Cassedy and Thampi, 1973), a collection of rhymes from India. The children could write their own rhymes about the moon.

6.   Read *Calendar Moon* (Belting, 1964). This book explains in poetry some of the names for the months from stories of different people around the world. Children could think about their own activities at different times of the year, select their own name for a month, and write an explanation of their chosen name.

7.   Read "The Moon and a Star" from *The Moon and a Star* (Livingston, 1965). This poem describes a child's experiences with the changing position of the moon in the night sky. Children could relate and write about their own experiences.

8.   Read the section on the moon from *Flower Moon Snow* (Mizumura, 1977), a collection of haiku. Children could write their own haiku after having heard or read these verses. This book is illustrated with woodcuts; children might make their own print illustrations for their haiku.

9.   Read *Full Moons: Indian Legends of the Seasons* (Budd, 1971) and *The Moon in Fact and Fancy* (Slote, 1971). Compare the moon myths that have been collected from various cultures. Children could write a myth explaining the phases of the moon.

10.   Read MacDonald's (1953) poem "The Wind and the Moon." Children can talk about times when they thought they did something that they did not actually do. Find other stories in which one of the characters thinks that he or she is in control of some element of nature.

11.   Make reference books about the moon available to the children. Encourage them to share information from the books that they are reading. Compare pictures, photographs, and facts from various books, such as these:

The Moon: For Young Explorers (Fenton, 1963)
Project Apollo: Mission to the Moon (Coombs, 1965)
The First Travel Guide to the Moon (Blumberg, 1980)
The Moon (Brenna, 1964)
We Land on the Moon: NASA's Project Apollo (Raymond, 1963)
The New Moon (Zim, 1980)
The Moon Seems to Change (Branley, 1960)

These books vary in reading difficulty and complexity of content. Children of many different abilities should be able to find something appropriate for them and share information with their classmates through reports, charts, songs, radio broadcasts, newspaper articles, and other writing.

12. Use the card catalog in the media center or library to find other books about the moon or with "moon" in the title. Examine their classifications and determine why they were classified as they were.

13. Look up "moon" in the encyclopedia. Compare the information provided there with what is in some of the reference books. How is the information organized? Write a class encyclopedia of facts about the moon.

14. Find other poems about the moon in anthologies of poetry. Compare some of the styles and forms. Write some poetry about the moon.

15. Ask the music specialist to help find songs about the moon. Learn some of them. The children could put together a booklet of their favorite songs and/or poetry about the moon.

16. Learn about the relationship of the moon and ocean tides. If you live near the ocean, learn to read the tide tables and discuss the importance of knowing about the tides to fishermen, visitors to the coast, industry, and so on.

Themes can be very simple or very complex and can last for varying lengths of time, depending on the age and interests of the class. Some teachers use themes for enrichment activities accompanying textbook studies; others organize their reading and writing programs around a theme in literature. Whichever the choice, a wide variety of literature can make the curriculum come alive.

Figure 7.11 is a packet of activities developed for fifth-graders by one teacher to accompany a theme based on nature. Each child would have selected an individual adventure book, and every child would be given a copy of the packet of activities to complete. Generally children are given two weeks in which to complete the reading and the activities. Some weeks in each year are open for children to choose a genre themselves and plan their own activities.

As you can see, this theme incorporates reading, language arts, and science instruction. It also provides for individual work and instruction in both small and large groups. Children would be working on their theme activities for a large part of each day. In fact, some teachers alternate themes that have an emphasis on science with themes that emphasize social studies and do not otherwise provide instruction in either science or social studies. The advantages of this approach include letting children make choices about their reading, permitting flexibility and choice in when to do the reading, being able to meet individual needs through packet materials, and allowing the opportunity to provide both group and individual instruction. The disadvantages include the amount of time the teacher must spend in developing the packets and the limitation that individual

ADVENTURE READING PACKET

NAME: _____

DUE DATE: _____

TEACHER CHECKS HERE	STUDENT CHECKS HERE	ASSIGNMENTS TO BE COMPLETED...
		1. Name of your adventure book: _____ _____ Author of your adventure book: _____ Number of chapters in your book: _____
		2. Copy the <u>definition</u> of "adventure" from the bulletin board:
		3. What does the word "summary" mean?
		4. Write a good <u>summary</u> of every chapter of your adventure book. Remember, a summary is a shortened form of what happened in the chapter, written in your OWN words. Write down the number of chapters you have and then cross off each one as your finish the summary:
		5. <u>Add one card to the class time line.</u> Have the teacher sign here when you've shown her the card and it is complete: _____ The item on your card must be about some adventure that really happened in history and does <u>not</u> have to have anything to do with the book you are reading. <u>What was your time line card about?</u>

Figure 7.11   Sample activities packet for a theme.
SOURCE: Developed by Lynda Hatch.

(continues)

ADVENTURE READING PACKET   NAME: _____

TEACHER CHECKS HERE	STUDENT CHECKS HERE	ASSIGNMENTS TO BE COMPLETED...
		6. Add five words to your personal dictionary.

The words are to come from the adventure book you are reading. You choose the words. Choose words that are new or interesting to you. List the five words here. Tell the page number where they were found in your book.

Have the teacher sign here when she has seen your completed dictionary and it has been done right: _____

Word   Page number

_____   _____

_____   _____

_____   _____

_____   _____

_____   _____

7. Write a pretend letter to one of the characters in your book.

This can be you writing the letter to a character OR it can be written as if it is from one character to another character.

Look on the class bulletin board to see how a "friendly letter" is written. Use that form when writing this pretend letter.

If you'd like to make the letter look old, ask the teacher to help you burn around the edges of your paper, after lightly painting it tan. If you do this, it is extra credit. Have the teacher sign here if you do this extra credit: _____

(NOTE: You must do a rough copy that is to be checked by the teacher. This needs to then be recopied on plain white ditto paper. Then paint the letter, burn the edges, and glue it on black construction paper.)

8. Complete the group "adventure-building" activity.

This activity will be done together in class on: _____.

After the stories are written, decorate your paper. Turn it in to the teacher as soon as it is done. Have the teacher sign here when your story is written and decorated: _____

9. Read and summarize an adventure article from one of the tubs on the reading table. Choose an article from either the regular tub or the careers tub. What was the title of the article you chose?

_____

(Remember, a magazine summary needs to be at least six sentences or a half page, minimum. Write it in your own words.)

Figure 7.11   (continues)

ADVENTURE READING PACKET

NAME: _____

TEACHER CHECKS HERE	STUDENT CHECKS HERE	ASSIGNMENTS TO BE COMPLETED...

10. Draw and color a picture of either:

    a) An adventure that happened to you, your family, or your friends. This is something that really happened.

    b) OR, about some part of the adventure book you read.

    Write a label on the picture to tell about it.

11. Answer this question in a good paragraph on your own paper.

    Why do you think the book you read is called an "adventure story?"

    In other words, why was it exciting with unusual challenges to the characters? If your book turned out to NOT be an adventure, explain why it was not.

    This question needs to be answered in a detailed PARAGRAPH, using complete sentences. Be sure to wait to answer this question until you've finished your book and summaries.

EXTRA CREDIT EXTRA CREDIT EXTRA CREDIT EXTRA CREDIT EXTRA CREDIT

A. Read another adventure book and write very brief chapter summaries OR one big summary at the end. You will get more extra credit if you do chapter summaries.

B. Do more than one time line card. Each card needs to be on a different topic. If you do an extra time line card, have the teacher sign here when it is done: _____

C. Add more words to your personal dictionary. On a separate paper, list the words and page numbers. Have the teacher sign here if you do this extra credit:
    Teacher's signature: _____
    Number of extra words: _____

D. Write an extra letter, as described in #7.

E. Draw and label another adventure picture, as described in #10.

F. Read and summarize another magazine article, as described in #9.

G. Watch an adventure story on TV or at the movies. It must be done during the two weeks of this packet. It is an adventure story only if it fits the definition from #2. Do the following:

    1. Have a parent sign to show you saw it: _____
    2. On paper, summarize the show.
    3. Tell the name of the show, date, time, and channel if it was on TV.
    4. Tell WHY the show fit the definition of adventure.

H. If you can think of any other extra credit adventure projects, check with the teacher first and then enjoy doing them. HAVE FUN!

Figure 7.11   (continues)

ADVENTURE
READING
PACKET

NAME: _____

WEEKS: _____

DUE DATE: _____

Have the teacher sign here when your
book is returned. (Or, have the
librarian sign if it's a library book
or a parent sign if it's a book from
home.)
Signature: _____

+3 points extra!
Have a parent sign here to show
he/she has seen the packet on the
1st or 2nd night. This will help
your parents know what work you have
to do.
Parent's signature: _____
Date: _____

Have another student in class (or) a parent sign here to show the following is done:

Signature: _____

-All work is completely done

-All extra papers that were added, have your name, project title, and assignment number
 on them. (You decide the title of the project.)

-All blanks filled in

-Each "Student Checks Here" box is checked off or colored in

-All extra papers are stapled behind the packet, in the order in which they occured
 on the packet

Have the teacher sign one of these boxes to show whether your packet was turned in
early, on time, or late. This must be signed at the time you turn in your packet!

Early	On Time	Late
+20 extra points if it is turned in on or before:	-0 if it is turned in at any time on the due date:	-10 points if it is turned in on or after

Figure 7.11 (continued)

reading selections places on the children's chances to interact with others who are sharing their reading experience.

Themes can be built around the work of a single author, letting the children choose which of the author's books to read. Children can discuss significant features of the author's work, themes that the author chooses, and other points of comparison and contrast in the author's work. For example, several of the works of Cynthia Voight feature the same characters. Usually the main character in one story is a supporting character in another story. Several of her books retell the same incident from the perspectives of different characters. Another author whose work might be used for thematic study is Katherine Paterson. Her books do not share the same characters, but they express important themes that the children could explore. So many others come to mind—the survival books of Scott O'Dell and Jean Craighead George, the historical fiction of Jean Fritz, the Anastasia books of Lois Lowry. Perhaps the children would enjoy reading *your* favorite childhood author.

In most classrooms, teachers will devote some reading time to each type of reading. For example, teachers will spend some time in group discussions of common reading material. They will plan for small-group or individualized reading of material that they and the children select cooperatively and provide opportunities for instruction and peer interaction. And they will encourage independent reading activities in which the children choose their own reading material and learn individually. "A total reading program should contain various combinations of teacher and student interaction and selection of literature so that children develop as thoughtful, proficient readers" (Hiebert and Colt, 1989, p. 19).

■ Major Ideas in This Chapter

- ■ Children's literature is important in providing motivation and interest in the reading/writing program. Children will be more likely to want to read real books than portions of a book designed for reading instruction.

- ■ Picture books help children learn sight vocabulary and story structure, and they can inspire writing experiences for both younger and older children. Picture books are available about a wide range of topics and for audiences of different ages.

- ■ Books for reading aloud should be carefully selected by the teacher. Reading aloud can contribute to improved reading ability, heighten interest in reading, and broaden children's exposure to various genres.

- Experiences of writing in many formats, such as diaries, journals, letters, stories, and poems can be encouraged through children's literature.

- Literature can serve as the core for developing curriculum by building activities around one book or around themes that encompass many books.

? Discussion Questions
Focusing on the Teacher You Are Becoming

1. How do you select books for your own reading? Can you use any of the same techniques to help children select books in a classroom?
2. Compare and contrast the various approaches to organizing reading instruction around literature presented in this chapter.
3. Many basal publishers are advertising their books as "whole language" readers because they include literature. Is that all that is needed to make a program "whole language?" If not, what other elements should be present?
4. Discuss the place of literature in the reading program: should it be the basic source of reading material or should literature activities be for enrichment?

✓ Field-Based Applications

1. Choose a picture book and develop plans for extended reading and writing activities based on the book.
2. Choose one of the Newbery medal-winning books and develop a study guide to accompany the book. Be sure that writing activities are included in your guide.
3. Plan one variation of the text of a book with predictable language that would help beginning readers master a sight vocabulary.
4. Plan a writing experience (not a narrative) based on children's literature.
5. Choose a book for reading aloud and practice reading it well. List as many possibilities as you can for children's growth from the reading experience (vocabulary, listening, language patterns, etc.).
6. Choose a topic in social studies or science and develop plans to enhance the study of that topic through children's literature.

7. Participate with some of your peers in a literature study group. Keep a log of your responses to your own reading and to the group's discussions.

⊡ References and Suggested Readings

Bond, Guy L., and Dykstra, Robert. "The Cooperative Program in First Grade Reading Instruction." *Reading Research Quarterly* 2 (1967): 5–142.

Bridge, Connie A.; Winograd, Peter N.; and Haley, Darliene. "Using Predictable Materials vs. Preprimers to Teach Beginning Sight Words." *The Reading Teacher* 36 (May 1983): 884–891.

Cullinan, Bernice E. "Books in the Classroom." *Horn Book* 62 (November/December 1986): 766–768.

Cullinan, Bernice E., ed. *Children's Literature in the Reading Program.* Newark, Del.: International Reading Association, 1987.

Cullinan, Bernice E. *Literature and the Child.* 2nd ed. New York: Harcourt Brace Jovanovich, 1989.

Cullum, Albert. *The Geranium on the Window Sill Just Died But Teacher You Went Right On.* Belgium: Harlin Quist, 1971.

Galda, Lee. "Teaching Higher Order Reading Skills with Literature: Intermediate Grades." In *Children's Literature in the Reading Program,* edited by Bernice Cullinan. Newark, Del.: International Reading Association, 1987.

Greenberg, David. *Teaching Poetry to Children.* Portland, Ore.: Continuing Education Publications, 1978.

Hiebert, Elfrieda, and Colt, Jacalyn. "Patterns of Literature-Based Reading Instruction." *The Reading Teacher* 43 (October 1989): 14–20.

Johnson, Terry D., and Louis, Daphne. *Literacy through Literature.* Portsmouth, N.H.: Heinemann Educational Books, 1987.

Lawrence, Paula, and Harris, Virginia. "A Strategy for Using Predictable Books." *Early Years* 16 (May 1986): 34–35.

May, Frank. *Reading as Communication: An Integrated Approach.* Columbus, Ohio: Charles E. Merrill, 1986.

Monson, Dianne L., ed. *Adventuring with Books.* Urbana, Ill.: National Council of Teachers of English, 1985.

Norton, Donna. *Through the Eyes of a Child: An Introduction to Children's Literature.* 2nd ed. Columbus, Ohio: Charles E. Merrill, 1987.

Rhodes, Lynn. "I Can Read! Predictable Books as Resources for Reading and Writing Instruction." *The Reading Teacher* 34 (February 1981): 511–518.

Roberts, Patricia. *Alphabet: A Handbook of ABC Books and Activities for the Elementary Classroom.* Metuchen, N.J.: Scarecrow Press, 1984.

Trelease, Jim. *The New Read-Aloud Handbook.* Newark, Del.: Penguin/International Reading Association, 1989.

Tway, Eileen. *Writing Is Reading: 26 Ways to Connect.* Urbana, Ill.: ERIC Clearinghouse on Reading and Communication and the National Council of Teachers of English, 1985.

Watson, Dorothy. Speech in Tucson, Ariz., December 1988.
Wuertenberg, Jacque. "Reading and Writing for Every Child." Seminar, Oregon
    State University, 1983.

Journals

Childhood Education
Association for Childhood Education International
11141 Georgia Ave., Suite 200
Wheaton, MD 20902

Horn Book
The Horn Book, Inc.
Park Square Building
31 St. James Ave.
Boston, MA 02116

Language Arts
National Council of Teachers of English
1111 Kenyon Rd.
Urbana, IL 61801

The Reading Teacher
International Reading Association
800 Barksdale Rd.
PO Box 8139
Newark, DE 19714

Young Children
National Association for the Education of Young Children
1834 Connecticut Ave., N.W.
Washington, DC 20009-5786

Children's Books

Ahlberg, Janet, and Ahlberg, Allan. *The Jolly Postman*. Boston: Little, Brown, 1986.
Ahlberg, Janet, and Ahlberg, Allan. *The Clothes Horse*. New York: Viking Kestrel,
    1987.
Alda, Arlene. *Arlene Alda's ABC Book*. Berkeley: Celestial Arts, 1981.
Aliki. *How a Book Is Made*. New York: Thomas Y. Crowell, 1986.
Anno, Mitsumasa. *Anno's Alphabet: An Adventure in Imagination*. New York:
    Thomas Y. Crowell, 1975.
Anno, Mitsumasa. *Anno's Journey*. New York: Philomel Books, 1977.
Anno, Mitsumasa. *Anno's Magical ABC: An Anamorphic Alphabet*. New York:
    Philomel Books, 1981.
Anno, Mitsumasa. *Anno's U.S.A.* New York: Philomel Books, 1983.

Armstrong, William H. *Sounder*. New York: Harper & Row, 1969.

Baylor, Byrd. *Hawk, I'm Your Brother*. New York: Macmillan, 1976.

Baylor, Byrd. *If You Are a Hunter of Fossils*. New York: Scribner's, 1980.

Baylor, Byrd. *I'm in Charge of Celebrations*. New York: Scribner's, 1986.

Baylor, Byrd. *Moon Song*. New York: Scribner's, 1982.

Baylor, Byrd. *The Way to Start a Day*. New York: Aladdin, 1977.

Baylor, Byrd. *Your Own Best Secret Place*. New York: Scribner's, 1979.

Belting, Natalia. *Calendar Moon*. New York: Holt, Rinehart & Winston, 1964.

Bisset, Donald J., ed. *Poetry and Verse for Urban Children*. 3 vols. New York: Chandler Publishing, 1967.

Blos, Joan. *A Gathering of Days*. New York: Macmillan, 1979.

Blumberg, Rhoda. *The First Travel Guide to the Moon*. New York: Four Winds Press, 1980.

Branley, Franklyn M. *The Moon Seems to Change*. New York: Thomas Y. Crowell, 1960.

Brenna, Virgilio. *The Moon*. New York: Golden Press, 1964.

Brown, Marcia. *Cinderella*. New York: Atheneum, 1954.

Budd, Lillian. *Full Moons: Indian Legends of the Seasons*. New York: Rand McNally, 1971.

Byars, Betsy. *Cracker Jackson*. New York: Puffin Books, 1985.

Carle, Eric. *Papa, Please Get the Moon for Me*. Natick, Mass.: Picture Book Studio USA, 1986.

Cassedy, Sylvia, and Thampi, Parvathi. *Moon-Uncle, Moon-Uncle: Rhymes from India*. Garden City, N.Y.: Doubleday, 1973.

Cleary, Beverly. *Dear Mr. Henshaw*. New York: Dell, 1983.

Comenius, John Amos. *Orbis Pictus: The World Illustrated*. 1657.

Coombs, Charles. *Project Apollo: Mission to the Moon*. New York: Morrow, 1965.

dePaola, Tomie. *The Cloud Book*. New York: Holiday House, 1975.

dePaola, Tomie. *The Popcorn Book*. New York: Scholastic Book Services, 1978.

dePaola, Tomie. *The Quicksand Book*. New York: Holiday House, 1977.

Dragonwagon, Crescent. *Alligator Arrived with Apples: A Potluck Alphabet Feast*. New York: Macmillan, 1987.

Elting, Mary, and Folsum, Michael. *Q Is for Duck: An Alphabet Guessing Game*. New York: Clarion Books, 1980.

Emberly, Barbara. *Drummer Hoff*. Englewood Cliffs, N.J.: Prentice-Hall, 1967.

Evans, C. S. *Cinderella*. New York: Viking Press, 1919, 1972.

Farber, Norma. *As I Was Crossing Boston Common*. Berkeley: Creative Arts Book Company, 1973.

Fenton, Carroll L. *The Moon: For Young Explorers*. New York: John Day, 1963.

Hoguet, Susan R. *I Unpacked My Grandmother's Trunk*. New York: Dutton, 1983.

Hooks, William H. *Moss Gown*. New York: Clarion Books, 1987.

Irvine, Joan. *How to Make Pop-Ups*. New York: Morrow Junior Books, 1987.

Keats, Ezra Jack. *The Snowy Day*. New York: Scholastic Book Services, 1962.

Kitamura, Satoshi. *What's Inside? The Alphabet Book*. New York: Farrar, Straus & Giroux, 1987.

Lauber, Patricia. *The News about Dinosaurs*. New York: Bradbury Press, 1989.

Lee, Dennis. *Alligator Pie*. Toronto: Macmillan of Canada, 1974.

Lee, Dennis. *Garbage Delight*. Boston: Houghton Mifflin, 1977.

L'Engle, Madeleine. *A Swiftly Tilting Planet*. New York: Dell, 1978.

L'Engle, Madeleine. *A Wind in the Door*. New York: Dell, 1973.

L'Engle, Madeleine. *A Wrinkle in Time*. New York: Dell, 1962.

Lewis, C. S. *The Lion, the Witch and the Wardrobe*. (Book 1 of *The Chronicles of Narnia*.) New York: Collier, 1950.

Lionni, Leo. *Frederick's Fables*. New York: Pantheon Books, 1985.

Livingston, Myra Cohn. *The Moon and a Star*. New York: Harcourt, Brace & World, 1965.

Lobel, Arnold. *Fables*. New York: Harper & Row, 1980.

Louie, Al-Ling. *Yeh-Shen*. New York: Philomel Books, 1982.

Lucas, Mrs. E. V.; Crane, Lucy; and Edwards, Marian, trans. *Grimms' Fairy Tales*. New York: Grosset & Dunlap, 1925.

McCloskey, Robert. *Blueberries for Sal*. New York: Viking, 1948.

MacDonald, George. "The Wind and the Moon." In *The Moon Is Shining Bright as Day*, compiled by Ogden Nash. New York: Lippincott, 1953.

MacLachlin, Patricia. *Sarah Plain and Tall*. New York: Harper & Row, 1985.

Martin, Bill, Jr. *Brown Bear, Brown Bear*. New York: Holt, Rinehart & Winston, 1970.

Mizumura, Kazue. *Flower Moon Snow*. New York: Thomas Y. Crowell, 1977.

Musgrove, Margaret. *Ashanti to Zulu: African Traditions*. New York: Dial Press, 1976.

O'Neill, Mary. *Hailstones and Halibut Bones: An Adventure in Color*. Garden City, N.Y.: Doubleday, 1961.

Prelutsky, Jack. *It's Valentine's Day*. New York: Scholastic, 1983.

Prelutsky, Jack. *My Parents Think I'm Sleeping*. New York: Greenwillow, 1985.

Prelutsky, Jack. *The New Kid on the Block*. New York: Greenwillow, 1984.

Provensen, Alice, and Provensen, Martin. *A Peaceable Kingdom: The Shaker Abecedarius*. New York: Viking, 1978.

Raymond, John. *We Land on the Moon: NASA's Project Apollo*. Long Island, N.Y.: Child Guide Publications, 1963.

Ryden, Hope. *Wild Animals of America ABC*. New York: Dutton, 1988.

Sendak, Maurice. *Where the Wild Things Are*. New York: Scholastic Book Services, 1963.

Silverstein, Shel. *A Light in the Attic*. New York: Harper & Row, 1981.

Silverstein, Shel. *Where the Sidewalk Ends*. New York: Harper & Row, 1974.

Slote, Alfred. *The Moon in Fact and Fancy*. New York: World Publishing Company, 1971.

Speare, Elizabeth. *The Witch of Blackbird Pond*. New York: Dell, 1958.

Steig, William. *Roland the Minstrel Pig*. New York: Windmill Books, 1968.

Steptoe, John. *Mufaro's Beautiful Daughters*. New York: Lothrop, Lee and Shepard, 1987.

Sutherland, Zena, and Livingston, Myra Cohn. *The Scott, Foresman Anthology of Children's Literature*. Glenview, Ill.: Scott, Foresman, 1984.

Tafuri, Nancy. *Jungle Walk*. New York: Greenwillow, 1988.

Thurber, James. *Many Moons*. New York: Harcourt Brace Jovanovich, 1943.

Van Allsburg, Chris. *Jumanji*. Boston: Houghton Mifflin, 1981.

Van Allsburg, Chris. *The Mysteries of Harris Burdick*. Boston: Houghton Mifflin, 1984.

Vuong, Lynette Dyer. *The Brocaded Slipper and Other Vietnamese Tales*. Menlo Park, Calif.: Addison-Wesley, 1982.

White, E. B. *Charlotte's Web*. New York: Scholastic, 1952.

Wilder, Laura Ingalls. *Little House on the Prairie*. New York: Harper & Row, 1953.

Willard, Nancy. *The Nightgown of the Sullen Moon*. New York: Harcourt Brace Jovanovich, 1983.

Williams, Vera. *Cherries and Cherry Pits*. New York: Greenwillow, 1986.

Williams, Vera, and Williams, Jennifer. *Stringbean's Trip to the Shining Sea*. New York: Greenwillow, 1988.

Yolen, Jane. *Owl Moon*. New York: Philomel Books, 1987.

Yorinks, Arthur. *Hey, Al!* New York: Farrar, Straus & Giroux, 1986.

Zim, Herbert S. *The New Moon*. New York: Morrow, 1980.

Chapter 8

![black bar]

When Children Write Their Own Reading Material

Chapter Overview

- Language experience is a method of teaching reading in which children write material that is then used for reading instruction.

- Language-experience methodology is supported by psychological research and research on the contributions that writing makes to the development of reading.

- Language-experience and whole-language advocates share many beliefs about the reading process and learning to read.

- Teaching children about specific skills is part of the cycle of instruction in the language-experience approach.

- Language experience activities can easily be integrated with other aspects of classroom instruction, including use of a basal reader and writing with a word processor. Children edit, polish, and publish their writings in various forms for various audiences.

- Teaching reading with the language-experience approach requires structure and organization in the classroom, in record keeping, and in communicating with parents and with other teachers.

Observing in your local elementary school, you have been visiting different classes all day. This morning you were in a kindergarten classroom and a primary classroom, and now you are in a fifth-grade class. All day you have seen children busily working on various writing and reading projects. The kindergarten children were dictating their observations of their visit to a local dairy farm as their teacher was recording them on a large piece of paper. Afterwards she read all the comments back to the group, moving her hand under each phrase. Then she asked all the children to read with her what the class had said about the trip. You wondered what further use, if any, the teacher plans to make of the chart.

In the primary classroom, the teacher was reading *Chicken Soup with Rice* (Sendak, 1962). After several repetitions, you realized that the children were not hearing this story for the first time; most of them knew it by heart. The teacher then brought out a chart showing the months of the year and asked the children to think about things that are part of their experience in each of the months. They brainstormed several ideas for each month while the teacher wrote their suggestions on the chalkboard. After a few minutes, the teacher asked the children to select a month that they wish to write about. Reminding them of the refrain " . . . once, . . . twice, . . . chicken soup with rice" repeated in the Sendak book, she encourages the children to follow this model in writing their own descriptions of the months.

The fifth-grade children are busy with a variety of projects that revolve around their study of the United States. Some are making travel posters for a region of the nation, some are writing letters to tourist bureaus in various places to get information, some are using the resources of the media center in writing reports about various states or regions, and some are making charts and graphs that compare information about the various regions. It is obvious to you that these children are gaining skill in finding and presenting information. Are there also specific reading and writing skills that they are developing through these experiences?

Language Experience

Definition

What is happening in each of these classrooms is called the *language-experience approach* to reading instruction. In simple terms, using the language-experience approach in reading instruction means presenting children with some sort of stimulus to which they write a response, or they write about something they choose to write about. The writing that they produce is used for teaching the various skills of reading. The kindergarten class had experienced a trip to the dairy farm (probably with some advance preparation, such as seeing pictures of dairy cows, milking machinery, and hay and talking about the source of the milk at snack time). After the trip, the children stated their observations. The teacher recorded their words on a chart, read their words back to them, and then invited them to read along with her.

The next day, the teacher could use the chart for skills instruction. After a short discussion of the trip and their report on it, the teacher would reread the chart. Then, depending on the children's needs, the teacher could have them find all the words that began with a given sound, perhaps /f/, and underline or highlight them. Individual children could be asked to match word cards with words on the chart. They could find all the punctuation marks and think about why they were used, identify all the capital letters, or practice whatever other skills the teacher felt they needed. After perhaps another reading or two, the teacher might bring in books about dairy farms or farms of other kinds and read them to the children, who would compare their own descriptions with the descriptions written by other authors. Maybe they would add their report to a large scrapbook about their experiences; maybe the teacher would type the text onto pages that could be made into booklets for each child. The decisions about the direction of instruction in language-experience strategies rest with the teacher; this approach is truly teacher dependent.

Language experience for older children usually would not include the taking of dictation. Even in kindergarten, children would do the writing much of the time. Dictation is used for specific purposes by the teacher and is not always a part of the instruction. Having written their first draft, children would work through the writing process and share materials for reading. Older children would also have some group instruction in skills as needed. For example, they could compare the writing styles of reference books and newspapers, or they could be led to think about the vocabulary needed for persuading tourists to spend their travel money in a certain state.

Some of us taught ourselves to use the language-experience approach long before we had a name for this strategy. We learned it when faced with children who did not respond well to basal reader instruction and who had had many failures in their reading experiences. Language experience offered a way to tap these children's interests and vocabulary and to make reading something meaningful and relevant to their lives. Many teachers choose language experience for readers who are not progressing as well as they might in the basal program. Other teachers turn to language experience for those readers who need a challenge and whose interests do not conform to the selections in the basal. For gifted children, language experience offers the opportunity to move along the reading continuum as quickly as they can while writing and reading about topics that are personally interesting.

■ Advantages of Language-Experience Reading

As a method of reading instruction, language experience has many advantages. In Chapter 2, we described reading as a developmental process, one that is closely related to the child's understanding of language. In Chapter 3, we further described writing as a developmental process related to the child's understanding of language and how it works. The language-experience approach to reading brings together the child's experiences and the child's expressions about experiences through the processes of speaking, reading, and writing. This connection between experience and language is the greatest advantage of using language experience. When asked to read a basal reader, children may face a selection for which they have no background experience. Some children can produce a letter-perfect decoding of the material without any real understanding of the message. Remember that reading is constructing a message from print (Goodman, 1986). Materials for reading instruction in language experience are always relevant, current, and meaningful—characteristics not always found in other types of material. Figure 8.1 is a reproduction of a first-grader's story about science. This child was not succeeding in reading the basal reader, but he loved anything about science.

Language experience builds on the child's knowledge of language and how it works. For example, as children write their own reading material, they reveal their understanding of the conventions of word spacing, capitalization, punctuation, and paragraphing. A teacher attempting to help children become more skillful readers will not spend instructional time on teaching capitalization to children who have demonstrated that they understand it; for them, that instruction is redundant. (As new instances of need for capitalization arise, such as words in a title, instruction will be given.) For children who do not yet write sentences at all, however, instruction in capitalization is useless because they cannot yet apply it. The children who need such instruction—those just beginning to write sentences—can be easily identified using a language-experience approach.

Another advantage of the language-experience approach is that it treats language as a whole, not as bits and pieces. Children learning through language experience do not practice language skills outside the act of communication. Practice of a "proper" form, such as the old drills on *can* and *may,* when the form is not needed for communication is not useful in helping children speak or write more effectively. A teacher can insist that a young child repeat the form "My brother and I," but until the child can hear the difference between "Me and my brother" and "My brother and I" and has a need to use the more mature form, practicing the skill will not change the child's oral or written language. In the same way, children do not need to practice letter–sound relationships outside meaningful text. Children have learned a great deal about language before they ever have any formal instruction in it; language experience allows the teacher to build on that knowledge.

Language experience has some psychological advantages, too, as a method of reading instruction. One of them is the feeling of success that is possible for every child. Children are compared only with themselves, not with other children, and success is measured in terms of individual growth rather than ranking in the class. Research has found that success is necessary for more success (Berliner, 1984). Too often teachers, striving to challenge students, have given them tasks that result in failure. What is needed for maximum achievement is the opportunity to be successful over and

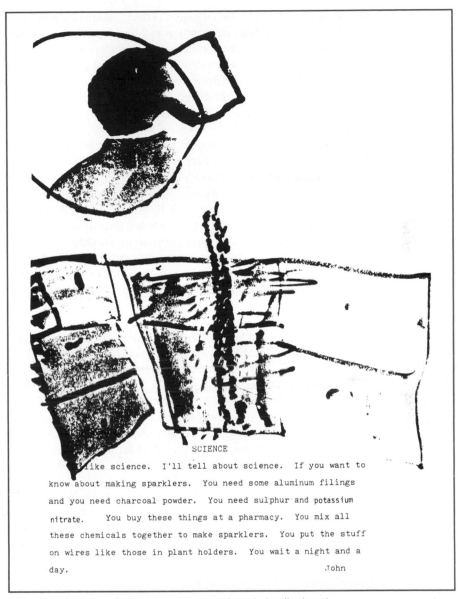

SCIENCE

...ike science. I'll tell about science. If you want to know about making sparklers. You need some aluminum filings and you need charcoal powder. You need sulphur and potassium nitrate.   You buy these things at a pharmacy. You mix all these chemicals together to make sparklers. You put the stuff on wires like those in plant holders. You wait a night and a day.   John

Figure 8.1   Story by a first-grader who was not mastering the basal.

over. In many classrooms, all the children know who reads the most diffi-cult material and who does not. In language-experience classrooms, such comparisons are not easily made.

Language experience is also highly motivating. No words are quite as precious to us as our own words. One group of low-achieving readers in first grade wrote their own stories. When the stories were returned to them typed and bound, their response was a joyous "These are *our* words!" Children need to feel that their own words are important.

Using language experience as a method for teaching reading will not necessarily raise children's reading scores on standardized tests, but studies have shown that children participating in language experience have better concepts of themselves as readers and a more positive attitude toward reading (Harris, 1969; Wilson and Parkey, 1970). Children who feel more capable as readers are much more likely to choose reading when given a choice of activities. Just as adults do not like to participate in activities in which they do not do well, children prefer those activities in which they perceive their performance to be positive. Lillian Katz (1986) has said that one of our jobs in education is to help children develop the disposition to continue an activity when they are not required to do so. We want readers who can read, and who choose to read outside of school. Language experience, because of its close connection to real experience, tends to help children view reading and writing as responses to events in their lives, not as something one does for a short period of time in school. One young man of about six must have had a teacher who used language experience in his classroom. Exploring the tide pools at the coast with his father one July, he was overheard to exclaim, "We can make a book about this when we get home!" He had the idea about reading and writing!

Teachers who choose language experience must have respect for the children and their language and thinking. One way to demonstrate that respect is to share children's own written materials with other class members and use them for instruction. Children who come to school from different cultural or linguistic backgrounds may be required to read in the basal a language far removed from their home language. Teachers must accept the child's language as a vital part of the child and then help the child gain competence in using more standard English. A child's reading experience may vary dramatically, depending on the level of acceptance and respect accorded his or her language in school. Some children may not be allowed to speak their home language at school and may be forced to begin reading instruction in a language that is very foreign to them.

■ Research on Language Experience

There is not much current research on language experience as an approach to reading instruction, primarily because research for the past few years has focused on whole-language instruction. Researchers who compared groups using language experience and basal readers reported that children in language-experience programs made gains in oral language (Stauffer and Pikulski, 1974; Cox, 1971). When they used language experience with a

Children's own art work can serve as a potent stimulus for writing.
© *Janice Fullman/The Picture Cube*

low-achieving reading group, Bridge, Winograd, and Haley (1983) found that it spurred children in their acquisition of sight vocabulary, encouraged the use of contextual clues, and created more positive feelings about reading aloud. As one would expect, children's writing abilities increase when they write their own material (Oehlkers, 1971; M. Stauffer, 1973). Children who do more writing also tend to be better spellers (Cramer, 1970). Children do develop a satisfactory reading vocabulary when they are engaged in language-experience instruction (Hall, 1965; Kelly, 1975).

In a study that found most independent skill-practice exercises to be ineffective in fostering beginning reading, Evans and Carr (1985) identified writing as an exception to that pattern. They recorded a positive relationship between reading achievement and activities that involved writing, which helps children gain insight into letter–sound correspondences and therefore serves to reinforce practice in word analysis. These and many other studies have confirmed that the language-experience approach can help children develop as competent readers and better writers with more positive feelings about reading.

The authors of *Becoming a Nation of Readers* (Anderson, Hiebert, Scott, and Wilkinson, 1985, p. 79) speak in support of writing in the reading program:

> Opportunities to write have been found to contribute to knowledge of how written and oral language are related, and to growth in phonics, spelling, vocabulary development, and reading comprehension. Students who write frequently and discuss their writing with others approach reading with what has been termed the "eye of the writer."

The first-grader who wrote "Seagulls" (Figure 8.2) demonstrates both knowledge of how language works and a wonderful sense of the poetic. Not all the spelling is conventional, and neither is the placement of words on the page, but surely every teacher would value the child's abilities.

Both Calkins (1986) and Graves (1983), in their work with children's writing, have observed that when children write they also read. They read to get started writing again, they read to enjoy what they have written, they read to edit, and they read to share their writing. Reading contributes to growth in writing and writing contributes to success in reading. Children develop strategies in their writing that transfer to their reading. Boutwell

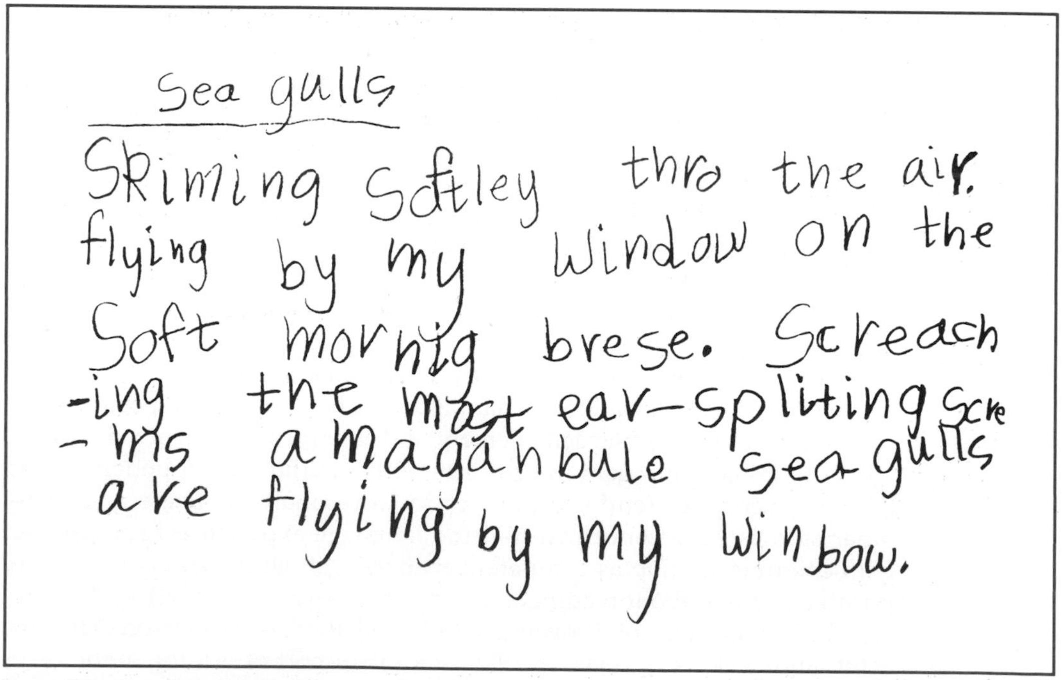

> Sea gulls
>
> Skiming softley thro the air.
> flying by my window on the
> soft mornig brese. Screach
> -ing the most ear-spliting scre
> -ms a magahbule sea gulls
> are flying by my winbow.

Figure 8.2   Story by a first-grader.

(1983) described the strategy used by one child when she met a confusing passage in her reading (p. 725): "When Marta encountered confusing parts, she reread them. This strategy sprang from the same question she asked in reading her own writing: Does this make sense?"

The Language-Experience Approach

Relationship to Whole-Language Instruction

More than once in this book, we have talked about whole-language instruction as instruction that begins with meaningful material and then helps children with the skills of reading as they are needed in order to achieve meaning. This progression from whole to part to whole is, by definition, required in the language-experience approach. Points at which language-experience advocates and whole-language advocates diverge are the follow-up activities planned for the children's writing and the strong emphasis of whole language on genre restrictions on writing. In whole-language instruction, writing would most typically follow reading instruction. For example, children might read a story and then write a review of that story or use the story as a model for their writing. In language experience, the writing usually comes first, and reading instruction is based on the children's writing.

Advocates of whole language believe that all writing is bound by the rules of the genre. In other words, all narratives have certain structures in common, an essay has certain structures that define it as an essay, and textbooks or reference books have certain structures. Some teachers using language experience have not been especially aware of the restraints on writing that are imposed by the genre and have therefore failed to help children become aware of the genre and the audience for their writing. Language experience at its best always extends the children's work to the work of other authors who have written on the same or similar topics and uses the literature as a model for future writing. For example, if children have written about their experience in making soup, the teacher might then read *Stone Soup* (Brown, 1947) and encourage some children to write in narrative style rather than "report" style. Others might find a soup cookbook and write an introduction to their own collection of favorite family soup recipes. There are numerous opportunities for connecting children's experiences, their writing, their reading, and the worlds of literature and expository writing.

In other respects, the language-experience approach and whole-language instruction are very much alike. They both honor language and believe that reading is for meaning. Both treat skills instruction in a meaningful context and want children actively involved in learning to read. They both believe that language, reading, and writing are learned through children's involvement in using them, not through activities that are separated from real communication.

■ Experience and Language—Bringing Them Together

If you choose language experience as a strategy for teaching reading, how do you get all the instruction done? How do you arrange for enough experiences and group the students for skills instruction? Must everything be taught individually? How will you keep records? If one of the children in your class transfers to another school, how will you report to the child's new teacher? What about next year's teacher? What about how to inform parents about their children's progress in reading? This section is a brief "how-to-do-it" guide offering some ideas for how to manage language experience. However, each teacher must work out his or her own system; following a set pattern is not what language experience is about. It is about making professional decisions concerning reading instruction and being

Instruction in the conventions of writing is still an important part of the reading/writing program.
© Elizabeth Hamlin/Stock, Boston

accountable for those decisions. These are the basic steps in language experience for young children:

1. selection of the purpose for instruction
2. presentation of the stimuli
3. discussion
4. writing
5. reading
6. skills instruction as needed
7. extension to the work of other authors.

Selection of Purpose

The first step in language-experience instruction is to determine the focus of instruction. Suppose a child had brought a frog to school and the children were excited about the frog and wanted to write about it. You would consider the age, experience, and previous writing of the children in establishing the most important goals of this specific writing experience. If the children were just beginning to read and write, you might want to emphasize the /fr/ blend; if they were beginning independent readers, you might want to concentrate on the sight words that they recognize; if they have a little more experience, you might focus on the different story structures of reports about frogs and toads, narratives about frogs, and personal observations about frogs. The purpose for instruction will serve as a guide in determining how the other steps are implemented.

Presentation of Stimuli

Finding something for children to write about should not become a problem for a teacher when interesting things are going on all the time. In a classroom where there are animals, visitors, and activities evolving out of the teacher's and children's interests, the stimuli for language experience are just daily activities. In response to the children's interest in frogs and toads, the teacher finds books and poems about frogs. The children take a walk to a nearby pond and collect some tadpoles, which they put into an aquarium in the classroom. The tadpoles, frogs, and books about toads and frogs all become the stimuli for writing. While taking advantage of an expressed interest of the children, the teacher has arranged for the stimuli within the realm of usual classroom activities.

Depending on their needs, the teacher might help the children think of and record on the chalkboard some words they could use in writing about frogs. The words would simply be available to them, but not required in their writings.

Discussion

After a common experience, the teacher will want to engage the children in discussing it, so that the group has a common direction. Usually the discussion is short, sometimes to help the children focus on the experience, sometimes to share ideas about format or audience for their writing, sometimes to explore pertinent words. If in the class with the new frog the teacher wanted to focus on the structure of reports about frogs, the discussion would include reminders about the scope, contents, and presentation of reports.

Writing

Let's say the children are obviously interested in the frogs, toads, and tadpoles. Some want to write about the trip to collect the tadpoles. The teacher might help them think about adventure stories and use one as a model for their accounts. Others might keep a pictorial and written record of the changes they observe in the tadpoles. The teacher will help these children think about scientific reports, including the information necessary to enable other scientists to replicate their findings. Some children will decide to record the facts they have learned about frogs and toads. The teacher will help them think about reference materials and how they are written and arranged, suggesting that they compile a class encyclopedia about amphibians. Others might want to model their writing on stories such as *Frog and Toad Together* (Lobel, 1972). The teacher would give group instruction to children working on each kind of writing and encourage them to help one another as they worked through their writing problems.

The choice of taking dictation from the students or asking them to write independently depends on the goals of instruction and/or the age and ability of the students. Dictation would be preferred if the goal were to help younger children record their words quickly so that instruction could focus on learning to recognize given words on sight. Dictation might also be the choice if the teacher wanted to help the children create a group story or to assist a child whose motor disabilities make writing a struggle. However, most of the time the children, even the younger ones, should write independently.

Taking dictation for a specific purpose does not mean that children cannot do their own writing on the same topic. After the teacher had taken dictation about the tadpole-collecting expedition, for example, the children could be encouraged to do their own writing as they painted frog pictures or prepared the aquarium. The main use of dictation should be to record group responses rather than individual responses.

Teachers taking dictation have an obligation to record children's words as they are dictated. If the child's language forms are not standard English constructions, the teacher may help the child (over a period of time) think about alternate ways of expressing a thought in more standard English. If the point of taking dictation is to help children see that thoughts can be recorded in print and that print can serve as a way of storing those thoughts for later reading, then the words must be exact. The words of a child who speaks a dialect should be spelled in conventional spelling. When the child reads the passage aloud, the teacher must expect dialectal pronunciation. Making changes in the children's words gives children the message that their words are not good enough and that they cannot communicate successfully. This to not to say that teachers should not help children move toward competence in standard English; but for a beginning reader, it is important to remember the purpose of taking dictation, which is to let children see their own ideas in print.

Reading

The children would be involved in reading as the process of writing continued. They would listen as a response group to a piece read by the author and they would read their own compositions to the class. They would read their own and other children's work as members of an editing group or editing committee or simply as part of a reading audience. Some pieces would be bound into books, to become a part of the class library for any child to check out and read. The children would also read many of the reference books and trade books that the teacher had helped them to locate.

In the language-experience approach, both oral reading by the teacher and choral reading are important. The teacher would read aloud to the children frequently. Read-aloud sessions would include reading the children's work and reading narrative or information books related to the topic. Children can be involved in choral reading as they read a chart that has been dictated or as they read a book that has been composed by one child or by the class. Both listening to the teacher read and choral reading will aid the development of fluent, efficient reading.

Skills Instruction

Skills instruction in language experience is a natural outgrowth of the reading, not an overlay. Instruction can encompass the full range of skills presented in any basal reading series. Skills might be as simple as letter–sound relationships or directionality of print or as complex as examining the development of fictional characters or analyzing the language used to achieve a particular mood. In between those extremes, instruction can focus on phonics, sight words, clarity, coherence of text, story structure, assumptions of prior knowledge by the author, changes needed to adapt the text for different audiences, and so on. Instruction can also focus on the mechanics of writing, such as capitalization, punctuation, and paragraphing. Children's vocabularies certainly present as many opportunities for teaching skills as does the basal reader. The difference is that their vocabularies are not controlled, nor is there the planned redundancy found in basal readers. Children who learn to read through the language-experience approach may read a selection over many times before they finish with it, so repeated exposure to the same words is very likely even though the words themselves are not repeated.

Large-group instruction in skills is appropriate when a new topic is introduced to the class. For example, the teacher might determine that the entire class needed instruction in recognizing the point of view of the author. The class might read and compare two passages on the same topic, written from different points of view. If some, but not all, children needed instruction in letter–sound relationships, it would make sense to use small-group instruction in skills. Individual instruction in skills would also take place on a regular basis as teachers talked with individual children about the content of their reading or listened to the child read orally.

Assume that the children in our frog example are in fourth grade. The teacher checks the basal reading manual adopted by the school district and finds that outlining is one of the skills to be introduced in fourth grade. Having provided the class with copies of a selected piece from a reference book about frogs, therefore, the teacher leads the children through the steps of outlining the material. Then the children who have written factual information about frogs and toads share their material, and the class outlines the information they have presented. Finally, the teacher helps the children to see how the authors of factual material construct an outline to help them write more clearly. Perhaps all the children will make an outline of what they would say if they were to write about frogs and toads.

To use the same topic with older children, the teacher would follow the same basic procedures but provide more sophisticated literature. For example, older children might read Mark Twain's "The Notorious Jumping Frog of Calaveras County" (Neider, 1957) and use reference books that contain overlays of the digestive and circulatory systems of a frog. They might then have a jumping frog contest or they might dissect a frog and keep accurate scientific records of their work. The skills instruction would probably include an examination of the writing style of Mark Twain, figurative language, and the importance of accuracy in scientific writing.

In general, older children may read individually, without oral reading by the teacher, and participate in a more extensive writing process, employing response groups and editing groups in the revision stage. The products of language experience may include any type of material, from directions for making things to poetry. The outcomes may include books, dictionaries, encyclopedias, journals, pamphlets, and posters.

Extension to the Work of Other Authors

All through this study of frogs, the teacher has been reading aloud books and poetry about frogs and tadpoles. The children compare the genres and styles of several of the works during class discussions. They are asked to share the works they like best and perhaps read aloud a passage that they believe will encourage others to read their favorite book. The children might also study the writings of a particular author and think about common elements of his or her style. Perhaps all the books or poetry on this topic would be collected on a table or special shelves and made available to the children to read silently or at home.

■ Key Words and Word Banks

One approach to language experience was developed in New Zealand by Sylvia Ashton-Warner (1963), who was working with Maori children whose first language was not English. She began recording their words of the day—each child's daily choice of an important word he or she wanted to learn. She felt that these words were of real interest and meaning to the children. Every few days she would have the children read back their collections of words. The words that a child could not remember were dis-

A word bank, a collection of personally meaningful words, is an excellent resource for writing.
© Paul Conklin/Monkmeyer Press Photo Service

carded. She felt that the words they remembered were especially significant to the individual child. Over a period of a few weeks, the children
would build their own collections of words that they could read on sight.
This strategy has been called the *key word* technique. The collection of
words that become part of the child's sight vocabulary is called a *word bank*.

Teachers use the key-word technique in several ways. Children
may be asked to dictate their word of the day as they enter the classroom
each day. The teacher writes the word on a card, involving the child by asking him or her to tell the teacher what letters to write or to identify the
sounds in the word. After recording the word, some teachers ask the child
to copy the word into a booklet with a title like "My Important Word Book"
or "My Beautiful Word Book." The child may then draw an illustration or
write a sentence about the word. Over a period of time, the children can
read and reread their books and recall their words. This technique works
especially well with children whose first language is not English; these
words they know in English have a special significance.

Figure 8.3 is a sample page of a child's "important word book." The
key word is *tidepool*. Please note that the important word was taken from a
classroom activity—the creation of a tidepool in the classroom.

Figure 8.3   Key word entry in a student's booklet.

Word banks—the words children collect as sight words—can inspire a variety of activities. Teachers will be able to think of many meaningful ways for the children to use their word banks. These are just examples:

- Use the word bank as a dictionary when writing.
- Choose your favorite word and write about it.
- Tell a friend why you chose one or two of the words.
- Look for one or two of the words in a newspaper.
- Draw a picture to illustrate a word.
- Build a model with clay or blocks to illustrate a word.
- Find three objects in the classroom that rhyme with one of the words.
- Group words that are related and explain how they are related.

Integrating Language Experience with the Reading/Writing Program

The Basal Reader

Teachers who use the basal reader, whether by choice or by necessity, often choose to integrate language experience with it. One technique for accomplishing this is to present a stimulus, ask the children to write about it, and have them read their own and other children's stories or read the group compositions. At the step of extension to the work of other authors, the story in the basal is presented. A good example of this technique is described by Jones and Nessel (1985): the teacher presented the children with several hats, they wrote stories about hats, and then they read the basal story about hats.

The process might also be reversed. Children could read the story in the basal reader, and using it as a stimulus or model, write their own story on the same topic. For example, *Landmarks* (1987) contains two biographies. After reading them, the class could study the characteristics of a well-written biography and then write a short biography of someone they know or someone in their community.

Teachers may also elect to alternate use of the basal with language experience, allocating, for example, three weeks of each month to the basal and the fourth to language experience. This format permits staggering groups so that only one group is involved in language-experience activities at any given time. Other teachers use language experience and basal readers in alternating weeks.

■ The Computer

Language experience works well in conjunction with use of a word processor, one of the major advantages being the ease of making revisions and corrections. The laborious work of recopying is eliminated when children write with a word processor. Having the flexibility to choose among type fonts and arrangements of words on the paper is another plus. When the teacher is taking dictation on a word processor, it is now possible to project the image that appears on the monitor onto a movie screen in the classroom. The teacher can lead the children to revise their dictated sentences in ways that would make the writing more effective and can demonstrate rewriting strategies for the children to use in their own composition efforts.

Word processors are also valuable to children who are engaged in individual writing projects. Newman (1984) has noted that children using word processors consider organizational changes and word choices more freely. To be able to choose a synonym for a given word and have the computer replace every occurrence of the given word so that one can consider how the composition sounds using the synonym is just one example of creative use of the word processor. Children learn about language each time they engage in writing; the word processor can make that learning even more enjoyable.

Some word processors are now capable of drawing figures or shapes at the stroke of a key. These programs have been used with very young children, who select the drawings they want, arrange them, and then dictate to the teacher what they want to say about their drawings. The teacher types the words and prints out a copy for the child. Children tend to produce more words about their computer drawings than about their drawings by hand. They also sustain interest in the computer over the year and do not tire of participating in the drawing and dictating activities (Warash, 1984).

When the teacher wants children to share their compositions for use in reading instruction, the services of a word processor and printer are especially helpful. Children can readily print one or more paper copies of their work for distribution to an instructional group. Later a copy can be placed in a class binder or the author's own. It is also very convenient to be able to store the work on the computer disk for future reference or revision. If every child has a diskette, keeping a file of each one's progress becomes very simple. (Be sure to make frequent backup copies of the children's diskettes so their valuable work won't be lost.)

Many word processing programs have built-in features for checking the spelling of common words. Teachers must make a professional decision about using spelling checkers with their children. Since the more times one sees a word spelled correctly, the more likely one is to learn to spell it, a spelling checker may have some legitimate use. The teacher

In many classrooms, children acquire competence at the computer keyboard while gaining proficiency as writers.
© Robert V. Eckert, Jr./The Picture Cube

would also have to help children recognize the limitations of spelling checkers: they cannot distinguish between correctly spelled but incorrectly used words, such as *their* and *there*. Errors you notice in the local newspaper, where all the type is set and checked by computer, can provide confirming examples of this fact.

One of the limitations of word processing is the cost. At this time, most schools cannot afford many computers and printers per classroom. That means that children cannot have a turn on the word processor very often. As the prices of computer equipment and word processing software become more reasonable, perhaps more children will have ready access to them.

Another problem with using the word processor for writing is the necessity of having keyboarding skills and the controversy over whether young children should be allowed to type without first learning proper keyboarding skills. Most typing teachers would prefer that children not be allowed to "hunt and peck" because they must break all those habits when learning to type correctly. Some schools are successfully teaching keyboarding skills to elementary children. Teachers who want to make the word processor available to their students must decide how they feel about keyboarding skills for young children and consider not just the advantages but the disadvantages of using a word processing program to enhance the writing component in language experience.

■ Literature

The "extension" step in the language-experience sequence of instruction calls for children to read the works of other authors. Now, reading what others have written on the same topics they are writing about, children read "like a writer." They pay more attention to the structure and style of a composition if they are involved in writing something themselves in the same genre.

Sometimes the teacher may wish to begin the instruction with literature, using a book or poem or other piece of writing as the stimulus for the children's writing. We offer a few suggestions for helping children write compositions based on children's literature. These ideas only scratch the surface of possibilities; teachers who want to use language experience will think of many more ways to base writing and reading opportunities on books their classes enjoy.

- *Free Fall* (Wiesner, 1988). One of the many wordless books available, this selection allows children to produce their own text to tell the story. Some wordless books are open to very diverse interpretations. Several children could write a story for the same illustrations, or each child could write a story for a different wordless book.
- *The Doorbell Rang* (Hutchins, 1986). Children could write their own stories about times when they have had to share something that was special to them. In this book, the two children are given a plate of cookies; as more and more people come to their door, fewer and fewer cookies remain. Children could also write some real-life math story problems for other children to solve.
- *The Talking Eggs* (San Souci, 1989). Children can compare this folk tale with others in which something plain turns out to be very valuable. They can use the folk tale structure to create a story of their own.
- *The Relatives Came* (Rylant, 1985). This book describes a visit by the relatives. Children can write about visits to or from their own relatives. It would be a good story to use for discussing point of view in writing.
- *The Devil's Arithmetic* (Yolen, 1988). The author uses changes in time to tell this story of a Jewish girl caught in the Holo-

caust. After studying her techniques and reading other books in which characters move from one time period to another, children could write a story employing this device.

- *The Legend of the Bluebonnet* (dePaola, 1983). The children can compare this account of how bluebonnets came into being with many other books that explain the how or why of some common event or object and then write their own stories to explain their observations of nature.
- *Number the Stars* (Lowry, 1989). A young girl during World War II learns what it means to be brave. Children could describe characters whom they believe to have been brave even if their actions would not have been described as heroic by others.
- *The Napping House* (Wood, 1986). In this cumulative tale, one character after another sleeps and wakes in the napping house. Children could write their own cumulative stories following this pattern or the pattern in *This Is the House That Jack Built* (Underhill, 1987) or *Drummer Hoff* (Emberley, 1967).
- *The King Who Rained* (Gwynne, 1970). In imitation of this book's play on words, children could make illustrations that play on the literal meanings of homophones.
- *Guess Who My Favorite Person Is* (Baylor, 1977). A child and an adult play the "favorite" game, naming their favorite things and telling why they are their favorites. Children could write about their own favorite things in response to the questions in the book or could write about their favorite things in other categories.

Figure 8.4 is an example of a child's writing based on the pattern found in *The Important Book* (Margaret Brown, 1949). After the teacher had read the book several times and discussed the pattern, the children selected individual topics for their own writing. A parent volunteer typed the entries before they were bound into a class book. Figure 8.5 reproduces a page from a class book called *The ABC's of Water*. Each child selected a letter of the alphabet and wrote an entry that was related to water. The entries were typed, bound into a book, and placed in the school library.

Writing experiences are not limited to creating repetitive books and alphabet books, of course. Children can write and publish a variety of books based on all kinds of picture books. They can be encouraged to use unusual page cutouts or fold-outs (as in the Eric Carle books) and make their own pop-up books. *How to Make Pop-Ups* (Irvine, 1987) gives clear directions for helping children produce such books. *How a Book Is Made* (Aliki, 1986) explains the process of publishing a book.

The most important thing about a school is the children. There are many desks at school. There are many classrooms. There are many classes like math, reading, spelling, and art. But the most important thing about school is the children.

By Levi

Figure 8.4   Composition modeled after a patterned book.

Children involved in the writing process will relate to the bat in *The Bat Poet* (Jarrell, 1963). The bat is excited about the things he sees around him and struggles to write poems that express his feelings. Children can empathize with his feelings when the reactions he gets from the other bats are not helpful. Let them talk about how he felt, how they feel in their writ-

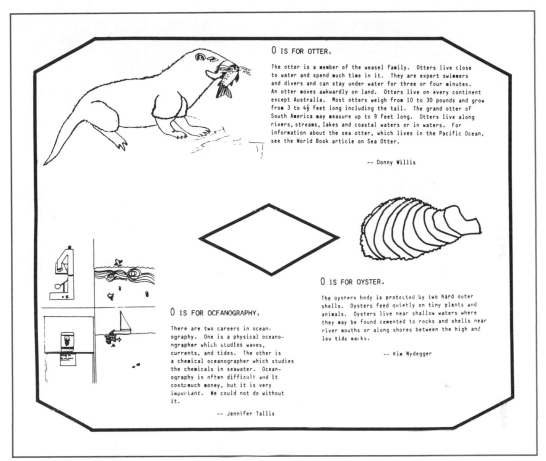

Figure 8.5   Composition modeled after an ABC book.

ing conferences, and how they can better help each other. The book will also remind them that writing is a time-consuming and sometimes difficult process.

There are many, many more books that are exciting aids for writing experiences. Teachers need to think about using trade books in order to extend children's reading to the works of other authors, as well as to stimulate writing.

Publishing Children's Writing

Whether or not to publish a child's writing is an instructional decision based on the child's needs and interests and the instructional uses of the material. In Chapter 3, we talked about how children need to select for

Publication of an original hand-bound book is a proud accomplishment for a student author.
© *Michael Hagan*

publication certain pieces of their work and noted that not every writing experience has to culminate in publication. In teaching reading with children's writing, teachers may help children to select some of their own work for binding and placement in the classroom library. They may also assist children who are interested in submitting their material to magazines that publish children's work. Three such magazines are *Stone Soup* (Children's Art Foundation, P.O. Box 83, Santa Cruz, CA 95063), *Cricket* (Carus Corporation, 315 Fifth Street, Peru, Illinois 61354), and *Stepping Stones* (Aprovecho Institute, 80574 Hazelton Rd., Cottage Grove, OR 97424). Subscribing to these magazines so that children can read the work of other children motivates children's writing regardless of their interest in submitting work.

Meeting the Challenges of Language Experience

Language experience is not a random teaching method in which children are never instructed in reading. Language experience can be done poorly, just as any other method can be done poorly. But when it is done well, children do learn to read skillfully. Teachers are responsible for selecting the skills to be taught and for carrying out large-group, small-group, and individual instruction. Language experience requires careful planning and thought by the teacher.

Language experience does not imply a chaotic classroom lacking in discipline. In a well-run classroom there will be many planned experiences to involve the children. Time, space, and materials are arranged to encourage reading and writing about those experiences. A program that includes skills development and extending the children's reading to the works of other authors is certainly not automatically chaotic. It may involve more child-to-child interaction than some other methods, and more moving about as children gather resources and complete their work, but these activities are not without goals. In fact, we think a classroom that is *too* orderly and disciplined is in danger of stagnation.

Teaching reading through language experience does present some challenges for the teacher. For example, recording and remembering what each individual child has learned is a formidable task, and so is communicating that information to others who need it. One method of tracking children's progress is to keep a file of their writing over a period of time. Each child's file should contain evidence of the child's growing ability to express meanings effectively and increasing knowledge of the conventions of written language, such as spelling, capitalization, punctuation, and paragraphing, together with a checklist of skills and the date on which instruction was given in each skill. As children mature in writing skills, their files would reveal their understanding of voice, point of view, and intended audience for a piece of writing. The file can record books they have read and samples of drawings, book jackets, and other indicators of reading comprehension. Anecdotal records of children's oral reading or notes from discussions of what the child was reading would belong in the file. File maintenance is no more time consuming than giving basal tests regularly and recording the scores.

Carefully keeping the file for each child facilitates communication with parents and other teachers. Reporting to parents is easiest if it is done in a conference format so that parents can look at the files and see the progress the child has made. Writing a summary of the child's progress is the next-best method of communicating with parents.

Communicating with other teachers about the children's growth in language experience involves a little more than recording each child's reading level in a basal series. It usually takes a short narrative to explain what the child has learned and what the child has currently been working on. By the same token, the information is far more useful to next year's teacher than a check mark beside a book title would be. It might also be helpful to keep a running list of topics that the class had chosen to read and write about and make a photocopy of the child's file (or parts of it) to send on to the next teacher. A little thought and time will solve the problems of communication, and the child will certainly benefit.

■ Major Ideas in This Chapter

- ■ The language-experience approach to reading instruction means that children write on topics of interest to them and that the products of their writing are used for reading instruction.

- ■ The language-experience approach does not necessarily raise scores on standardized reading tests, but children do have better concepts of themselves as readers and more positive attitudes toward reading. They also read and write more, growing in ability as a result.

- ■ Language experience is a teacher-dependent approach to reading instruction. Teachers must make professional decisions about the purpose of lessons, the sequence of skills instruction, and the activities that will enrich the lesson.

- ■ Language experience can be integrated successfully with a basal program of reading instruction. Use of a word processor can enhance language-experience activities. Literature occupies a significant place in language-experience instruction.

- ■ Language experience is not a haphazard, chaotic program; it requires careful planning and organization in order to be successful. Planning includes selecting the purpose of the activity, choosing the stimuli, deciding whether the children will write or dictate, and instructing in needed skills.

- ■ Communication with parents and other teachers about a child's progress in reading when language-experience instruction is used may be time consuming but will also reveal much about the child's learning.

? Discussion Questions
Focusing on the Teacher You Are Becoming

1. Discuss with your classmates what you consider to be the most significant reasons for choosing to use the language-experience approach and the major challenges.
2. Decide on the most important pieces of information you would like to have about a child's reading if a child were moving into your classroom

and discuss how one teacher might share that information with another teacher.

3. Talk to one or two teachers who use language experience. What elements do they find most difficult to manage? How do they solve the problems?

4. Discuss the elements of language-experience instruction that most closely match your emerging philosophy about how children learn to read.

☑ Field-Based Applications

1. Choose one of your favorite picture books. Plan a language-experience lesson based on the book. Be sure to include the purpose of the lesson in your plan.

2. Compare the vocabulary and length of sentences in a basal reader with those in samples of children's writing from the same grade level. How would you use this information in planning instruction?

3. Collect samples of children's writing and design-skills instruction lessons that could be done using the samples for instructional material.

4. Look at the skills sequence chart of a basal reader and select a specific skill. Plan a language-experience activity involving instruction in that skill.

5. Design a chart on which records of skills instruction could be kept.

6. Choose a selection from a basal reader and plan a language-experience lesson that would precede or follow the reading of the selection.

7. Plan a language-experience lesson in reading that would focus on a topic from science or social studies.

8. If possible, participate in a language-experience activity in which the child uses a word processor. Note the advantages and disadvantages of using the word processor.

⊡ References and Suggested Readings

Aliki. *How a Book Is Made*. New York: Thomas Y. Crowell, 1986.

Anderson, Robert; Hiebert, Elfrieda H.; Scott, Judith A.; and Wilkinson, Ian A. G. *Becoming a Nation of Readers*. Washington, D.C.: National Institute of Education, 1985.

Ashton-Warner, Sylvia. *Teacher*. New York: Simon & Schuster, 1963.

Berliner, David. "Making the Right Changes in Preservice Teacher Education." *Phi Delta Kappan* 66 (October 1984): 94–96.

Boutwell, Marilyn. "Reading and Writing Process: A Reciprocal Agreement." *Language Arts* 60 (September 1983): 723–730.

Bridge, Connie; Winograd, Peter N.; and Haley, Darliene. "Using Predictable Material vs. Preprimers to Teach Beginning Sight Words." *The Reading Teacher* 36 (May 1983): 884–891.

Brown, Marcia. *Stone Soup.* New York: Scribner's, 1947.

Brown, Margaret. *The Important Book.* New York: Harper & Row, 1949.

Calkins, Lucy. *The Art of Teaching Writing.* Portsmouth, N.H.: Heinemann Educational Books, 1986.

Cox, Vivian. "Reciprocal Oracy/Literacy Recognition Skills in the Language Production of Language Experience Students." Doctoral dissertation, University of Arizona, 1971.

Cramer, Ronald L. "An Investigation of First-Grade Spelling Achievement." *Elementary English* 47 (February 1970): 230–237.

dePaola, Tomie. *The Legend of the Bluebonnet.* New York: Putnam's, 1983.

Emberley, Barbara. *Drummer Hoff.* Englewood Cliffs, N.J.: Prentice-Hall, 1967.

Evans, Mary Ann, and Carr, Thomas. "Early Development of Reading." *Reading Research Quarterly* 20 (Spring 1985): 327–347.

Gillet, Jean, and Gentry, J. Richard. "Bridges between Nonstandard and Standard English with Extensions of Dictated Stories." *The Reading Teacher* 36 (January 1983): 360–364.

Goodman, Kenneth. *What's Whole in Whole Language?* Portsmouth, N.H.: Heinemann Educational Books, 1986.

Graves, Donald. *Writing: Teachers and Children at Work.* Portsmouth, N.H.: Heinemann Educational Books, 1983.

Gwynne, Fred. *The King Who Rained.* New York: Simon & Schuster, 1970.

Hall, MaryAnne. "The Development and Evaluation of a Language Experience Approach to Reading with First-Grade Culturally Disadvantaged Children." Doctoral dissertation, University of Maryland, 1965.

Hall, MaryAnne. *Teaching Reading as a Language Experience.* 3rd ed. Columbus, Ohio: Charles E. Merrill, 1981.

Harris, Albert. "The Effective Teacher of Reading." *The Reading Teacher* 23 (December 1969): 195–204, 238.

Hoberman, Mary. *A House Is a House for Me.* Cedar Grove, N.J.: Rae Publishing, 1978.

Hutchins, Pat. *The Doorbell Rang.* New York: Greenwillow, 1986.

Irvine, Joan. *How to Make Pop-Ups.* New York: Morrow Junior Books, 1987.

Jarrell, Randall. *The Bat Poet.* New York: Macmillan, 1963.

Jones, Margaret, and Nessel, Denise. "Enhancing the Curriculum with Experience Stories." *The Reading Teacher* 39 (October 1985): 18–22.

Katz, Lillian. Speech in Salem, Ore., May 1, 1986.

Kelly, Ann Marie. "Sight Vocabularies and Experience Stories." *Elementary English* 52 (March 1975): 327–328.

Landmarks. Orlando, Fla.: Harcourt Brace Jovanovich, 1987.

Lobel, Arnold. *Frog and Toad Together.* New York: Harper & Row, 1972.

Lowry, Lois. *Number the Stars.* Boston: Houghton Mifflin, 1989.

McCracken, Robert, and McCracken, Marlene. *Reading Is Only the Tiger's Tail.* San Rafael, Calif.: Leswing Press, 1972.

Neider, Charles, ed. *The Complete Short Stories of Mark Twain.* Garden City, N.Y.: Doubleday, 1957.

Nessel, Denise, and Jones, Margaret. *The Language-Experience Approach to Reading: A Handbook for Teachers.* New York: Teachers College Press, 1981.

Newman, Judith. "Language Learning and Computers." *Language Arts* 61 (September 1984): 494–497.

Oehlkers, William. "The Contribution of Creative Writing to Reading Achievement in the Language Experience Approach." Doctoral dissertation, University of Delaware, 1971.

Rylant, Cynthia. *The Relatives Came.* New York: Bradbury Press, 1985.

San Souci, Robert D. *The Talking Eggs.* New York: Dial Books for Young Readers, 1989.

Sendak, Maurice. *Chicken Soup with Rice.* New York: Scholastic Book Services, 1962.

Stauffer, Marian. "Comparative Effects of a Language Arts Approach and Basal Reader Approach to First Grade Reading Achievement." Doctoral dissertation, University of Delaware, 1973.

Stauffer, Russell G. *The Language-Experience Approach to the Teaching of Reading.* 2nd ed. New York: Harper & Row, 1980.

Stauffer, Russell G., and Pikulski, John. "A Comparison and Measure of Oral Language Growth." *Elementary English* 51 (November/December 1974): 1151–1155.

Underhill, Liz. *This Is the House That Jack Built.* New York: Holt, Rinehart & Winston, 1987.

Veatch, Jeanette; Sawicki, Florence; Elliott, Geraldine; Flake, Eleanor; and Blakey, Janis. *Key Words to Reading: The Language Experience Approach Begins.* 2nd ed. Columbus, Ohio: Charles E. Merrill, 1979.

Warash, Barbara. "Computer Language Experience Approach." Paper presented at the annual meeting of National Council of Teachers of English, Columbus, Ohio, April 1984. (ERIC Document Reproduction Service No. ED 244 264).

Wiesner, David. *Free Fall.* New York: Lothrop, Lee & Shepard Books, 1988.

Wilson, Robert, and Parkey, Nancy. "A Modified Reading Program in a Middle School." *Journal of Reading* 13 (March 1970): 447–552.

Wood, Audrey. *The Napping House.* Orlando, Fla.: Harcourt Brace Jovanovich, 1986.

Yolen, Jane. *The Devil's Arithmetic.* New York: Viking Kistrel, 1988.

Part IV

Developing Reading/Writing Abilities

In the preceding sections you have learned about the development of language, reading, and writing; about the decisions you must make as a teacher; and about different approaches to teaching reading.

This section will discuss what reading teachers commonly call *skills*—all the parts of reading that together should lead to accomplishing the whole process. Experts do not argue about the importance of children's knowing all the skills; they argue about the place of skills instruction and how skills are to be taught. These chapters will help you learn the bits and pieces that contribute to the reading process. Knowing about these skills will aid you in understanding how best to assist developing readers and writers in their growth.

By including these chapters, we run the risk of encouraging the misguided notion that skills are the focus of reading instruction. We believe that learning to read is much more than mastering a given set of skills. The reason for knowing skills is to read more effectively—not to know skills. Skills are a means, not an end.

Chapter 9

Using Cueing Systems

Chapter Overview

- Moving from print to language in reading is a very complicated process. It relies on a variety of cues found on the printed page. Readers use only a small portion of the available cues.

- Word identification requires the use of several cueing systems—sight vocabulary, context cues, and word-attack cues—that help the reader create meaning.

- A teacher's view of the reading process determines the kinds of curricular decisions the teacher makes. In one view, reading should be taught beginning with sounds, then words, then sentences and stories. In another, reading instruction should begin with whole stories.

- Word-identification instruction should be guided by a set of principles to ensure that in the course of skills instruction the teacher never loses sight of the reading process.

- Skills lessons (regardless of the skill being taught) should consist of activities to develop knowledge, promote practice, provide application, and permit reinforcement.

- Learning the strategies of the reading process is more valuable than learning individual subskills. Instruction in reading strategies should be an important part of the reading program.

How do we get from print to language en route to creating meaning when we read? We accomplish this complicated task by the simultaneous use of a variety of cueing systems. Cueing systems are all the data we use to "cue" us as to the meaning of the text—some of them resident in the text, some in the mind of the reader. Those in the text itself are context cueing systems: syntactic cues, semantic cues, and graphophonic cues. Reader-based cues are the schematic cues the reader brings to the text—all the things the reader knows as a result of experience. All the strategies readers use to move from print to language are grouped under the global term *word identification*, also known as *decoding* (signifying "breaking the print code"—moving from the print symbol to its language equivalent) and *word recognition* (containing the sense of word identification and decoding, and including the idea that a word is in one's listening vocabulary; that is, its meaning is understood when it is heard).

The Cueing Systems

A page of print is rich in cues to help the reader decode the print and construct meaning—far more, in fact, than readers usually need. Mature readers rely on the various cues as needs dictate. Our use of the components of word identification varies with the difficulty of the text. The components of word identification are our sight vocabulary, language cues (semantic, syntactic, and graphophonic), and schematic cues.

Sight Vocabulary

The most frequently used component of word identification is *sight vocabulary*, composed of all of the words we recognize instantly when we see them in print. We do not have to look at individual letters within the words or think about the sounds that make up the words. The process of going from written symbol to language is virtually instantaneous. As a mature reader, you will have in your sight vocabulary most of the words you see in print. Some of the technical terms in this text will not be in your sight vocabulary, and probably even more words might be unfamiliar to you in a zoology text or a book of Elizabethan sonnets. Most of the words in your sight vocabulary are in your listening vocabulary—those words you understand when you hear them. Many of the words in your sight vocabulary are in your speaking and writing vocabularies, but usually one's sight vocabulary is larger than one's speaking or writing vocabulary.

Language or Context Cues

Language or context cues are the cues resident in the text that we are able to use because of our knowledge about how language works. To understand context cues, think about what you do while reading when you come to a word that is not in your sight vocabulary. Chances are that you skip it and go on, in the hope (or on the assumption) that the word is not important. When you realize that you are not understanding the author's message, you finally stop and go back to deal with the unknown word. Maybe you even feel as if you'd been caught in the act of trying to evade the unfamiliar word. To deal with it at that point, you usually rely on (1) the structure of the sentence in which the word occurs, (2) the meanings of other words in the sentence, and (3) the meanings of words in nearby sentences.

Syntactic Cues

The structure of the sentence in which the word occurs can sometimes cue us to the identification of the unfamiliar word. The term for the arrangement of words in a sentence and the relationship among the words is *syntax*. The principles that describe how words may be arranged make up the syntax of our language, and the cues they provide are called *syntactic cues*. Consider this sentence:

> The rambunctious boys broke the lamp.

Suppose the word *rambunctious* were not in your sight vocabulary. How could the structure of the sentence cue you to identify the word? The first word in the sentence provides some help. *The* is a noun marker, indicating that a noun follows. Other examples of noun markers are *those, this, that, some, his, her,* and *their*. When you see a noun marker, you know that a noun will follow it next or very soon. In the sample sentence, you realize that *boys* is a noun. That means that the unknown word has to be an adjective—a word that describes or modifies a noun. Now you ask yourself what words you know that can describe boys. At this point you probably consider the beginning sounds in the unknown word to limit the possible *boy* descriptors you will consider. As a start in identifying the unknown word, syntactic cues are helpful because of what you know about how the language works.

Semantic Cues

The meanings of words around the unknown word, in the same or nearby sentences, often provide cues called *semantic cues* to help identify the word. Known meanings of other words can help you predict the identity of an unfamiliar word. Semantic cues could help you identify *rambunctious* in the sample sentence if you considered what breaking the lamp suggests about the boys' behavior and the nature and level of their activity. Cues to the identity of *rambunctious* exist in the meaning of *broke the lamp*.

Words within a sentence often cue other words semantically. In the following examples, semantic cues occur in the same sentence as the unknown word:

> His sock was worn through; the _____ was growing larger with each step he took.
> He put the milk in the _____ to keep it cool.
> It was an easy book, and reading it was not _____ at all.

Those sentences have such clear semantic cues that you probably correctly predicted the missing words to be *hole, refrigerator,* and *difficult.* Semantic cues are not always that clear, but they are still helpful in identifying an unknown word. Consider these examples:

His favorite dessert was _____.
The girls' favorite team sport was _____.

Here, semantic cues occur in a sentence that follows the unknown word:

The student who was the team's best center was supercilious. Some of the fans called him a supercilious jerk. In
fact, he was the most haughty member of the team.

If you did not know the meaning of *supercilious,* how would the surrounding sentences help you identify the word? The idea that the player is supercilious is in essence repeated two sentences later with the word *haughty.* This would cue you that *supercilious* must have a meaning like *haughty.*

Graphophonic Cues

When a word is not in your sight vocabulary and the use of syntactic and semantic cues fails to help you identify it, the next step is to use word-attack skills. The violent sound of the term is not inappropriate: the reader does rip the word apart—attack it—to identify its parts and then, we hope, the whole word. Word attack involves structural cues, syllabic cues, and graphophonic cues.

Structural cues arise from base or root words, prefixes, and suffixes. The first step in word attack is to examine the unknown word to see if a possible prefix or suffix can be separated from a recognizable root word. Try dropping anything that looks like a prefix or suffix, and ask if the predicted root word sounds like a word you have ever heard. Because prefixes and suffixes usually form separate syllables, it is helpful to identify the root and then apply syllabic cues.

Syllabic cues are provided by dividing the unknown word into syllables based on a set of typical syllable patterns. For example, the vowel, consonant, consonant, vowel (VC/CV) pattern suggests that when two like consonants fall between two vowels, the syllable break usually occurs between the consonants. Suppose we came upon the following unfamiliar (not in our sight vocabulary) word:

subcommittee.

To apply our knowledge of structural word attack, we would first have to ask whether or not we see a possible prefix. *Sub* is certainly a candidate for a prefix. Removing it leaves a predicted root word, *committee*. At this point we apply our knowledge of syllabic cues by looking for familiar syllable patterns. We know that prefixes usually form syllables. If *sub* is a prefix, there is our first syllable. We notice two consonants (*mm*) between two vowels (*o* and *i*). We predict the first syllable break to be between the two *m*'s. Then we see two other consonants (*tt*) between two vowels (*i* and *e*). We predict the second syllable break to occur between the two *t*'s. Our prediction of the syllabic breakdown of this word is

sub   com   mit   tee.

Our use of structural cues and syllabic cues has led to a set of predicted syllables. What happens next?

Graphophonic cues are the cues that exist because letters (graphemes) represent sounds (phonemes) in our alphabetic language. Each letter on the page represents one or more sounds or the absence of sound. To be sure, inconsistency is a problem. Think of the letters *ea* in *great* and *eat*. What's more, not all letters have equal weight in cueing the word. We know that consonants provide more cues than vowels, that beginnings of words are more important than middles and ends, and that ends of words are more helpful than middles. Nevertheless, at this point we need to deal with the sounds represented by the letters in our unknown word.

Syllables are important in the word-attack process because the structure of the syllable signals the sound of a vowel. The fact that our syllables *sub, com,* and *mit* all end in a consonant preceded by a single vowel suggests that the vowel sounds will be short. The *ee* structure in the final syllable suggests that the vowel sound will be a long *e*. Now, if we are very lucky, we can pronounce the syllables and therefore the word! We will then need to go back to semantic cues and possibly even syntactic cues to determine the meaning of the word once we have decoded (pronounced) it.

Context cues help us identify (name) words in our speaking vocabulary that we do not immediately recognize in print. Context cues also help us assign meaning to words that we might not otherwise have understood. Young readers must learn to use context within and beyond the sentence as they predict and confirm meaning. Those who do not become proficient at using the language-based context cues are likely not to become independent readers.

Our intuitive knowledge about how language works—grammar, word order, function words, endings of words—cues us to identify words. These syntactic cues are supplemented by semantic cues, the meaning of words and the relationships among words. Graphophonic cues (especially the first sound of a word) help us further (Weaver, 1988). In addition to using these language-based cues in identifying words and creating meaning, we bring our knowledge of the world, born of our personal experiences, to bear on what we read. These reader-based cues are what we call *schematic cues*.

■ Schematic Cues

Schematic cues are all the information, assumptions, and theories (schemata) about the world that the reader brings to the act of reading. The reader creates meaning through the interaction of the ideas of the writer and the background experiences and knowledge of the reader. Consider a typical example of the way in which the schemata two readers bring to the text dramatically affect the interpretation of that text.

Suppose that Chris and Sean have both been to dog shows. Chris's experience at the dog show was wonderful. She enjoyed seeing all the different breeds, even got to pet a few dogs, and loved trying to predict which dog would be the winner in each event. Sean, who had been seriously bitten by a large dog a year earlier, saw the dog show with very different eyes. The barking reminded him of the dog that bit him. He was uncomfortable the whole time he was at the show.

Chris and Sean would read stories about dogs and dog shows very differently because of the background experiences and mental images (schemata) they have for dogs. They could each begin with the same printed text, but they would individually create very different meanings.

The process of using word-identification cueing systems can be very rapid. Although we have taken it apart in order to discuss the components, the reader may in fact combine them so speedily that the separations are not apparent. If the separations of the components are not apparent in use, then why separate them in teaching them? This question has generated heated debate within the reading profession. Where do readers look first? Do they move from the whole of a written piece to sentences, words, and then sounds, or do they begin with the smallest units—sounds—and build to words, sentences, and paragraphs? Do they begin from the top and work down or from the bottom and build up?

Whole versus Parts

How teachers see the reading process very much determines the kinds of curriculum decisions they make and the goals they set for students. For the past sixty-five years a behavioristic view of learning has dominated the teaching of reading (May, 1986): learning has been seen as a response to a stimulus, which, when reinforced, is finally remembered. The stimulus/ response approach to learning sought to break the learning act down into its smallest pieces and then reinforce the student's learning of each piece. In reading, the smallest pieces are the sound–symbol relationships. Therefore, the behaviorist teacher of reading would begin by teaching letters, then sounds represented by those letters, then words, and finally sentences and longer discourse. Typically, the vocabulary in beginning materials was carefully controlled so that once students learned a sound–symbol relationship they did not encounter variations in that relationship in textual materials. This part-to-whole approach to the teaching of reading has been challenged in the past ten years by those who believe that the reading process works from the top down. In their view, the most significant element within the reading process is not sound–symbol relationships but sentences, which represent meaning.

What has now come to be known as the *whole-language movement* originated in the view of learning suggested by Gestalt psychology: learning moves from wholes to parts. The learner is seen as looking for wholes— complete forms—Gestalts. Our perceptions are dominated by our schemata. When we witness an event, look at a picture, or pick up a book, we do so with expectations of what we will see, hear, find. Expectations created by our background experiences color our perceptions. As we read, we continually make predictions about what the author is saying to us. We use the fewest possible cues on the printed page to confirm our predictions. Mature readers do not even decode all the words in a sentence. In attempting to proofread a paper, you have probably had to fight the urge to skim. Only when we become aware that the reading process has broken down do we begin to use more of the cues, ultimately resorting to a careful examination of the sound–symbol relationships. Since the early 1980s this whole-language, top down, whole-to-part view of the reading process has gained wider and wider acceptance.

The question of whether to engage in part-to-whole or whole-to-part instruction in word identification is best answered by considering what you want children to believe about the reading process. Answer each of the following questions to determine where you stand on the issue.

1. Do you want young readers to believe that reading is constructing meaning or unlocking sounds?
2. Do you believe that children should first read their own language or first read a controlled vocabulary so that sound–symbol relationships are consistent?
3. Do you believe that before children read a selection they should hear it well read by another, or should children always decode a selection on their own?

4. Do you believe that children learn to read by reading and writing, or do you believe that they must master word-identification skills before they can read?

5. Do you believe that the information children bring to the printed page affects their understanding, or do you believe that all the meaning resides in the words?

6. Do you believe that children understand an author's ideas without reading every word, or must they understand every word in order to comprehend a selection?

7. Do you believe that when children read aloud they may substitute meaningful alternatives to the printed words, or must they read every word accurately?

8. Do you believe that when a child reads incorrectly you should say, "Here is what you read, does that make sense?" or should you simply correct the child's errors?

9. In reading, are the basic units of instruction sentences and paragraphs, or are the basic units of instruction sounds, letters, and words?

10. Do you believe that the structure of a sentence often determines the meanings of words, or are word meanings independently stable?

If you answered yes to the first part of each question you have sided with the whole-to-part advocates. Agreement with the second half of each question puts you in the part-to-whole camp. When you examine the five principles we state here, you will see that we advocate whole-to-part instruction. One of our goals is to convince the part-to-whole advocates of the benefits of a whole-to-part approach.

Instruction in Word Identification

Principles

The teaching of word identification should be guided by the following principles.

Principle 1.   Instruction in word identification should be seen as an aid to constructing meaning, not as an end in itself. We do not teach children the sound(s) represented by a certain letter because that knowledge is important as such. We teach the sound–letter correspondence so that the process of constructing meaning may go on as effortlessly as possible.

Principle 2.   What we do in skills instruction should be as much like the reading act as possible. In skills instruction we should use examples taken from meaningful texts, preferably texts written by children.

Principle 3.   Before instruction of young children in phonic word attack can begin, three conditions must be met: (1) the children must be at the onset of concrete operational thinking, (2) the children must have auditory and visual discrimination abilities, and (3) the children must understand that reading is a process of constructing meaning.

Principle 4.   While engaging in skills instruction, we must respect the reading process. Having broken the process down in order to examine individual steps, we should put it back together before ending the instruction, so children can see the relationships between the parts and the whole.

Principle 5.   Word identification is useful only when the words identified are in the reader's listening or speaking vocabulary. The use of word-identification cues will not be effective if children cannot recognize miscues when they make them and self-correct. Word identification is useless if readers do not know the words they have identified.

■ Strategies

The only justification for engaging in word-identification instruction is to help readers construct meaning when they read. Increasing a child's sight vocabulary helps in constructing meaning. Giving children strategies for using context cues aids the cause of unlocking unfamiliar words and constructing meaning. Teaching children how the sound–symbol system works is justified only in that such knowledge may facilitate decoding unfamiliar words and assist in constructing meaning. Aiding comprehension must be the rationale for and focus of word-identification instruction.

Developing Sight Vocabulary

What are words? Many words are language labels for the concepts we have in our heads. Words provide a convenient medium for us to use when thinking about, discussing, and sharing our concepts with others. Working with children, it is important to be focused on concept attainment when discussing vocabulary. Teaching children words without making certain that they know what the words mean and how to use them is truly a waste of time. In junior high, one of our daughters used to ask her father to give her a practice test every week the night before her spelling test. Asked, "What does that word mean?" she frequently answered, "I don't know." Her father was always struck by the futility of the exercise. Children who are taught to identify words without understanding what they mean and how to use them will be unable to use them!

Verbal Knowledge versus Experience

Some children have very well-developed auditory memories. After hearing something on television or in a conversation, they are able to recall the words and repeat them fluently. This ability is called *verbal knowledge*. When you probe the depth of this knowledge, you sometimes discover shallow understanding. Lacking the background experiences upon which to develop concepts, such children often use the concept labels without understanding the concepts. For them, the teacher's role here is to provide the experiences, *either real or vicarious,* to undergird the verbal knowledge. For example, in order to learn *bud* children may need to take a walk outside and examine buds or find pictures of budding flowers in books. As the children examine the buds, the teacher asks questions to focus their attention on the salient characteristics. Thus the concept will develop and the language level will finally become meaningful. A young friend recently went deep-sea fishing for the first time. He was very ill during the trip, and as he climbed back onto the wharf he said, "Before today, 'seasickness' was only a word!"

Just as some children need assistance in developing concepts for the language labels they already use, other children require help in learning the language labels for concepts they are developing. Interaction with others is a key. When I share my view of the world with you and get your reaction, I either have confirmation of my concepts or have to alter my concepts to accommodate your view. Oral communication is vital to the development of concepts and the association of the appropriate labels with the concepts. Communication about ideas and concepts is a hallmark of the classroom in which the teacher is sincerely concerned about development of sight vocabulary.

Focusing on Word Meanings

Sight-vocabulary development happens best in classrooms where the teacher focuses attention on word meanings. The teacher is excited about words and takes every opportunity to call them to the attention of the children in real, meaningful ways. These are some activities that serve the cause of word advocacy:

1.   *Meaningful introduction of vocabulary.* Before the children read a selection, present important words to them using a sentence from the selection. Have someone read aloud the sentence containing the word, and invite volunteers to tell what the word means. Ask the children to use the word in their own sentences to show that they understand it. If the children cannot respond, then you define the word and use it in a sentence. Always end this activity by having children use the words in sentences of

The act of reading is the act of creating meaning from the interaction of the ideas of the author and the background of the reader.
© Gary Walts/The Image Works

their own that illustrate *meaningful* understanding of the word rather than just the ability to parrot it back. This activity is especially important when dealing with words of multiple meanings.

2.   *Special word lists.* During the teaching of a unit or theme, keep an ongoing list of important words (in sentences) on a large sheet of paper hanging in the classroom. Take time periodically to examine the growing list and talk about the words added recently. Older children can keep their own lists.

3.   *Important word books.* Children maintain their own books of words that have become important to them in some way. The words may then be used in writing activities.

4.   *Structured overview.* Present vocabulary to children in a way that shows the interrelationships between and among terms. (See Chapter 10.)

5.   *Semantic mapping.* To use this device for building word meanings and connections, select a concept such as "camping." Have the chil-

dren tell all of the words that are related to that concept and map them to show the relationships. The technique is similar to a structured overview, but in semantic mapping the words usually come from the children. Figure 9.1 illustrates a semantic map for *camping*.

    6. *Revisiting of important words.* At the completion of a reading selection, revisit important words with children to establish their understanding based on the context of the selection.

    7. *Figures of speech.* Focus on figures of speech, colloquial expressions, and idioms. Frequently discuss the difference between literal meanings and figurative language. Create a class book of favorite expressions. Establish a pen-pal activity with students in a different dialectal region. Exchange expressions and their uses and meanings.

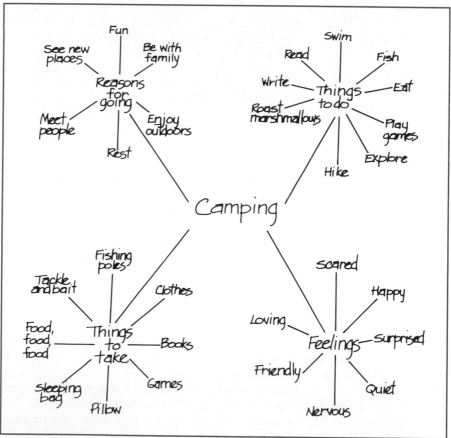

Figure 9.1   Semantic map for *Camping*.

Teachers who focus on the importance of vocabulary development in both planned and impromptu activities enhance their students' reading and writing vocabularies.

Developing the Use of Context Cues

The importance of context cues was made clear by Durkin (1978–1979), who stressed that English is a *positional language* in which meaning very often depends on word order. She pointed out the importance of word order in sentences such as these:

The boy fed the kitten.

The kitten fed the boy.

and in such expressions as *day off* and *off day*. Because meaning is so dependent on word order, the structure of sentences signals meaning. However, the importance of context cues must not be overestimated. Context assists readers in understanding the meaning of words that are primarily redundant. Frequently, words whose meaning is signaled by context are words that contribute little new meaning to the text (Hittleman, 1988). The effectiveness of context cues is dependent on readers' ability to see connections, to solve problems, and to recognize a word as being in their listening vocabulary once they have decoded it. We suggest activities like these to develop children's use of context cues:

1. Play word games in which the order of words is changed to illustrate the positional nature of our language. Show that word order sometimes changes the meaning and other times renders the sentence meaningless.
2. Teach the concept of noun markers. Have children brainstorm and later predict the words that can occupy a slot following a noun marker. For example, which words could go in this empty slot?

    The _____ were sweet and juicy and made wonderful juice.

3. Teach the concept of the preposition as a noun marker and do activities similar to the ones suggested in activity 2.
4. Teach the concept that some words signal the meaning of other nearby words (semantic cues). Have children predict possible words signaled by semantic cues in sentences such as this:

    The _____ did not cover the sides of the window.

Extend this activity to show that the meaning of the word may be illustrated in sentences other than the one in which the word is found. Activities like this one may be simplified by indicating the beginning sound in the unknown word—information that is always available in actual reading situations.

5. Demonstrate that in some sentences words are simply defined; for example,

A carpenter's square is a device to measure or create 90-degree angles.

6. Demonstrate that in some sentences the meaning of words is explained by examples introduced by words such as *such*, *like*, *such as*, and *for example:*

Many cities are altering their skylines with towers such as Toronto's CN tower and the Space Needle in Seattle.

7. Develop modified cloze activities using text from which words have been omitted not randomly but systematically: those words that are contextually cued are removed. Again, this activity may be simplified by indicating the initial letter of each omitted word. Figure 9.2 is an example of a modified cloze activity. As you predict the words that might fit in the blanks, consider all the contextual and other language information you are using. It is interesting to do this activity with a partner and discuss the reasons for your predictions.

THE CIRCUS

For a week the circus posters had been displayed on the Stanfield signboards. Billy had stood by while the men _____ them on, and he and Larry almost knew the different _____ by heart.

"It ain't as _____ as Barnum's," said Robert. "I saw that at Madison Square Garden. I tell you it was _____!"

The Brandenberg children were not _____ to argue on this subject. It was to be their first _____, and if it proved as good as the posters represented, it would be _____.

"How do you suppose he can _____ on such a thin wire way up in the _____?" asked Billy.

"She's a star if she can _____ on a _____ when he is on the gallop. Look there, she's going to _____ through _____ and land on _____ on the other side!" exclaimed Tom.

Figure 9.2   Modified cloze.

8. Have students create their own examples as modeled on those discussed in activities 2 through 7.

Developing the Use of Word-Attack Cues

A Word of Caution

It is important for you as a teacher of reading to have background knowledge of how the graphophonic system works in reading. Under appropriate conditions, instruction in the use of graphophonic cues is necessary in reading education. However, the amount of space basal teacher guides devote to instruction in word-attack skills would suggest that such instruction is far more important than it is. Durkin's (1978–1979) research showed that the greatest amount of instructional time in reading is spent on phonics instruction. The following discussion of the teaching of word-attack skills is offered here *primarily* as background information for the teacher-in-training. Please note that the amount of space it requires is out of proportion to its significance.

Assumptions

Word-attack instruction should be based on the following assumptions:

1. Breaking words apart to "sound them out" is usually not a very helpful way to identify an unknown word. The combination of context cues, schematic cues, and beginning sound is usually more powerful than sounding out a word letter by letter, sound by sound.
2. Mature readers (those beyond the stages of emerging and developing readers) rarely sound out the individual sounds within a unfamiliar word. If context cues combined with schematic cues and initial sounds do not reveal the word, the dictionary, the glossary, the teacher, or a friend is usually consulted.
3. Before phonic word-attack instruction is begun with young children, certainty is established regarding their abilities in auditory discrimination, visual discrimination, and the onset of concrete operational thinking.
4. Children have had many meaningful interactions with print and understand that reading is a meaning-constructing process before instruction in word attack begins.
5. Word-attack instruction is derived from a meaningful text that is taken apart and studied. The instruction ends with a reading of the text. Instruction proceeds from whole to part to whole.

■ Components of a Skills Lesson

The components of a skills lesson are here presented as steps in teaching graphophonic skills. In fact, the skills lesson format is appropriate for teaching any skill—a reading skill, a writing skill, or even a manual skill such as typing. A skills lesson has four components: development of knowledge, practice, application, and reinforcement.

Development of Knowledge

To begin, the skill is demonstrated, explained, memorized, or discovered. Decisions regarding instructional strategy must be made at this point: knowledge of some skills is best developed deductively; of others, inductively.

Using a deductive strategy, the teacher makes a statement such as, "The sound of *m* is the sound you read at the beginning of *mommy, monkey,* and *make.*" (Some teachers ignore Principle 1 and 2 of instruction in word identification by breaking the reading process down even further, saying, "The sound of *m* is /mmmm/." We believe that sound–symbol relationships should be taught in the context of words.) The teacher then presents several examples of words that begin with /m/. Students are guided to state the sound–symbol relationship themselves. The deductive strategy, sometimes called *rote learning,* is best employed in phonic word-attack instruction rather than in structural or syllabic word attack.

Using the inductive strategy, the teacher presents several examples of words illustrating the skill (a pattern or generalization) and guides students' examination of the samples until they discover the pattern. Inductive learning is often called *discovery learning.* To teach the generality that a syllable formed by a consonant, vowel, and consonant (CVC) usually has a short vowel sound, the teacher presents to the children examples of words (preferably from a story they have recently read) such as *cat, hid,* and *had.* The children are asked to read the words and then to describe how the words are alike. After carefully guiding the children's observation, the teacher encourages them to state the pattern in their own words. Clearly, inductive learning takes longer than deductive learning. The good news is that it is also longer lasting and more readily transferable. The time spent in inductive strategies is therefore worthwhile.

Practice

The children practice with words that are already in their sight vocabulary, looking for examples of the skill demonstrated in the development-of-knowledge stage. For example, they might search through stories they had recently dictated or written and peruse magazines or newspapers in search of instances of the pattern. They might suggest alternative ways to state the generalization they had just discovered.

Children may also practice with words that are not their sight vo-cabularies, but the teacher must take care to see that they are not frustrated in their efforts. Practice activities could be planned on a continuum from very easy, using known words, to more challenging, using unfamiliar words. Often it is helpful for the teacher to guide the children's practice, especially in initial or very challenging activities.

Practice is important because it helps lock the use of a skill into long-term memory. Easy skills require relatively little practice. Complicated skills call for massed practice initially, followed by spaced practice. Some practice activities can be presented in game format that groups of children can use.

Application

The teacher assesses the mastery of a skill by asking children to apply it to words not in their sight vocabulary. The only purpose for teaching word-attack skills is to enable children to decode words not already in their sight vocabulary. Therefore, the ultimate application of any word-attack skill is the decoding of an unfamiliar word. The teacher must now make instructional decisions regarding how controlled or "strict" the application is to be. Application activities can be distributed over a continuum from very controlled to very uncontrolled, or assumed (Figure 9.3).

Reinforcement

All teachers have had the painful experience of teaching a skills lesson they are certain would earn them the "Teacher of the Year" award, only to have the children the next day appear never to have heard of the skill! Skills instruction requires a great deal of patience from both the teacher and the learner. Sometimes additional practice is all it takes for retention; other times it is necessary to reteach a skill. We know that the best way to ensure that children retain skill knowledge is to provide massed practice initially, followed by intermittent practice. Reviewing a skills lesson the next day and walking through practice activities with children is helpful. This review should usually be followed by opportunities to read. We have known

Very controlled	Somewhat controlled	Assumed
Completing a test made with nonsense words guaranteed to be unfamiliar.	Playing a game or completing a worksheet, with application carefully observed by the teacher.	Reading a book.

Figure 9.3 Continuum of skills applications.

for some time that READING, READING, READING is clearly the best form of reinforcement (Schneider, 1979).

■ Teaching Graphophonic Cues

In preparing to teach graphophonic cues, the teacher must make an instructional strategy decision, choosing between synthetic and analytic phonics instruction. Synthetic phonics involves teaching sound–symbol relationships in isolation and then teaching children to blend the sounds into words. Analytic phonics involves teaching children sounds in the con-

Graphophonic cues constitute one cueing system among several that the reader relies on for the creation of meaning.
© *Steve Takatsuno/The Picture Cube*

Development of knowledge

1. Write the letters *sh, i,* and *p* on the board.
2. Say, "Today we are going to learn some new sounds. Listen as I read the sounds to you." Say each of the sounds in isolation.
3. Ask the children to repeat the sounds with you.
4. Write the word *ship* on the board. Say, "Now let's say the sounds together faster. Faster. Faster."
5. Say, "You now know all the sounds in the word *ship.*"

Practice

1. Write phonograms (clusters of letters) that the children know on the board, such as *ut, out,* and *ot.*
2. Write *sh* on the board. Have them practice the /sh/ sound and then add it to the front of each of the known phonograms.

Application

Give the children a test in which they must decode the /sh/ sound in nonsense words.

Reinforcement

Repeat the practice portion of the lesson the next day.

Figure 9.4   Synthetic phonics lesson.

text of words and then blending sounds known from two or more words into the sounds of an unknown word. Figures 9.4 and 9.5 illustrate the two strategies.

Choice of Strategy

Which strategy should the teacher select? Our preferences are strong here. The synthetic strategy has several disadvantages. It violates Principles 1, 2, and 4 set forth earlier in this chapter. Sounds in isolation have no meaning, look nothing like the reading act, and are the least important aspect of the reading process. Many consonant sounds produced in isolation are distorted because they must be voiced with a vowel sound. For example, the sound of *p* is rendered /puh/. Sounds are much more useful to the decoding goal when they are considered in patterns (May, 1986; Hittleman, 1988).

Development of knowledge

1. From a recently read or dictated story, select sentences that use words containing the sounds on which you wish to focus.
2. Write the sentences on the board, underlining the target words.
3. Ask for volunteers to read the sentences, or have the children read each sentence after you.

The *shark* has very *sharp* teeth.

The *shark flips* its tail in the water.

4. Have the children read the underlined words with you. Ask them to listen carefully to the *sh* sound and the sounds in *flips*.

Practice

1. Have the children repeat the underlined words with you.
2. Ask them to name other words that have the same sounds. Reinforce the sound–symbol relationship within each word correctly suggested.

Application

Write the words *shark* and *flips* on the board. Under those words write the word *ship*. Say, "If you know the *sh* sound from *shark* and the *ips* sound from *flips*, what is this new word?"

Reinforcement

1. Have children blend sounds from other words in their sight vocabularies.
2. Practice reading sentences containing the word *ships*.
3. Reread the two sentences about sharks introduced in the development-of-knowledge step.

Figure 9.5   Analytic phonics lesson.

Drill on isolated sounds may well signal to young readers that the most important part of reading is making *sounds* rather than making *sense*.

There is some research to show that the synthetic method works for some children (Bond and Dykstra, 1966–1967) and that some children who cannot learn to decode using the analytic method can learn using the synthetic method (Bond and Dykstra, 1966–1967; Weaver, 1988). However, teaching word-attack skills using the analytic method is much more consistent with the principles of word-identification instruction outlined in this chapter. We recommend that when it is necessary to teach word-attack skills the analytic method be used first. Because of its many limitations, the synthetic method should be used only as a last resort.

A Skills Sequence

After resolving the analytic/synthetic debate, the next issue in planning graphophonic skills instruction is a scope and sequence decision. There is no widely agreed-upon skills sequence for graphophonic instruction. The sequence is best determined by the needs of students. In practice, the sequence is generally determined by the publisher of the basal reading series used in a given classroom. One typical sequence follows.

I. **Letter names.** Although it is not necessary for children to know letter names in order to learn graphophonic word attack, the ability to talk about letters facilitates instruction.

II. **Consonant sounds.** Most publishers begin with consonant sounds because the consonants in a sentence carry the bulk of the message. To illustrate this point, read the following sentences:

_ _ e _ oy _ i_ _ _e _ a_ _.

Th_ b_ _ _ h_t th_ b_ll.

The sentence containing only consonants is much easier to decode than the sentence with only vowels.

A. Initial single consonants.

B. Initial consonant blends. Consonant blends, sometimes called clusters, are two or more consonants pronounced rapidly together. Examples: *bl, br, cr, dr, fl, sp, st, str*.

C. Initial consonant digraphs. Digraphs are two consonants that represent only one sound. Examples: *ch, ph, sh, th, wh*.

D. Some programs reteach these three categories of consonants in final positions in words.

III. **Vowels.** Vowel sounds are more variable and thus more difficult for children to learn than consonants. In many classrooms a great deal of time is spent teaching vowel sounds, even though consonant sounds are demonstrably more important.
   A. Vowel sounds in syllable patterns.
      1. VC and CVC.[1] Syllable ends with a consonant; vowel sound is usually short.

         at   cat

      2. VCe and CVCe. Syllable ends with an *e* preceded by a single consonant and a vowel; vowel sound is usually long.

         ate   rake

      3. CV and CVV. Syllable ends with a vowel; vowel sound is usually long.

         go   buy

   B. Vowel sounds in other patterns.
      1. Vowel digraphs. Two vowels, only one of which is sounded. Examples: *ai, ea, ee, oa, wait, each, speech, oats.*
      2. Diphthong. Two vowels that make a new sound composed of the vowel plus glide. Examples: *ow, oi, oy, ou, how, oil, toy, out.*
      3. Consonant-controlled vowel. The sound of a vowel is distorted by the following consonant sound so that the vowel sound is neither long nor short. Examples: *fir, far, call.*

Utility of Graphophonic Generalizations

One of the most important decisions regarding instruction in graphophonic skills is which skills to teach. Although a scope and sequence decision is the traditional guide here, research conducted by three investigators in the sixties may be more helpful. Ted Clymer, Mildred Bailey, and Robert Emans independently conducted research to determine the utility of phonic generalizations (general rules to guide pronunciation of written words, such as, "When a word begins with *wr*, the *w* is silent"). Clymer examined primary-grade materials, Bailey looked at first- through sixth-grade materials, and Emans studied intermediate-grade materials. In each study the

---

1. V = vowel; C = consonant; e = silent *e*.

question was, "In what percentage of the time that a particular generalization could apply does it apply?" Of the forty-five generalizations studied, only ten applied in 100 percent of the instances in which they could apply. Many fell short of reasonable utility. For example, a generalization commonly taught in first grade is, "When two vowels go walking, the first one does the talking" (another way to describe vowel digraphs). In the primary materials this generalization held up 45 percent of the time; in grades one through six, 34 percent of the time; and in intermediate-grade materials, only 18 percent of the time. A composite of these studies is found in Appendix G. We suggest that generalizations not be taught unless they have a minimal utility of 75 percent.

Sorenson (1983) did an updated study of the utility of thirty-eight generalizations in five primary-level basal reader series. Of those, only twenty-two met our recommended level of 75 percent. Years ago, Dolores Durkin (1976, p. 28) offered teachers advice that is still valid today:

1. Commercial materials (especially workbooks) commonly have children work on tasks that will not advance their ability to read. It is important, therefore, that teachers constantly ask, "Is this essential?" when they preview materials. . . .
2. Teachers should be knowledgeable about a great many things, but that does not mean they should try to teach everything they know. . . .

Degree of Emphasis

So how much graphophonic instruction should we do?

This question is the cause of a great deal of debate within our profession. We believe that the answer becomes clear if you consider these important points:

1. We have researched the utility of graphophonic generalizations and discovered that few are highly dependable. Most of these rules do not need to be taught to children because most children will internalize graphophonic patterns through reading and writing.
2. Children cannot remember complex phonics terms and patterns, though they can apply such rules or generalizations unconsciously in their reading (Tovey, 1980).
3. Since children can apply phonics rules that they cannot articulate, it appears that the usual amount of instruction in phonics terminology and rules far exceeds what is necessary. Weaver (1988, p. 77) underscores this point, saying, "We do not expect

toddlers to *consciously* learn rules for putting sounds together in order to form words, and neither need we expect young school-age children to consciously learn rules for taking words apart and putting them back together again."

4. We need to help children learn basic sound–symbol relationships, but that instruction should be done only as we see a need for it.

■ Teaching the Use of Letter Clusters

The value of letter clusters—groups of letters whose pronunciation is consistent from one word to the next—has received renewed attention from authors of reading textbooks (May, 1986; Hittleman, 1988). Drawing on research done in the early seventies, these authors have suggested that children notice letter clusters naturally with little instruction, if any (Cunningham, 1975–1976), and that readers seem to rely more on word structures than on generalizations regarding syllables or vowels when unlocking an unfamiliar word (Glass and Burton, 1973). Hittleman (1988, p. 186) stressed the value of using word clusters in word-identification instruction:

It is possible and natural for students to learn three- and four-letter clusters as easily as they learn single-letter phonic units. These letter clusters are learned by examining words in students' listening vocabularies that are not immediately recognized. This system helps alleviate the problem of teaching vowel sounds. A vowel has a sound as part of a cluster and not because of a rule.

The teacher should present the clusters as part of whole words. Through direct teaching, students can learn to recognize the cluster and associate it with a common phonological unit.

The idea of teaching letter clusters, while gaining support in the literature, presents a dilemma to the teacher who is sensitive to the five principles of word-identification instruction. Work with word clusters may help children learn vowel sounds, but drilling children on lists of words is far removed from the reading act. Drill on words like *cast, mast, fast, past,* and *last* may reinforce the short sound of *a,* but it does not relate word identification to constructing meaning. The value of any word-identification teaching strategy must be weighed against how closely that activity is related to the reading act. Word-identification instruction must be related to the reading and writing children are doing. For example, instead of drilling on letter clusters with words in isolation, the teacher could select a word representative of a cluster from a child's writing or from the day's story. Children could be asked to make as many other words as they can by substituting for the initial consonant. Playing rhyming games and reading the rhymed Dr. Seuss stories (with pauses for the children to fill in words) are also good practice. Work with the letter cluster is then more closely related to the reading or writing the children are doing.

■ Teaching Structural Word-Attack Cues

When a reader fails to recognize an unfamiliar word through context cues and/or a combination of context cues, schematic cues, and initial-letter cues, the next strategy is to apply knowledge of structural cues. Often called *structural word attack*, this procedure involves the identification of prefixes, suffixes, and root or base words in an attempt to decode a word not in the reader's sight vocabulary. The instructional goal is to teach the reader to examine the unfamiliar word for the possible inclusion of prefixes and suffixes so that the root may be identified. Then syllabic word attack and phonic word attack may be applied to the root.

Roots

The basic structural unit in English words is the root. Roots are units that cannot be reduced and still maintain the same meaning relationship to other words in the same family. For example, *hit* is a root word. If we removed the *h* we would alter the meaning, and the result could no longer belong to the family of words made from the root *hit*, such as *hits*, *hitter*, and *hitting*.

Prefixes

Prefixes are groups of letters added to the beginning of words to alter the meaning of the root. Examples are *re-* (meaning "again" or "back," as in *recall*), *im-* (meaning "not," as in *immature*), and *un-* (meaning "not," as in *unhappy*). The teaching of a prefix should follow the same strategy as the teaching of a sight word and should include an explanation of the way in which the prefix alters the meaning of the root. The following steps may be included in a prefix lesson:

1. Present the complete word drawn from a recently read selection.
2. Have children read the word or read it to them.
3. Ask children to identify the root if they can; if not, show them the root and prefix.
4. Have children read the prefix and then the root. Ask what the root means.

5. Ask if anyone knows what the prefix means. Establish the meaning of the prefix and demonstrate how it alters the root.
6. Demonstrate the function of the prefix with other roots familiar to the children.
7. Ask for volunteers to suggest other words bearing the same prefix.

Suffixes

Suffixes are groups of letters added to the ends of words either to alter the meaning of the root or to change the function the root may perform in a sentence. The suffixes that alter the meaning of a root are called *derivational suffixes*. Those that alter the function of a word are called *inflectional suffixes*. Examples of derivational suffixes include *-able* (meaning "capable of being," as in *loveable*) and *-less* (meaning "without," as in *penniless, senseless,* and *careless*). Inflectional suffixes change nouns to indicate number, gender, or possession; verbs to indicate tense or voice; and adjectives or adverbs to indicate comparison (Durkin, 1976). These are some examples:

Noun	*house* to *houses; girl* to *girls'*
Verb	*hit* to *hits* or *hitting; paint* to *paints, painted, painting*
Adjective	*happy* to *happier* or *happiest*
Adverb	*quick* to *quickly.*

The suggestions for teaching prefixes apply to the teaching of suffixes.

■ Teaching Syllabic Word-Attack Cues

Syllabic word attack applies generalizations describing ways in which words are divided into syllables. Once an unknown word is divided into syllables, graphophonic analysis may be applied at the syllabic level.

These generalizations describe how words may be divided into syllables:

1. When two like consonants stand between two vowels, the word is usually divided between the consonants:

   pup py   stag ger   pep per   com mon

2. When two unlike consonants stand between two vowels, the word is usually divided between the consonants:

   wal rus   cir cus   pic nic   trum pet

3. When one consonant stands between two vowels, the consonant usually goes with the second syllable:

   pi rate   si lent   pa per   mi ser

4. When a word ends in a consonant and *le*, the consonant usually begins the last syllable:

   ea gle   ta ble   no ble   ket tle

5. Compound words are usually divided between the parts and between syllables within those parts:

   po lice man   blind fold   sun shine   snow man

6. Prefixes and suffixes are usually separate syllables:

   dis own   re sold   swift ly   re pay ment

Some reading programs teach each of these syllabic generalizations. Nevertheless, we suspect that readers usually identify unfamiliar words through the use of context cues and the first letter of the word. We doubt the utility of drill and practice on syllabic generalizations. When you see a situation in which teaching a syllabic generalization would help a child, do it, and then move on to real reading activities.

Developing the Use of the Dictionary

Most mature readers do not know the formal rules of word identification. When we do get caught trying to ignore a word that is not in our sight vocabulary, and comprehension fails, we usually turn to the dictionary. In fact, next to the use of context cues, the use of the dictionary may be the most helpful route to the pronunciation and meaning of an unfamiliar word. It is important that children see the dictionary as a valuable tool early in their reading and writing experiences; its use will then, we hope, pose no threat in later grades. These are some ways to help young children become comfortable with the dictionary:

1. Make alphabetized important-word books or language-experience dictionaries in which to record words that children have wanted to use in their writing. Working with them, children become accustomed to alphabetical order early.
2. Place picture dictionaries and beginning dictionaries in the classroom reading corner and model their use with young readers and authors.

A dictionary serves as a useful tool when children are writing.
© *Dan Chidester/The Image Works*

3. Share larger dictionaries in the media center with children and talk about their use.
4. Help children to see that words have more than one meaning and that those meanings are defined in the dictionary.

Some children who are struggling with learning to read find it very difficult to use a dictionary. It is appropriate, we believe, to teach children that when they cannot decode a word they may ask a friend or the teacher for help. Let children know that they may make use of the "last resort" resources.

■ Skills Lessons versus Integrated Use

How should dictionary use be taught? Should teachers plan isolated lessons in dictionary skills, or should reference to the dictionary be integrated with real reading and writing activities? In a sense, the answer is yes to both alternatives. We believe that the use of the dictionary should be integrated with reading and writing activities through carefully planned lessons on dictionary use. When an unknown word turns up while the teacher is sharing a reading experience with children, that is the time for the teacher to help children turn to the dictionary. Keeping dictionaries on the reading table or in the writing center facilitates this integration. Consulting the dictionary for real purposes in real situations will foster its use far better than skill-and-drill activities in workbooks or with worksheets, which, in our observation, transfer to real uses minimally at best. Therefore, teachers should present lessons in dictionary use as part of the reading and writing program and should reinforce those lessons with regular reference to the dictionary during reading and writing activities.

■ Dictionary Skills

The skilled use of the dictionary is a developmental process that continues throughout the grades. Consulting the curriculum guide for a given grade level will determine the skills to be taught at that grade level. Most elementary school programs include the following goals for dictionary use:

1. Use alphabetical order for everyday things; at first, go only by initial letter, and later add second, third, and more letters.
2. Learn to open the dictionary near the word sought.
3. Use guide words to find the page on which the desired word is located.
4. Use accent marks to produce the correct pronunciation of words.
5. Use the pronunciation key and phonetic respellings of words.
6. Identify several meanings of words.
7. Be able to select the meaning that fits the text being read.
8. Develop an attitude that says, "Let's look it up!"

Real purposes for using alphabetical order are common in the classroom; for example, recording absentees, replacing encyclopedia volumes, determining one's place in a rotation, and ordering supplies.

Reading Skills versus Reading Strategies

Traditionally, reading programs have been skill based or skill driven. The assumption was that if children learned a sequence of subskills, then eventually they would learn to read. This skill-based view of reading has been challenged by those who have carefully studied the reading process (Goodman, 1968; Rumelhart, 1977; Smith, 1982; Weaver, 1988). These researchers have suggested that readers make use of an array of strategies that are very different from, and much more useful than, subskills.

When readers interact with print, they are bombarded with language cues—syntactic, semantic, and graphophonic. Their reading strategy is to *predict* from syntactic and semantic cues what will be said, to *sample* the minimum number of graphophonic cues required to support the prediction, and then to *confirm or correct* the prediction as necessary. The reader moves on, employing semantic and syntactic cues to make another prediction in a continuing cycle of steps. The steps are used simultaneously as readers construct a text and create meaning (Goodman, Watson, and Burke, 1987). At each point, the use of the strategy is influenced by the reader's schemata. This three-part strategy of predicting, sampling, and confirming/correcting is much more essential to the reading process than are subskills.

The strategy is taught through a variety of activities, one of the most useful of which is what Dorothy Watson and Paul Crowley call "bringing the reading process to a conscious level" (Watson and Crowley, 1988, p. 257). Teachers help children bring the reading process to a conscious level by talking about it in both formal and informal ways. For example, noticing that a reader has stopped reading and gone back in the text because the reading did not make sense, the teacher can talk about the strategy of checking for sense as you read.

During an individual conference, the teacher can ask a child to recall a story and then talk about how the reading process worked. Asking questions such as, "How did you learn from the story? What part of the story was easy for you to read? Why? What part was difficult? What made it difficult? How did you overcome the difficulty? What did you do when you came to words you did not know?" helps the reader focus on the reading process and the strategies used in reading. The teacher talks about the process and reinforces the use of strategies with the student. The discussion allows the teacher to focus on the reader's strengths while making note of weaknesses to address in the future.

The modified cloze activity (such as the one in Figure 9.2) is a helpful tool in bringing the reading process to a conscious level. It is important that only highly predictable words be deleted so that the activity goes smoothly, allowing focus on the reading process and not on individual words.

Another useful strategy for bringing the reading process to a conscious level is putting schema stories together. Schema stories are texts with highly predictable structures (first, second, third; or Once upon a time, then, finally) that are physically cut apart so that reading each section will permit the student to predict what comes next. A group of children (each holding a piece of the story) then decides how to put the pieces together. Discussing the reasons for their predictions and their use of the reading process is central to the activity.

Our experience has been that children are willing to talk about the reading process and are eager to extend their understanding. They lose interest in reading only when they have been drilled on skills until they are bored and their enthusiasm has waned.

Word Identification and the Reading/Writing Connection

The difficulty in talking about any one part of the reading process is that literacy is a complicated fabric of interdependent strands. The knowledge a child has of the sound–symbol relationships in our language is as important in writing as in reading. Logic argues that when we keep children's literacy experiences whole, the warp and woof of the fabric reinforce each other. So it is that we urge the use of real, meaningful exercises in the reading/writing program. The best practice of word-identification skills is found in actual reading experiences, not in worksheets and workbooks. The knowledge of how our sound–symbol system works is reinforced in writing activities.

Here it seems appropriate to recall three of the recommendations made in *Becoming a Nation of Readers,* the 1985 report of the Commission on Reading. First, children should spend less time completing workbooks and skills sheets. Second, children should spend more time in independent reading. Third, children should spend more time writing. Inherent in the third recommendation is the recognition not only that writing is valuable in its own right but that it promotes ability in reading. Teachers must always weigh the value of skills instruction against the cost of time taken away from reading and writing.

Major Ideas in This Chapter

- The reader moves from print to language by means of word-identification cues: sight words and context cues (syntactic, semantic, and graphophonic). The use of word-identification cues should be taught in meaningful contexts with as little disruption to the reading process as possible.

- A teacher's stance on the whole-to-part versus part-to-whole debate governs his or her approach to teaching reading. The issue is really whether we want children to believe reading is unlocking sounds or creating meaning. We advocate a whole-to-part approach.

- Skills lessons, whether inductive or deductive, proceed through development of knowledge, practice, application, and reinforcement. The preferred use of word-identification cues occurs in real reading activities supported by writing experiences. Skills instruction should take place in response to a child's specific need.

- The reading strategy of prediction, sampling cues, and confirming and correcting, followed by another prediction, is the heart of the reading process. Helping children learn to use these steps is more valuable than teaching isolated subskills.

- The best way to learn to read is to read; to write is to write. The value of skills instruction must always be weighed against the time it takes away from reading and writing activities.

? Discussion Questions
Focusing on the Teacher You Are Becoming

1. How much instructional time should be given to syntactic cues, semantic cues, and graphophonic cues? How does a teacher decide on the answer to this important question?
2. "How teachers view the reading process very much determines the kinds of curriculum decisions they make." Discuss this statement, generating as many examples as you can.
3. Review the five principles of word identification presented on pages 294–295. What specific differences would you observe in comparing classrooms where these principles are honored with classrooms where they are ignored?
4. Why is there no agreed-upon sequence of word-identification skills? Should there be one? Why or why not?
5. Should reading teachers teach reading strategies *instead of* reading subskills? Is there a place for both? Take a position on the question and argue it in a small discussion group.

✔ Field-Based Applications

1. Interview three classroom teachers at three different grade levels to find out how they determine which word-identification skills to teach.
2. Compare the skills sequences presented in three basal reading series. How much agreement is there? How do you account for this?

3. Plan six word-identification lessons: two each on graphophonic cues, structural cues, and syllabic cues. In each pair, make one lesson inductive and one lesson deductive. Compare the children's responses to each kind of lesson with your own.

4. Engage in some of the reading strategy activities identified in the section headed "Reading Skills versus Reading Strategies." Discuss reading with three children, trying out your skill in helping them bring the reading process to a conscious level.

5. Plan two dictionary-use lessons that are integrated with reading/writing activities. Think about the differences between dictionary lessons that stand alone and those that are incorporated into meaningful activities.

6. Observe two classrooms, one in which skills are taught part-to-whole, and one in which skills are taught whole-to-part. List all the comparisons and contrasts you can find.

▣ References and Suggested Readings

Anderson, Richard C.; Hiebert, Elfrieda H.; Scott, Judith A.; and Wilkinson, Ian A. *Becoming a Nation of Readers*. Washington, D.C.: National Institute of Education, 1985.

Bailey, Mildred H. "The Utility of Phonics Generalization in Grades One through Six." *The Reading Teacher* 20 (February 1967): 413–418.

Bond, Guy L., and Dykstra, Robert. "The Cooperative Research Program in First-Grade Reading Instruction." *Reading Research Quarterly* 2 (1966–1967): 5–142.

Clymer, Theodore. "The Utility of Phonic Generalizations in the Primary Grades." *The Reading Teacher* 16 (January 1963): 252–258.

Cunningham, Patricia M. "Investigating a Synthesized Theory of Mediated Word Identification." *Reading Research Quarterly* 11 (1975–1976): 127–143.

Durkin, Dolores. "What Classroom Observations Reveal about Reading Comprehension Instruction." *Reading Research Quarterly* 14 (1978–1979): 481–527.

Durkin, Dolores. *Strategies for Identifying Words*. Boston: Allyn & Bacon, 1976.

Emans, Robert. "The Usefulness of Phonic Generalizations above the Primary Grades." *The Reading Teacher* 20 (February 1967): 419–425.

Glass, Gerald G., and Burton, Elizabeth H. "How Do They Decode? Verbalizations and Observed Behaviors of Successful Decoders." *Education* 94 (September/October 1973): 58–64.

Goodman, Kenneth S., ed. *The Psycholinguistic Nature of the Reading Process*. Detroit: Wayne State University Press, 1968.

Goodman, Yetta; Watson, Dorothy; and Burke, Carolyn. *Reading Miscue Inventory: Alternative Procedures*. New York: Richard C. Owen, 1987.

Hittleman, Daniel R. *Developmental Reading, K–8, Teaching from a Whole Language Perspective*. 3rd edition. Columbus, Ohio: Charles E. Merrill, 1988.

May, Frank. *Reading as Communication: An Interactive Approach.* Columbus, Ohio: Charles E. Merrill, 1986.

Rumelhart, David E. "Toward an Interactive Model of Reading." In *Attention and Performance VI,* edited by Stanislov Dornic. Hillsdale, N.J.: Erlbaum, 1977, pp. 573–603.

Schneider, E. Joseph. "Researchers Discover Formula for Success in Student Learning." *Educational Research and Development Report 2,* Fall 1979, pp. 1–6.

Smith, Frank. *Understanding Reading.* Hillsdale, N.J.: Erlbaum, 1982.

Sorenson, Nancy. *A Study of the Reliability of Phonic Generalizations in Five Primary-Level Basal Reading Programs.* Unpublished doctoral dissertation, Arizona State University, 1983.

Tovey, Duane R. "Children's Grasp of Phonics Terms vs. Sound–Symbol Relationships." *The Reading Teacher* 33 (January 1980): 431–437.

Watson, Dorothy, and Crowley, Paul. "How Can We Implement a Whole-Language Approach?" In *Reading Process and Practice from Sociopsycholinguistics to Whole Language,* edited by Constance Weaver. Portsmouth, N.H.: Heinemann Educational Books, 1988, pp. 232–279.

Weaver, Constance, ed. *Reading Process and Practice from Sociopsycholinguistics to Whole Language.* Portsmouth, N.J.: Heinemann Educational Books, 1988.

Weaver, Phyllis, and Shankoff, Fred. *Research within Reach: A Research-Guided Response to Concerns of Reading Educators.* ERIC Document Reproduction Service No. ED 162 283, 1978.

Chapter 10

Assisting Children with Comprehension

Chapter Overview

- Comprehension is a very complex subject about which our views are changing as we learn more about the reading process.

- Helping children think about their own comprehension before, during, and after reading is a critically important aspect of comprehension instruction. Thinking about their own thinking is more important than studying specific comprehension subskills.

- Teachers must carefully plan for activities in guided reading, skills development, and enrichment. The Guided Metacomprehension Strategy, a form of guided reading activity, combines what we currently know about the reading process with the traditional practice of asking comprehension questions.

- Relating background experiences and knowledge to a text, making predictions, and bringing the reading process to a conscious level are especially important comprehension skills.

- Effective teachers of comprehension model the comprehension process for their students, provide cues to help them understand what they are reading, help children know what they know about the topic, generate useful independent activities, and enrich children's vocabularies.

- Enrichment activities in comprehension include writing, drama, and art, all of which offer students opportunities to enhance and extend their comprehension of story content.

When you talk with other teachers-in-training about your work with children in a reading practicum, one word that comes up frequently is *comprehension*. Teachers, too, use it often in talking about their students' progress in reading. What do we all really mean when we speak of comprehension? This chapter will explain the concept of comprehension and show you ways of teaching it. Of all the things we do in reading instruction, understanding comprehension and teaching it are the most challenging.

The Meaning of Comprehension

The simplest definition of comprehension is that comprehension is thinking—the thinking we do when we read or listen. The dictionary definition of comprehension is "the act or action of grasping with the intellect: understanding." Although each of these definitions may be clear, neither is sufficient for us to understand the nature of comprehension as it relates to the reading process. To say that comprehension is the thinking we do when we read is too simple. Comprehension certainly involves thinking, but it is much more complex than that. Read the following passage and *think* about what it means. We predict that the thinking you do as you read will not be enough in itself to enable you to say that you *comprehended* the passage.

The procedure is actually quite simple. First, you arrange things into different groups. Of course, one pile may be sufficient depending on how much there is to do. If you have to go somewhere else due to lack of facilities that is the next step, otherwise you are pretty well set. It is important not to overdo things. That is, it is better to do a few things at one time than too many. In the short run this may not seem important, but complications can arise. A mistake can be expensive as well. At first the whole procedure will seem complicated. Soon, however, it will become just another facet of life. It is difficult to foresee an end to the necessity for this task in the immediate future, but then one can never tell. After the procedure is completed one arranges the materials into different groups again. Then they can be put into their appropriate places. Eventually they will be used once more and the whole cycle will then have to be repeated. However, that is part of life. [Bransford and Johnson, 1973]

Did you "grasp with the intellect: understand?" Did you comprehend? If not, then we must conclude that comprehension involves more than just thinking when you read. It also involves much more than just pronouncing or recognizing the words. See what happens to your understanding of the selection when we tell you that it is a very "technical" description of how to sort the laundry before and after doing the wash. Now that you know this, go back and reread the description. Why will you be able to read it this time with solid understanding?

You now read the selection with solid understanding because of *what you brought to the reading act.* You approached the print with a history of personal laundry-sorting experiences on which you could draw once you knew what the topic was. This is what we should do all the time when we read. We draw on our remembered experiences to *bring* meaning to the text, provided that something or someone triggers our perception of the

A first-grader gives a whole new meaning to the expression "reading to yourself."
© Elizabeth Crews/The Image Works

relationship between the text and our background. These understandings and applications of background experiences are what we have referred to as *schemata*, defined by May (1986) as minitheories about things, people, language, places, and other phenomena in our background of experiences. Frank Smith (1978) says that we cannot read what we do not already have in our heads. In other words, we cannot read something about which we have no knowledge at all and expect to comprehend it. We call this same idea the *Velcro theory:* if we do not have at least some prior knowledge to bring to the reading experience, the new words and ideas do not stick. (Our term itself illustrates the idea!)

So comprehension is much more than just thinking when we read. It is the application of our schemata to the act of reading. We comprehend when we are able to combine the words (ideas) of the author with our own schemata (minitheories about the world). Interaction is central to the process. We define *comprehension* thus: the interaction of the author's ideas and the reader's schemata that results in the creation of meaning.

Comprehension occurs on more than one level at a time. For example, literal comprehension of the laundry-sorting description yields specific information that you might be able to recall if questioned. At another level is inferential comprehension, a more creative process in which we use our own prior knowledge to supply missing information or information that might have been assumed by the author. Rumelhart (1984, p. 3) suggests that a reader is "constantly evaluating hypotheses about the most plausible interpretation of the text. Readers are said to have understood the text when they are able to find a configuration of hypotheses which offer a coherent account for the various aspects of the text." Critical comprehension is the level at which the reader evaluates the author's ideas in terms of the reader's prior experience, the author's authority in writing about the subject, and the quality of expression in comparison with a standard. All these levels of comprehension are directly related to the purpose that the reader brings to the reading task. How you read *this* text will differ greatly depending on whether you expect to take a test on it or you just happen to be skimming it casually. You may also read it differently if you are a veteran classroom teacher applying your own experience to the teaching of reading. Comprehension is clearly an interactive process that occurs when a reader with a unique set of purposes and experiences meets a given text.

The complex task of comprehension is a topic of considerable discussion in our profession. Our view of the comprehension process is still evolving.

Our Developing View of the Comprehension Process

What you believe about the process of comprehension will certainly dictate how you design and carry out comprehension activities with your students. In their research, Jerome Harste and Robert Carey (1984) clearly demonstrated that what a teacher believes about the process of learning to read "strongly affects what instructional strategies are employed" (p. 32). The First Grade Studies conducted by the U.S. Office of Education (Stauffer, 1966) in the late 1960s attempted to identify the best approach to beginning reading. No best approach was found, but one of the major conclusions of the researchers was that the single most influential variable in the teaching of reading is the teacher. What you believe is very important. Now is the time for you to begin to formulate your position regarding instruction in comprehension.

An examination of the literature on teaching comprehension and a look at current classroom practices suggest that instructional strategies are changing as our understanding of the comprehension process becomes more complete. In the past we have thought that the way to know children have comprehended a text is to ask comprehension questions after they read. Now we are understanding that whereas asking comprehension questions has value, we can help readers even more if we bring the reading process to a conscious level and teach them to monitor their own comprehension. In Chapter 9 we said helping readers to use strategies is more important than teaching subskills. This principle applies just as emphatically to comprehension as it does to using the four cueing systems. We now understand that being able to predict, sample, and confirm or correct hypotheses is essential to good comprehension. When readers monitor their own comprehension of a text, they are using metacomprehension strategies.

■ Using Metacomprehension Strategies

Metacomprehension means "along with" and "after" comprehension. It signifies thinking while reading (or just afterward) about how we are comprehending what we read. Lowenthal (1986) has called this process "private, silent speech." Metacomprehension is our own personal monitoring of comprehension (May, 1986). Good readers seem to engage in the process of metacomprehension rather effortlessly. However, the skill is slow to develop. Baker and Brown (1984) have discovered that it is very hard for children in primary grades to explain why they are having trouble understanding something they have read. Intermediate-grade children who are good readers can usually tell you that they don't know a word or know what the word means. All children, and especially poor readers, would benefit from instructional strategies that improve metacomprehension ability.

Monitoring Comprehension

As you proceed through this text you are probably reading quite easily. In fact, you are likely to be using very few of the many, many graphophonic, semantic, and syntactic cues that are on this printed page. As a mature reader, you are probably relying most heavily on the semantic cues, followed by a combination of syntactic cues and your own schematic cues; you are paying little attention to individual words and almost none to the sounds in the words. In fact, in addition to using few of the cues on this page, you are probably making ongoing predictions about what we are going to say _____.

Did you predict that the word in the blank would be *next?* That is because as you read or listen to a speaker you are continually making predictions about what will follow. Ken Goodman (1967) has called reading a "psycholinguistic guessing game." Like Rumelhart's interactive hypotheses, this term refers to the prediction-making aspect of reading. As long as

What can you predict about this book, having seen only the cover?
© Elizabeth Crews/The Image Works

your reading confirms your predictions, you have comprehended. Frank Smith (1978) has said that evidence of comprehension is the state of having no unanswered questions. When we ask ourselves what the author is going to say next, make the prediction, and then confirm that prediction by reading, comprehension has occurred.

What does all this have to do with metacomprehension? When your predictions have not been confirmed—and you know it—you are engaged in metacomprehension. To say to yourself, "Hey, this isn't making any sense. I'd better go back and read more carefully" or to say, "I'm following this author's arguments every step of the way" is to engage in a personal comprehension-monitoring task known as *metacomprehension*. Realizing that you are in trouble as a comprehender, you then begin to use more of the cues on the printed page. Whereas you might have been relying heavily on semantic and syntactic cues as long as your reading flowed smoothly and logically, you must now slow down and make careful use of graphophonic cues to get you out of comprehension difficulty. Good readers do this kind of comprehension monitoring. Poor readers do not.

Here is another example of how metacomprehension works. Suppose you were reading this text:

The boy ran to the house. It was yellow with white shutters.

If you read, "The boy ran to the horse. It was yellow with white shutters," and did not notice that you had made a terrible mistake, you would be reading much as poor readers often do. In this case you would have been relying on the graphophonic cues without regard to meaning. A poor reader who makes this kind of error is not doing metacomprehension probably because he or she does not know that, first and foremost, reading is supposed to make sense.

Now suppose that when you read *horse* for *house* you very quickly noticed that the sentence was not making sense. Your background experiences have taught you that horses are not yellow (except on merry-go-rounds) and they never have shutters. You say something to yourself such as, "Hey, this is not making sense." You then reread more carefully and understand the author's message. You have engaged in metacomprehension. You thought about how you were comprehending while you were comprehending. It is important to help readers do this kind of self-monitoring and to correct breakdowns in comprehension when they occur.

Good readers tend to use the four cueing systems with considerable facility, relying here on one, there on another, and often integrating all four. The good reader's ability to use the cueing systems goes hand in hand with the ability to engage in metacomprehension. It is comprehension monitoring that signals the failure of one system and the need to shift to another. When the reader who has been relying primarily on schematic and syntactic cues suddenly realizes that comprehension has failed, making the switch to more intense use of semantic or graphophonic cues is a clear indication of good metacomprehension skill.

Making Inferences

Lapp and Flood (1984) have identified several ways in which good readers differ from poor readers. One of those ways is that good readers are adept at drawing inferences, and they know when they have failed to draw inferences. Most of the time, we rely heavily on our ability to draw inferences in order to make sense of what we read. The following example will provide some insight into the importance of inference in reading comprehension.

Susan and Michael have taken their allowance money to the local mall, where they are shopping for a sweater to give their mother for her birthday.

"Look at that one," said Susan. "It's perfect."

"No, it's not," said Michael. "It's not right at all."

To understand these two lines, you must make several inferences. You might infer, for example, that Susan is pointing to some kind of sweater in a shop window or a store display when she says, "Look at that one." From "It's perfect" you might infer that it appears to be the right size, the right color, and a style that she thinks their mother would like. When Michael says, "No, it's not," he may mean that it is not the right size, color, or style or that it costs too much or that he doesn't like the store or that he doesn't want Susan to be the one to make the selection. You would certainly make numerous inferences just in understanding those two simple statements.

In their 1984 research, Lapp and Flood also concluded that good readers are adept at predicting what authors are going to say next (Goodman's psycholinguistic guessing game). In both cases of inference drawing—reading between the lines of the text and predicting what comes next—metacomprehension is at the heart of the matter.

To summarize, it is very important that the teacher help children become interactive readers who monitor their own comprehension. In other words, they need to know that they don't know, to know why they might try certain strategies, and to know how well they are doing. We will discuss how this can be done later in this chapter.

■ Asking Comprehension Questions

Before recent gains in our understanding of the comprehension process, the traditional view held that the teacher's job in comprehension was to monitor the kind of thinking students could do in response to what they had read. The assumption was that comprehension consists of discrete skills—thinking skills—that can be identified, measured, and taught. This traditional view is built into practically all basal reader programs. Typically, when you observe a teacher guiding the reading of children in a basal, you will hear the teacher asking questions of the children. We are sure that this often seems *to the children* to be a great "I gotcha" game in which the teacher is trying to expose the children who have not read the story. In fact, the questions attempt to determine the kinds of thinking children can do in response to what they have read. At least, that is *supposed* to be the reason for them.

What place does the asking of comprehension questions have in helping children with comprehension? We believe that *after* children have been assisted in the process of prediction, sampling, and confirming or correcting, then it is appropriate to ask comprehension questions. Our first job is to help children use metacomprehension strategies; then we can refine the comprehension process through the use of comprehension questions.

Components of Comprehension

Where do the teachers' comprehension questions come from? They come from research that has attempted to define the components of comprehension and from efforts by authors to categorize various kinds of thinking tasks into groupings called *taxonomies*. We will look at one piece of significant research that defines the components of comprehension, and then we will examine two comprehension taxonomies.

One of the most significant pieces of research on identifying the components of comprehension was done by Frederick Davis in 1968. Davis used a very complicated statistical procedure called *factor analysis* to isolate those factors that make up this thing called comprehension and discover the extent to which each of them contributes to the whole. Of the five

Guided reading activities foster comprehension.
© Ellis Herwig/Stock, Boston

comprehension skills Davis identified, the most powerful contributor was knowledge of word meanings and the least powerful was the ability to answer recall questions. This is the order in which they contribute to comprehension:

1. Recalling word meanings; knowledge of word meanings
2. Drawing inferences from the text
3. Following the structure of a passage
4. Recognizing an author's purpose, attitude, tone, and/or mood
5. Answering recall questions—questions whose answers are found in the text.

To monitor the kinds of thinking students do in response to what they read, teachers should formulate questions from each of the five categories.

We know with certainty that each of those five factors does contribute to comprehension. However, we should recognize that the number of comprehension *skills* exceeds five: each of the factors could be broken down into component skills. It is important to take great care in identifying subskills so that we do not reduce the reading process to the point of meaninglessness. The danger in breaking the process down into hundreds of subskills (as some programs do) is that we create situations in which children cannot see the forest for the trees. We take so long assessing and teaching the individual subskills that children do not have enough time to read.

Taxonomies

The need to make the monitoring of comprehension manageable has motivated several authors to create taxonomies (classifications) of comprehension (thinking) skills or tasks. Educators have vigorously debated whether these taxonomies are just classifications or actual hierarchies of learning tasks in comprehension. If a taxonomy were simply a classification of comprehension tasks, then presumably a child who was an accomplished reader could answer questions drawn from any point within the taxonomy. If the taxonomy were a hierarchy, however, then it would follow that a child's ability to answer questions drawn from the first level should precede the ability to answer questions from the second, and so on. Tatham (1978, p. 193) asserted that taxonomies are "misused whenever it is believed that they describe developmental stages in children's cognitive responses to written materials." Research has not produced a definitive ordering of comprehension skills and comprehension skills are not taught in a hierarchical fashion in commercial materials.

From our work with children, we know that children can often answer questions of evaluation or judgment ("Was it right for Goldilocks to sample the porridge?") even when they have considerable difficulty answering a recall question ("What were the first three things Goldilocks did when she went into the bears' house?"). If taxonomies were hierarchical, the child would have to be able to answer the recall question (and several other kinds of questions) before being able to answer the evaluation question. Our conclusion is that comprehension taxonomies are not hierarchies, and should not be viewed as a means of describing developmental stages in comprehension. Rather, they should be used simply as a way to tap a variety of comprehension tasks, a teacher's guide to formulating questions about children's reading, challenging the thinking of readers, and identifying areas in which to concentrate instruction. A child's consistent difficulty with questions from one category tells us where to focus our instruction. We will talk about instructional issues later in this chapter. For now, consider two well-known comprehension taxonomies.

Dr. Wallen (1972) developed the Wallen taxonomy when asked to help a school move from a basal reading program to a literature-based reading program. Patterned after Bloom's *Taxonomy of the Cognitive Domain*, the Wallen taxonomy (Wallen, 1972, pp. 510–511) covers a wide range of comprehension tasks.

Wallen taxonomy[1]

I. Recall
   A. Identification. Recall specific items; facts and details.
      Cue words: who, what, where, when, how
   B. Organization. Recall events in sequence.
      Cue words: Tell in order, what happened.
                 Put these events in order. . . .
                 What happened after _____ did _____?

II. Interpretation
   A. Summarization. Student tells main idea of a selection in a title, sentence, paragraph.
      Cue words: What would be a good title for _____?
                 In two sentences, summarize this passage.
   B. Conclusion. Student infers underlying ideas in form of cause–effect relationship.
      Cue words: What happened because of _____?
                 What motivated _____ to _____?
                 As a result of _____, what _____?
                 What was the effect of _____ on _____?

---

1. From *Competency in Teaching Reading* by Carl Wallen. Copyright © 1972 by Science Research Associates, Inc. Reprinted by permission.

III. **Extrapolation**

    A. **Consequences.** Student predicts what would happen in cause–effect relationship if one element is changed.

       Cue words: What would happen if _____?

                  How might the story have changed if _____?

    B. **Corollaries.** Student is asked to draw from own experience related to the story.

       Cue words: Have you ever had an experience like _____?

                  Can you think of a time when you _____?

                  What is similar about _____ and _____?

IV. **Evaluation**

    A. **Objective evaluation.** Student makes judgments of soundness of statements or events in a selection based on an internal criterion such as supporting evidence, reasons, or logic provided.

       Cue words: Based on information from the story, should _____ have _____? Why or why not?

    B. **Subjective evaluation.** Student makes judgments about statements or events presented based on criteria external to the selection, such as own biases, beliefs, or preferences.

       Cue words: Do you think it was right for _____ to _____? Why or why not?

The Wallen taxonomy provides a good basis on which teachers can formulate discussion questions that monitor a variety of thought processes. The one shortcoming on the Wallen taxonomy that is addressed in the Barrett taxonomy (Brunner and Campbell, 1978, pp. 199–202) is the lack of questions in the affective domain. The Barrett taxonomy is unique in that it includes comprehension tasks in both the cognitive and affective domains.

Taxonomy of reading comprehension[2]

1.0 *Literal recognition or recall.* Literal comprehension requires the recognition or recall of ideas, information, and happenings that are explicitly stated in the materials read. *Recognition tasks*, which frequently take the form of purposes for reading,

---

2. From *A Taxonomy of Reading Comprehension* by Thomas C. Barrett, a Reading 360 Monograph. Copyright © 1972 by Ginn and Company. Reprinted by permission of Silver, Burdett & Ginn, Inc.

require the student to locate or identify explicit statements in the reading selection itself or in exercises that use the explicit content of the reading selection. *Recall tasks* demand the student to produce from memory explicit statements from a selection; such tasks are often in the form of questions teachers pose to students after a reading is completed. Two additional comments seem warranted with regard to literal comprehension tasks. First, although literal comprehension tasks can be overused, their importance cannot be denied, since a student's ability to deal with such tasks is fundamental to his ability to deal with other types of comprehension tasks. Second, all literal comprehension tasks are not necessarily of equal difficulty. For example, the recognition or recall of a single fact or incident may be somewhat easier than the recognition or recall of a number of facts or incidents, while a more difficult task than either of these two may be the recognition or recall of a number of events or incidents and the sequence of their occurrence. Also related to this concern is the hypothesis that a recall task is usually more difficult than a recognition task, when the two tasks deal with the same content and are of the same nature. Some examples[3] of literal comprehension tasks are:

1.1 *Recognition or recall of details.* The student is required to locate or identify or to call up from memory such facts as the names of characters, the time a story took place, the setting of a story, or an incident described in the story, when such facts are explicitly stated in the selection.

1.2 *Recognition or recall of main ideas.* The student is asked to locate or identify or to produce from memory an explicit statement in or from a selection which is the main idea of a paragraph or a larger portion from the selection.

1.3 *Recognition or recall of sequence.* The student is required to locate or identify or to call up from memory the order of incidents or actions explicitly stated in the selection.

---

3. Although the examples in each of the categories are logically ordered from easy to difficult, it is recognized that such a finite hierarchy has not been validated. Therefore, the user of the Taxonomy should view the examples as some of the tasks that might be used to help students produce comprehension products that relate to the type of comprehension described in each of the four major categories of the Taxonomy.

    1.4 *Recognition or recall of comparisons.* The student is requested to locate or identify or to produce from memory likenesses and differences among characters, times in history, or places that are explicitly compared by an author.

    1.5 *Recognition or recall of cause and effect relationships.* The student in this instance may be required to locate or identify or to produce from memory reasons for certain incidents, events, or characters' actions explicitly stated in the selection.

    1.6 *Recognition or recall of character traits.* The student is requested to identify or locate or to call up from memory statements about a character which help to point up the type of person he was, when such statements were made by the author of the selection.

2.0 *Inference.* Inferential comprehension is demonstrated by the student when he uses a synthesis of the literal content of a selection, his personal knowledge, his intuition and his imagination as a basis for conjectures or hypotheses. Conjectures or hypotheses derived in this manner may be along convergent or divergent lines depending on the nature of the task and the reading materials involved. For example, inferential tasks related to narrative selections may permit more divergent or creative conjectures because of the open-ended possibilities provided by such writing. On the other hand, expository selections, because of their content, may call for convergent hypotheses more often than not. In either instance, students may or may not be called upon to indicate the rationale underlying their hypotheses or conjectures, although such a requirement would seem to be more appropriate for convergent rather than divergent hypotheses. Generally, then, inferential comprehension is elicited by purposes for reading, and by teachers' questions which demand thinking and imagination stimulated by, but going beyond the printed page. Examples of inferential tasks related to reading are:

    2.1 *Inferring supporting details.* In this instance, the student is asked to conjecture about additional facts the author might have included in the selection which would have made it more informative, interesting or appealing.

    2.2 *Inferring the main idea.* The student is required to provide the main idea, general significance, theme, or moral which is not explicitly stated in the selection.

    2.3 *Inferring sequence.* The student, in this case, may be requested to conjecture as to what action or incident might have taken place between two explicitly stated actions or incidents; he may be asked to hypothesize about what would happen next; or he may be asked to hypothesize about the beginning of a story if the author had not started where he did.

2.4 *Inferring comparisons*. The student is required to infer likenesses and differences in characters, times, or places. Such inferential comparisons revolve around ideas such as: "here and there," "then and now," "he and he," "he and she," and "she and she."

2.5 *Inferring cause and effect relationships*. The student is required to hypothesize about the motives of characters and their interactions with others and with time and place. He may also be required to conjecture as to what caused the author to include certain ideas, words, characterizations and actions in this writing.

2.6 *Inferring character traits*. In this case, the student may be asked to hypothesize about the nature of characters on the basis of explicit clues presented in the selection.

2.7 *Predicting outcomes*. The student is requested to read an initial portion of the selection, and on the basis of this reading he conjectures about the outcome of the selection.

2.8 *Inferring about figurative language*. The student, in this instance, is asked to infer literal meanings from the author's figurative use of language.

3.0 *Evaluation*. Evaluation is demonstrated by a student when he makes judgments about the content of a reading selection by comparing it with external criteria, e.g., information provided by the teacher on the subject, authorities on the subject, or by accredited written sources on the subject; or with internal criteria, e.g., the reader's experience, knowledge, or values related to the subject under consideration. In essence, evaluation requires students to make judgments about the content of their reading, judgments that have to do with its accuracy, acceptability, worth, desirability, completeness, suitability, timeliness, quality, truthfulness, or probability of occurrence. Examples of evaluation tasks related to reading are:

3.1 *Judgments of reality or fantasy*. The student is requested to determine whether incidents, events, or characters in a selection could have existed or occurred in real life on the basis of his experience.

3.2 *Judgments of fact or opinion*. In this case the student is asked to decide whether the author is presenting information which can be supported with objective data or whether the author is attempting to sway the reader's thinking through the use of subjective content that has overtones of propaganda.

3.3 *Judgments of adequacy or validity.* Tasks of this type call for the reader to judge whether the author's treatment of a subject is accurate and complete when compared to other sources on the subject. In this instance, then, the reader is called upon to compare written sources of information with an eye toward their agreements or disagreements, their completeness or incompleteness, and their thoroughness or superficiality in dealing with a subject.

3.4 *Judgments of appropriateness.* Evaluation tasks of this type require the student to determine whether certain selections or parts of selections are relevant and can contribute to resolving an issue or a problem. For example, a student may be requested to judge the part of a selection which most appropriately describes a character. Or he may be called upon to determine which references will make significant contributions to a report he is preparing.

3.5 *Judgments of worth, desirability, or acceptability.* In this instance, the student may be requested to pass judgments on the suitability of a character's action in a particular incident or episode. Was the character right or wrong, good or bad, or somewhere in between? Tasks of this nature call for opinions based on the values the reader has acquired through his personal experiences.

4.0 *Appreciation.* Appreciation involves all the previously cited cognitive dimensions of reading, for it deals with the psychological and aesthetic impact of the selection on the reader. Appreciation calls for the student to be emotionally and aesthetically sensitive to the work and to have a reaction to the worth of its psychological and artistic elements. Appreciation includes both knowledge of and emotional response to literary techniques, forms, styles, and structures. Examples of tasks that involve appreciation are:

4.1 *Emotional response to the content.* The student is requested to demonstrate his reaction to a selection in terms of the visceral effect it had upon him. The emotional impact of a work may have to do with such things as its ability to stimulate and sustain interest, ex-

citement, boredom, fear, hate, or amusement on the
part of the reader.

4.2 *Identification with characters and incidents.* Tasks of this
nature will elicit responses from the reader that demonstrate his sensitivity to, sympathy for, or empathy with
characters and events portrayed by the author.

4.3 *Reactions to the author's use of language.* In this instance,
the student is required to recognize and respond to the
author's craftsmanship in his use of words. Such tasks
deal with the semantic dimensions of a selection, e.g.,
the connotations and denotations of words.

4.4 *Imagery.* In this instance, the reader is called upon to
recognize and respond to the author's artistic ability to
"paint word pictures" that cause him to visualize, smell,
taste, hear, or feel the things the author is describing.

In order to become better acquainted with the comprehension categories in the Davis research, the Wallen taxonomy, and the Barrett taxonomy, try writing a question for "Goldilocks and the Three Bears" from
each of the steps in one or more of these comprehension classifications.

Issues in Comprehension Instruction

Three very important issues with which you must deal in comprehension
instruction are key elements of instruction, teacher effectiveness, and development of vocabulary.

Key Elements of Instruction

Your planning for instruction in comprehension, like most other aspects of
reading instruction, must take into account three of the key elements discussed in Chapter 5: guided reading activities, skill-development activities,
and enrichment activities. Guided reading activities are those activities in
which you guide an individual child or a group of children through a reading selection. Skill-development activities are those in which you break the
reading process into its component subskills and teach or reinforce those
subskills. Enrichment activities are the things you do to build bridges between reading and other areas of the curriculum. Guided reading and skill-
development activities focus primarily on assisting children with comprehension; enrichment activities deepen and refine it. All three are important
to comprehension instruction.

■ Teacher Effectiveness

Heilman, Blair, and Rupley (1981) analyzed the research on teacher effectiveness and drew implications for the teaching of reading. From researchers' attempts to define characteristics of effective teachers in terms of pupil growth, Heilman et al. concluded (1981, pp. 35–37) that effective teachers of reading

- ■ maximize students' involvement in tasks or academic activities related specifically to lesson content and desired outcomes;
- ■ control students' behavior by the use of task-related comments rather than criticizing or scolding pupils for not focusing on learning tasks;
- ■ monitor and guide the direction of students' learning;
- ■ employ a pattern of instruction at the primary level that allows them to be accessible to students, to work in small groups, and to use a variety of materials;
- ■ use a pattern of instruction at the intermediate level that allows for larger instructional groups, more discussion at higher cognitive levels, less teacher direction, and greater student-initiated learning;
- ■ provide for application of reading skills in silent reading tasks that ensure maximum success for students;
- ■ assure that students understand how to apply their reading skills for the purpose of reading enjoyment.

Of the important implications Heilman derived, these seven characteristics of effective teachers seem to be particularly applicable to the teaching of comprehension.

■ Development of Vocabulary

To address the issue of vocabulary development, we discuss the strategies used by teachers to help children understand word meanings when they read. The fact that the knowledge of word meanings is the single most powerful contributor to overall comprehension (Davis, 1968) gives teachers permission to spend considerable time working to develop children's understanding of words. In fact, teachers must become word advocates.

Oral Language Activities

As a teacher you need to be excited about words. Your focus on and excitement about words should begin with oral language and continue on a *daily basis* throughout the year. "That's an interesting word. What does it mean?" should be heard *frequently* in your classroom, as well as questions like this: "Can anyone think of another word to describe that color? Who knows what *russet* means? How can we talk about the shape or the texture, the feel, of the bark? What are some words we can use?"

When you are engaged in class discussions, one of your jobs as a teacher is to focus on language and build interest and excitement in your students about words and their meanings. You must take time to listen carefully to children and respond to both their ideas and their language. Hang a long strip of paper in front of the room for children to add interesting words to as they encounter them. Use another strip to display words related to a unit of study in social studies or science. Refer to these words frequently in class discussion—be excited about them!

Recognize, too, that silent reading contributes to vocabulary growth, and be sure to build into the daily schedule time for silent reading.

Words in Reading Selections

At times it will be important to deal with the meanings of words in a particular selection before or after children read the selection. These words may either be new to the children or be so important to comprehending the selection that they warrant special attention.

How do you develop vocabulary knowledge when children are dealing with a reading selection, as opposed to a class discussion? The steps we follow are fairly common across reading programs:

1. Show the children a sentence containing the word, printed on a card or the chalkboard. It is helpful to underline the word. Presenting the word in a sentence permits children to make use of multiple cues.
2. Ask: "Who can read this sentence?" If no one responds, read the sentence to the children.
3. Ask: "Who can tell us what this underlined word means?" If no one responds, tell the children the meaning of the word.
4. Say: "Listen, and I will use the word in another sentence." Note that the definition given in Step 3 and the sentence used in Step 4 should be consistent with the meaning of the word as used in the reading selection.
5. Ask: "Who can use this word in a sentence of your own?" Listen to several volunteers.
6. Discuss the meaning of the word with the group. Discussions of word meanings are important because through the discussion children begin to "own" the word.

As you develop knowledge of word meanings with children, encourage them to use the new words in their writing. You should always be looking for ways to link the words children are learning to read with the words they *may* choose to use as they write. The links must come from the children, however, and *never* from an assignment to "use all your new words in your story," a practice that denies the essence of the writing process. Writers always begin with ideas and then select the language (words) to express those ideas. It is a violation of that principle to tell children they *must* use given words in their writing.

Structured Overviews

A structured overview is a way of presenting vocabulary terms that shows the interrelationships among the terms. It is best used when presenting information to students as a part of a unit of instruction in one of the content areas (such as social studies, science or health). Using an overhead projector or the chalkboard, you place the terms on a diagram as you present them in order to show their relationship to each other. Suppose you were introducing a unit on westward expansion. Your structured overview might look like that in Figure 10.1.

Not just as you begin the unit but as you proceed through it, you can use the structured overview to introduce new topics of study, expanding the original diagram as needed. The main idea is that students see the relationships among terms that are new to them and important in their study. We suggest that you put the structured overview on paper so that it can be displayed throughout the unit of study. You will find students referring to it as they come across the terms in their reading.

Developing Comprehension Ability

Metacomprehension is a process—an ongoing process occurring simultaneously with reading. It is the interaction between the words of the author and the schemata of the reader. Comprehension is not an accomplishment to *test* after the child has read; it is a process that the reader *monitors* during the act of reading.

Instructional Goals

Our primary task in teaching comprehension is to ensure that our students can monitor their own reading comprehension. We want readers to know when they understand what they are reading, to know when they are not understanding what they are reading, and to be able to do something about

As you introduce the unit ("Today we are going to begin our study of westward expansion"), the diagram looks like this:

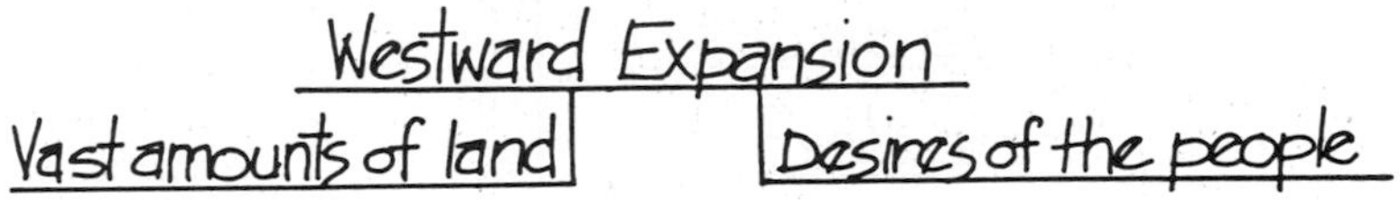

Westward Expansion
Vast amounts of land | Desires of the people

As you tell students about Manifest Destiny, the diagram begins to look like this:

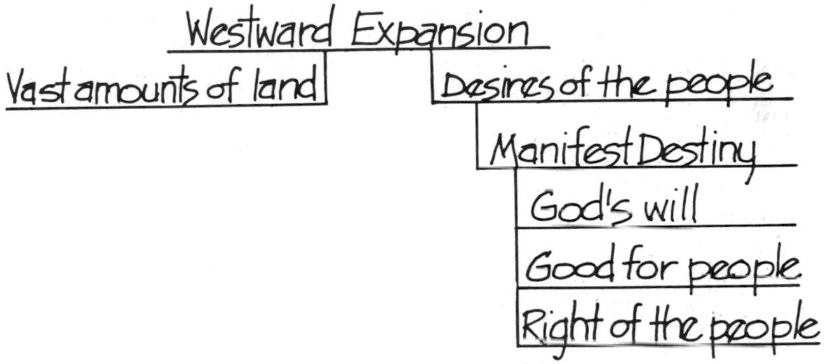

Westward Expansion
Vast amounts of land | Desires of the people
Manifest Destiny
God's will
Good for people
Right of the people

As you discuss the incentive to westward expansion created by the offer of free land, your structured overview looks like this:

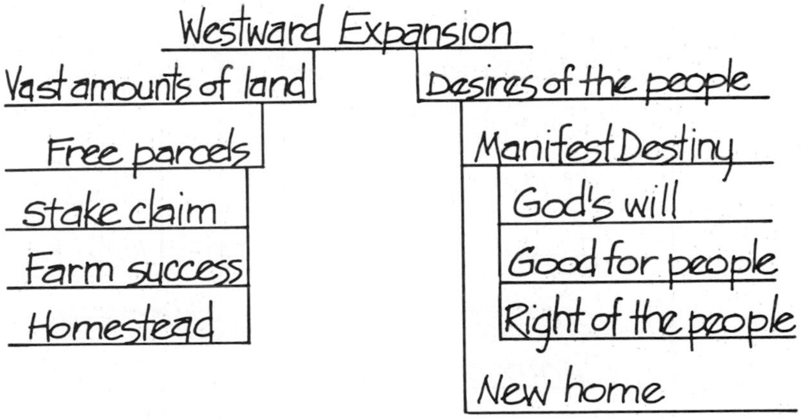

Westward Expansion
Vast amounts of land | Desires of the people
Free parcels | Manifest Destiny
Stake claim | God's will
Farm success | Good for people
Homestead | Right of the people
New home

Figure 10.1   Structured overview.

(continues)

As you speak about the modes of travel used by the pioneers, your structured overview looks like this:

Westward Expansion

Vast amounts of land
- Free parcels
- Stake claim
- Farm success
- Homestead

Travel
- Conestoga wagons
- Teams of oxen
- 10 miles per day

Desires of the people
- Manifest Destiny
  - God's will
  - Good for people
  - Right of the people
- New home

As you explain the hardships suffered by the pioneers, your diagram looks like this:

Westward Expansion

Vast amounts of land
- Free parcels
- Stake claim
- Farm success
- Homestead

Travel
- Conestoga wagons
- Teams of oxen
- 10 miles per day

Desires of the people
- Manifest Destiny
  - God's will
  - Good for people
  - Right of the people
- New home

Hardships
- Illness
- Indians
- Weather

Figure 10.1   (continued)

the problem. "Comprehension monitoring entails keeping track of the success with which one's comprehension is proceeding, ensuring that the process continues smoothly, and taking remedial action if necessary" (Baker and Brown, 1984, p. 22).

What, then, are the goals of comprehension instruction? The major ones are these:

1. Readers will be able to monitor their comprehension during the reading act and take necessary corrective action.
2. Readers will be able to establish their own purposes for reading a selection and then choose the most appropriate reading strategies.
3. Readers will be able to adjust their reading rate to fit their purposes for reading the selection.
4. Readers will draw on their schemata to interact with the ideas of the writer. They will construct meaning from this interaction.
5. Readers will recognize when comprehension has failed, will then read on, reread, or consult an expert source (book or person), and will apply the most efficient corrective strategy.
6. Readers will ask for help when the comprehension process has faltered.
7. Readers will be able to respond to questions drawn from a comprehension taxonomy.

With respect to Goal 4, the research of Baker and Brown (1984) suggests that many readers do not even know they are supposed to interact with the text.

■ Instructional Strategies

Two major instructional strategies are important to the realization of these goals: helping children draw on their own schemata before and during the reading of a selection and helping them learn to play the psycholinguistic guessing game of predictions. We may combine these strategies in practice, but here we will examine them separately.

Using Schemata

Helping readers learn to relate their background experiences to a reading selection speaks directly to Instructional Goal 4, and to some degree to Goal 2. Readers must learn to relate their experiences to the ideas of the

Children's native interest in the phenomena of the real world provides an ideal starting point for literacy-related activities.
© *David S. Strickler/The Picture Cube*

author if reading is to be an interactive process. Too, they need to learn to establish their own purposes for reading a selection. One purpose is formed when the reader sees a link between the topic and his or her background experiences ("Gee, I know something about that—I'll read to find out more.").

We help readers use their schemata through the questioning we do before, during, and after the reading of a selection. In traditional instruction in comprehension, we simply introduced vocabulary beforehand and asked comprehension questions afterwards. But these practices flatly do not suffice to help readers draw on their background experiences. They do not promote an interactive process in reading. To encourage interaction of the reader's experience and the author's ideas, we need to ask questions such as those in the following example.

Let's say you are going to have a group of students read a selection from *Ira Sleeps Over,* by Bernard Waber (1972). First you introduce the story to the group:

You:	*Today we are going to read a story called* Ira Sleeps Over. *How many of you have ever stayed overnight at a friend's house? Who can tell us about it?*
Katie:	*One time when my mom and dad were going to a convention I got to stay with Rochelle. She is my best friend.*
You:	*Katie, can you tell us some of the things you and Rochelle did?*
Katie:	*We played with her dolls, we went for long bike rides, and we raked up leaf piles to jump in.*
You:	*That sounds as if it were lots of fun. Can someone else tell us about a time you stayed overnight at a friend's?*
Randy:	*I stayed at my cousin Jim's place for two nights. We played computer games and helped his mother bake cookies, and we played army in his fort. We got to sleep in the fort, but Jim got scared.*
You:	*What happened after Jim got scared?*
Randy:	*We had to go sleep in his room. That was okay, though.*
You:	*Today we are going to read a story about a boy named Ira who goes to stay overnight at his neighbor's house. It is the first time he has ever stayed overnight away from home. Before you read the story, think about the first time you stayed away from home for the night. Think about the things you did and how it felt. If you haven't gotten to stay overnight at a friend's house, think about what you would want it to be like.*

After you have finished introducing the story, the children read to the point when Ira is grappling with the decision of whether or not to take his Teddy bear to his friend's house. The discussion might proceed like this:

You:	*How many of you have a Teddy Bear or a favorite stuffed animal? It is all right to say so—no one in our group will laugh or make fun.*
You:	*How do people feel about their favorite stuffed toys?*
Steve:	*I think kids have them for friends.*
Tricia:	*Sometimes stuffed toys are someone to hold on to when you are sad or afraid.*
You:	*When you read the part in the story where Ira is trying to decide to take his bear with him, think about how you feel about your favorite stuffed toy if you have one. What do you think you would do if you were Ira?*

This example illustrates how you can draw on children's background experiences both to prepare them for reading a selection and to sustain involvement in the middle of it. We cannot stress enough the importance of helping children draw on their own schemata as a fundamental part of the comprehension process. Bringing one's own experiences to bear on a selection and seeing how they fit are an essential part of the metacomprehension process. Children can be taught to use metacomprehension processes. Good reading instruction must include this schemata–reading link. By leading children in discussions like the one about Ira, you *model* for them the kinds of interactions they must have *on their own* with print. Each time you do this kind of schemata enhancement before and during the reading of a selection, you should remind the children that this is what they must learn to do themselves when they are reading on their own. They have to learn to answer the following questions for themselves:

1. What do I know about this topic?
2. Have I ever done what these characters are doing, or have I ever known of someone who has done this?
3. What do I need to remember while I read this?
4. How does this selection fit with my past experiences?

Reading Interactively—Making Predictions

Recall Frank Smith's (1978) evidence of comprehension as the state of having no unanswered questions. The questions he means are the questions you as a reader ask yourself before, during, and after reading a selection. In answering those questions, you are making the predictions we talked about earlier. Russell Stauffer (1975) described a process for guiding the reading of a selection that invokes this prediction-making/confirming or rejecting strategy. Called the Directed Reading Thinking Activity (DRTA), this form of guided reading is designed to model for students the ways in which the mature reader interacts with print. It trains students to be interactive readers.

Guided Metacomprehension Strategy

We have used Stauffer's important ideas about having children make predictions in our Guided Metacomprehension Strategy (GMS). The GMS is a way of doing a guided reading activity with a group of children that draws on what we know about the reading process.

Guided Metacomprehension Strategy

1. **Schemata enhancement.** Focus: drawing on the reader's schemata to assist in relating the text to his or her background experiences.
   A. Tell readers the topic or theme of the selection. Probe their background experiences and knowledge about the topic or theme.
   B. Ask them to think about three questions: (1) What do I know about the topic? (2) What experiences have I had with the topic? (3) What will I need to remember from my experience as I read?

C. *Important:* Engage them in thought about the purposes for reading the text—for information, for entertainment, to be persuaded, etc. Purpose depends on the nature of the text; for example, the purpose of reading an expository piece on Egypt would be very different from the purpose of reading a poem.

2. **Prediction making.** Focus: drawing on available clues, the reader makes predictions about the story.

   A. Give readers clues—the title, a picture, a sample sentence or paragraph, an incident.

   B. Get predictions. Ask, "What do you think will happen in this story?" Be sure to get a prediction, or at least concurrence with another child's prediction, from each child in the group. (Note: Do not try this prediction strategy with children who have already read the story. It will not work!) As children are making predictions, point out to them the ways in which they are drawing on their background knowledge in the process. Underscore this important schemata–reading link.

3. **Silent reading.** Assign specified pages. You decide the most interesting way to segment the selection.

4. **Discussion and oral rereading.** Focus: proving or disproving predictions.

   A. Ask, " Which of our predictions can we prove? Which ones were not proven?" Ask, "Can you read aloud the part that proves or makes us change our predictions?"

   B. This is a good time for questions about story structure (Where are we in the plot? Who are the central characters? What is the conflict? Where does the story take place?).

5. **Prediction making.**

   A. Invite reflection on the story so far; it is now a clue to what will follow.

   B. Ask, "What do you think will happen next?" We suggest that you note students' predictions on a pad of paper or the chalkboard so that you do not accidentally overlook a prediction.

6. **Silent reading.** Assign further specified pages.

7. **Continuing to conclusion.** Recycle through Steps 4, 5, and 6 as many times as necessary to complete the story.

8. **Bringing reading to a conscious level.** Focus: helping readers think about how they used the reading process.

   A. Ask readers to retell as much as they can remember about the story.

    B. Ask readers questions about how they dealt with the reading process:

      (1) How did you learn from the story?

      (2) What parts of the story were easy to read? Why? Difficult? Why?

      (3) How did you overcome difficulties you had with the text?

      (4) What did you do when you came to a part that was not making sense?

      (5) What did you do when you came to words you did not know?

9. **Concept Development.** Focus: broadening understandings of important concepts.

    A. Students' understandings can be broadened and deepened by modeling, drawing, explaining, demonstrating, examining, and acting.

    B. Questions can be drawn from a comprehension taxonomy to check students' abilities to do particular kinds of thinking in response to their reading.

Here is how the dialogue about *Ira Sleeps Over* might sound using the GMS. The teacher's first step, as before, is schemata enhancement. Remember, GMS will not work with a story the children have already read.

You:	*Today we are going to read a story about a boy who is invited to stay overnight at a neighbor's house. How many of you have ever stayed overnight at a friend's house? Who can tell us about it?*
Katie:	*One time when my mom and dad were going to a convention I got to stay with Rochelle. She is my best friend.*
You:	*Katie, can you tell us some of the things you and Rochelle did?*
Katie:	*We played with her dolls, we went for long bike rides, and we raked up leaf piles to jump in.*
You:	*That sounds as if it were lots of fun. Can someone else tell us about a time you stayed overnight at a friend's?*
Randy:	*I stayed at my cousin Jim's place for two nights. We played computer games and helped his mother bake cookies, and we played army in his fort. We got to sleep in the fort, but Jim got scared.*
You:	*What happened after Jim got scared?*
Randy:	*We had to go sleep in his room. That was okay, though.*
You:	*Today we are going to read a story called Ira Sleeps Over. (Show children the picture on the cover of the book.) What do you think might happen in this story?*
Mariko:	*I think it will be about boys who get bored watching TV and get into trouble.*
You:	*That is an interesting idea, Mariko. Who else has a prediction?*

Explain to students that predictions are "educated guesses," and discourage wild guessing. Invite children to draw on their background experiences in formulating predictions.

> Joel: It looks like this story is going to be about friends.
> You: Joel, do you have any ideas about what these friends are going to do or what is going to happen?
> Joel: I guess they are going to have a big secret.

At this point you would gather any other predictions and then get everyone to make a commitment to one or more predictions; that is, to signal their agreement with the predictions they favor as you review the list. Even if each child did not offer a prediction, it is important that each child commit to at least one. Insist if necessary; do not let children "sit behind their eyes." The commitment to a prediction creates what we have called a "cognitive itch"—a desire to know if one's predictions are right. Thinking, "I think I know what this story will be about. It will be about . . ." is exactly how the interactive reader establishes purposes for reading (our Instructional Goal 2).

> You: Let's read the first x pages to see which of our predictions we can prove. Count up x pages in the book, put your bookmark there, and then close the book when you come to the bookmark.

Insist that none of your students read ahead. Competition to make "perfect" predictions by reading ahead is harmful to the interactive process.

> You: Which of our predictions can we prove?
> Mariko: Joel said it was going to be about friends, and he was right. But I don't think they will have a big secret.
> You: Mariko, can you read us the part of the story that proves what you think?

After Mariko reads, take this opportunity to have children draw on their schemata to relate to the story. Discuss times children in the group have stayed overnight at a friend's home. Then take each of the original predictions in turn, discussing which can be proven and which cannot. Invite oral reading to prove or disprove the predictions.

> You: Well, what do you think is going to happen next in the story?
> Carlos: I think Ira is not going to take his bear.
> You: Carlos, have you ever had to decide whether or not to take a stuffed animal to a friend's house? Tell us about it.
> Carlos: One time my mom told me not to take my elephant to my cousin's house. She thought my cousin would wreck it.

You:	*Well, what did you decide? Did you take the elephant or leave it at home?*
Carlos:	*I took it, but I should have left it at home 'cause my cousin did pull one of his ears off. I think Ira will leave his bear at home. He'd better.*
You:	*Are there any other predictions?*
Joel:	*I think Ira will take his bear with him.*
You:	*How many of you think Ira will leave his bear at home? How many think he will take it with him?*
	Let's read the next x pages to find out what happens.

Remember that it is important to get a commitment to a prediction from each child in the group whether that child made a prediction or not.

You continue to cycle through the GMS in this fashion until the children have finished the story. Then, following Steps 8 and 9 of the GMS outline, you bring reading to a conscious level and do concept development.

Endorsing the practice of asking children to read carefully to prove their predictions, Nessel (1987) states that requiring students to use information from the text to make logical predictions about outcomes actively engages the readers in problem solving and surmises that their arguments over the merits of various predictions may be the most compelling type of motivation to read further. Good reading instruction must include this schemata–reading link.

Prediction Mapping

Another way of guiding metacomprehension is prediction mapping, a strategy in which you record children's predictions on a diagram. Walker (1985) found that prediction mapping was useful in helping children follow the internal thought processes that good readers use automatically. This technique is very similar to the GMS, except that as the predictions are made they are written on an overhead projector or chalkboard and then revised as the children read the sections of the story. For *Ira Sleeps Over*, the map might look like the one in Figure 10.2.

Selection of Material

Selecting material for use in teaching children to make predictions requires thought and care. Obviously the materials must be sensible and be written so that the outcomes are at least probable from the information given. Leu, De Groff, and Simons (1986, p. 352) have recommended patterned books as a good source of material for primary grades because "when reading predictable text, attention for both good and poor readers is available for comprehension processing but for different reasons. Good readers are able to attend to the meaning of a story because of their automatic, context-free word-recognition skills. Poor readers are able to attend to the meaning of a story because of their automatic use of repetitive sentence context.

Figure 10.2   Prediction map for *Ira Sleeps Over* (Waber, 1972).

Thus, some thought should be given to using predictable texts in helping poor readers develop important comprehension skills. Predictable texts may give poor readers important early opportunities to make inferences, draw conclusions, predict outcomes, and engage in other processes traditionally associated with comprehension instruction, opportunities that they seldom have because their attention is often occupied by word-recognition demands." Repetitive-language books were discussed in some detail in Chapter 7.

One good source of such material for intermediate-grade children is well-constructed mystery stories. Children can make predictions about the outcomes at various points in the story and then read on to verify their predictions. And sometimes when the solution is revealed they will have to backtrack, just as adult mystery fans often have to do, to find the clues they might have missed or misinterpreted.

Recognizing Story Structure

An awareness of the development of story structure (Fitzgerald and Spiegel, 1983) is an aid to metacomprehension. Knowledge of story structure involves an understanding of plot, character development, setting, theme, and time. It can help children make predictions and apply previous experience as they read. Folk tales are excellent examples from which to teach story structure. Mandler and Johnson (1977) have demonstrated that young children have some knowledge of story structure, which varies with developmental level, and that children's abilities to recall stories differ qualitatively. In other words, as children gain ability to analyze stories they can begin to organize information from new stories into familiar story structures. Knowing that children already possess a basic grasp of story structure, Fitzgerald, Spiegel, and Webb (1985) found that the only new skill fifth- and sixth-graders exhibited after instruction in story structure was recognition of more complex structures such as subplots and embedded episodes.

Smith and Bean (1983) have suggested that teachers help children recognize the patterns in stories, sketching a diagram of the sequence of events to enable the children to visualize them. Figure 10.3 illustrates simple depictions of structure in two stories: *The Turnip* (Tolstoi, no date) and *Millions of Cats* (Gag, 1928). *The Turnip* can be illustrated in a vertical sequence, showing only one character in the first box, two in the second, and so on until the conclusion of the story. *Millions of Cats* follows a circular pattern. In a circular story, the character comes back after various adventures to the place where he or she began. *The Runaway Bunny* (Brown, 1942) and *Journey Cake, Ho* (Sawyer, 1953) are circular stories. Once children can recognize these patterns, they can base predictions on them and also apply them in their own writing.

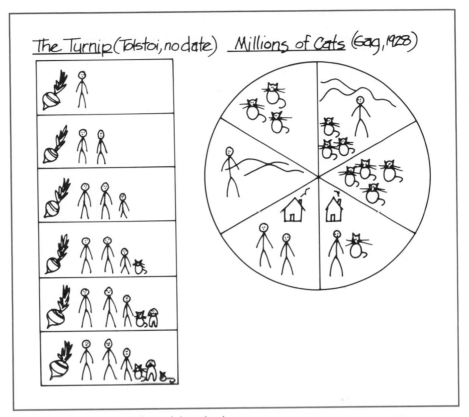

Figure 10.3 Simple depictions of story structure.

One good device for helping youngsters analyze stories is a simplified drawing of a nursery rhyme, such as Figure 10.4, "Little Miss Muffet" (Gatheral, 1984). Each box represents a story element—the main character, the setting, exposition, the introduction of the antagonist, the conflict or problem, and the resolution of the story. In the first box, the circle represents Miss Muffet, the main character. In the second box, the tuffet represents the setting. The exposition tells us what is going on. The spider is the antagonist, and sitting down beside her is the problem. Resolution comes when Miss Muffet runs away. We prefer to draw these pictures on separate 8″ × 10″ cards to match each story because not every story begins with the introduction of the main character. Even young children, we find, can begin to recognize the parts of the story and relate them to story structure in general. This skill is important for both reading and writing. As children read, they form expectations about what will happen next; as they write, they need to think about story elements and the arrangement of those elements.

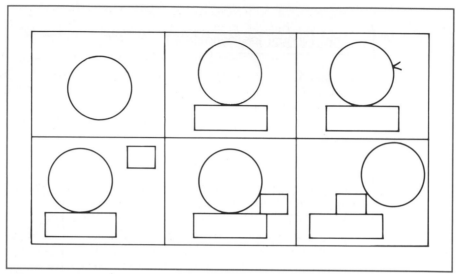

Figure 10.4   Simplified drawing of "Little Miss Muffet."
Source: Maryanne Gatheral, "Teaching Gifted Children in the Regular Classroom." Speech, Albany, Ore., 1984.

Modeling the Comprehension Process

To help students develop better comprehension, teachers have successfully used the technique of thinking through the comprehension process aloud and training the children to ask themselves questions as they read. Nolte and Singer (1985) reported that children trained to question themselves about their own comprehension were able to improve their scores on comprehension tests and that the improvement had some transfer to materials not included in the training. First the teacher reviewed with the students their knowledge of story structure. Then, as the students read the material, she modeled appropriate questions such as, "Is this what I expected to happen?" After a limited number of modeling experiences, the teacher grouped the children and had one child lead the questioning in each group. The children worked next in pairs, and finally independently. The training was completed in fifteen days.

Nist and Kirby (1986) used a similar technique, suggesting that the teacher first introduce any new terms in the reading material and then explain the purpose for the reading. The next step is probably the most important: the teacher thinks aloud for the students, showing them how a mature reader/thinker solves reading problems and constantly monitors comprehension. Next, the students go through the process themselves, find out where their techniques are ineffective, and, with help from the teacher, adopt a more effective method. Most students will require more than one demonstration before they can effectively carry out the thinking processes independently.

Miller (1985) found that self-instruction is also an effective technique for improving comprehension. In common with other studies, she used an initial guidance stage modeled by the teacher, followed by a self-verbalization stage that stressed the generation of questions and a gradual transfer of task responsibility to the readers.

Guided Imagery

Another strategy for helping students achieve the metacomprehension abilities used so unconsciously by mature readers is that of guided imagery or mental imagery. Children learn to visualize the people, events, places, or things they encounter in their reading. Of course, the usefulness of the technique is related to the purposes of the reading and the reader's experience. Gambrell and Koskinen (1982) found that helping children form mental images produced better literal comprehension when done prior to the reading experiences than when done afterwards. Fredericks (1986) encourages teachers to follow a progression: children first create images of concrete objects, then images of objects or experiences from recall, then images of their predictions on the next events while listening to stories. Finally they think about the relationship between the images in their minds and the words on the page when they read. Teachers can invent a series of activities that will help children move through these stages of imagery. Walker (1985) suggests that creating guided imagery before the reading may help some readers access their previous experiences more easily than they would with direct questioning. For example, the teacher develops guided imagery in which the children are asked to visualize the main points in a reading selection. The children are encouraged to visualize the resolution of the story before they read and to write how they solved the problem. They are then eager to read the story to compare the author's version with their own.

Fredericks (1986, p. 81) lists the following guidelines for imaging:

1. Children need to understand that everyone's images are different and are affected by their own experience.
2. There are no right or wrong images. Teachers should not attempt to change individual images, but they can help children reformulate images through rereading or relistening to a story.
3. Provide sufficient opportunities for children to create their images prior to discussion. Children who need a long time to create or embellish their mind pictures should be encouraged

to draw illustrations of their images, which can then be shared with the teacher or the class.

4. Provide adequate time for students to discuss their images—not to arrive at a "correct" image but to encourage sharing of ideas in a supportive atmosphere.

5. Stimulate image development through a series of open-ended questions. The questions provide structure to the child's image formation by soliciting details.

■ Metacomprehension and the Young Child

Metacomprehension is linked to the child's level of cognitive development. A child who, in Piagetian terms, is not yet concrete operational cannot decode symbols and at the same time think consciously about prior experience and semantic and other cues as easily as the operative child (Wadsworth, 1984). For young children, metacomprehension strategies should include applying children's knowledge of story structure to the stories they read. They can compare and contrast versions of familiar folk tales, as well as stories that have similar plots or themes. For example, even young children can recognize similarities between *Too Much Noise* (McGovern, 1967) and *It Could Always Be Worse* (Zemach, 1976). Young children can also benefit from collective composition: members take turns dictating lines that make sense when added to the group's story in progress. Of course, young children also need to spend time in vocabulary development and in making their own dictionaries and word banks, as described in Chapter 8.

Using language-experience techniques assures that the print material the children meet has a direct connection with their own experiential backgrounds, rather than material for which they lack schemata. Perhaps the most important task of the teacher of young children is to make sure that these readers know that reading is supposed to make sense—it is not merely pronouncing words.

■ Comprehension and the Basal Reader

Our collective professional understanding of the reading process is developing constantly. New strategies are added to our instruction all the time. However, the view of comprehension embodied in most basal reader programs is that the primary job of the teacher is to *monitor* the children's thinking in *response* to their reading rather than to *help* the children *engage in metacomprehension*. This traditional view of comprehension is found in the teacher's guide of virtually every basal reader in use today. The reading of a selection is followed by the answering of questions drawn from one of the comprehension taxonomies. Ideally, the teacher notes which kinds of thinking tasks pose problems for individual children, and then plans instruction for that particular comprehension subskill. Unfortunately, this comprehension teaching step is frequently omitted. We fear that teachers often think they have taught comprehension by monitoring the thinking children can do—that is, by asking them questions. In fact, the asking of questions following the reading of a selection is *testing* comprehension rather than *teaching* it.

In contrast to the Guided Metacomprehension Strategy, the traditional Directed Reading Activity is the model found in most basal teacher's guides.

■ Using the Directed Reading Activity

The primary purpose of the Directed Reading Activity (DRA) is to monitor the kinds of thought tasks children can do in response to what they read. This procedure has come to be fairly standardized in its use in basal reader programs. Here the steps in the DRA are followed by our own descriptive text and commentary:

1. **Readiness for reading**
   A. **Introduction of vocabulary.** Teacher introduces words that may cause difficulty for the reader—in basal terminology, "new words" because they have not previously been used in the series. Applicable procedures for the introduction of vocabulary are listed on page 339.
   B. **Purpose setting.** Teacher gives children a reason for reading the first segment of the selection. Typically calls their attention to the title or the first picture, engages them in attention-focusing discussion, and then gives them a reason for reading the first x pages of the selection.
2. **Silent reading.** Teacher instructs children to read silently from page x to y, reminding readers to ask for help if they need it.
3. **Discussion and oral rereading.** The heart of the DRA. Teacher asks comprehension questions drawn from one of the taxonomies, not to see if the children have read the selection but to ascertain the kinds of thinking they can do. Oral rereading is selective and based on necessities arising from the discussion.
4. **Skill development.** Teacher gives instruction in new reading skills or reinforces previously taught skills.

5. **Enrichment activities.** Teacher initiates activities that build bridges between reading and other curricular areas, activities that extend and refine comprehension.

With respect to Step 3, the teacher should have in mind the *kind* of thinking task each comprehension question is designed to monitor. The nature of the questions is of supreme importance in a DRA, as is the nature of responses to students' answers, if they are to promote comprehension growth. Students must have time to think through an answer before they respond. Heilman et al. (1981, p. 247) reported a study by Sarason indicating that whereas elementary teachers thought they asked between 12 and 20 questions in a 30-minute period, the actual number ranged from 45 to 150. Observers have noted that of the questions teachers formulate on their own, the preponderance require recall. Therefore, we believe that it is important that you use one of the taxonomies in formulating discussion questions.

Notice that the silent reading is followed by discussion, not by oral reading. We have spoken strongly against the practice known as round-robin reading. In a DRA, oral rereading proves the answers to comprehension questions and highlights certain features of the selection. The teacher should frequently ask, "Who can read us the part of the story that proves that answer is correct (or incorrect)?" It is also worthwhile to reread particularly interesting or moving dialogue, especially bold or colorful descriptions, and any other skillfully handled passages that the students might emulate.

■ Example from a Basal Text

Figure 10.5 is a selection entitled "The 23rd Street School" from a basal reader by the same name, part of Addison-Wesley's series entitled *The Nitty Gritty Rather Pretty City* (Rowland, 1982). Please enjoy reading this story, and then examine the reprint of the accompanying teacher's guide to see how the Directed Reading Activity was handled. Compare it with the outline we have just presented.

■ Comparing DRA and GMS

When you compared the outline for the Directed Reading Activity with the teacher's guide for "The 23rd Street School" you undoubtedly found clear similarity. Vocabulary was introduced, children were given a purpose for reading, and after they read the teacher was instructed to ask questions to monitor thinking: questions designed for "identifying main idea," "identifying details," "inferring details," and so on.

LESSON 6

Story Summary

Niki Pappas is unhappy because his family has moved to The Nitty Gritty City. Niki's plan is to pretend that he can speak only Greek so that his family will take him back to their old home. When some new classmates show that they care enough to try to teach Niki English and to include him in their plans, Niki decides to stop pretending and to enjoy his new situation.

Step 1 · Word Preview page 245

Sketch an opened notebook on the chalkboard, and write the headings to the left of the traffic light on page 245 at the top of the notebook pages. Call on students to use page 245 in their Readers to help them fill in the words below the headings on the chalkboard. Then have the students read aloud each word on the notebook pages.

Review the story words *school* and *English* by writing the following question on the chalkboard and asking the children to read it and then answer it: *Do you study English in school?*

Step 2 · Vocabulary

Before the students read "The 23rd Street School," introduce them to the following words and phrase.

Greece; Greek.   Write *Greece* and *Greek* on the chalkboard, and have the children read the words. Explain that Greece is a country and that Greek is the language spoken by the people who live in Greece. You may wish to use a globe or an atlas to show the students where Greece is.

Then kata loveno.   Write the words on the chalkboard, and read them with the children. Explain that these words are Greek words that mean *I don't understand.*

records.   Write the following sentence on the chalkboard: *Your school records tell about the work you did in first grade.* After the children read the sentence, underline the word *records,* and have the children reread the word. Explain that records are charts that tell about each student's work.

Figure 10.5   Basal reader example.   (continues)

SOURCE: Pleasant T. Rowland, *The Nitty Gritty Rather Pretty City* (Menlo Park: Calif.: Addison-Wesley, 1982).

Reader

"The 23rd Street School," pages 258–265   **page 258**

Step 3 · Directed Reading
pages 258–265

Have the students turn to page 245 in their Readers, locate the title "The 23rd Street School," and turn to the page on which the story begins. (page 258) Tell the children that they can read the story to find out why Niki Pappas learns how to speak English very quickly.

Before you ask the questions in the Directed Reading section that follows, read the story with the students. Have them support their responses by reading the words or sentences that prove their answers.

The
23rd Street
School

where Niki Pappas refuses to speak English

Niki Pappas kicked the garbage pail next to his apartment house. This time he was really mad at his father. It hadn't been so bad the first time they left an old home for a new one. When they left Greece, he was too little to miss it very much. But this time was different. His best friend was back in the other city, and he didn't know anyone here. He didn't understand why his father had to buy a new store in The Nitty Gritty City.

258

Inferring cause
- Why did Niki kick the garbage pail? (He was mad.)
- Why was Niki mad? (His family had moved to The Nitty Gritty City where he didn't know anyone, and his best friend was in the other city.)

Identifying details
- Where had Niki lived when he was very little? (Greece)

Figure 10.5 (*continues*)

page 259

Niki had a plan that would make his father take him back to the other city. "I will stop speaking English," Niki said to himself. "I still know how to speak Greek. If no one in my new school can understand me, I will be kicked out. I will tell my dad that I won't ever speak English again unless we go back."

On the first day at his new school, Niki started his plan.

"We have someone new today," Mr. Kelly said to the class. "Niki Pappas comes from another city, but he was born in Greece. Welcome to our class, Niki."

259

page 260

Niki chuckled to himself. "Then kata loveno," he said to Mr. Kelly in Greek. (That means "I don't understand.")

Mr. Kelly looked puzzled. "But, Niki," he said, "you've been in the United States for five and a half years. Your teacher in the other school wrote me that your English is perfect. You do understand me, don't you?"

Niki tried hard to look as if he didn't understand. "Then kata loveno," he repeated.

Mr. Kelly frowned. "O.K., Niki," he said at last, "it looks as if you really can't speak English, so I shall try to teach you. You can sit in the second seat in the first row for now."

"Ha," thought Niki to himself, "he thinks he can fool me that easily!" Niki didn't go to the second seat in the first row. He just stood there, calmly smiling at Mr. Kelly.

260

Identifying main idea
- What was Niki's plan? (He was going to stop speaking English so that he would be kicked out of school.)

Identifying details
- When would Niki start speaking English again? (When his family moved back to the other city.)

Inferring details
- Who was Mr. Kelly? (Mr. Kelly was Niki's teacher.)

Predicting outcomes
- Do you think that Niki will carry out his plan? (Answers will vary.)

Inferring cause
- Why did Niki say, "Then kata loveno?" (He was pretending that he could speak and understand only Greek.)
- Why was Mr. Kelly puzzled? (Niki's school records showed that he was able to speak perfect English.)

Drawing conclusions
- How can you tell that Mr. Kelly thought Niki could speak English? (Mr. Kelly told rather than showed Niki where to sit.)

Figure 10.5 (*continues*)

page 261

Mr. Kelly pulled Niki gently by the hand to a seat. Then Mr. Kelly started the math lesson. He kept looking over at Niki, but Niki just stared out the window. Why pay attention if you can't understand? Niki acted the same way during the reading lesson and the spelling lesson.

page 262

Then it was time to go out to the school yard. It was lonely just standing around and not talking to anyone. But Niki knew he couldn't stop his plan now. A bunch of kids were standing off in a corner of the yard. They were whispering and looking at him. Finally one of the kids walked over and smiled.

"I am Carl," said the boy. "Maybe we can help you with your English. After school today, we're all going to play softball. Do you want to play?"

Inferring cause
- Why didn't Niki take a seat? (If he had taken a seat, Mr. Kelly would have known that he understood English.)

Identifying details
- What did Niki do during the math lesson? (He looked out the window.)

Inferring cause
- Why did Niki look out the window during Mr. Kelly's lessons? (Niki was pretending not to understand English by not paying attention.)

Identifying details
- How did Niki act in the school yard? (He stood by himself and didn't talk to anyone.)

Identifying mood
- How did Niki feel? (He felt lonely.)

Identifying details
- What did Carl say to Niki? (Carl offered to help Niki learn English and invited him to play softball.)

Inferring character traits
- What was Carl like? (friendly; kind)

Giving opinions
- How do you think Niki felt about his plan now? Why?

Figure 10.5 (*continues*)

page 263

Niki did want to play. Carl and the other kids seemed nice and friendly. But Niki had to pretend he didn't understand what Carl said. "Then kata loveno," mumbled Niki.

"He can't understand you, Carl," said a boy with curly red hair.

"CAN YOU PLAY SOFTBALL AFTER SCHOOL?" repeated Carl, very loudly and very slowly.

Niki had to work hard to keep from chuckling. "Then kata loveno," he said again.

"Oh, you're doing it all wrong!" said the boy with red hair. "We have to start from the beginning." He pointed to himself and said, "Billy."

"Billy," Niki repeated. He tried to say it oddly, as if he were saying the word for the first time.

"Carl," said Billy pointing to the other boy.

"Carl," repeated Niki.

263

page 264

Billy went on with his lesson, teaching Niki the words <u>school</u>, <u>friend</u>, and <u>ball</u>. Niki began to feel rather bored. "How long will it take them to teach me English all over again?" he said to himself. But Billy went on and on with the lesson, and the other kids helped him.

"I can't stand it!" Niki said to himself at last. "I don't want to be taught English all over again. I just want to play softball with them."

So quickly, before Billy tried to teach him another word, Niki whispered to him, "Do you want me to tell you a secret?"

"Yes," said Billy. "What is it?"

264

Inferring cause	• Why did Carl shout? (He thought that Niki would understand him better.)
Identifying sequence	• What did Billy teach Niki first? (Billy's name)
Identifying cause	• Why did Niki try to say "Billy" oddly? (to make it seem as if it were the first time he had ever said the word)

Identifying details	• What other words did Billy teach Niki? (school; friend; ball)
Inferring cause	• Why was Niki bored? (He already knew how to speak English.)
	• Why did Niki decide to admit that he spoke English? (He didn't want to learn English again; he wanted to play ball.)
Predicting outcomes	• What secret do you think Niki is going to tell Billy? (that he knows how to speak English)

Figure 10.5 (*continues*)

page 265

"I do know how to speak English," said Niki.

"You do!" yelled Billy. "That's terrific!"

When it was time to go back into the classroom, Niki walked in with his new friends.

"You know what?" Billy said to Mr. Kelly. "Niki knows how to speak English now!"

"Does he?" said Mr. Kelly. He didn't seem very surprised. "How did that happen?"

"We taught him out in the school yard," said Billy. "He learns very quickly!"

Interpreting the Second Title

Review "The 23rd Street School" with the students. Then have them turn back to page 258 and read the second title. Have them discuss what "where Niki Pappas refuses to speak English" means to them now that they have read the story. (Niki Pappas thinks that by refusing to speak English in school he will get his family to go back to where they used to live. Then he realizes that he is missing out on some fun, so he decides to speak English.)

Inferring mood • How did Billy feel when he learned that Niki could speak English? (very happy)

Identifying details • What did Billy tell Mr. Kelly? (He told Mr. Kelly that Niki could speak English.)

Inferring cause • Why do you think Mr. Kelly wasn't surprised? (He knew that Niki spoke English from Niki's school records.)

Giving opinions • Do you think that Mr. Kelly was right not to force Niki to speak English? Why?

Figure 10.5 (*continued*)

DRA	GMS
Introduction of vocabulary	Schemata enhancement
Purpose given for reading	Prediction making
Silent reading	Silent reading
Discussion and oral rereading (discussion of questions from a comprehension taxonomy)	Discussion and oral rereading (discussion of predictions)
Skill development	Bringing reading to a conscious level (retelling and looking at the reading process)
Enrichment activities	Concept development (questions can be asked from a comprehension taxonomy)

Figure 10.6   Comparison of directed reading activity and guided metacomprehension strategy.

Now consider the differences between the Directed Reading Activity and the Guided Metacomprehension Strategy, compared in Figure 10.6. The traditional DRA does not include schemata enhancement before reading the story. When using a basal we suggest that you make this addition to the DRA. Also include the making of predictions (note that this was done in the basal example when children were asked, "Do you think that Niki will carry out his plan?"). The addition of more prediction making will help readers learn to use metacomprehension strategies. Finally, you can strengthen the DRA by adding a discussion to help readers bring reading to a conscious level.

■ Record Keeping in the Directed Reading Activity

To save and use information about individual children's ability to do various thought tasks in response to their reading, you need to devise a record-keeping system. The one illustrated in Figure 10.7 allows you to track which children are able and which unable to answer a given kind of comprehension question. You can then identify children who need instruction in a given skill and those to whom you need not direct a certain kind of question very often.

The data collection process is simple. List the names of the children down the side and the kinds of thinking tasks (drawn from a taxonomy or the basal teacher's guide) across the top. When a child successfully answers a question, write a plus in the child's row name under the appropriate heading. Note a failure with a minus. The pattern that emerges will give

	Recall—Identification	Recall—Organization	Interpretation—Summary	Interpretation—Conclusion
Katie	+ + / +	+ + / −	− − / −	+ / − +
Randy	+ + / + +	+ + / +	+ − / −	+ + / − +
Steve	− − / − +	+ + / + − +	− + / + −	+ − / − +
Tricia	± − / − +	+ + / − − −	+ + / − −	± + / −
Mariko	+ + / + +	+ / − +	+ − / + +	− − / − +

Figure 10.7   A portion of a sample record-keeping system. The complete record would have ten columns.

you direction in planning comprehension instruction. The spaces to the right of the columns are for further notes about strengths, interests, and skill needs.

▮▮▮ Direct Instruction in Comprehension

Can comprehension be taught? Some would argue that we can only teach children to use the four cueing systems and that comprehension will follow. Others contend that comprehension can be taught only by breaking the reading process down into its irreducible components and teaching those pieces (subskills). We take the position that comprehension can be taught by continually bringing the reading process to a conscious level, by modeling interaction with print for children, and by arranging instructional strategies that help them develop metacomprehension abilities. Pearson and Johnson (1978, p. 4) listed the following things we can do to *teach* comprehension:

1. Model comprehension processes for students.
2. Provide cues to help them understand what they are reading.
3. Guide discussion to help children know what they know.
4. Ask pointed, penetrating, or directional questions, offer feedback.
5. Generate useful independent practice activities.
6. Help expand and clarify children's vocabularies.

7. Teach children how to handle various formats (charts, graphs, tables).
8. Offer guidance about how to study a text.

Dolores Durkin (1978–1979) conducted research that examined how much time elementary classroom teachers actually spend in comprehension instruction. She reported that whereas teachers asked a great many questions, very little actual instruction in comprehension took place. Most of what teachers considered to be comprehension instruction was directing children's use of workbook pages and duplicated materials. Durkin concluded that completing worksheets and getting "right" answers was valued over learning word meanings and learning and applying other comprehension skills.

Direct instruction in comprehension must involve teaching children to do a certain kind of thinking. Asking them questions and assigning workbook pages will not meet this goal! In fact, most basal reader workbook pages should be used as a teaching tool rather than as an independent assignment. By walking children through a workbook page, engaging them in discussion of the assignment as they work on it, you can implement some of the suggested instructional strategies. The focus of comprehension instruction is one of problem solving. We are actually teaching children how to solve the problem of answering a certain kind of question—a question designed to promote a certain kind of thinking. In order for comprehension to occur, children must always be able to relate the text to what they already know.

Lessons in a comprehension subskill should consist of careful instruction followed by practice and application of the skill. Heilman et al. (1981, p. 256) suggested four steps in the well-planned comprehension skills lesson:

1. Readiness—review of previous lessons, explanation and illustration of lesson objective, why it is important to learn this ability, and how it relates directly to immediate application in meaningful reading.
2. Step-by-step explanation and illustration of skill or ability using familiar materials.
3. Supervised practice with the teacher.
4. Application of skill or ability—independent assignment or group activity closely monitored by the teacher.

We consider Step 1 to be an extremely important step that informs students of things often kept secret from them.

Please review the story entitled "The 23rd Street School" in Figure 10.5. The following excerpt from the teacher's guide for the Addison-Wesley Reading Program (Rowland, 1982, p. 27) suggests a skills lesson to present after reading the story. The comprehension subskill developed in this lesson is from Section 2.6 of the Barrett taxonomy: inferring character traits. Note the extent to which each of the steps Heilman, Blair, and Rupley outlined are included in this guide's plan.

Skills Spinoff

Comprehension: identifying and inferring character traits

Review "The 23rd Street School" with the children. Discuss with them what kind of person Niki was and what kind of people Billy and Mr. Kelly were.

Have the children discuss what each character was like. Ask them whether they would like to have Billy or Niki for a friend, and have them share their answers and their reasons for the answers. Have them name things they like or dislike about each character.

Then ask the children whether they would like to have Mr. Kelly for a teacher, and have them share their answers and reasons with the group.

This example is typical of the ways in which comprehension lessons are structured in basal reader teacher's guides. In addition to discussion lessons like this, many lessons use a workbook. Figure 10.8 is an excerpt from the *Skills Book* accompanying the student text for 23rd and 24th Street of *The Nitty Gritty Rather Pretty City* (Rowland, 1982, p. 100). Please note that the teacher's guide instructs the teacher to use the workbook page as a teaching device.

Note also the directions to the teacher to discuss answers with the children. This recommendation is part of what Pearson and Johnson (1978) meant when they said that teachers should guide discussion to help children know what they know and provide cues to help them understand what they are reading, or provide feedback. We assist children with comprehension only when we are interacting with them about their reading, not when giving them worksheets to be done silently and independently at their desks.

Where do you learn which comprehension skills to teach? There are three important sources. The most important source is your observation of your students. Every interaction you have with readers should be diagnostic in the sense that you are constantly on the lookout for reading strengths and weaknesses. You monitor carefully the reading strategies your students are using, as well as the kinds of comprehension questions they can answer. You listen closely to comments when you bring the reading process to a conscious level and you pay concentrated attention to their story retellings. The second source is your school district's curriculum guide, which tells you which comprehension objectives are to be devel-

LESSON 5

Step 1 · Page 100

Objectives
- *to identify and infer details*
- *to identify main idea*
- *to express opinions*

page 100

Check the correct boxes.

1 What secrets did the girls in the club have?
- They said their names backwards.
- They wore their hair the same way.
- They ate lunch together every day.
- They wrote secrets in their secret book.

2 Why did the girls stop enjoying the secret club meetings?
- They wanted to do other things after school.
- They began to like more kids at school.
- The basement was too cold.
- They were bored.

3 What was the main idea of the story?
- It is not much fun to have secrets from other people. It is more fun to be friendly.
- You should not say mean things about other people, because they will not like you.

4 What do you think was wrong with the secret club?

(Child will write sentences.)

100 Use after reading "The Basement of Linda's House."

Do page 100. Review "The Basement of Linda's House" with the children. Recall with them what secrets the girls had, where the club met, and why the girls got tired of the club. Ask the children whether they have ever belonged to a club. Have those who wish to do so share their experiences.

Have the children open their Skills Books to page 100. Tell the children that the questions on this page are about "The Basement of Linda's House." Have someone read aloud the direction at the top of the page. Tell the children that they are going to read each question and the sentences that follow it and then write a check mark in the box in front of the sentence or sentences that correctly answer the question.

Have the children read question 1 aloud. Then have them read and discuss the four sentences that follow the question. Have the children write a check mark inside the box in front of each sentence that answers the question. Then have the children follow a similar procedure with questions 2 and 3.

Have someone read question 4 aloud. Ask the children to share their answers in a group discussion. Then tell the children to write on the lines what they think was wrong with the club. When the children have finished, have volunteers write their responses on the chalkboard.

Figure 10.8 *Skills Book* excerpt.

SOURCE: Pleasant T. Rowland, *The Nitty Gritty Rather Pretty City* (Menlo Park: Calif.: Addison-Wesley, 1982).

oped in your assigned grade level. The third source is the teacher's guide to the basal reader you are using, if any. All these sources are likely to have rather extensive listings of comprehension skills.

Enrichment Activities

Enrichment activities—those activities that build bridges between reading and other curricular areas—offer students opportunities to enrich and extend their comprehension of story content. For example, the child who dons an old police officer's hat in the dramatic play center and pretends to hand out parking tickets or help children cross the street will have a much better understanding of the roles and relationships of police officers when he or she meets the helpful policeman in *Make Way for Ducklings* (McCloskey, 1941). Making finger puppets of two dogs and acting out their quarrel over a bone helps a child to comprehend the story in *Finders Keepers* (Lipkind, 1951). Comprehension of *Where the Wild Things Are* (Sendak, 1963) is enhanced when the reader writes a sequel telling of another (perhaps personal) dream experience. Meeting a challenge to write a story about his or her own fears equips a child to relate to Mafatu's struggle to overcome his fears in *Call It Courage* (Sperry, 1940).

Writing

Writing improves reading comprehension. When children write, they gain awareness of style, thematic elements, and authors' development of the parts of story structure. These are just a few examples of useful writing activities:

1. Write a help-wanted advertisement for a job that a character in a book might apply for.
2. Write what might happen if characters from two different books met each other.
3. Write an adventure a character might have if moved forward or backward in time.
4. Write an obituary for a character in a book.
5. Write riddles whose answers are book characters.
6. Develop scripts for skits, plays, or puppet plays.

Drama

Dramatic activities not only increase comprehension and retention but provide a means to assess them. The way children act out a portion of their reading material makes obvious their understanding or lack of it. For ex-

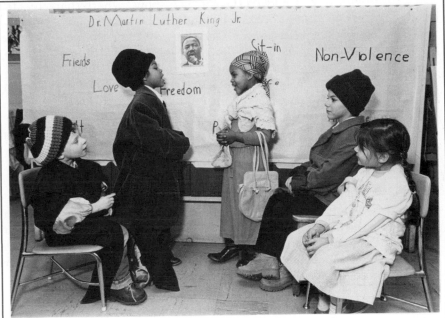

Schemata enhancement through drama helps children acquire background knowledge
of concepts outside their range of experience.
© Roberta Hershenson/Photo Researchers, Inc.

ample, if the bird in the story is supposed to glide, but the children are
flapping their arms as they act the part, then they probably do not understand *glide*. Drama allows children to take the part of another person, as-
suming character traits and perhaps even a language register different from
their own. This experience aids comprehension by helping the child learn
to identify with a character. Children also remember episodes that they
have acted out much longer than comparable ones they have only read.
Both planned and spontaneous dramatic activities are good for extending
comprehension. Here we suggest but a few ways of using drama:

1. One child or a small group pantomimes a character or event
   from a story, and the rest of the class tries to guess who or
   what it is.
2. Children can adapt a story or an excerpt from a story and
   present it as a puppet play for the other children. Young children can make simple stick puppets; older ones can handle
   even very elaborate papier-mâché figures.
3. Using a "talk show" format, the "host" interviews the "guest"
   as if he or she were a character in a book.

4. Children stage a "talk show" where characters from two different books meet and discuss a topic. For example, a girl from *A Gathering of Days* (Blos, 1979) might meet Margaret from *Are You There, God? It's Me, Margaret* (Blume, 1970) to discuss what is expected of them in their daily lives.

5. Children dramatize what might have happened next if the story had gone on to another episode.

6. Children choose an exciting excerpt to present to the class in the format of a movie preview to arouse the others' interest in reading the book.

■ Art

Another strategy for enriching reading and enhancing comprehension is the use of art to extend understanding. Art and craft activities can encourage others to read the books on which the activities are based, as well as clarifying the reader's images of the words portrayed in the writing. We suggest activities like these:

1. Design a book jacket or an advertising poster to "sell" the book or story.

2. Draw a map that illustrates the travels of a character in a book or story.

3. Make murals that depict events in a book or story as the murals in the Capitol building depict American history.

4. Make a collage of images that represent characters or events in reading materials.

5. Make a puppet to represent a character in a story.

6. Make a mobile of figures representing the major characters from a story.

7. Construct a diorama or shadow box representing a scene from a book.

8. Dress dolls in costumes to represent characters in books or stories.

9. Stitch a quilt or wall hanging with each square representing a scene from a book or from different books.

10. Design props for a theme for the reading center; for example, a space ship for books about space, a covered wagon for the Laura Ingalls Wilder books, a castle for fairy tales, a closet for the *Chronicles of Narnia*, a safe or a Sherlock Holmes hat for detective stories.

11. Draw the dress you would design for Cinderella if you were her fairy godmother.

Book knowledge about dinosaurs translates into a vivid diorama with the aid of realistic scenic effects.
© Howard Dratch/The Image Works

12. Make a mask for a character in a book.
13. Design a home for a character in a book; for example, a miniature house for *The Borrowers* (Norton, 1953) or a mouse house for *Whose Mouse Are You?* (Kraus, 1970).

You are the key to your students' success in terms of the instructional planning you do. Careful planning of guided reading activities, skill-development activities, and enrichment activities is essential to a good reading program. We wish you the greatest success!

■ Major Ideas in This Chapter

■ Comprehension—the interaction of our schemata with the ideas of the author—occurs on more than one level at a time. Recall and interpretation of a text are influenced by the reader's background.

■ Mature readers use as few as possible of the cues on the printed page to confirm or reject the predictions they are continually making about the text.

■ On the assumption that comprehension is a learnable process, your job as a teacher is to help students develop strategies to monitor their own comprehension: that is, engage in metacomprehension. Bringing the reading process to a conscious level is critically important.

■ Comprehension can be taught by a variety of strategies, including modeling comprehension processes for children, providing cues to help them understand what they are reading, helping them to know what they know about a topic, and helping them expand their vocabularies.

■ In order to monitor the kinds of thinking your students do in response to their reading, you should draw questions from taxonomies such as Wallen's or Barrett's.

■ The planning of comprehension instruction should include guided reading activities, skill-development activities, and enrichment activities.

? Discussion Questions
Focusing on the Teacher You Are Becoming

1. How do you think you would respond to a colleague who asserted that comprehension can be taught by teaching a series of subskill lessons based on a taxonomy?
2. Set up a debate within your class: "Metacomprehension strategies are of utmost importance in teaching comprehension" versus "Asking questions from a taxonomy is of utmost importance in teaching comprehension."
3. Describe the differences you see between the recommendations made in this chapter and what you remember about learning to read. How do you account for the changes?
4. What proportions of time should be allocated to skills lessons, guided reading activities, and enrichment activities? Would your answer depend on grade level? How?

☑ Field-Based Applications

1. Select a trade book to read to a small group of children. Prepare plans for introduction of vocabulary as outlined in this chapter.
2. Plan a Directed Reading Activity for a selection from a basal reader. Follow the reading of the selection with a comprehension skills lesson from the basal. Repeat the DRA activity with another story, but this time plan your own follow-up comprehension skills lesson.

3. Plan a Guided Metacomprehension Strategy for a selection from a basal reader. Repeat the GMS with another story, adding the use of prediction mapping. Repeat these two steps using favorite trade books.
4. Either read a story to children or plan a guided reading activity and then follow it with an enrichment activity in art. Select two other stories and follow them with activities in writing and drama.
5. Select two groups of children who can read the same story. Guide the reading of one group with DRA strategies, using questions from the Wallen or Barrett taxonomy. Guide the reading of the other group with GMS strategies. Observe the differences in responses from the children. Draw some conclusions about metacomprehension.
6. Choose a well-known folk tale that involves a journey. Draw a diagram of the events in the story. Have the children find a similar folk story and draw their own diagram of the events.

⊡ References and Suggested Readings

Baker, Linda, and Brown, Ann L. "Cognitive Monitoring in Reading." In *Understanding Reading Comprehension*, edited by J. Flood. Newark, Del.: International Reading Association, 1984, pp. 21–44.

Blos, Joan. *A Gathering of Days: A New England Girl's Journal 1830–32.* New York: Scribner's, 1979.

Blume, Judy. *Are You There, God? It's Me, Margaret.* New York: Bradbury Press, 1970.

Bransford, John D., and Johnson, Marcia K. "Considerations of Some Problems of Comprehension." In *Visual Information Processing*, edited by W. C. Chase. New York: Academic Press, 1973.

Brown, Margaret Wise. *The Runaway Bunny.* New York: Harper & Row, 1942.

Brunner, Joseph F., and Campbell, J. J. *Participating in Secondary Reading: A Practical Approach.* Englewood Cliffs, N.J.: Prentice-Hall, 1978.

Davis, Frederick B. "Research in Comprehension in Reading." *Reading Research Quarterly* 3 (1968), 185–197.

Durkin, Dolores. "Is There a Match between What Elementary Teachers Do and What Basal Reader Manuals Recommend?" *The Reading Teacher* 37 (April 1984): 734–744.

Durkin, Dolores. "What Classroom Observations Reveal about Reading Comprehension Instruction." *Reading Research Quarterly* (1978–1979): 481–533.

Fitzgerald, Jill, and Spiegel, Dixie Lee. "Enhancing Children's Reading Comprehension through Instruction in Narrative Structure." *Journal of Reading Behavior* 15 (1983): 1–17.

Fitzgerald, Jill; Spiegel, Dixie Lee; and Webb, Tamsen Banks. "Development of Children's Knowledge of Story Structure and Content." *Journal of Educational Research* 79 (November/December 1985): 101–108.

Fredericks, Anthony D. "Mental Imagery Activities to Improve Comprehension." *The Reading Teacher* 40 (October 1986): 78–81.

Gag, Wanda. *Millions of Cats.* New York: Coward, McCann & Geoghegan, 1928.

Gambrell, Linda B., and Koskinen, Patricia S. "Mental Imagery and the Reading Comprehension of below Average Readers, Situational Variables and Sex Differences." Paper presented at the annual meeting of the American Educational Research Association, New York, March 1982.

Gatheral, Maryanne. "Teaching Gifted Children in the Regular Classroom." Speech, Albany, Ore., 1984.

Goodman, Kenneth S. "Reading: A Psycholinguistic Guessing Game." *Journal of the Reading Specialist* 4 (1967): 126–135.

Harste, Jerome C., and Carey, Robert F. "Classroom Constraints and the Language Process." In *Promoting Reading Comprehension*, edited by J. Flood. Newark, Del.: International Reading Association, 1984, pp. 30–47.

Heilman, Arthur W.; Blair, Timothy; and Rupley, William H. *Principles and Practices of Teaching Reading*. Columbus, Ohio: Charles E. Merrill, 1981.

Kraus, Robert. *Whose Mouse Are You?* New York: Macmillan, 1970.

Lapp, Diane, and Flood, James. "Promoting Reading Comprehension: Instruction Which Insures Continuous Reader Growth." In *Promoting Reading Comprehension*, edited by J. Flood. Newark, Del.: International Reading Association, 1984, pp. 273–288.

Leu, Donald J.; De Groff, Linda-Jo; and Simons, Herbert D. "Predictable Texts and Interactive-Compensatory Hypotheses: Evaluating Individual Differences in Reading Ability, Context Use, and Comprehension." *Journal of Educational Psychology* 78 (October 1986): 347–352.

Lipkind, William. *Finders Keepers*. New York: Harcourt Brace, 1951.

Lowenthal, Barbara. "Planning Activities to Aid Metacognition." *Academic Therapy* 22 (November 1986): 199–203.

Mandler, Jean M., and Johnson, Nancy S. "Remembrance of Things Parsed: Story Structure and Recall." *Cognitive Psychology* 9 (January 1977): 111–151.

May, Frank B. *Reading as Communication: An Interactive Approach*. 2nd ed. Columbus, Ohio: Charles E. Merrill, 1986.

McCloskey, Robert. *Make Way for Ducklings*. New York: Puffin Books, 1941.

McGovern, Ann. *Too Much Noise*. New York: Scholastic Book Services, 1967.

Miller, George. "The Effects of General and Specific Self-Instruction Training on Children's Comprehension Monitoring Performances during Reading." *Reading Research Quarterly* 20 (Fall 1985): 616–628.

Nessel, Denise. "Reading Comprehension: Asking the Right Questions." *Phi Delta Kappan* 68 (February 1987): 442–445.

Nist, Sherri L., and Kirby, Kate. "Teaching Comprehension and Study Strategies through Modeling and Thinking Aloud." *Reading Research and Instruction* 25 (Summer 1986): 254–264.

Nolte, Ruth Y., and Singer, Harry. "Active Comprehension: Teaching a Process of Reading Comprehension and Its Effects on Reading Achievement." *The Reading Teacher* 39 (October 1985): 24–31.

Norton, Mary. *The Borrowers*. New York: Harcourt Brace, 1953.

Pearson, P. David, and Johnson, Dale D. *Teaching Reading Comprehension*. New York: Holt, Rinehart & Winston, 1978.

Rowland, Pleasant T. *The Nitty Gritty Rather Pretty City: 13th–24th Street*. Menlo Park, Calif.: Addison-Wesley, 1982.

Rumelhart, David E. "Understanding Understanding." In *Understanding Reading Comprehension,* edited by J. Flood. Newark, Del.: International Reading Association, 1984, pp. 1–20.

Sawyer, Ruth. *Journey Cake, Ho.* New York: Viking Press, 1953.

Sendak, Maurice. *Where the Wild Things Are.* New York: Scholastic Book Services, 1963.

Smith, Frank. *Reading without Nonsense.* New York: Teachers College Press, Columbia University, 1978.

Smith, Marilyn, and Bean, Thomas W. "Four Strategies That Develop Children's Story Comprehension and Writing." *The Reading Teacher* 36 (December 1983): 295–300.

Sperry, Armstrong. *Call It Courage.* New York: Collier Books, 1940.

Stauffer, Russell G. *Directing the Reading-Thinking Process.* New York: Harper & Row, 1975.

Stauffer, Russell G. "The Verdict: Speculative Controversy." *The Reading Teacher* 19 (May 1966): 563–575.

Tatham, Susan M. "Comprehension Taxonomies: Their Uses and Abuses." *The Reading Teacher* 32 (November 1978): 190–194.

Tolstoi, A. *The Turnip.* Moscow: Malysh Publishers, no date.

Waber, Bernard. *Ira Sleeps Over.* New York: Scholastic Book Services, 1972.

Wadsworth, Barry J. *Piaget's Theory of Cognitive and Affective Development.* New York: Longman, 1984.

Walker, Barbara J. "Right-Brained Strategies for Teaching Comprehension." *Academic Therapy* 21 (November 1985): 133–141.

Wallen, Carl J. *Competency in Teaching Reading.* Chicago: Science Research Associates, 1972.

Zemach, Margot. *It Could Always Be Worse.* New York: Scholastic Book Services, 1976.

Chapter 11

Assisting Children with Content-Area Reading

Chapter Overview

- Content-area reading—the reading of expository texts—presents challenges to the reader not found in narrative texts. Our job has been done well when students can draw on their background experiences and create meaning while interacting with expository texts.

- Content-area texts challenge readers with special text structures, a heavy concept load and thus a difficult vocabulary, and special text features such as graphs and charts, calling for a variety of instructional strategies.

- Content-area instruction presents special writing challenges to children. Writing activities need to be linked to content-area instruction so that the content texts become models for expository writing.

Reading in the content areas has become a common topic in reading instruction. What does the term *content areas* mean? The concept of "content areas" is confusing because *all* reading has content. Mystery stories have content. Poetry has content. A grocery list has content! Without content, we cannot read. So why call certain reading selections "content-area reading?" We do not have a really good answer. Traditionally, those subjects that involve factual, expository writing, such as science, social studies, and health, have come to be known as "content areas." This usage is not intended to imply that other kinds of writing, such as fictional prose or poetry, lack content.

Let's reexamine our definition of reading comprehension. In Chapter 10 we said: "We define *comprehension* thus: the interaction of the author's ideas and the reader's schemata that results in the creation of meaning." It is crucial, as students read in the content areas, that we keep this definition of comprehension—and therefore of reading, because reading is comprehension—in mind. Since comprehension is the primary objective in content-area reading, we need to help the student draw on his or her background experiences to create meaning in interacting with the text. The following conditions optimize the comprehension of content texts:

1.   Readers' comprehension of content texts is enhanced by strong motivation to read the material. This condition assumes that teachers create background experiences—and ways to draw on students' background experiences—so that readers approach text with heightened interest and motivation. Field trips, television, film, trade books, magazines, speakers, news media, and artifacts all work to build interest in, and schemata for, reading content texts. Therefore, exposure to them increases students' likelihood of success.

2.   Comprehension is heightened by authentic classroom activities that draw on content-area knowledge, among them activities that provide real reasons to write. The guiding of content reading will be effective when children see real reasons to read and real, authentic activities that grow out of that reading. An assignment to "read and answer the questions" is not enough. Content materials should be read as resource materials in instructional units and thematic units and as part of real problem-solving situations.

3.   Just as we cannot teach children to ride a tricycle by giving pedaling lessons first, then steering lessons, so we cannot teach children to read content texts by teaching them first to read isolated, specialized vocabulary, then to read headings and subheadings, and then to read the text. "Content-area reading skills" are learned by reading content-area texts. Helping students deal with the challenges of content texts *as they read them* will help them learn to read content material effectively.

Reading Challenges in Content Areas

Reading and writing about content-area subjects present challenges to students far greater than those posed by the reading and writing of fiction texts. Flood and Lapp (1987) report that the content of basal readers is almost exclusively literary. Sixty-five percent of the selections and 72 percent of the pages in eight basal programs studied were either narratives or poems. Expository selections were rarely included. The expository reading that is required in science, social studies, mathematics, and health presents text structures, sentence structures, and specialized vocabulary that are foreign to narrative reading. Writing about content subjects requires the use of new formats, sentence structures, and vocabulary. The schemata that children bring to content-area reading may not accommodate the new concepts presented. In fact, children may have no background, very limited

Literacy skills form the foundation for learning in all subject areas.
© *Frank Siteman/The Picture Cube*

background, or inaccurate information about topics covered in content-area texts. In these cases teachers have to plan activities that provide the experiences children need to build the images required to make sense of expository writing. Teachers must be aware that reading instruction should begin with developmental, recreational, and functional reading and that reading instruction of all these types continues throughout the grades. The old saying that children learn to read in primary grades and read to learn in intermediate grades is not true.

The reading of content-area texts presents special challenges to the reader. Three major reading challenges posed by content-area texts are that of text structure, that of specialized vocabulary occasioned by heavy concept load, and that of special text features.

■ First Challenge: Text Structure

The overall organization of an expository text, as well as its sentence and paragraph structures, differs from the features of narrative writing, with which children have typically had more experience. Compare the excerpts from a fifth-grade story about a boy who is trying to photograph cranes and an expository piece about cranes in Figures 11.1 and 11.2. What differences do you see in the structures of the two passages?

The story selection has a plot, setting, and characters. There is dialogue that helps the reader create meaning. In the expository piece there is no plot, no setting, and no story characters. Instead, each sentence presents one or more facts. In the narrative piece, the facts about cranes are woven into the story. In the expository piece the facts are simply presented, to be remembered by the reader. The mental images that are built by the reader in the story selection are very different from those that must be built in the expository selection. The reading challenge is to move from dealing with story structure to dealing with processing facts in such a way that they make sense to the reader.

IN SEARCH OF A SANDHILL CRANE

Link cooked an early dinner at his campsite and then, with his sleeping bag and enough food for breakfast, he hiked back through the woods to a spot not far from the "blind" he had made—a hiding place of cut bushes from which he could watch the birds without being seen. He slept well and got up a short while before dawn and ate a cold breakfast of a banana, two pieces of bread, and a slice of cold ham. He would have liked a cup of hot coffee and an egg, but he did not want any smoke rising from a campfire to alarm the cranes. When he had finished he carried his sleeping bag out to his blind and made a comfortable spot where he could sit or lie while he waited. He had scarcely settled himself when Olson appeared. The wildlife expert had come up quietly and Link had no idea he was around until he was within a few feet of the blind. . . .

Olson inspected and loaded his gun—not with bullets, but with tranquilizing darts. Link checked his camera as the field grew lighter.

"Cranes eat seeds, berries, roots, worms, bugs, almost anything," Olson said. "My guess is that at this time of the year it's grasshoppers and bugs that they're after in a place like this. You'll want to wait until the sun gets up a ways so you will have good light for your pictures. They'll hang around for several hours if they come, so there's plenty of time."

Figure 11.1 Sample narrative text.
Source: Excerpted from "In Search of a Sandhill Crane," by Keith Robertson. Copyright © 1973 by Keith Robertson. Reprinted by permission of the publisher, Viking Penguin, a division of Penguin Books USA Inc.

SANDHILL CRANES

Each year, sandhill cranes migrate from their nesting grounds in the North to wintering grounds in the Southwest. They sometimes fly at altitudes of 10,000 feet or more.

After the eggs—usually two—are laid, the mother and father crane take turns sitting on the nest. The eggs, three to four inches long, hatch in about 32 days. The crane chick can walk and swim when it is a few hours old.

The crane's long toes keep it from sinking into mud at the bottom of the marsh. Its long legs, long neck and long bill help it to walk about in marshlands and catch fish. Cranes eat a great variety of foods, including worms, frogs, small snakes, and grasshoppers, as well as grain and other vegetation. A sandhill crane will sometimes eat 500 grasshoppers and worms a day.

Figure 11.2   Sample expository text.
SOURCE: Excerpted from "Sandhill Cranes," *Landmarks* (Orlando, Fla.: Harcourt Brace Jovanovich Reading Program, 1987), pp. 100–102.

■ Second Challenge: Specialized Vocabulary

Comprehending a text heavily laden with concepts, which are labeled by a specialized vocabulary, presents a challenge to the reader. It is impossible to write about content subjects without using specialized vocabularies. Despite authors' attempts to write in simple language, the expository selection must inevitably present the reader with vocabulary challenges. It would be ridiculous, for example, to write a piece about the Constitution and avoid the multisyllabic word *Constitution* by referring to it as "the big paper."

Figure 11.3 is an excerpt from a third-grade science selection. Consider the specialized vocabulary that the author must use in order to write accurately about precipitation, and that the reader must relate to his or her schemata in order to create meaning.

Reexamine the selection in Figure 11.3, asking the question "Can this selection be made any easier?" Our answer is no. When authors attempt to write expository material without using the necessary technical vocabulary, they have "dumbed down" the selection—often to the point of rendering it meaningless. An editorial in the *San Francisco Chronicle* on September 13, 1988, decried the practice of dumbing down books, calling it "insulting." Reporting an example in which Goldilocks ate fish when she entered the three bears' house, the editors suggested that the book's publishers had apparently decided children could not understand—or learn—

PRECIPITATION

Both the waterdrops or ice crystals in clouds are very small. They are so small they hang in the air. Sometimes the drops or crystals grow too large. When they grow large enough, they are too heavy to stay in the air. The drops or crystals fall to the ground. Water that falls from clouds is called precipitation (prih sihp uh TAY shun).

Rain and snow are two kinds of precipitation. Rain is liquid water that falls when the air is warmer than 0 degrees C. Snow is made of ice crystals that fall when the air is colder.

Sleet and hail are two other kinds of precipitation. Sleet is frozen rain. Some hail is formed from many layers of ice. The picture shows hailstones. Why might it be dangerous to be out in a hailstorm?

Figure 11.3 Vocabulary challenge.
SOURCE: *Accent on Science* (Columbus, Ohio: Charles E. Merrill, 1983), p. 123.

what porridge is. Such violations of the original language of a story occur when publishers rely too heavily on readability formulas to simplify the text.

Readability formulas are based on a shaky hypothesis that language complexity can be assessed by measuring sentence length and by counting syllables (Brewer, Jenkins, and Harp, 1984). The hypothesis is that longer sentences and multisyllabic words are more difficult to read than shorter sentences and one-syllable words. Yet experienced teachers readily acknowledge that children can read words like *airplane, transformer, Tyrannosaurus Rex,* and *birthday* much more easily than shorter words such as *these, this, there,* and *their.* When we try to write nonfiction without using the essential vocabulary, we have dumbed down the text past all usefulness. Instead of counting syllables and words per sentence, we should be asking whether the children for whom a piece is written can understand it. Perhaps even more important is the question of whether or not children will find their expectations about how language works confirmed by the text. Dumbed-down texts do not meet children's expectations about how language works.

■ Third Challenge: Special Text Features

Content-area reading assignments require students to attend to features of the text that are unique to expository writing. Charts, graphs, tables, and maps, as well as subheadings and special ways of highlighting information, are all challenges to readers of expository material. Often the reader

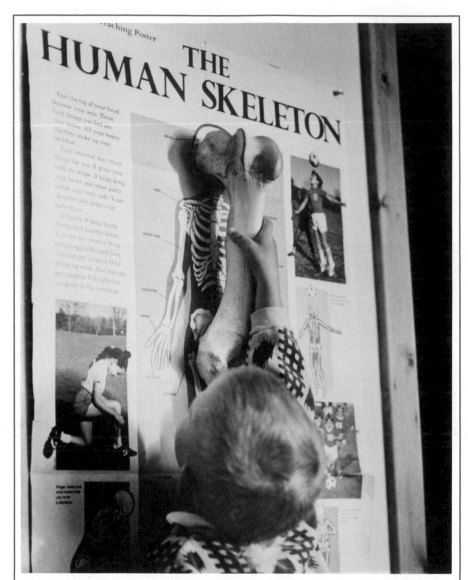

Reading in the content areas typically involves mastery of a specialized vocabulary.
© *Crystal Images/Monkmeyer Press Photo Service*

must learn to rely on the special-text features to make up for a lack of background experience and thus of schemata with which to relate to the text. Read the fifth-grade science selection in Figure 11.4 and then examine the illustration in Figure 11.5. It is easy to imagine that a child would be able to create much more meaning with the aid of the illustration than without it.

DERMIS

The dermis is much thicker than the epidermis. It may be three or more millimeters thick. The dermis is made of living cells. Nerves and blood vessels are in this layer of skin. Blood supplies food and oxygen to the skin cells. The blood also takes away cell wastes.

The dermis contains hair roots and some glands. **Glands** are special groups of cells which produce and store substances. Some glands are oil glands. They release an oily liquid which keeps the skin soft and smooth.

The oil rises to the skin's surface through pores. **Pores** are small openings in the skin. The pores let the oil travel from the glands in the dermis to the skin's surface.

Figure 11.4   Sample text: dermis.
SOURCE: *Accent on Science*, Grade 5 (Columbus, Ohio: Charles E. Merrill, 1983), pp. 138–139.

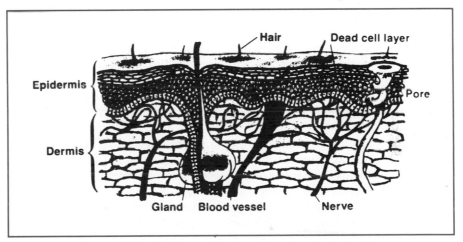

Figure 11.5   Sample illustration: dermis.
SOURCE: *Accent on Science*, Grade 5 (Columbus, Ohio: Charles E. Merrill, 1983), p. 138.

However, children have to be taught how to make use of special text features. Otherwise they tend to ignore them! By teaching we mean pointing out the features to young readers and explaining how they may make use of them to better understand the text. Only if children understand *how* charts, graphs, tables, and maps improve their understanding will they use them independently. Your reference to them in class discussions (including displaying some special text features with the overhead projector) will illustrate their importance.

Meeting Content-Area Reading Challenges

The activities used to meet content-area reading challenges are either *teacher-directed* or *independent* activities. Teacher-directed activities are those the teacher does with children to assist their reading of content texts. Independent activities are things that children can learn to do on their own to increase their understanding and use of content texts.

Teacher-Directed Activities

Ability to Grasp the Text

The teacher must know for whom the text is too difficult. Not every child in a class can read the social studies or science text with comfort and understanding. For example, the fact that a child is in fourth grade does not mean that he or she can read the fourth-grade social studies text. The fourth-grade text will contain a considerable range of difficulty, perhaps from third- to eighth- or ninth-grade readability. The range of reading achievement levels in a typical fourth-grade class stretches from first to sixth or higher. As we move up through the grades, the ranges become even broader.

An effective and efficient way to determine which children will be unable to read a text with good comprehension is the cloze procedure. Studied extensively by John Bormuth (1968), the procedure is based on the assumption that reading is interactive. As readers predict words to fill in blanks, they are calling on their knowledge of syntax as well as their relevant schemata to demonstrate their understanding of the syntactic and semantic relationships within the text.

To construct a cloze test, select a passage of about 250 words in length from each of several places within a textbook. Type the selections, leaving the first and last sentences intact but omitting every fifth or seventh word in the rest of the text. Type a blank line of about fifteen spaces where each word is removed. For the process to be reliable, you need a passage incorporating fifty blanks. Have students fill in the blanks.

To score a cloze exercise, count the number of blanks in which the student replaced the *exact* word that had been omitted. If the student exactly replaces 45 to 59 percent of the words, the selection is probably at the student's instructional level; if 60 percent or more, at the independent level. If the correct replacements amount to less than 45 percent, the book is at the reader's frustration level and should not be used as assigned reading.

Once you know for which of your students the adopted text is too difficult, you can make arrangements for them to read easier material or get the necessary information in another way. Having identified material that your students can read, you should engage in important schemata-enhancement activities to assist them in bringing what they know about a topic to a conscious level and to relate their knowledge to their reading.

Schemata Enhancement

Because comprehension *depends* on the reader's ability to integrate his or her past experiences (schemata) with the author's ideas, it is essential that we attend to schemata before children read content texts. Schemata can be enhanced by providing children with experiences by which they may build new schemata or refine existing schemata. Edgar Dale (1969) proposed a Cone of Experience (Figure 11.6, as modified by Rodgers [1975]) that may be helpful to teachers in designing schemata-enhancement activities. Clearly the best schemata-enhancement activities would be "direct, purposeful experiences." Working in a lumber mill before reading about the role the lumber industry plays in the economy of Pacific Rim countries would be the best form of schemata enhancement. But barring that possibility, a computer simulation of the lumber milling process might be the next best option, followed next by dramatization of working in the lumber mill or of the importance of lumber to economic development. As the teacher's planned activities move up Dale's cone, the likelihood of truly enhancing schemata diminishes. Each step up the cone moves the experience to a more abstract level. The most abstract experience, of course, will be reading the text. The further down the cone the teacher can design schemata-enhancement activities, the more effective they are likely to be.

Text Structure

Techniques that help children focus on the organization of content texts will assist their understanding. Expository texts are very different from the narratives most children have been reading. Comparing and contrasting these two kinds of texts and looking at patterns of organization will not only increase comprehension of expository texts but improve the writing of expository material.

Compare and Contrast Narrative and Exposition
Just as we illustrated in Figures 11.1 and 11.2, share with children both narrative and expository texts and compare their distinguishing characteristics. After reading examples of both types of writing, children can analyze

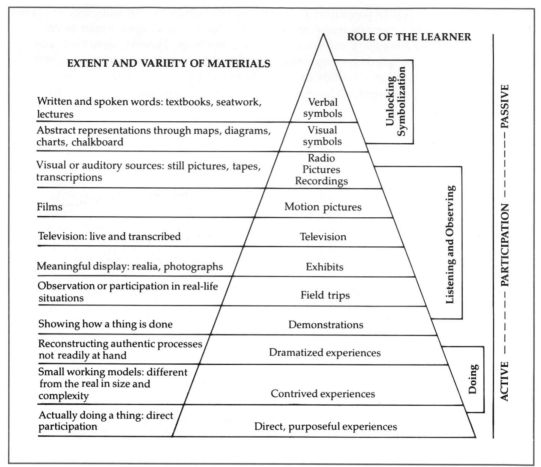

Figure 11.6   Dale's Cone of Experience.

SOURCE: From *Curriculum and Instruction in the Elementary School* by Frederick A. Rodgers. Macmillan Publishing Company. Copyright © 1975 by the author. Reprinted by permission.

the major differences, such as presence of plot, setting, and characterization versus organization around facts, and look for similarities. Children's understanding of expository writing will be aided by exposure to many models of it, as well as by opportunities to write expository material.

Study Patterns of Text Organization

Authors of expository materials choose from a variety of organizational patterns, each of which may be a topic of study and a focus of writing experiences as examples arise in textbooks. Comprehension of texts is enhanced by a reader's recognition of the text's organization (Weaver, 1988).

After learning about organizational patterns, a group of ninth-graders remembered two times as much from their reading as they could before (Meyer, 1982). Authors rarely confine themselves to a single organizational pattern; a text normally reveals several. These are some patterns of text organization:

Major idea/supporting details	Author states the major idea or conclusion and then offers the evidence to support it.
Details/conclusion	Author offers the data first, then draws conclusions.
Time order	Author relates events in the sequence in which they occurred, using chronological order or ordinal markers such as "first, second, third" or "then, then, and finally."
Cause/effect	Author explains events or phenomena in terms of conditions that create them and follow from them.
Comparison/contrast	Author examines similarities and differences between things.
Flashback	Author sequences information by beginning in the present and then moving to an exposition of past events that led up to the present events.
Question/answer	Author asks a question and then answers it, perhaps repeating the device throughout the text.

Children understand these patterns best if they use them in their own writing after studying them. When do they study them? We suggest that as you are assigning an expository selection, you point out the organizational patterns the author uses. For example, discuss the pattern of organization based on cause and effect before the students read a text arranged that way. Then have the students perform a science experiment that demonstrates a cause–effect relationship and write about it using the model you have provided. Practicing the use of various patterns in class discussions of topics important to the children is another helpful strategy. When a class discussion exhibits a particular pattern, be sure to point that out to your students.

Variety of Materials and Resources

In order to meet the challenges of expository structure and specialized vocabulary, teachers have to locate a variety of materials for children to read in the content areas. This task can be difficult, but it is not impossible. Here are some suggestions for meeting the materials challenge.

Use Child-Authored Texts

Each time you teach a unit, duplicate a selection of the books that the children have published and keep them in the classroom library for next year's class to read during the study of the unit. Our experience has been that child authors produce some of the clearest, most readable content-area materials. Individually written or group-authored books produced to culminate a unit of study not only will be informative but will provide writing models for the next group of students.

Use Trade Books

The media specialist can be an invaluable partner in the search for materials that supplement the content-area texts. A few weeks before you begin a social studies or science unit, talk with the media specialist about the kinds of trade books (books published for noninstructional purposes) you would like to have in your classroom during the study. He or she will probably be able to pull together an assortment of books ranging from picture books to reference materials that relate to your topic. When the library corner or learning center is filled with trade books related to the current topic of study, children of varying reading abilities will be able to find information that is pertinent and interesting to them. You can read trade books to your students as a way of building background that makes it easier for them to read other texts.

Use Periodicals

In addition to the popular weekly magazines, which often have pictures that can be used in content areas, there are many periodicals published for children. Many of their articles on content topics are written at levels more easily read than textbooks. These are children's periodicals that teachers have found useful:

> *International Wildlife* (National Wildlife Federation)
> *National Wildlife* (National Wildlife Federation)
> *Ranger Rick* (National Wildlife Federation)
> *Faces* (Cobblestone Publishing)
> *Cobblestone* (Cobblestone Publishing)

Scienceland (Sekai Bunka Publishing)
Zoo Books (Wildlife Education Ltd.)
National Geographic World (National Geographic Society)
Owl (The Young Naturalist Foundation)
3-2-1 Contact (The Children's Television Workshop)

Use Recorded Texts

Some expository materials are so well written or distinctive that a teacher wants the children to experience them just the way they are, not simplified or recast as a series of illustrations. It is effective (and efficient) to ask a volunteer who enjoys oral reading to tape-record those selections. The tapes can be played for the whole class or placed in the listening center for small groups of children to hear, with or without copies of the text in which to follow along.

Use Other Media

Ask the media specialist to identify filmstrips, films, and videotapes that can be used to supplement the written material in the content areas. Computer software is even available to simulate certain real-life situations, letting children experience the flavor of a given time and place. Using other media in conjunction with written material can help children develop concepts in the content areas. However, the teacher must carefully prepare for the use of audiovisual media by previewing them and planning strategies for children to respond to them. Showing a film without careful planning is of no more value than simply turning on the television!

Use Guest Speakers and Field Trips

Make a study of the resources available in your community, such as business people who are willing to make free presentations to schools. Recognize that taking children on a trip to actually *see* what they are studying will make the study much more relevant to them. Resourceful teachers often find worthwhile destinations within easy walking distance of their schools so field trips are not costly.

Guided Metacomprehension Strategy

The Guided Metacomprehension Strategy, introduced in Chapter 10, is a way to help children become interactive readers, assisting them in the vital metacomprehension functions that set good readers apart from poor ones. Stauffer (1975, p. 33) argued that when children are not engaged in reading strategies that develop self-generated learning about the reading process, "reading and thinking deteriorate into a waste of energy through an idle

Field trips enable children to acquire personal experiences of significance not only to their careers as students but to their lives as inhabitants of the world.
© Rhoda Sidney/Monkmeyer Press Photo Service

recital of facts and a round-the-robin oral reading that incline pupils toward dogma and cant and a mindless disregard for thoughtful reading.''

We illustrated the GMS strategy with the reading of *Ira Sleeps Over*. The key questions asked by the teacher were, ''What do you think this story will be about?'' and, ''What do you think will happen next?'' These questions lend themselves to narrative text but not to expository text. Asking children, ''What will this story be about?'' before they read a social studies selection on the transcontinental railroad would be silly, given that the selection is not a story and the title tells what the selection will be about. However, we can still use the GMS before children read an expository selection by asking questions that direct their thinking to certain key facts or concepts it contains. Like the GMS for narrative material, the expository GMS engages the readers in schemata enhancement, predicting, reading, and proving their predictions. The teacher asks what the readers think and why they think so, and invites them to read aloud to prove their answers. The important steps in bringing reading to a conscious level are still included when reading expository texts.

The following application of the GMS with fifth-grade students involves expository material.

Teacher:	*What can you tell me about what causes us to have seasons such as fall and winter?*
Jessica:	*The earth tilts on its axis, so sometimes one part of the world is having summer when another part is having winter.*
Ethan:	*The earth goes around the sun. That's what makes seasons.*
Teacher:	*Today we are going to read a selection about how the position of the earth affects the seasons on the earth. What answers do you think you will find to these questions? What determines a day?*
Robert:	*24 hours.*
Patti:	*One daytime and one night time.*
Damon:	*When the earth turns away from the sun.*
Teacher:	*Why are the days hotter and longer in the summer?*
Andrea:	*Because the earth is closer to the sun.*
Joanne:	*The days are hotter because they are longer.*
Teacher:	*What is meant by "summer solstice"?*
Sonja:	*It's a party in the summer.*
Robert:	*It's the beginning of summer.*
Damon:	*It has something to do with where the earth is to the sun.*
Teacher:	*Let's read from page 202 through page 205 to see which of your predictions you can prove and which ones you will want to change.*

Now the children read the selection from which Figure 11.7 is excerpted.

Teacher:	*One of your predictions was that a day was determined when the earth turns away from the sun. Can anyone read a part of the selection that proves or disproves that prediction?*
Patti:	*It says, "Earth makes one complete rotation in 24 hours. This amount of time is called a day."*
Teacher:	*Does that prove or disprove the prediction?*
Ethan:	*It sort of proves it because we said the earth turns away from the sun, and that is what it does when it rotates. One part of the earth turns away from the sun. All of our first predictions were partly right. We just didn't explain enough.*
Teacher:	*You said that days are hotter and longer in the summer because the earth is closer to the sun. Can someone read us the part of the text that proves or disproves that prediction?*
	(Discussion continues.)
Teacher:	*Who can tell me what you learned from reading this selection?*
Joanne:	*We learned that we were right about what makes a day.*
Lupe:	*We learned about the four seasons and the revolution of the earth around the sun.*
Vinh:	*We learned that summer solstice is not a party. (Laughter.)*
Teacher:	*How did you make use of the illustrations in the selection?*
Andrea:	*That one picture helped me see how one side of the earth is dark when the other side is sunny.*
	(Discussion continues.)

CHAPTER

THE EARTH AND THE MOON

1 DAYTIME, NIGHTTIME, AND SEASONS

What time of the day is it now? Is the sky bright or dark? How will the sky look twelve hours from now? Why do you think a change occurs?

When you finish this lesson, you should be able to:

○ Tell how Earth moves in space.

○ Explain how Earth's movements cause daytime, nighttime, and seasons.

Figure 11.7   Passage from a fifth-grade science text.   (continues)

SOURCE: Joseph Abruscato, Jack Hassard, Joan Wade Fossaceca, and Donald Peck, *Holt Elementary Science* (New York: Holt, Rinehart, and Winston, 1980), pp. 202–205.

Earth is a **planet**. A *planet* is a solid body in space that does not give off its own light. Earth gets its light from the sun.

Earth is shaped like a ball. Therefore, only the half of Earth that faces the sun gets light. Places on the half that is lit have daytime. Places on the other half are dark and have nighttime.

Earth moves in space. It spins, or **rotates** (row-tates). Do you feel the movement? Earth makes one complete *rotation* in 24 hours. This amount of time is called a day. Within 24 hours, or one day, most places on Earth have a daytime and a nighttime.

Earth rotates from west to east. That is why the sun seems to rise in the east and set in the west.

Planet: A solid body in space that does not give off its own light.

Rotate: To spin.

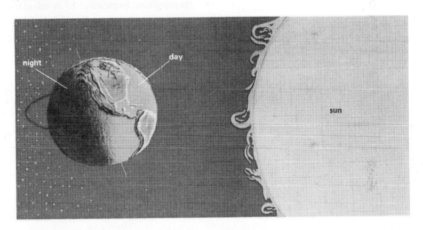

Earth also **revolves** (ree-volvs), or moves around, the sun. Earth makes one complete *revolution* around the sun every 365¼ days. This amount of time is called a year. Within one year, most places on Earth have four seasons. Can you name them?

Earth tilts toward or away from the sun at different times of the year.

Revolve: To move around something.

Figure 11.7   (*continues*)

Summer soltice: The first day of summer in the Northern Hemisphere.

Winter solstice: The first day of winter in the Northern Hemisphere.

Vernal equinox: The first day of spring in the Northern Hemisphere.

Autumnal equinox: The first day of fall in the Northern Hemisphere.

On June 21, Earth's North Pole is tilted toward the sun. In the Northern Hemisphere, this is the first day of summer. June 21 is called the **summer solstice** (sole-stis).

On December 22, Earth's North Pole is tilted away from the sun. In the Northern Hemisphere, this is the first day of winter. December 22 is called the **winter solstice** (sole-stis). Look at the diagram below. Can you find the position of Earth at the *summer solstice* and *winter solstice?*

In the spring and fall, Earth is not tilted toward or away from the sun. In the Northern Hemisphere, March 21 is the first day of spring, or the **vernal equinox** (vernal ee-kwi-noks). The first day of fall in the Northern Hemisphere, September 23, is called the **autumnal equinox** (awe-tum-nal ee-kwi-noks). Look at the diagram again. What is the position of Earth at the *vernal equinox* and *autumnal equinox?*

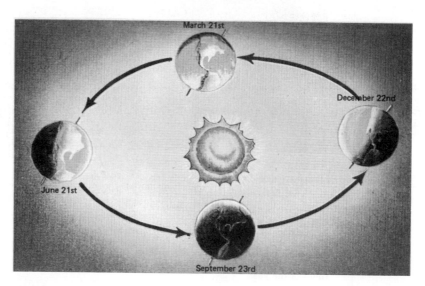

Figure 11.7   (*continues*)

How is a summer's day different from a winter's day? Why do you think the days are hotter and longer in the summer than in the winter? This activity may help you find out.

A. Place one sheet of paper on your desk. Hold the lit flashlight over the paper as shown in the first picture below.

B. With the chalk draw a line around the lit area.

C. Place the other sheet of paper on your desk. Hold the lit flashlight over the paper as shown in the second picture. Then draw a line around the lit area.

1. How are the lines you drew different from each other?

Materials
chalk
flashlight
2 sheets of black
  construction paper

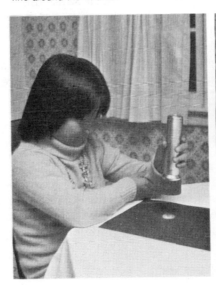

Figure 11.7   (*continued*)

Words and Concepts

Word Study

For the duration of a unit, keep a large sheet of paper hanging in the classroom where children may record interesting words and their meanings. Take time during class discussions to zero in on words—to point out uncommon uses of words and alternate ways of expressing something. It is important to help children see the multimeaning vocabulary in content areas. Vocabulary knowledge needs to grow vertically by adding new words and horizontally by adding new meanings to known words (for example, cabinet, act, and apron). To explore the true extent of multiple meanings, look up *run* in your dictionary. Ours devotes nearly a whole page to the meanings of *run*. Amazing!

Structured Overviews and Semantic Maps

Both structured overviews and semantic maps can help children with complex concepts and the language labels attached to them. Refer again to our discussion of structured overviews in Chapter 10. Semantic maps, less complex than structured overviews, are likewise intended to show the interrelationships among ideas. Introduced as a note-taking and study technique by Hanf (1971), the semantic map can provide a way for children to organize what they know about a topic before the reading, can be developed during the reading of a selection, or can follow it as a part of a group discussion. Figure 11.8 is a semantic map based on the excerpt from "Sandhill Cranes" presented in Figure 11.2.

■ Independent Activities

Independent activities are those things children can do on their own to make content-area reading more meaningful. We have labeled them "independent" because once you have taught them to do these things, they can do them without further instruction from you. For the most part, the activities described in this section are the traditional "study skills."

Identify Purposes for Reading

Children need to understand that we read texts for a variety of purposes. If the aim is to find specific pieces of information, we will approach the reading process very differently from the way we would when reading to understand a difficult concept. We will read about Egyptian history one way if it is for a hobby and another if it is for a school assignment and we know that we will be tested on the information. Clearly, children will be more highly

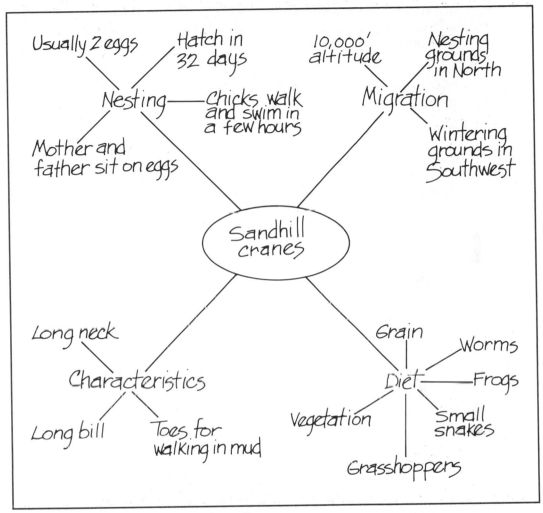

Figure 11.8 Semantic map of "Sandhill Cranes."

motivated to read a piece if they have a purpose or purposes for doing so. We know that comprehension is increased when readers have a purpose for reading.

The best purposes often grow out of the student's own questions. The teacher also asks leading questions: "Why would reading this be helpful? What do you expect to learn from reading this selection? What kinds of information do you expect to find here? How will you approach this reading—will you skim or will you read very carefully?" By asking questions like these each time you assign expository reading, you model the kind of "purpose for reading" thinking that children need to learn to do on their own.

Recognize Prior Knowledge and Knowledge Desired

The schemata-enhancement activities you do as part of the GMS are intended to help children focus on what they know before they read. You can combine this activity with writing by having pairs or small groups of children write down what they know about a topic before they read the text (Hammond, 1986). This step leads naturally to identifying the things they are not sure about and the things they want to find out when they read. After reading the selection they can determine the accuracy of their prior knowledge and note which of their questions have been answered. Confirming what children know and finding answers to their questions are two very compelling purposes for reading. Heller (1986) proposes that students make a chart with the reading topic and purpose for reading written at the top. Three columns are then headed "What I already know," "What I now know," and "What I want to know" (or the equivalent in question form). The columns are completed before and after reading, and finally the answer to the purpose question is written at the bottom of the chart. Heller recommends that teachers verbally walk students through the charting process as a way of teaching metacomprehension strategies.

We can invoke the power of prediction by having children predict answers to their questions in the third column of the chart, or by getting their predictions to questions at the start of a unit of study. Suppose the next unit of study is the space shuttle and related concepts. Instead of *telling* children what they are going to learn about the space shuttle and space travel during the next two weeks, you might begin the unit by letting them help plan it: "We are going to spend the next two weeks studying space travel and the space shuttle. What would you like to know?"

Organize children's questions into categories and ask them to predict what the answers will be. This example might yield categories like these: eating on the shuttle, steering the shuttle, takeoffs and landings, daily life on the shuttle, and miscellaneous. Record the questions and predicted answers for reference throughout the study. This record could be kept on the chalkboard or on a large piece of paper. Have the children form groups to research the answers to questions in a given category. As the children discover the answers, they write them into the group record below the question. Finally, the group selects a way to present its findings to the whole class.

Invoke SQ3R

The processes of having children generate questions and predictions before they read are intended to model ways in which mature readers interact with print. As you guide your students through these processes, they will see the value in questioning and predicting and begin to do so on their own. A strategy helpful in focusing reader attention to the ideas in a text is the SQ3R technique (survey, question, read, recite, review). Often labeled a "study strategy," the SQ3R is a way to help children read and learn expository material (Robinson, 1962).

To *survey* is to examine the selection to be read, noticing title and subheadings, illustrations, graphs, charts, labels, and questions at the beginning or at the end. Next, students turn the headings into *questions* that become purposes for reading. Students then *read* the text in search of the answers to the questions formulated in the second step. During the *recite* step, the students recite to themselves the answers to the questions. If the answers are not available or clear, they do additional reading. In *review*, the readers go over their answers to the questions, revisit the major points in the selection, and make sure of their understanding.

Locate and Select Information

The instructional strategies that help children deal with charts, graphs, indexes, glossaries, illustrations, maps, and so on are often played out as self-contained "skills" lessons. A worksheet on the card catalog or on the use of a glossary assumes that the study skills can be effectively taught in isolation and then transferred to real reading and study situations.

The purpose of instructional strategies in the area of study skills is to help children engage in independent study in which they make maximum use of the available resources. They have to learn to locate information, select the information that is most useful, organize the information they select, and then retain that information in some practical, meaningful way. These skills should not be taught in isolation. They should be taught and practiced while students engage in *real* units of study with *real* reasons for reading and writing and *real* needs to know.

Table of Contents

A table of contents is useful in locating and selecting information. Figure 11.9 illustrates a table of contents from a fifth-grade social studies text.

Appropriate instructional strategies include large- or whole-group instruction on the nature of the table of contents and its use. Children should be helped to understand that the table of contents demonstrates

Contents

Figure 11.9 Sample table of contents.

SOURCE: From *Heath Social Studies: The United States Past and Present, Grade 5.* Copyright © 1985 by D. C. Heath & Co. Reprinted by permission.

how the book is organized and the kind of information it contains. Essential questions in using the table of contents are "Does this book contain the information I need?" and "Where is it?" Large-group instruction should then be followed by the actual use of tables of contents as students engage in research during a thematic unit or as the teacher instructs children to locate selections in books. Giving children a worksheet on which a table of contents is reproduced and having children answer questions about the table is not an effective strategy. Transfer of the knowledge about tables of contents to practice will occur only when children are given many opportunities to actually use tables of contents in real study situations.

Index

The index is another tool for locating and selecting information. Children should recognize that the index provides more detailed information about the contents of a book than does the table of contents. Index entries show the page locations of specific topics, as well as the breakdown of entries by subtopic. By consulting the index, a student can often determine quickly the relevance of a book to the current study. To use indexes effectively and efficiently, children must be able to deal with alphabetical order, carefully predict key words in a domain of study, and see relationships among topics. These skills can be developed through specific instruction by the teacher, but they must be applied frequently in actual research use. The best instructional strategy is to guide the children's reference to indexes *as they use them* in their research, reminding them frequently of their potential value. Figure 11.10 is a portion of an index from a fifth-grade social studies text.

Card Catalog

The card catalog is an indispensable aid in content-area reading and research. Instructional strategies must include familiarization with the nature and use of the three kinds of cards found in the library's card catalog: author, subject, and title. Students will need instruction in reading the text of each kind of card. Practicing using the card catalog in real research situations will be far more effective than isolated drill with worksheets. Figure 11.11 illustrates a subject card from a card catalog.

Other Resources

Other research tools that will be helpful to students as they study in the content areas include glossaries, charts, graphs, maps, encyclopedias, atlases, dictionaries, and the *Readers' Guide to Periodical Literature*. Their use is taught over years of school as students' need for them increases. For example, the concept of table of contents may be taught in first grade as an aid to locating favorite stories in books. Later, as the learning is reinforced, it will have wider application. Instruction in the use of tools for locating

Impeachment trial, of Andrew Johnson, 303

Incan empire, 49m, 50, 430–431

Indentured servants, 122, 153

Independence, Latin American struggles for, 437–440

Independence, Missouri, 259, 267

India, American trade with, 221

Indian alliances, 85–86, 228–229

Indiana Territory, 229

Indian cultures: in the Americas, 32, 38m, 39–41, 75; of Andes, 430–431; in Canada, 412–413, 414; of Caribbean, 432, 433; of Great Plains, 311–313; of Ohio Valley, 168; of Piedmont, 127. *See also* Old Northwest.

Indian land claims, 168–169, 390

Indian languages, 39

Indian reservations, 314g

Indians: citizenship for, 361; slaves, 54; in Spanish-American War, 345

Indies, 31, 34. *See also* Cuba; Hispaniola; West Indies.

Indigo, 119, 120, 220

Industrial Revolution, 327–340; and cities, 335; inventions of, 329g; jobs created by, 332–333; population growth during, 332

Industry, in Latin America, 450–452

Inuit, 414, 419, 424

Inventions, in Industrial Revolution, 329g. *See also* Computers; Jet airplane.

Iroquois, 85–86, 133

Isabella, queen of Spain, 28

Isthmus of Panama, 268, 350

Italy, 379, 381

J

Jackson, Andrew, 233, 248–249

Jamaica, 435

James I, king of England, 64

James II, king of England, 136

Jamestown, Virginia, 65–67, 69

Japan, 379, 380–384

Japanese Americans, in World War II, 381–382

Jefferson, Thomas, 171, 183, 215, 230–231, 250, 252, 278

Jet airplane, effect of, 394, 396

Jews, 322, 362, 378–379

Johnson, Andrew, 302–303

Joint-stock companies, 63

Joliet, Louis, 86

Jones, John Paul, 195–196

Judicial branch, of government, 209

K

Kansas, 285, 293

Kaskaskia, Illinois, capture of, 193–194

Kearney, Stephen, 245

Keelboats, 241

Kelly, William, 330

Kennedy, John F., 398

Kentucky, 193, 227, 245

Key, Francis Scott, 232

King, Martin Luther, Jr., 389

Knox, Henry, 215

Korea, war in, 386

Ku Klux Klan, 305, 362

L

Labor unions, 337–338

Land claims: in North America, 167m; Dutch, 90m; English, 87m, 119, 133, 166, 260; French, 87m, 133, 166; Mexican, 263, 265–266; Spanish, 119. *See also* Indian land claims.

Land giveaways, 322, 324

Land ownership, in colonies, 92, 100–101, 153

La Salle, Lord (Robert Cavalier), 86–87

Latin America, 427–441; agriculture of, 444–446, 451m; cities of, 448–449; class structure in, 434; and colonial rule, 433–436; family life in, 448; independence of, 437–439; Indians of, 412–413, 429–431; industry in, 450–453; land use in, 451m; naming of, 427; natural resources of, 450; revolutions in, 439–440; vegetation of, 428m

League of Nations, 356

Lee, Robert E., 292, 298–299

Legislative branch, of government, 209

Legislatures, colonial, 161–162

Lewis, Meriweather, 250–252

Lewis and Clark expedition, 250–252

Lexington, Battle of, 176–178

Liliuokalani, queen of Hawaii, 349

Lima, Peru, 54, 56–57

Lincoln, Abraham, 245–247, 286; president, 287, 297, 301, 302

Lincoln, Mary Todd, 292

Little Big Horn, Battle of, 313–314

London Company, 64, 67, 69–70, 72

Long drive, the, 319

Longhorn cattle, 319

Louis XIV, king of France, 87

Louisiana, 245

Louisiana Purchase, 230m, 250

Louisiana Territory, 87, 230, 232, 253

Loyalists, 184, 185

Lusitania, The, 355

M

Machine gun, 355

Madison, James, 209, 231

Maine, 99, 104, 277

Maine, The, 344–345

Mandans, 250–251

Manila, Philippines, 345

Manitoba, 422

Marion, Colonel Francis, 196

Marquette, Father Jacques, 86

Marshall, John, 287

Maryland, 74–75, 116–117, 219

Massachusetts, 69–74, 100–102, 207–208

Massachusetts Bay Colony, 73–74

Massachusetts Bay Company, 73

Massasoit, 71

Mayflower, The, 70, 72

Mayflower Compact, 70, 160

McCoy, Joseph G., 320

McKinley, William, 349

Merchants, American. *See* China trade; Fur trade; Slave trade.

Methodist Church, 260

Mexican-American War, 265–266

Mexican rights, in Republic of Texas, 266

Mexican territories, in North America, 261, 262

Mexico, 46–48, 433, 437, 440, 450, 452

Mexico City, 54, 57, 265

Miami (people), 228

Middle colonies, 131–137; farming in, 134, 136, 138–139;

Answering your own questions is the best reason for learning how to look up information.
© *Spencer Grant/The Picture Cube*

and selecting information begins in kindergarten and culminates in high school with the accessing of computerized information systems. Along this continuum, teachers should instruct and guide children in the use of the tools while challenging them to ask more and more questions—and to seek the answers.

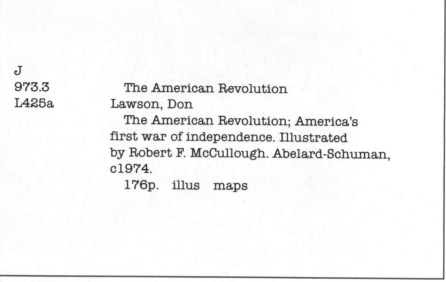

J
973.3   The American Revolution
L425a   Lawson, Don
               The American Revolution; America's
               first war of independence. Illustrated
               by Robert F. McCullough. Abelard-Schuman,
               c1974.
                  176p.   illus   maps

Figure 11.11   Sample card catalog entry. This is a subject card.

Organize Information

The organization of information involves posing questions and research hypotheses, taking notes, outlining, and planning the presentation of the information. We suggest that as part of the introduction to any unit of study, children be asked to *pose their own questions,* which they hope the study will answer. Certainly the teacher has the right and responsibility to add questions to the list, but the initial questions should come from the children. Drawing on the schemata the children bring to the study, this approach makes the study their own. It suggests that children are responsible for their learning, not just the teacher.

Once the questions for a unit of study have been organized, the strategies for locating and selecting information come into play. Then the information gathered must be organized in a way that is helpful to the learner. Techniques of retaining and organizing information should be taught together. The way in which information is retained should be related to the purpose of collecting the information. For a report, notes and an outline may be most useful. For a mural or diorama, sketches might be the best way. A science experiment would require notes and diagrams produced in a carefully timed sequence. Data collected for a report on an historical event could be organized by cause and effect. We believe that it is as important and beneficial to children to present the information gained in

Giving children the tools for independent learning is a major function of education.
© *Steve Takasuno/The Picture Cube*

content-area study as it is to do the research. Children should know before beginning the unit of study that they will be responsible for presenting information to others. They should have a major say in how to do it.

Having decided on the form of presentation, they should identify the best ways to retain important information. This is where both note-taking and outlining skills are helpful. We recommend these instructional strategies:

1. Help children discriminate between information related to their questions and information that is irrelevant.
2. Help children identify the patterns of text organization described earlier in this chapter. Discuss the ways in which text organization may affect the kinds of notes they take.
3. Show children how to take notes on 5″ × 8″ cards, one topic per card.
4. Show children how to outline information. First, use a two-stage outline like this:

Care of a dog

I. Feeding
   A. Kinds of food
   B. Water

    II. Living conditions
      A. Kennel
      B. Dog house

5. Follow this simple outlining with much more complex three- and four-stage outlines. Underscore the relationship between the pattern of text organization and the outline.
6. Help children decide on the level of detail necessary in notes and outlines, depending on the nature of the research questions.
7. Help children see the relationships among semantic maps, structured overviews, and outlining. Whole-group lessons can be built around turning a semantic map into an outline.

Note taking seems to follow a developmental sequence. From kindergarten through grade two, the teacher makes class notes. Children can make notes in groups in grades three and four and finally can work individually in grades five and six.

Writing Challenges in Content Areas

The "integration of reading and writing" and "writing across the curriculum" are increasingly popular topics in educational circles. In some classrooms, however, writing is used for very limited purposes (Langer, 1986). Writing can be used in the content areas for important purposes beyond determining what children have learned: it can make students aware of what they know, what they do not know, and what they need to learn. Content-area writing presents challenges to the young author that are just as great as the reading challenges. In the primary grades, most of the children's writing is narrative. From third grade on, children are asked to do increasingly more writing in the content areas, so they must learn to deal with new writing formats and new sentence and paragraph structures.

Teachers who carefully guide the reading of expository material are preparing children to use it as a model for their writing. Writing activities should be planned in terms of both content and format. While establishing reasons for children to write expository material, teachers must be sure they understand both the content and the format they are to use.

Establishing a purpose for writing about expository topics is a challenge to the teacher. Getting a grade is not a legitimate purpose. In planning instructional units, teachers need to think of purposes for expository writing, such as presenting reports to an interested audience, doing write-ups for the class newspaper, dramatizing scripts based on real-life experiences, and creating captions for items in a display. Writing about content topics can involve the use of note taking, outlining, report writing, caption writing, and the creation of charts and graphs. Each of these formats needs to be taught and used in situations in which real communication occurs. Children should practice note taking, for example, during the preparation of a report, not as an isolated workbook exercise. They should exercise their outlining skills during the process of taking real notes rather than during a contrived drill on a worksheet. Children will see the value of writing in these formats when that writing is purposeful.

Meeting Content-Area Writing Challenges

In this section we present three strategies to help children meet the challenges of content-area writing: writer's workshop, repertoire of writing formats, and use of paragraph frames. A period of time in the instructional day is reserved for writers' workshop, in which all children are engaged in writing-related activities, including conferences with the teacher. Writers' workshop gives children time to write, affords them ownership of their writing, and allows time for responses of teacher and classmates to their writing. The use of various expository formats is a valuable strategy because children can learn to write expository material more easily when they have understood the formats that expository texts take. Finally, for helping children write in certain text structures, the strategy of paragraph frames assists children in organizing information.

Writers' Workshop

Nancie Atwell (1987) tells the story of the day noted writing teacher Don Graves visited her middle school class while her students were engaged in writing workshop. Graves told Atwell that the reason she was such a good writing teacher was that she was "so damned organized" (p. 54). The key to helping children become good writers in expository areas is organization! Atwell's chief organizational secret is observing carefully to discover what writers need and then providing plenty of it. Writers, according to Atwell, need time, ownership, and response. Nowhere are these requisites more essential than in expository writing. Time, ownership, and response are provided through what Atwell calls writers' workshops. In writers' workshops topics are not assigned. The challenge in content-area study is to motivate children to *choose* to write expository texts.

As children are working in thematic units, they need time to think about the writing they might do, as well as the time to do it. They need time to rehearse what they might write about, how they might write it, and how others might respond to it. At minimum they need three hours of writing time per week. They should write daily.

The degree to which children will own their writing depends on the instructional decisions made by the teacher. If the scope and sequence decisions allow for children to have input into what they will study, ownership will be enhanced. If the classroom organization decisions invite student involvement, they will have ownership. If it is clearly communicated to children that the classroom is theirs, the learning is theirs, and the responsibility is theirs, they will experience ownership.

Writers' workshops are characterized by immediate verbal response from the teacher. If the purpose of writers' workshops is to help children improve as writers, they need immediate, specific, careful feedback. Again, students need ownership to some degree in the response. For this reason Calkins (1983, p. 132) begins the conference with two questions: "Tell me about your piece" and "How's it coming?" Of the conference, Atwell (1987, p. 70) says: "I wait, listen hard, tell what I heard, ask questions about things I don't understand or would like to know more about, ask what the writer might do next, and offer any options I might know of." Response of this kind, necessary for all writing to develop, is especially necessary for expository writing.

■ Writing Formats

Teachers need to plan activities that teach writing formats and invite children to use those formats in purposeful ways. Consider each of the writing formats listed below in terms of the unique characteristics—and challenges—it presents to the author.

Format	Characteristics	Purpose
Outline	• Highly prescribed • Sequential	Collecting information
Note taking	• Personal • Must be accurate • Information must be useful later	Organizing information
Captions	• Essence of main idea must be captured	Helping others understand what we know
News report	• Who, what, when, where	Classroom or school newspaper

| Script | • Set and stage specifications, dialogue, costume specifications | Skit, videotape, or full stage play to present what we've learned in a unit |
| Book of facts | • Very accurate, well-documented, clear writing
• In the form of ABC books, reference books, fact sheets | A culminating activity for a unit |

Children learning to write in various formats should see examples from content texts, trade books, and periodicals. With exposure to many good models, time, ownership, and response, and real communicative purpose, children will be able to write expository material as well as they write narratives. Direct instruction and feedback on the use of each format will be necessary.

■ Paragraph Frames

The gap between narrative and expository reading and writing can be bridged with the use of paragraph frames (Cudd and Roberts, 1989). An adaptation of the cloze procedure, the paragraph frame begins with a sentence that is written by the teacher and that includes specific signal words or phrases. Students then proceed on their own, following one of the text organization patterns discussed in the section on "Text Structure" earlier in this chapter. A paragraph frame used by Cudd and Roberts (1989, p. 393) began with "Before a frog is grown, it goes through many changes." This was followed by the key words used in organizing a paragraph through sequential ordering: "First, the mother frog. . . . Next, . . . Then, . . . Finally, . . . Now they. . . ." A second-grader named Elena wrote:

Before a frog is grown, it goes through many stages. First, the mother frog lays the eggs. Next, the eggs hatch and turn into tadpoles. Then, slowly the tadpoles legs begin to grow. Finally, the tadpole turns into a frog. Now and then they have to go into the water to keep their skin moist.

The paragraph frame strategy is a demonstrably successful way to guide children's writing of expository material.

A single well-chosen topic such as insects ties reading and writing in with science, art, and even math and music.
© *Bohdan Hrynewych/Stock, Boston*

■ Major Ideas in This Chapter

■ Our major objective in content reading is to help the student draw on personal background experiences to create meaning in interaction with the text. Content-area reading presents special challenges to the reader.

■ Challenges to the content text reader are presented by text structure, specialized vocabulary and concept load, and special text features.

■ A variety of instructional strategies may be employed to meet the challenges of content-area reading. In any case, comprehension of content texts is enhanced by motivation to read, authentic classroom activities that draw on content-area knowledge, and real quests for information.

■ Content-area study presents writing challenges to students. Writing activities should be planned in terms of both content and format. Writers need time, ownership, and response when writing in the content areas.

[?] Discussion Questions
Focusing on the Teacher You Are Becoming

1. Should primary-grade children (beginning readers) have experiences with expository writing? Build your most convincing argument.
2. What are the most common text features of the textbooks you are using in your other college classes? If you were asked to tutor a college freshman who was having difficulty comprehending a science text, what are the first three steps you would take?
3. Were you surprised to discover that some of the strategies for helping children comprehend content material were ones you use in your own studying? Which strategies did you rediscover?
4. Discuss the content-area reading strategies that you think would be most helpful in adult life outside of school.

[V] Field-Based Applications

1. Develop and use a cloze procedure to determine the children for whom a social studies or science text is too difficult. When scoring the procedure, analyze the extent to which readers relied on semantic and syntactic cues.
2. Select a chapter from a social studies, science, or health text and plan instructional strategies to help learners meet the reading challenges.
3. Plan lessons that help students locate information, select information, organize the information, and present the information to others.
4. Plan authentic content-area writing activities that provide time, ownership, and response for the writer. Include the use of paragraph frames to guide expository writing.

[·] References and Suggested Readings

Atwell, Nancie. *In the Middle: Writing, Reading and Learning with Adolescents*. Portsmouth, N.H.: Boynton/Cook Publishers, Heinemann, 1987.

Bormuth, John R. "The Cloze Readability Procedure." *Elementary English* 45 (April 1968): 429–436.

Brewer, Jo Ann; Jenkins, Lee; and Harp, Bill. "Ten Points You Should Know about Readability Formulas." *The School Administrator*, June 1984, pp. 23–24.

Calkins, Lucy M. *Lessons from a Child: On the Teaching and Learning of Writing*. Portsmouth, N.H.: Heinemann, 1983.

Cudd, Evelyn T., and Roberts, Leslie. "Using Writing to Enhance Content Area Learning in the Primary Grades." *The Reading Teacher* 42 (February 1989): 392–404.

Dale, Edgar. *Audiovisual Methods in Teaching*. 3rd ed. New York: Holt, Rinehart & Winston, 1969.

Flood, James, and Lapp, Diane. "Forms of Discourse in Basal Readers." *The Elementary School Journal* 87 (January 1987): 299–306.

Hammond, Dorsey. "Common Questions on Reading Comprehension." *Learning* 14 (January 1986): 49–51.

Hanf, M. Buckley. "Mapping: A Technique for Translating Reading into Thinking." *Journal of Reading* 13 (January 1971): 225–230.

Heller, Mary F. "How Do You Know What You Know? Metacognitive Modeling in the Content Areas." *Journal of Reading* 30 (February 1986): 415–422.

Johnson, Dale D.; Pittleman, Susan D.; and Heimlich, Joan E. "Semantic Mapping." *The Reading Teacher* 39 (April 1986): 778–783.

Langer, Judith. "Learning through Writing: Study Skills in the Content Areas." *Journal of Reading* 30 (February 1986): 400–406.

Meyer, Bonnie. "Reading Research and the Composition Teacher: The Importance of Plans." *College Composition and Communication* 33 (February 1982): 37–49.

Robinson, Francis P. *Effective Reading*. New York: Harper & Row, 1962.

Rodgers, Frederick A. *Curriculum and Instruction in the Elementary School*. New York: Macmillan, 1975.

Stauffer, Russell G. *Directing the Reading-Thinking Process*. New York: Harper & Row, 1975.

Weaver, Constance. *Reading Process and Practice from Socio-Linguistics to Whole Language*. Portsmouth, N.H.: Heinemann Educational Books, 1988.

Part V

Building Reading/Writing Connections

You have learned about language, the development of literacy, planning for instruction, approaches to reading instruction, and teaching the skills of reading. In Part 5 you will learn how all that information is applied in the classroom.

As you teach science and social studies, you can incorporate literacy skills and provide children with authentic reasons for reading and writing. You will learn how art, music, and drama can help you teach children to read and write as they participate actively in experiences in the arts. Finally, you will learn how four practicing teachers really plan for and implement literacy instruction in their classrooms.

Chapter 12

Teaching Reading and Writing through Social Studies and the Sciences

Chapter Overview

- Many reading and writing goals can be achieved through instruction based on material from social studies and science.

- A unit of study, typically a set of activities or experiences to help children gain facts and develop concepts about a given topic, normally occupies one instructional period of the school day.

- A theme has a focus or topic but cuts across subject-matter areas and spans much of the school day.

- A wide variety of activities can meet both content and literacy goals: doing library research, recording and analyzing observations, reading reference materials, writing responses to reading, and many others.

Social studies and science content material can serve specific literacy goals. Many teachers help children read and comprehend social studies or science material by organizing the topics into instructional units or themes. However teachers approach social studies or science, these content areas offer multiple opportunities for meeting literacy goals. Using real content material is much more effective in helping children learn the important reading and writing skills than providing children with workbook pages in which skills are practiced outside other activities.

Teachers planning social studies and science instruction that also meets the goals of literacy instruction should follow these steps:

Step 1. Review state and district guides for the literacy skills appropriate to the grade level.

Step 2. In planning a unit of instruction, review the curriculum guide for social studies or science; in planning a theme, review the guides for goals from multiple subject-matter areas.

Step 3. Identify major literacy and content goals of the unit or theme.

Step 4. Specify important objectives, recognizing that children will determine some of them as they choose areas of personal interest to study in depth.

Step 5. Collaborate with the media teacher to review library and media resources available in the school or district. Select appropriate resources.

Step 6. Consult with local resource people, such as Chamber of Commerce, historical society, local speaker's bureau, educational director of museum, and so on.

Step 7. Develop a time line for the unit or theme.

Step 8. Plan specific activities for each lesson.

Step 9. Develop a scheme for monitoring students' progress.

Step 10. Plan evaluation strategies for each lesson, activity, and unit or theme.

Guidelines for Selecting Instructional Activities

Preparing content-area instruction typically means developing plans for classroom activities that help children build concepts and learn facts about a given topic. Each of the units, which generally takes several days or several weeks to complete, is planned for a certain time period in the school day. Units usually include a variety of activities, such as reading from a textbook, viewing a film, listening to a guest speaker, creating art projects, and participating in drama or role playing. The Cone of Experience illustrated in Figure 11.6 is a helpful planning tool.

In selecting activities for inclusion in a unit or theme, teachers will find the following guidelines valuable:

1. *Activities should help connect new information to the knowledge that children already have.* For example, having selected the solar system as a topic for a unit or theme, the teacher might use a variety of means to ascertain what the children know: asking direct questions, having children dictate what they know about the solar system, asking children to write individually about the solar system, or having children pool their knowledge in small groups and report to the class. The teacher can then select activities to help children gain new knowledge and make connections with what they originally knew by revising dictated charts, rewriting reports, or resuming discussions.

2.   *Activities should be of interest to the children.* When Dewey (1938) suggested that children would more easily learn what they were interested in, he was putting forward a relatively novel idea. Students' interest can be the result of some happening in the school or world, or it can be generated by the teacher. For example, as reports from the Voyager spacecraft first hit the news, they would surely awaken interest in the solar system. If the teacher had selected rocks as a theme, bringing in rocks of many types would probably generate considerable interest.

3.   *Activities should involve the children in as many direct, hands-on experiences as possible.* Children can't go fight in the American Revolution, but they can make candles, quilts, and posters appropriate to the period, and they can read from as many original documents as possible. Some schools are located within field-trip distance of Revolutionary War sites.

4.   *As much as possible, children should be allowed to select individual activities that interest them most.* For example, if the teacher had chosen amphibians as a suitable topic of study, then the children might pick a specific

Children who are encouraged to follow up on their own interests acquire an unconstrained love of learning.
© *The Picture Cube*

amphibian for intense study. In small study groups, children might divide up the task according to personal interests, such as reading reference material, recording careful observations of the animal subject, making scientific drawings, and studying the animal in a broader context, such as its place in the ecosystem or food chain.

5.   *Activities should have multiple outcomes.* An activity such as reading information in a textbook and answering review questions at the end of the selection may have a limited outcome—primarily the recall of factual information. But if the children are learning to use headings and subheadings to locate specific information in the text, practice skimming the text for selected information, compare the structure of the text with the structure of another genre of writing, and use the review questions to guide their reading for information, then reading the text and answering the questions will have multiple outcomes. Most hands-on activities, such as making

Election of the "Ten Greatest Americans" involves sixth-graders in campaigning as well as in reading to make informed choices.
© *David S. Strickler/The Picture Cube*

candles, have multiple outcomes. For example, children will learn some scientific concepts, such as how wax changes when subjected to heat and how different wax and wick materials affect the quality of the product. At the same time they will find out that producing goods and services to meet daily needs in Colonial times required a large investment of time and that most goods were made at home. Of course, the activity will also reinforce the importance of reading and following directions.

6. *Activities should involve a genuine need for literacy skills.* For example, if the instructional goal is to teach children to take notes from written material for use in writing a report, then the children should actually be involved in writing a report that will be presented to an audience and provide a communicative experience in sharing information.

7. *Activities should give children opportunities to learn and to share what they have learned through various modes of presentation.* For example, children should be encouraged to construct (models, maps), create (puppets, posters, paintings, collages), and dramatize (role plays, puppet plays), as well as write.

Social Studies and the Literacy Connection

Suppose that you have reviewed the district and state goals in social studies and found that a unit on the American Revolution would be appropriate at your grade level. You follow the planning steps we recommended and decide that the resources are available for a unit of study focused on the American Revolution.

Unit Approach

The broad goals of the unit could include content goals such as the learning of facts about the Revolution (participants, battles, military strategies, chronology of events) and the development of concepts about the causes of the Revolution. Literacy goals might include making and using maps, conducting library research, and taking notes. The goal of all the instruction would be for the learners to be able to evaluate the importance of the Revolution in the development of our democratic form of government and to apply their knowledge of the American Revolution to current world situations.

Once the broad goals and time frame of the unit are established, then for each instructional period short-term goals are set that will help the students meet the unit goals. For example, during one instructional period the students could write a newspaper article describing the Boston Massacre from the point of view of a Colonial or a British reporter. The goals for the instructional period would include learning factual information about the Boston Massacre, placing the event in a chronology, reviewing the structure of writing in newspapers, and recognizing a given point of view.

Let's assume a six-week schedule of instruction for the unit. The following plan illustrates the range of possibilities for teaching the unit and highlights the literacy goals that can be achieved.

Introduction of the Unit

Introduce the unit with a poster of a Minuteman. Discuss the poster and as a group list on a large chart things that the students know about the American Revolution. Separate students into smaller groups to develop questions that they have about the Revolution. Categorize the questions into broad areas, such as life in Revolutionary times, information about battles, causes of the Revolution. The charts will be reviewed and revised as children gain new information from films, filmstrips, videotapes, reading materials, and reports.

Presentation of Information

Show films, filmstrips, or videotapes that present information about the American Revolution. Assign selected portions of the social studies textbook. Have children read facsimiles of original documents from the Revolutionary period, such as the Declaration of Independence, records kept by the Colonial army, and diaries and letters. Let individuals or small groups make reports to the class.

Individual or Small-Group Activities

1.   After viewing films and reading for background information, select an event from the Revolution to learn more about. The children conduct library research on the event and prepare to make an oral presentation, such as a report or newscast, to the class. They would have to write an outline or script for the presentation and might also make maps or other supporting visuals.

2.   Participate in hands-on activities such as making quill pens, candles, a square for a quilt, a puppet of a participant in the Revolution, or a toy typical of the period. Each of these activities would require reading for information and directions, and each would encourage other literacy experiences. With the quill pen, for example, the children could write a letter to a friend describing some aspect of life in Colonial times; with the puppet of an historical character, they could create a play.

While learning how candles were made in colonial days, a fourth-grade boy heightens his understanding of early Americans.
© *Elizabeth Crews/The Image Works*

3.   Participate in choral readings and in dramatizing events of the Revolution. For example, the teacher could read some poetry from or about the Colonial period and encourage the children to participate in choral readings of other selections. Small groups could dramatize events such as the Boston Tea Party or could role-play a conversation between a loyal British colonist and a supporter of the Revolution as they discuss an event of the war.

4.   Write a newspaper account of an event in the Revolution. Write summaries of films or oral presentations. Write scripts for plays or reports. Write reports of research findings. Write journals.

5.   Read texts, newspapers, diaries, journals, government documents, biographies, reports, and reference materials.

Instructional Opportunities

The unit creates a variety of instructional opportunities. Some of the instruction would be presented to small groups, some to the whole group, and some individually. Instructional opportunities include helping students recognize the structure and organizational patterns of the text material, comparing readings in several genres, and skimming the text for specific information. The teacher might present techniques for taking notes on written and oral material and locating information in the library or in different reference books. Lessons might focus on making and reading maps, developing abilities in outlining and summarizing, and recognizing the special structure of newspaper writing and biographies. Another reading experience not likely to arise in the basal is the interpretation of charts and graphs that have real meaning to the readers. The difference in children's reading a graph that they have been involved in developing and a graph that is presented to teach how to read a graph is significant.

Structured this way, the unit would make a number of literacy experiences possible:

Literacy experiences

Skimming material to find relevant information
Predicting content of text material from headings/questions;
    confirming or rejecting predictions
Reading text material
Locating information in library
Reading newspaper reports
Taking notes on reference materials
Writing scripts for presentation
Summarizing material presented in oral form
Reading charts

Reading maps
Writing letters
Choral reading
Reading and following directions
Writing journal entries
Writing an ABC book.

Thematic Approach

A thematic approach to teaching could also focus on the American Revolution, but the content would not be confined to a social studies class period. The Revolution would be the theme that tied together instruction throughout the day—from language arts and fine arts to math and science.

The goals of a thematic unit would be quite broad. Many would involve the development of skills and abilities that cut across subject-matter areas. In addition to specific goals much like those of a unit (such as learning factual information about the American Revolution), the goals might be knowing how to choose sources of information, synthesizing information from several sources, using information to draw conclusions, reading critically and evaluating the content of the reading, and making decisions about presenting research to others.

A schedule of activities for thematic teaching occupies most of the school day. Figure 12.1 is a schedule from one school that uses a thematic approach to curriculum. Only those subject-matter areas that are not treated thoroughly in the theme (music, mathematics, and French, in this example) are scheduled separately. The large blocks of time devoted to the theme allow time for developing many different activities and for in-depth exploration of the topics.

A thematic plan focusing on the American Revolution might extend over a period of several weeks. Unit activities might also be included in a thematic approach, but the instruction would not be limited to one class period or instructional period each day. Activities can be chosen from the areas of social studies, arts, language arts, sciences, and math. Some of the possibilities are illustrated in Figure 12.2.

Daily Activities

Not all the ideas generated around a theme can be carried out in the classroom. The teacher and children will have to select the ideas that are the most interesting and that will help most to achieve the learning goals. For the Revolutionary War theme, the teacher might choose historical fiction, the textbook, selected official documents, and reference materials to complete research projects as the primary reading experiences. Responding to

WEEKLY TIMETABLE

	Monday	Tuesday	Wednesday	Thursday	Friday
9:00–10:30	Theme	Theme	Theme	Theme	Theme and Music
10:30–11:00	Recess				
11:00–12:15	Math and French / 11:45–12:15 Lunch	Math and Music	Theme	Math	Math and French
12:15–1:15	12:15–2:00 Swimming	Lunch			
1:15–1:35		Meeting			
1:35–2:45	2:00–3:05 Math	French and Theme	French and Math	French and Theme	Gym
2:45–3:05		Silent Reading			Reading in pairs
3:05–3:15	Clean-up				

NOTES

This timetable applies to all the children in the school.

Wherever two activities are listed in one time slot, it indicates that while some children are engaged in one activity, e.g., French or music, others are doing the other activity listed; this rotates so that all children do both.

The children are divided into two groups for math (about five hours a week for each group), two groups for music (one hour a week for each group), and three groups for French (one hour and forty minutes a week for each group).

Figure 12.1   School schedule constructed around a theme.

SOURCE: Ruth Gamberg et al., *Learning and Loving It: Theme Studies in the Classroom* (Portsmouth, N.H.: Heinemann Educational Books, 1988).

the students' interest, the teacher might also concentrate on clothing styles of the Colonial period rather than on architecture or silversmithing. Teachers are responsible for choosing among the many possibilities the activities that best meet the needs of their classes.

Themes can be introduced in a variety of ways. For example, to introduce a theme on the American Revolution, a teacher might show a film on the Revolution, take children on a field trip to one of the sites important in the Revolution, visit a museum that has a collection of artifacts from Colonial times, decorate the classroom for a Fourth of July celebration, or develop a Revolutionary subtheme as a part of study of American heroes.

As much as possible, thematic activities should be related and not isolated projects. For example, after reading the accounts of the Revolution

Language arts
Read historical fiction
Read biographies
Read/write poetry
Read official documents
Write letters, journals,
    diaries, reports, news-
    paper articles
Oral reports
Handwriting styles
Research: roles of women
    in Revolution, roles of
    minorities, grievances
    of colonists, events

Fine arts
Posters of the Revolution
Sketches
Colonial architecture
Colonial furniture
Silversmithing
Clothing styles

Music
Songs of the period
Folk dances of Colonial
    America

Math
Tesselations
Population charts
Calculating costs

Crafts
Make quill pens
Make candles
Spinning/weaving
Make toys
Quilting

Science
Physical and chemical
    changes in making
    candles
Weather

Social studies
Map study
Land forms that affected
    battles
Official documents
Information in text
Reports of participants
Causes of Revolution
Events in chronological
    order
Forms of government
Provisions for protest
Current protests

**Physical education/
wellness**
Colonial games,
    recreation
Field Day
Food preservation
Common foods

Figure 12.2   Activities related to a Revolutionary War theme.

presented in their books of historical fiction, students would compare those accounts with the information presented in their social studies texts and with reference material. They might also relate descriptions of the characters to what they are learning about clothing styles and perhaps create some costumes that would have been appropriate for the characters in their books. In social studies they could find out about the importance of quilt making in Colonial times, while in mathematics they learned about tesselations and in art they worked on the creation of aesthetically pleasing patterns as they participated in creating a quilt.

Selected Examples

Suppose the teacher has selected books of historical fiction to be presented to the class for reading in their literature groups. (Please review the specific steps for literature sets in Chapter 7.) The groups might choose among *Johnny Tremain* (Forbes, 1946), *My Brother Sam Is Dead* (Lincoln and Collier, 1974), *Sarah Bishop* (O'Dell, 1980), *Phoebe and the General* (Griffin, 1977), and *Peter Treegate's War* (Wibberley, 1960). If the theme schedule were to last two weeks or so, the students might be expected to read one book in that time frame. If longer, they might read one book of historical fiction and a biography of one of the participants in the Revolution. As they discuss their reading, they will discover differing accounts of events in the Revolutionary War. They can compare novelists' descriptions of the same events and compare the fictionalized accounts of those events with the factual descriptions in reference material. As culminating projects, students might create dioramas, collages, brief dramas or songs, bulletin boards, or filmstrips.

One topic appropriate to a theme on the American Revolution is Paul Revere. The teacher might introduce Paul Revere with a Revere bowl and pictures of Revere's house in Boston. After ascertaining through questions and discussions what the children knew about Paul Revere, the teacher might read Longfellow's (1985) poem *Paul Revere's Ride* to the class. Depending on the goals of the instruction, the students might then be asked to research the facts of Revere's ride and determine which historic incidents are represented accurately in the poem and which are poetic fictions. Or the teacher might present the factual information for comparison with the poem, or show a film that portrays the events factually. For independent research, students could use the encyclopedia, the textbook, and trade books such as *Midnight Alarm* (Phelan, 1968), *Picture Book of Revolutionary War Heroes* (Fisher, 1970) and *Two If by Sea* (Fisher, 1970).

In the process of doing research, students would consult the card catalog, use guide letters on the encyclopedia volumes, and search tables of contents and indexes. They would also gain experience in comparing the writing styles, points of view, intended audiences, and purposes of each of the sources of information. Writing possibilities focusing on Paul Revere's ride include the script for a newscast to report on it, a newspaper article, a prediction about how the event would be reported today, a descriptive journal entry, an entry for a class book on the American Revolution, a biography of Revere, and a narrative that tells the story of the midnight ride.

Many of the activities listed in Figure 12.2 overlap traditional subject-matter areas. For example, learning about food preservation would require that the students learn or practice the literacy skills of locating and reading reference materials, reproducing the information in some form, and, if they cooked the food, reading and following directions. The suggested activities include many opportunities for developing literacy skills and abilities in meaningful contexts as students learn about the American Revolution. Most of the following literacy skills would be employed in each subject-matter area and would be practiced in a wide variety of activities:

Literary experiences

Reading novels, poetry, biographies, song lyrics
Reading reference materials
Reading textbooks

Practicing research skills
Writing letters, journals, diaries, reports, newspaper articles
Reading/writing charts and graphs.

Science and the Literacy Connection

Now suppose the teacher finds that weather is one of the topics recommended by the state and district curriculum guides. The district literacy goals include learning to read a variety of functional materials, collecting and organizing data, locating information, and following directions. A study of weather would lend itself to meeting the knowledge goals in

The winning entry in a school science fair exhibits the productive partnership of science and literacy.
© David S. Strickler/The Picture Cube

science as well as furthering the literacy goals. Let's say that the science content goals specify students' ability to define the difference between weather and climate, describe conditions in air masses that cause weather, identify cloud types, describe various forms and types of precipitation, and relate effects of weather and climate to man.

■ Unit Approach

A unit of instruction in a subject-matter area, you'll recall, takes place in a given instructional period each day, and even though the activities may overlap other subject-matter areas, the focus remains on the subject. A unit on weather might last for two or three weeks. A plan for a study of weather might have the following features.

Introduction of the Unit

Show a tape of a weather report from television or turn on the weather channel for a few minutes if it is available. Use a semantic map with "weather" at the center to help students organize the information they already have about weather. Draw students' attention to weather information in newspapers, on radio, and on television. Elicit some reasons for taking an interest in weather.

Presentation of Information

Present information through films, filmstrips, or videotapes, the science textbook, resource people such as meteorologists, demonstrations, and peer presentations. For example, the teacher or a meteorologist might demonstrate the instruments used in gathering weather data and teach the children how to use the instruments.

Individual or Small-Group Activities

1. Gather weather data and record it each day.
2. Collect weather maps from the newspaper each day for a given period of time and learn to interpret the symbols used on the maps.
3. Collect newspaper stories about weather for a given period of time. The stories might include accounts of droughts, sports events affected by weather, and other human-interest stories in which weather is important.
4. Participate in demonstrations such as making a cloud. Preparation would require reading for directions and gathering information from reference sources.
5. Correspond with pen pals in other regions of the country or the world, exchanging summaries of weather conditions.

6. Learn about weather-related safety precautions and share the information with the class in the form of a skit, a newscast, a report, or a slogan.
7. Find examples of weather as a significant element in narratives. For example, in *James and the Giant Peach* (Dahl, 1961) the weather is important for the voyage. *The Wizard of Oz* wouldn't have been much of a story without the cyclone.
8. Write the script for weather reports and present the reports to a primary class.
9. Write informational reports on a particular aspect of weather.

Instructional Opportunities

The teacher can provide instruction in analyzing the structure of the text, using the index and headings of the text to find specific information, interpreting symbols on weather maps, and skimming material in order to locate desired information, and can supply facts about weather instruments and conditions. The class can use Tomie dePaola's *The Cloud Book* (1975) as a model for their writing of informational reports. Children can practice recognizing figurative language through reading poetry about weather and comparing the poet's descriptions of weather with accounts in the newspaper or on television.

Notice that the literacy experiences afforded by a science unit include some uncommon ones:

Literacy experiences

Writing/reading charts of information and questions
Reading text, poetry, narratives, newspaper articles
Reading instruments, recording readings
Writing letters, reports, summaries.

■ Thematic Approach

With weather as the focus, a thematic approach to curriculum could include the activities listed in Figure 12.3.

Again, the teacher and students must be selective about which activities to carry out. The content goals of the theme might be the same as those of the unit on weather, but a theme offers more possibilities for tying together content goals in other subject matter areas while meeting goals in science instruction. Choose activities that will fulfill as many of those goals as possible. For example, weather is an excellent topic for accomplishing a variety of goals in mathematics. Weather provides occasions for measuring, comparing, and graphing data. As children maintain weather records, they learn the importance of keeping accurate information. They discover the

Language arts
Read books, poetry
Weather as an element of
    setting in narratives
Read/write newspaper
    articles
Reference material
Text material
Read almanacs
Vocabulary terms
Writing reports, nar-
    ratives, poetry
Composing scripts for
    weather reports
Symbols on weather
    maps
Write a recipe for a cloud

Social studies
Jobs related to weather
Effect of weather on life-
    styles, habits
Weather effects on
    agriculture
Map skills

Fine arts
Light effects (e.g.,
    Monet's studies)
Light, shadows, color
Visibility of colors under
    different light
    conditions

Music
Weather songs
Rhythms
Movement

Math
Measuring, comparing
    temperature, relative
    humidity, barometric
    pressure, wind speed,
    precipitation
Graphing measurements

Science
Weather instruments
Identification of cloud
    formations
Cause/effect of air
    masses on weather
Forms/causes of
    precipitation
Work of meteorologist
Visiting a weather station
Weather/climate
    relationship
Weather effects on
    people/animals
Pollution/ozone layer/
    acid rain

**Physical education/
wellness**
Weather safety
Activities in different
    weather conditions
Caloric needs

Figure 12.3   Activities related to a weather theme.

utility of various formats for presenting information, such as circle graphs, bar graphs, percentages, averages, and tables. Science topics offer oppor-tunities for reading a variety of materials, such as almanacs and diagrams, and for writing in several styles.

If the children and teacher are interested, they might decide to ex-plore the area of jobs related to the weather. A meteorologist, a weather reporter, or a rescue team member could be invited to the classroom to talk about his or her work. Children could research job requirements and find out what knowledge is necessary to perform the job well. They could write letters of invitation to the speakers and appropriate thank-you letters after the presentations. Some children might write a factual report on the oc-cupations, to be added to a class book on career choices.

Children might also look for descriptions of weather in fictional literature as an element of the setting. For example, in *Time of Wonder*

McCloskey (1957) describes a summer storm on the coast of Maine. The weather is important in *Sam, Bangs and Moonshine* (Ness, 1966). The shapes of clouds figure in *I'm in Charge of Celebrations* (Baylor, 1986) and *It Looked Like Spilt Milk* (Shaw, 1947). Children can write about their own observations of clouds and their own experiences with weather. Poetry, especially cinquain and haiku, lends itself to descriptions of weather.

A science theme is a rich source of literacy experiences, especially those that are far beyond the scope of the typical basal reader.

Literacy experiences

Reading narratives, text material, poetry, reference material, newspapers with focus on author's intended audience, point of view, sources of information

Reading maps, charts, graphs

Writing reports, poetry, comparisons, narratives, letters

Listing known facts and questions

Library research

Getting information from visual media

Comparing and contrasting writing styles.

When used to record the real data of children's observations, abstractions such as charts, graphs, and maps become relevant tools.
© *Steve Takasuno/The Picture Cube*

■ Major Ideas in This Chapter

■ Some literacy goals can best be achieved through developing units or themes in social studies or science and including many opportunities for reading and writing experiences.

■ Writing activities at the beginning of units or themes can help children organize their current knowledge and think of questions they would like answered in studying the unit or theme.

■ Social studies and science material are excellent for teaching differences in text organizational patterns, use of subheadings, and use of special material such as charts and graphs.

■ Children are interested in science and social studies topics. Instruction that captures that interest gives them authentic reasons to read and write.

■ Literacy abilities in recognizing writing styles, intended audiences, and points of view can be achieved through subject-matter material.

■ Activities in the study of science and social studies have multiple outcomes. Children can practice literacy skills; learn art and music, and learn factual content at the same time.

? Discussion Questions
Focusing on the Teacher You Are Becoming

1. This chapter argues the case for developing some literacy abilities through social studies and the sciences. Discuss the differences between materials included in basal readers and materials found in social studies and science texts.
2. Discuss the advantages of organizing social studies and science instruction so that you can help children gain abilities in literacy while they learn content.
3. Some curriculum planners are worried that the content of social studies and the sciences will be neglected if they are included in thematic approaches. Discuss ways in which you could make sure that children learned content material well.

☑ Field-Based Applications

1. Borrow a social studies curriculum guide from a school district. Choose a social studies topic that is recommended and develop a list of

possible activities around that topic. Highlight the activities that would help achieve goals in literacy.

2. Choose a science topic from the local curriculum guide and develop a list of possible activities around the topic. Include as many literacy skills as you can.

3. Review two or three social studies and science textbooks. Check for the aids to the reader, the organizational patterns, and the use of illustrative material. Develop a plan for helping children recognize these features of the text.

4. Become familiar with the trade books that would be useful in developing a social studies or science topic. Compare the writing with that in a text and an encyclopedia.

5. Interview several intermediate-grade students about their interests in social studies and science topics. Relate what you find to the topics in the textbooks for their grade.

◉ References and Suggested Readings

Baylor, Byrd. *I'm in Charge of Celebrations.* New York: Scribner's, 1986.

Dahl, Roald. *James and the Giant Peach.* New York: Puffin Books, 1961.

dePaola, Tomie. *The Cloud Book.* New York: Holiday House, 1975.

Dewey, John. *Experience and Education.* New York: Macmillan, 1938.

Fisher, Leonard Everett. *Picture Book of Revolutionary War Heroes.* Harrisburg, Pa.: Stackpole Books, 1970.

Fisher, Leonard Everett. *Two If by Sea.* New York: Random House, 1970.

Forbes, Esther. *Johnny Tremain.* Boston: Houghton Mifflin, 1946.

Gamberg, Ruth, et al. *Learning and Loving It: Theme Studies in the Classroom.* Portsmouth, N.H.: Heinemann Educational Books, 1988.

Griffin, Judith B. *Phoebe and the General.* New York: Coward McCann & Geoghegan, 1977.

Lincoln, James, and Collier, Christopher. *My Brother Sam Is Dead.* New York: Four Winds, 1974.

Longfellow, Henry Wadsworth. *Paul Revere's Ride.* Illustrated by Nancy Winslow Parker. New York: Greenwillow, 1985.

McCloskey, Robert. *Time of Wonder.* New York: Viking, 1957.

Ness, Evaline. *Sam, Bangs and Moonshine.* New York: Holt, Rinehart & Winston, 1966.

O'Dell, Scott. *Sarah Bishop.* Boston: Houghton Mifflin, 1980.

Phelan, Mary Kay. *Midnight Alarm: The Story of Paul Revere's Ride.* Illustrated by Leonard Weisgard. New York: Thomas Y. Crowell, 1968.

Shaw, Charles. *It Looked Like Spilt Milk.* New York: Harper & Row, 1947.

Wibberley, Leonard. *Peter Treegate's War.* New York: Farrar, Straus & Giroux, 1960.

Chapter 13

Teaching Reading and Writing through the Arts

Chapter Overview

- Many important connections exist between the arts—music, art and drama—and the literacy program. Far from stealing time from literacy, the arts enhance the reading/writing connection.

- Music and literacy are natural companions. Children like to sing. Once they have learned a song by rote, they can read the lyrics in print. Experiencing this success with reading can then bridge to activities that extend comprehension and involve writing, art, and drama.

- Parallels exist between learning to read music and learning to read and write text. Interpretation by the listener/reader occurs in both music and literature. The listener/reader brings past experiences to music and literature, both of which involve imagery.

- The mental processes involved in art and reading are similar: children are taking in information, evaluating it against their experience, and constructing symbol systems for representing what they know. The similarity of processes enhances the integration of art and reading.

- Drama and reading share the creation of meaning from words, the use of language to express meanings, and the requirement that the participant bring his or her own experience to the material in order to interpret it.

- Each of the forms that drama takes in the elementary school classroom provides rich experiences for both reading and writing.

Music and the Literacy Connection

A Natural Pairing

Singing is a celebration of language. Language naturally has rhythm and melody. One need only listen to the language of children to hear its rhythms and melodies. Children bring this natural music of language with them to the task of learning to read, and so using singing to teach reading draws on the native understanding of language that all children share. They may not be able to verbalize their knowledge about language, but they demonstrate their understanding as they begin to speak. It makes sense to integrate music and reading in the elementary school classroom: language and music go together like walking and dancing.

Spontaneous Expression

Music is a natural part of children's play. The next time you visit a playground or park, pause and listen to the things children are saying. There and in the backyard and on the street, you will hear children making up songs, chanting rhymes, and caroling tunes that are a part of their lives. Music belongs in the classroom, too—not as a frill but as a serious educational tool.

Using singing to teach reading may sound like a simplistic approach to what some see as a very complex task. Holdaway (1980) has said that too often we become confused by the complexities of teaching reading and find it hard to see the "wood for the trees." In teaching reading, he says, we must provide for the most "sensible and obvious things first." Holdaway continues (p. 13):

What are the simple and obvious things? What *is* common sense in teaching reading? Perhaps we could agree as a starting point that reading is a language activity and that *anything we do in the teaching of reading should be consistent with the nature and purposes of language.* Most importantly, reading is the accomplishment of full, accurate and satisfying meanings. [Italics in original.]

We believe that using songs to teach reading is consistent with the nature and purposes of language. Song puts readers in touch with satisfying meanings.

Music is so natural for children that it can be described in the same terms applied in current literature on emergent literacy to the act of reading: it's a natural extension of children's language and experience. Children learn to use written language in much the same way that they learn to use oral language—through constructing their own rules and relationships (Graves, 1982; Goodman and Goodman, 1983). The more language, especially "book" language, children can hear, the more opportunities they have for constructing their own rules.

Teaching reading holistically, through whole-language instruction, requires that the materials used be meaningful to the child, that the language be treated as a meaningful message from an author to a reader, and

Singing is a natural adjunct to reading as children associate sounds, gestures, and feelings with the words they learn.
© *Michael Weisbrot/Stock, Boston*

that the teacher's role be one of assisting the child in the endeavor, much as a parent assists a child in learning to talk. In holistic instruction in reading and writing, the units of language are sentences and story units (Hall, 1981). Music and singing readily fit the needs of whole-language instruction. The songs can come from the child's environment, experience, or imagination and can have very personal meaning. Even the nonsense songs of childhood can be meaningful to a child, as well as fun to play with. The teacher's role is that of helping children learn at their own pace and fitting the songs to the needs of the individual.

Aid to Learning

The most compelling reasons to use music in reading instruction are that it provides a likelihood that children will experience success and that it represents another way of allowing children to experience language as a whole. There is also evidence that music instruction contributes to learning discrete skills in reading. Movsesian (1967) showed that children in an experimental group who learned how to read music made a larger gain in learning basic reading skills than did the control group that did not receive music instruction. Seides (1967) found that slow adolescent learners who were talented in music made greater achievement in reading when given music lessons. Nicholson (1972) discovered that children from six to eight years of age who had a special music program showed considerable improvement in some reading readiness skills, especially in increased attention span and discrimination for paired groups of letters. Along the same lines, Zinar (1976) found the following beneficial effects of music instruction on reading:

1. Slow readers learn to read music well.
2. Better music readers are better language readers.
3. High interest in music increases attention span.
4. Sensory activity is increased through music.
5. Self-concept is improved through successes in music.
6. Common connections exist between eye and ear understanding in both music and reading.

Lloyd (1978) noted that the combination of music and reading brings joy to children's learning and that there are many parallels between learning music and learning reading. Merrion (1981) also observed a parallel between music and reading: music has timbre and tonal nuances, and literature has vocabulary, usage, and innuendo of the language. In music there is rhythm and in literature there is style, including flow, pace, and transitions. Both the listener and the reader bring past experiences to the musical and reading events, and both experience a play of imagery as the music or story unfolds. Merrion points out that both listening and reading entail a pleasurable mood and involve the intellectual activity of following the unfolding musical structure or literary plot, themes, and characters. She asserts that once these parallels are better understood, they may be effectively used within instructional programs to help in bringing about a truly integrated education. The integration of curriculum is nowhere more important than in the teaching of reading and writing.

Using music to help children grow in their literacy abilities is not a technique whose application is limited to very young children. It is highly successful with beginning readers, but we know teachers of older readers, especially those who are having difficulty with reading, who use the lyrics of popular songs on the radio and MTV as texts for reading instruction. Songs are also a good way to teach specialized vocabulary, such as holiday words.

■ Activities Using Music

Activities that use music to teach reading and writing fall into five categories: learning favorite songs, meeting the lyrics in print, reading song charts and booklets, comprehension extension activities, and writing activities. Even if you don't think of yourself as especially musical, you can find suggestions here that will work for you.

Learning Favorite Songs

The first step in using singing to teach reading is filling the classroom with songs that will quickly become favorites. Children love to sing. Singing should be an important part of each day's activities in the classroom, and not reserved for the thirty minutes once a week that children spend with the music teacher. Bringing favorite songs to the classroom requires only that the teacher be willing to spend some time selecting the songs and to employ records, tapes, or an instrument in teaching the songs to children. Because of the ready availability of recorded music, one need not be an accomplished musician to use singing to teach reading. Teachers can also seek the music teacher's help or use songs that the children are learning in music. For now, the important point is that children should have repeated exposure to songs so that rote learning occurs.

The songs should be sung over and over again so that the language becomes as familiar to the children as if it were their own. A total of fifteen exposures to the words and music of a song over a two- or three-day period is not excessive. Learning to read by singing will be successful only if the children are totally familiar with the lyrics that they will eventually meet in print.

The following procedure may be used in teaching a new song by rote:

1. Explain to the children that they are going to learn a new song, or a song that they may have heard but have not sung in school.
2. Sing the song to the children, with accompaniment (such as autoharp, guitar, or piano), if possible. Or play a recording of the song.
3. Repeat Step 2 several times to increase the children's familiarity with the song.
4. If the lyrics are somewhat complicated, have the children repeat phrases after you as you say them.
5. Invite the children to sing the song with you or with the record.
6. Repeat Step 5 until the children can sing the song with enthusiasm, confidence, and comprehension.

Encourage children to sing musically, with good phrasing, from the beginning. If children are encouraged to sing softly enough so that they can listen to each other, it helps to develop their sense of pitch and tonal quality. Because folk songs were originally sung without accompaniment, do not hesitate to sing them that way. Figures 13.1 and 13.2 are examples of songs that are good to teach young children. Try them with the procedure we suggested.

Meeting the Lyrics in Print

When children have sung a song enough times to be comfortable with the tune and lyrics, they are ready to meet the lyrics in print. The easiest language for children to read is language with which they are very familiar. They delight in seeing the songs they know in print, and the teacher is truly rewarded when the children shout, "I can *read* this!" Their pleasure in their own success is an essential ingredient in any beginning or remedial reading experience.

Prepare for this activity by printing the song lyrics on large lined chart paper with a dark marker. The chart stand can hold your growing library of songs. Or print the lyrics on large pieces of tagboard that can be filed in a box and placed on an easel or chalktray for presentation.

Introduce the song charts by explaining to the children that they are now going to read the words to the song they have been singing. Show

Figure 13.1   Traditional song.
SOURCE: *Holt Music Grade 1 Teacher's Edition* (New York: Holt, Rinehart & Winston, 1988).

Figure 13.2   Traditional song.
Source: Kathleen M. Bayless and Marjorie E. Ramsey, *Music: A Way of Life for the Young Child,* 3rd ed. (Columbus, Ohio: Charles E. Merrill, 1989).

them the chart, and invite them to sing along as you move your hand or a pointer under each line of print. After singing the song once or twice using the chart, stop and encourage the children to celebrate the fact that they can *read* the words. Recognizing the words in this given context is an important step in learning to read.

Reading Song Charts and Booklets

These are some word-identification activities you can do with the song chart:

1. Invite individual children to come up to the chart to point to words pronounced by the teacher.
2. Invite individual children to come to the chart and identify words that they recognize.
3. Encourage children to locate words that appear in more than one place on the chart.
4. Write individual words of the song on separate pieces of tagboard, using the same size print as on the chart. Have children match the words on the cards with the words on the chart.

In writing about musical aids to literacy, Morris (1981, p. 660) underscored the importance of children's developing a sense of word—the concept of word—before attempting to read: "Children cannot learn to recognize words if they do not understand that words are printed units. . . . they cannot match written words with spoken words if they do not understand that words are bounded by white spaces." The development of a sight vocabulary in a language-based or contextual approach to reading, such as using singing to teach reading, requires that the child have a concept of word. The activities we have suggested can help to develop this concept.

Morris (1981) also identified a set of behaviors teachers should watch for as children use the song charts. By observing the following behaviors as children begin to read the charts, a teacher can determine their understanding of the concept of word.

1. Do they point to each word correctly as they sing (read) across the line?
2. When they mismatch spoken word to written word, do they self-correct without help from the teacher and continue singing?
3. Having read the entire song, can the children identify individual words throughout the song when the teacher points to them in random order?

Children who have trouble doing these things should not be forced to locate words in song charts, but should have many more exposures to the singing of the songs.

Once children have learned to sing the songs with confidence from the song charts, and the teacher is comfortable that a sense of the word has been developed, the children may be introduced to individual song booklets. The booklets can be made by duplicating the lyrics on sheets of $8\frac{1}{2}" \times 11"$ paper, cut in half, folded, and stapled along the fold. Print only a few lines of lyric on each page, leaving plenty of space for the children's illustrations.

When they use their own song booklets, the children know they are reading. And they are! The teacher can be confident that the children are developing a sight vocabulary when they point to words or phrases accurately as they sing along in their booklets. The booklets lend themselves to many activities that reinforce the learning of the words. These are some we recommend:

1. Sing (read) the song lyrics while sharing the song booklet with a friend.
2. Sing (read) the lyrics to a friend who does not know the song.
3. Follow the lyrics in the booklet while listening to the recorded song at the listening center.
4. Use the song booklet to locate the words of the songs in other books and magazines.

This last activity helps the children to understand that the same letters, same sounds, and same words that they now can read occur over and over again, in many places. It is fun to listen to the excitement of the children as they make this important discovery.

Comprehension Extension Activities

Reading has not really occurred until the reader interacts with the ideas represented by the words. Remembering the meanings of words read is one of the most valuable contributors to comprehension. It is appropriate to ask children about the meaning of words or phrases in the songs they have learned to sing and read. After the children have read and sung a song, select key words or phrases that are essential to understanding the ideas in the song, and ask children to tell what the words mean. When the children are unsure of meanings, explain the words or phrases to them.

Be certain that they can explain the word meanings in their own words and that they are not simply parroting back the definition that you gave them. Given the importance of memory of word meanings to overall comprehension (Davis, 1968), it is essential to spend time ensuring that children understand the songs they learn to sing and read.

Once you have established clear understandings of word meanings, it is time to engage children in a variety of activities that extend comprehension. These activities are important because they build bridges between reading and movement, reading and drama, and reading and art.

Using movement with the songs they have learned to sing and read is a wonderful way to extend comprehension. When the children do the movements to "I'm a Little Teapot," their animation shows their comprehension of the meaning.

Another song that lends itself to gestural interpretation is "This Old Man" (Figure 13.3). Children can dramatize it in trios, with one being the storyteller, one the old man, and one the dog, or they can sit all together in a circle and do the motions as a group. Reflecting ideas gained from the reading (singing) of a song is important here, but of even greater value may be the repeated opportunities to re-create situations—to discover and improvise (Allen, 1976).

Children can sometimes demonstrate their understanding of a song much more clearly in art than they can in words. Encourage them to use both ways. The number of ways art can be used to extend the comprehension of songs is probably limited only by our imaginations as teachers. Here are some possibilities:

1. Draw or paint a picture of the song.
2. Fingerpaint the way the song makes you feel.
3. Use clay to model a character from the song.
4. Create puppets (stick, finger, sock) to use in dramatizing the song.
5. Make posters to advertise a song party and invite another class to come hear you sing your favorite songs.
6. Illustrate song booklets.

Writing Activities

After children have read and sung a song, invite them to draw, color, or paint a picture to illustrate the song. Initially, ask each child what he or she wants to say about the picture, and write it on the bottom of the page. This gives them the opportunity to see that what they think, they can say; what they say can be written; and what can be written can be read by them and by others. We are acknowledging what Roach Van Allen (1976, p. 50) called *"the one big responsibility* of a teacher at any level of instruction: to help each child to conceptualize, to habituate, and to internalize a few truths about self and language" (italics in original). Asking the child what he or she

THIS OLD MAN

English singing game

This old man, he played one, He played nick-nack on my thumb,

Nick-nack, pad-dy whack, Give a dog a bone, This old man came roll-ing home.

2
This old man, he played two,
He played nick-nack on my shoe;
Nick-nack, paddy whack, Give a dog a bone,
This old man came rolling home.

3
This old man, he played three,
He played nick-nack on my knee;
Nick-nack, paddy whack, Give a dog a bone,
This old man came rolling home.

4
This old man, he played four,
He played nick-nack on my door; (Point to forehead.)

5
This old man, he played five,
He played nick-nack on my hive; (Fight the bees.)

6
This old man, he played six,
He played nick-nack on my sticks; (Hold up index fingers.)

7
This old man he played sev'n,
He played nick-nack up in heav'n; (Fly like angels.)

8
This old man, he played eight,
He played nick-nack on my pate; (Point to top of head.)

9
This old man, he played nine,
He played nick-nack on my spine; (Tap between shoulders.)

10
This old man, he played ten,
He played nick-nack once again;
Nick-nack, paddy whack, Give a dog a bone,
Now we'll all go running home.

Figure 13.3 Traditional song.
SOURCE: Kathleen M. Bayless and Marjorie E. Ramsey, *Music: A Way of Life for the Young Child,* 3rd ed. (Columbus, Ohio: Charles E. Merrill, 1989).

Children's art reveals their understandings and allows adults to glimpse what is important to them.
© Jean-Claude Lejeune/Stock, Boston

wants to say about the picture builds critical connections among speaking, listening, reading, and writing.

Soon the children will be able to do the writing on the pictures themselves. These beginning writing efforts will soon lead to the writing of stories about the songs and the characters in songs and the composing of additional song lyrics. We can suggest some writing activities that grow out of singing and reading:

1. Write invitations to parents to come hear the children sing their favorite songs.
2. Write books about a song or the characters in a song.
3. Write letters to the composer of a song.
4. Create new lyrics to a familiar tune.
5. Write a script for a play based on a favorite song.

■ Music in Trade Books

The joy of learning to read by singing can be extended to reading literature that is related to songs and reading patterned books with language that, like lyrics, is predictable.

A delightful piece of the rich world of children's literature is the category of song picture books, a selected listing of which appears in Appendix H. One example is Richard Schackburg's *Yankee Doodle* (1965), with woodcuts by Ed Emberley. This book has beautiful illustrations to accompany the song of the American Revolution, and it explains the history and meaning of the song in ways that children can understand. Even children who are too young to read the book themselves would benefit from having the teacher share it with them.

Spier (1973) has illustrated a wonderful version of *The Star-Spangled Banner* containing a reproduction of the poem as Francis Scott Key wrote it, a history of the battle, and a poster of flags of the American Revolution. Spier (1970) also illustrated *The Erie Canal*. John Langstaff illustrated a series of song books such as *Over in the Meadow* (1957) and *Frog Went A-Courtin'* (1956). Others of interest include *Over the River and through the Woods* (Child, 1974), *Old MacDonald Had a Farm* (Pearson, 1984), and *Once: A Lullaby* (Nichol, 1983). Both old favorites and new songs appear in picture song books, which have a place in the reading program.

■ Art and the Literacy Connection

At first glance it might seem that art and reading do not belong together and therefore that doing art activities during reading time would rob the reading program. However, closer examination reveals another picture. If reading is defined as an act of bringing individual experience to a printed text in order to construct ideas, then reading and art share some common characteristics. A reader must take in information and evaluate it in terms of his or her own experience. In doing art, too, the child is taking in information, evaluating it against personal experience, and constructing symbol systems for representing what he or she sees and knows. Therefore, the mental processes required in art and reading have some elements in common (Van Buren, 1986).

A review of the literature reveals only a handful of articles that deal with the relationship between art and reading. Most authors, such as Bookbinder (1975) and Macey (1978) describe ways to use art to motivate reading. Others, such as Jansson and Schillereff (1980), have reported using art activities with remedial readers. In most cases art is used as a subject of study leading to reading or as a way to add interest to the reading act.

A very limited number of authors report relationships between art activities and specific reading skills. McGuire (1984) presented strong evidence for the position that whereas the visual arts and music may diverge from the cognitive/perceptual process of language and reading in some aspects, they overlap in others. McGuire reported on others' work that shows interactions between language and drawing, between making associations in the arts and making associations in reading, between imagery in the arts and imagery in reading, and between arts-centered curricula and reading achievement.

Art may also help children clarify their experience in order to be able to write about it. Lucy Calkins (1986, p. 47) reports sitting down with a first-grade child and asking what he was going to write about that day. He responded, "I don't know. I haven't drawed it yet." Some experiences become focused enough for the child to begin to describe them through language after they have selected the elements of the experience and drawn them.

■ Art as Motivation

On a more practical level, the heart of the relationship between art and literacy seems to be motivation. Criscuolo (1985, p. 13) reports, "Most kids like art, and that's something you can capitalize on when it comes to the teaching of reading. Reading and art have one very important thing in common: both offer pleasure to the child." Criscuolo asserts that art can mean a welcome break from drill in reading because it lends itself to a whole host of activities. Four of the fifteen art activities he proposes to integrate with reading are drawing costumes for a favorite book character, making a collage to illustrate a favorite story, decorating a container such as a coffee can to reflect the theme of a book and putting into the container five or six objects mentioned in the book, and making shadow puppets with which to present a story.

A good example of art used to motivate reading was described by Cunningham (1982), who found a series of how-to-draw books that included interesting descriptive material in the text. In addition to furnishing the directions for the drawings, the books offered multiple opportunities for teaching vocabulary. *How to Draw Cats* (Rancan, 1981) includes the following informational passage about cats:

Persian cats originally came from Asia. Their luxurious coats can grow up to 5" (12 centimeters) long. These cats require a lot of brushing and special care to keep them looking well-groomed. Persians have short legs and stocky bodies. They are bred in a variety of colors.

In the directions for drawing cats, the instructions specify drawing "slanted eyes" and making fur that looks "soft, not hard and stiff." Reading these directions, children would learn vocabulary terms in a meaningful and interesting context.

Another series, the thumbprint books of Ed Emberley (1977), have also proved to be very useful in reading and writing instruction. Children have created thumbprint characters and then written narratives about them, as well as using the thumbprint characters to illustrate stories that they had already written. Children practice the reading skills of sequencing and following directions when they read and follow Emberley's instructions. They can also write their own directions for characters that they invent.

Classroom teachers can combine art and literacy instruction without the use of a set of books. Working with the district art specialist to plan thematic units, the classroom teacher chooses the content to be introduced to the children. The art teacher helps to plan related art experiences, such as sculpting and painting models of dinosaurs while the children are reading and writing about dinosaurs. As the children carry out the art activities, they review and expand their concepts and their ability to relate printed information to their own understandings.

■ Integration of Art and Literacy Activities

Some school programs combine art and reading. Rabson (1982) describes a program called Learning to Read through the Arts, in which a series of art/reading/writing experiences were based on a particular theme. Each student kept a journal in which original stories, vocabulary lists, and detailed directions for art projects were recorded. It is logical that involvement in describing experiences both visually and verbally helped children think and communicate more effectively.

Another strategy for integrating art with literacy is described by Thoms (1985). Children are encouraged to express through poetry their feelings about a selected painting. In writing poetry, the children are using one art form to express the complexities of human response to objects in another art form.

Writing about art and one's response to art could take other forms too. For example, children might write a factual report on the history of a painting or perhaps compose a letter explaining their response to a painting or a newspaper article critiquing the painting. Each of these writing experiences would require reading models of similar writing and gaining enough knowledge about the art object to write about it.

Illustration is an effective way to relate art and literacy. Many of the techniques of illustration can be introduced through picture books. The Caldecott Award–winning books (described in Chapter 7) provide examples of illustrations in many media. For instance, the artist of *Once a Mouse* (Brown, 1961) illustrates the fable with woodcuts. Although woodcuts are too difficult for elementary children, they could explore a medium like linoleum prints. Geometric shapes and bright colors characterize Gerald McDermott's (1974) *Arrow to the Sun*. Children could try making figures on graph paper or using pattern blocks to create shapes and figures. In *The Snowy Day*, Ezra Jack Keats (1962) works with collage and paint. Children might try sponge painting the background for their own illustrations and then adding paper cutouts. The list of Caldecott books alone is a rich source of ideas.

Preparing special paper on which to write poetry or to mount a page of poetry can add a dimension to children's art experiences. Doing a watercolor wash or preparing marbleized paper helps children feel that their work is valuable and increases the ways in which they can experience ownership of it. The poetry of *In a Spring Garden* (Lewis, 1965) is printed over beautiful washes and illustrations created by Ezra Jack Keats.

If art is often employed as a motivational tool in teaching reading and writing, art can also be the subject itself. Children can be encouraged to read about artists and about art techniques and styles. They could write a dictionary of art terminology. Catalogs from art galleries might serve as models for descriptions of pieces of art. Perhaps the students could prepare a catalog of works of public art to be used by the local chamber of commerce.

An art-related writing experience of another sort would be a "how to" manual for art techniques. For example, children could write all the directions for creating a crayon resist, a tempera wash over crayon, or a batik painting. The manual could be placed in the art center for use by children doing actual projects. Reading of various sources and then taking notes while observing the process during execution would be necessary before doing the writing. The skills of organization, thoroughness, and accuracy involved in writing "how to" directions are of enormous practical value in both scholastic and professional careers.

Clearly, art and reading can be instructional teammates. Art can be the motivating element in encouraging reading and writing experiences. Art can embellish the pieces of writing that the child chooses to publish and encourage pride in the presentation of ideas. Art can help children clarify and represent experiences about which they can then talk and write. Art can serve as the subject of reading and writing experiences that are interesting and meaningful.

Drama and the Literacy Connection

Literacy development and drama are natural partners. Booth (1985, p. 193) eloquently states the case for combining reading and drama:[1]

> As an act of learning, reading is basically a private experience and drama generally a shared one. When children read, they understand what the words say to them, translate the experience being read about into their own context, and conjure up feelings, attitudes, and ideas concerning everything from the author's values to their own life situations. They react and respond personally, free from outside intervention, to enter as deeply as they decide into this new world of meaning.
>
> The interactive, participating model of the drama experience helps children grow in a different way, moving them forward toward new, collective understanding. This does not mean, however, that drama is just an activity to be used after reading a story, as a check of comprehension, or as a means of motivating children to read a particular selection. It may assist in these goals, but it is, on its own, a powerful medium for helping children make learning happen.

■ Dramatic Activities

Drama and reading have in common the creation of meaning from words, the use of language to express meanings, and the requirement that the participant bring his or her own experience to the material in order to interpret it. Several forms of drama are useful in literacy instruction: improvised drama or role play, story dramatization, readers' theater, and dramatic play. These forms of drama also provide a meaningful context in which children can apply and extend their abilities in reading and writing.

Improvised Drama

Drama that is performed without benefit of script, costumes, or staging and with little or no rehearsal is improvised drama. This sort of drama takes place when children act out something they have read, either in a story or in content-area materials. Improvised drama may be very spontaneous. Just a quick enactment of something they are reading can help fix its mean-

---

1. From David Booth in *Theory and Practice* **24**(3), 193–198. Copyright © 1985 by College of Education, The Ohio State University. Reprinted by permission.

In dramatic play, children practice language appropriate to various situations.
© Irene Bayer/Monkmeyer Press Photo Service

ing in their minds. For example, if children are reading about magnets and two children demonstrate the actions of repelling and attracting, that is improvised drama. So is the role playing of a person's actions in a given situation, which can help children understand that person's responses or behaviors. Young children often act out the roles in which they've observed adults, such as that of clerk in the grocery store, including language and body language.

Older children can role-play various social situations to help them clarify their understandings of language use and the interactions of characters. For example, they could role-play a town hall meeting to decide where a new road should go through the city, taking the roles of citizens who would lose their homes, business owners who would reap financial gains, environmentalists who felt that the new road would destroy some animal habitats, and others. Each of these situations helps children see things from someone else's perspective and think about how others would use language to express themselves.

When used with intermediate-grade children in two economically disadvantaged regions of a large Eastern city, improvisational dramatics resulted in improved reading achievement and in more positive attitudes, specifically those regarding self-expression, trust, acceptance of others, self-awareness, and awareness of others (Gourgey, Bosseau, and Delgado, 1984).

Story Dramatization

Dramatizing stories can help motivate children to read. When children know that they are going to dramatize a story, they tend to read it with increased attention to detail and to think about the characters so that they will be able to bring life to them in the dramatization.

Story dramatization also leads to improved comprehension. Miccinati and Phelps (1980) suggest that drama provides a way for teachers to assess comprehension beyond the usual asking of questions. Martin, Cramond, and Safter (1982) theorize that dramatizing a story causes children to view the story in its entirety, whereas answering comprehension questions draws attention to only small parts of the reading. A landmark study, frequently referred to in the literature, was reported by Henderson and Shanker (1978). In this study both high and low achievers in reading who dramatized basal stories performed better on comprehension questions than did students who only read the stories. This study is often cited as evidence that dramatization is more powerful as an indicator of comprehension than is answering comprehension questions.

Other researchers have also found positive results on measures of comprehension when dramatization of stories was added to reading instruction. Yawkey (1980) and Pellegrini and Galda (1982) report improved comprehension as a result of role playing and fantasy. Kindergartners and first-graders demonstrated better story comprehension through fantasy play than through the typical discussion and drawing of pictures.

Other ways of dramatizing stories include pantomime and puppet shows. Pantomime experiences offer children an opportunity to express nonverbally the meanings they have taken in verbally, whether from literature or from a box of cards prepared for the purpose. For example, a child might pantomime the actions of Little Red Riding Hood as she wanders through the woods picking flowers, meets the wolf, knocks on her grandmother's door, and is surprised by the wolf. Or the child might select a card that describes an activity, read it, and present the pantomime for the class. Cards could call for such actions as eating a very long strand of spaghetti, walking a dog, lifting a very heavy box, and getting dressed to go out to a party.

Puppet plays can take a variety of forms. Children might be supplied with ready-made puppets representing characters in a well-known story, which they could then act out. They might also construct their own puppets and perform their own original stories. Hand-made puppets can be as complex as marionettes or as simple as paper cutout figures glued to sticks.

Readers' Theater

Larson (1976, p. 359) describes the characteristics of readers' theater:

1. The use of scenery and costumes is slight. Perhaps only a hat or held prop is used to identify a character.
2. There is not much physical movement or action. Instead, vocal inflections, gestures, and facial expressions suggest action and mood.
3. A narrator fills in much of the setting and action beyond what is carried by the dialogue.
4. A script is used, and the participants read the parts rather than memorizing them.
5. The readers communicate directly with the audience rather than with each other. As they read their parts they make eye contact with the audience.

Readers' theater requires in-depth comprehension of material, careful selection of pieces to be presented, thoughtful adaptations of stories not written for this kind of production, and, of course, much practice in reading as the material is rehearsed and presented.

Johnson (1987) suggests that the sequence of instruction in helping children make adaptations of material for readers' theater includes having an experienced person prepare an adaptation of a familiar story and then having the children compare the original story with the adaptation, noting and discussing the changes and reasons for them. He also suggests that children be taught to recognize the characteristics of stories that would be suitable for readers' theater—characteristics such as these (p. 147):

- It must be a good story.
- It needs plenty of conversation.
- It should have several characters.
- It can have a narrator but the narrator's part should not be too long.

Johnson concludes (p. 148): "To say that dramatization helps to develop comprehension is a colossal understatement. . . . Dramatic role-playing is the final word in comprehension."

Dramatic Play

Dramatic play is a form of play in which the child dramatizes life roles and situations. In contrast to a stage play, dramatic play is spontaneous and done without an audience. Children play out real-life parts in symbolic ways. The link between reading and dramatic play exists in the search for and creation of meaning (Collier, 1983). Sociodramatic play, a form of symbolic play, has the clearest link to reading because it involves both simple and complex uses of imagination and because through it a child manipulates reality and time.

Sociodramatic play has been thought to be important in the development of creativity, intellectual growth, and social skills (Smilansky, 1971).[2] According to Smilansky, six elements make up sociodramatic play:

1. Imitative role play. The child undertakes a make-believe role and expresses it in imitative action and/or verbalization.
2. Make-believe in regard to objects. Movements or verbal declarations are substituted for real objects.
3. Make-believe in regard to actions and situation.
4. Persistence. The child persists in a play episode for at least ten minutes. Fleeting incidents of play do not produce the same effects as sustained play.
5. Interaction. There are at least two real human players interacting.
6. Verbal communication.

In sociodramatic play children use symbols to create their own reality. A block becomes an airplane, the airport parking ticket machine, or the snack served by the flight attendant. This development of *representation* is the link between reading and play. Just as children manipulate objects to represent ideas, so words are representations of ideas. Both play and reading involve symbols. The quantity and quality of children's symbolic play influence the ability of the child to use symbolic representation. Simply put, the more a child engages in symbolic play, the greater is his or her ability to create representations—both in play and in reading (Collier, 1983; Wolfgang and Sanders, 1981).

One of the most compelling arguments for the link between dramatic play and reading proceeds from the research of Pellegrini (1980), who found that the sophistication of dramatic play in kindergarten was a better

---

2. From Sara Smilansky, *Play: The Child Strives Toward Self-Actualization*, G. Engstrom, ed. Copyright © 1971 by National Association for the Education of Young Children (Washington, D.C.). Reprinted by permission.

The importance of literacy to confident functioning in the real world is a suitable theme
for classroom exploration.
© David S. Strickler/The Picture Cube

predictor of first-grade reading and writing success than was IQ or socioeconomic status. Pellegrini noted that the same process of consciously assigning meaning to symbols takes place both in dramatic play and in reading. Wolfgang (1974) discovered that as first-grade males' achievement in
reading increases there is a corresponding decrease in dramatic play. He
theorized that the advanced readers had attained high levels of symbolic
play and essentially moved beyond the need for such symbolism.

Connections between sustained play and literacy were noted in
two ways by Roskos (1988). Her observations revealed that links to literacy
were found in both the "story making" and "literacy stance" of young children. Each dramatic episode was found to contain story-making elements
such as setting, characters, and a goal, concern, or conflict. Literacy stance
was observed in more than 450 distinct reading and writing acts displayed
during play. These acts were categorized into activities (such as reading
books), skills (such as printing letters and words), and knowledge (of ways
to use literacy in social settings).

Roskos suggested that teachers in daycare, preschool, and kindergarten do three things to help link dramatic play and literacy:

1. Create play centers that encourage symbolic play, including experimentation with literacy.
2. Convert children's pretend-play stories into language-experience charts.
3. Carefully observe children's play for indications of literacy understanding.

Teachers need to provide opportunities for symbolic sociodramatic play. Such play has clear links to literacy in primary grades; we need to consider connections in intermediate grades. Should all elementary classrooms have dress-up trunks? Perhaps so. The use of dramatic play for schemata enhancement before children read could be powerful throughout the elementary grades. Dramatizing what children know about a topic *before* they read or write would bring the existing schemata to the forefront of their thinking.

■ Benefits of the Drama Connection

Creative drama involves many forms of improvisation, each of which brings excitement to learning. Whether as story dramatization, pantomime, puppet shows, or dramatic play, drama is one of the best ways to integrate curriculum. Language skills become an important part of reading, social studies, and science when children dramatize the things they are learning.

Drama makes the use of language purposeful and meaningful. Children have valid reasons to read, speak, and listen when they are preparing for and presenting dramatizations. They see real reasons for reading when they know they are going to dramatize a story.

Drama is a natural companion to reading. When children dramatize they are drawing on the same language and thinking skills they use in reading. They must comprehend and express the details of story sequences, word meanings, plot, and character. Maybe the most important link is that in dramatizing a story they truly draw on their own background to bring meaning to the reading. As children struggle with how to make characters come alive and how to make situations real, they are working to find matches between the ideas in the story and their own experience. They learn that the meanings of words may be personal as they negotiate differing views of how a scene should be played.

■ Major Ideas in This Chapter

■ Reading and writing instruction integrates easily with the arts.

■ Music and literacy go naturally together, as do music and children. Acquisition of reading skills is supported by learning music. Many instructional opportunities to use music arise in the reading program. Trade books present music in enriching ways.

■ Art may be used to motivate reading and writing. It also enhances certain reading skills because of cognitive/perceptual commonalities between reading and art. Art helps children clarify their experiences so that they may write about them.

■ Drama is a powerful medium for making learning happen. Comprehension is deepened and extended when children dramatize events, literary or otherwise. Reading and drama both call for interpretation based on personal experience.

? Discussion Questions
Focusing on the Teacher You Are Becoming

1. The primary grades all follow the same daily schedule. You are teaching your children "I'm a Little Teapot" during the time allocated for reading. Hearing the singing, the principal asks, "Why are your kids singing during reading time?" What do you say?
2. More puzzled than critical, a parent inquires why his son is drawing at school when he should be learning the "basic skills." How will you respond?
3. A debate is going on around the lunch table in the staff room. The kindergarten teacher is trying to convince the fifth-grade teacher that dress-up boxes would be as appropriate in fifth grade as in kindergarten. What position would you take and how would you defend it?

☑ Field-Based Applications

1. Identify a social studies unit that will be taught to your class in the near future. With the help of the media specialist and music specialist, select some songs to include in the unit.
2. After children have learned a song well, suggest that they write new lyrics.
3. Encourage children to draw illustrations for a story before they write it so that you can see what the child meant when he said that he couldn't say what he would write because he hadn't "drawed it yet."
4. Assemble a collection of picture books that use a variety of media in their illustrations. Explore the various media with children and invite them to use them in their own illustrations.
5. Plan a way to use improvised drama with children in seeking a solution to a classroom or playground conflict or problem.

6. Experiment with the power of story dramatization. Have one group of children read a story without making any mention of dramatization before they read. Have another, similar group of students read the same story, but first talk with them about plans to dramatize the story later on. See how differently the two groups approach the reading activity.

⊡ References and Suggested Readings

Allen, Roach Van. *Language Experiences in Communication.* Boston: Houghton Mifflin, 1976.

Anderson, Betty, and Midgett, Jeanice. "Use the Arts: Add Lustre to the Reading Program." ERIC Document Reproduction Service No. ED 189 547, 1980.

Bayless, Kathleen M., and Ramsey, Marjorie E. *Music: A Way of Life for the Young Child.* 3rd ed. Columbus, Ohio: Charles E. Merrill, 1989.

Bookbinder, Jack. "Art and Reading." *Language Arts* 52 (September 1975): 783–785, 796.

Booth, David. "Imaginary Gardens with Real Toads: Reading and Drama in Education." *Theory into Practice* 24 (Summer 1985): 193–198.

Brown, Marcia. *Once a Mouse.* New York: Scribner's, 1961.

Calkins, Lucy. *The Art of Teaching Writing.* Portsmouth, N.H.: Heinemann Educational Books, 1986, p. 47.

Cardarelli, Aldo F. "Twenty-One Ways to Use Music in Teaching the Arts." ERIC Document Reproduction Service No. ED 176 268, 1979.

Child, Lydia Maria. *Over the River and through the Woods.* New York: Scholastic, 1974.

Clay, Marie M. *What Did I Write? Beginning Writing Behaviour.* Exeter, N.H.: Heinemann Educational Books, 1982.

Collier, Robert. "Reading, Thinking and Play: A Child's Search for Meaning." In *Claremont Reading Conference 47th Yearbook.* Claremont, Calif.: Claremont Reading Conference, 1983, pp. 124–189.

Criscuolo, Nicholas P. "Creative Approaches to Teaching Reading through Art." *Art Education* 38 (November 1985): 13–16.

Cunningham, Pat. "The Clip Sheet: Drawing Them into Reading." *The Reading Teacher* 35 (May 1982): 960–962.

Davis, Frederick B. "Research in Comprehension in Reading." *Reading Research Quarterly* 3 (1968): 499–545.

Emberley, Ed. *Ed Emberley's Great Thumbprint Drawing Book.* Boston: Little, Brown, 1977.

Goodman, Kenneth, and Goodman, Yetta. "Reading and Writing Relationships: Pragmatic Functions." *Language Arts* 60 (May 1983): 590–599.

Gourgey, Annette; Bosšeau, Jason; and Delgado, Judith. "The Impact of an Improvisational Dramatics Program on School Attitude and Achievement." ERIC Document Reproduction Service No. ED 244 245, 1984.

Graves, Donald H. *Writing Teachers and Children at Work.* Exeter, N.H.: Heinemann Educational Books, 1982.

Hall, MaryAnne. *Teaching Reading as a Language Experience*. 3rd ed. Columbus, Ohio: Charles E. Merrill, 1981.

Hartfree, Margareta. "Using Natural Rhythms: Scheme for Learning to Read with Music. *Times Educational Supplement*, 5413:26, November 27, 1981.

Henderson, Linda C., and Shanker, James L. "The Use of Interpretive Dramatics versus Basal Reader Workbooks for Developing Comprehension Skills." *Reading World* 17 (March 1978): 239–243.

Holdaway, Don. *Independence in Reading*. Exeter, N.H.: Heinemann Educational Books, 1980.

Holt Music Grade 1 Teacher's Edition. New York: Holt, Rinehart & Winston, 1988.

Jansson, Deborah, and Schillereff, Theresa. "Reinforcing Remedial Readers through Art Activities." *The Reading Teacher* 33 (February 1980): 548–551.

Johnson, Terry D. *Language through Literature*. Portsmouth, N.H.: Heinemann Educational Books, 1987.

Keats, Ezra Jack. *The Snowy Day*. New York: Viking, 1962.

Langstaff, John. *Frog Went A-Courtin'*. New York: Harcourt Brace Jovanovich, 1956.

Langstaff, John. *Over in the Meadow*. New York: Harcourt Brace Jovanovich, 1957.

Larrick, Nancy. "Pop/Rock Lyrics, Poetry and Reading." *Journal of Reading* 15 (December 1971): 184–190.

Larson, Martha L. "Readers' Theatre: New Vitality for Oral Reading." *The Reading Teacher* 29 (January 1976): 359–360.

Lawrence, Paula, and Harris, Virginia. "A Strategy for Using Predictable Books." *Early Years* 16 (May 1986): 34–35.

Lewis, Richard, ed. *In a Spring Garden*. New York: Dial Press, 1965.

Lloyd, Mavis. "Teach Music to Aid Beginning Readers." *The Reading Teacher* 32 (December 1978): 323–327.

Macey, Joan M. "Combining Word Recognition Skills and Art." *The Reading Teacher* 32 (October 1978): 64–65.

Martin, Charles E.; Cramond, Bonnie; and Safter, Tammy. "Developing Creativity through the Reading Program." *The Reading Teacher* 35 (February 1982): 568–572.

May, Frank. *Reading as Communication: An Integrated Approach*. Columbus, Ohio: Charles E. Merrill, 1986.

McDermott, Gerald. *Arrow to the Sun*. New York: Viking Press, 1974.

McGuire, Gary N. "How Arts Instruction Affects Reading and Language: Theory and Research." *The Reading Teacher* 37 (May 1984): 835–839.

Merrion, Margaret Dee. "Arts Integration Parallels between Music and Reading: Process, Product and Affective Response." ERIC Document Reproduction Service No. ED 212 986, 1981.

Miccinati, Jeanette L., and Phelps, Stephen. "Classroom Drama from Children's Reading: From the Page to the Stage." *The Reading Teacher* 34 (December 1980): 269–272.

Morris, Darrell. "Concept of Word: A Developmental Phenomenon in the Beginning Reading and Writing Process." *Language Arts* 58 (September 1981): 659–668.

Movsesian, Edwin A. "The Influence of Teaching Music Reading Skills on the Development of Basic Reading Skills in the Primary Grades." Unpublished doctoral dissertation, University of Southern California, 1967.

Nichol, bp. *Once: A Lullaby*. New York: Greenwillow Books, 1983.

Nicholson, Diana. "Music as an Aid to Learning." Unpublished doctoral dissertation, New York University, 1972.

Pearson, Tracey C. *Old MacDonald Had a Farm*. New York: Dial Books, 1984.

Pellegrini, Anthony D. "The Relationship between Kindergartners' Play and Achievement in Prereading, Language and Writing." *Psychology in the Schools* 17 (October 1980): 530–535.

Pellegrini, Anthony D., and Galda, Lee. "The Effect of Thematic-Fantasy Play Training on the Development of Children's Story Comprehension." *American Educational Research Journal* 19 (Fall 1982): 443–452.

Pikulski, John J. "Questions and Answers." *The Reading Teacher* 37 (October 1983): 111–112.

Rabson, B. "Reading and Writing at Guggenheim." *School Arts* 81 (April 1982): 13–15.

Rancan, Janet. *How to Draw Cats*. Mahwah, N.J.: Troll Associates, 1981.

Roskos, Kathleen. "Literacy at Work in Play." *The Reading Teacher* 41 (February 1988): 562–566.

Rumelhart, D. D. "Understanding Understanding." In *Understanding Reading Comprehension*, edited by J. Flood. Newark, Del.: International Reading Association, 1984, pp. 1–20.

Schackburg, Richard. *Yankee Doodle*. Englewood Cliffs, N.J.: Prentice-Hall, 1965.

Scofield, Twilo. *An American Sampler*. Eugene, Ore.: Cutthroat Press, 1981.

Seides, Esther. "The Effect of a Talent Class Placement on Slow Learners in the Seventh Grade of a New York City Junior High School." Unpublished doctoral dissertation, New York University, 1967.

Smilansky, Sara. "Can Adults Facilitate Play in Children?: Theoretical and Practical Considerations." In *Play: The Child Strives toward Self-Realization*, edited by G. Engstrom. Washington, D.C.: National Association for the Education of Young Children, 1971.

Smith, Frank. *Reading without Nonsense*. New York: Teachers College Press, Columbia University, 1979.

Spier, Peter. *The Erie Canal*. New York: Doubleday, 1970.

Spier, Peter. *The Star-Spangled Banner*. New York: Doubleday, 1973.

Stauffer, Russell G. *Directing Reading Maturity as a Cognitive Process*. New York: Harper & Row, 1969.

Stauffer, Russell G. *The Language Experience Approach to the Teaching of Reading*. 2nd ed. New York: Harper & Row, 1980.

Stewig, John W. "Drama and Comprehension." ERIC Document Reproduction Service No. ED 204 737, 1981.

Thoms, Hollis. "Creative Writing as Dialectical Interplay: Multiple Viewings of a Painting." *Art Education* 38 (November 1985): 10–12.

Tierney, Robert J., and Pearson, P. David. "Toward a Composing Model of Reading." *Language Arts* 60 (May 1983): 568–580.

Van Buren, Becky. "Improving Reading Skills through Elementary Art Experiences." *Art Education* 39 (January, 1986): 56, 59, 61.

Wolfgang, Charles. "An Exploration of the Relationship between the Cognitive Area of Reading and Selected Developmental Aspects of Children's Play." *Psychology in the Schools* 11 (July 1974): 338–343.

Wolfgang, Charles, and Sanders, Tobie. "Defending Young Children's Play as the Ladder to Literacy." *Theory into Practice* 20 (1981): 116–120.

Wood, Lucille. *Rhythms to Reading Picture Songbook.* Glendale, Calif.: Bowmar, 1972.

Wuertenburg, J. "Reading and Writing for Every Child." Seminar, Oregon State University, 1983.

Yawkey, Thomas D. "Effects of Social Relationships Curricula and Sex Differences on Reading and Imaginativeness in Young Children." *Alberta Journal of Educational Research* 26 (September 1980): 159–168.

Zinar, Ruth. "Reading Language and Reading Music: Is There a Connection?" *Music Educators Journal* 62 (March 1976): 71–74.

Epilogue

Putting It All Together

We have examined in great detail the ways in which literacy develops. We have encouraged, persuaded, and at times even admonished you to think about ways you can help children develop reading and writing ability in true communicative contexts. We have repeatedly asserted that children acquire literacy developmentally in settings that encourage the authentic uses of reading and writing. Sometimes we have been very theoretical, and sometimes we have been very practical. The purpose of the epilogue is to pull all that theory and some of the practice together in ways that will help you see that the vision we have can and does work in real classrooms.

Planning Thematic Units

We will introduce you to four very talented teachers. Each of them has written an explanation of how he or she uses thematic teaching to create for children the kinds of literacy experiences that we advocate. We hope that an understanding of how these teachers do thematic planning and teaching will give you the confidence to do it yourself.

Tying these narratives together are common threads that link them to the major ideas of the text. Look for them as you read each teacher's remarks. Thinking about the commonalities will help you distill from their work the suggestions that may be most helpful to you in your own planning. These are the common threads we see:

1. Children's interests and teacher's interests are accounted for in thematic planning and teaching.
2. Reading and writing are used both to learn and to communicate. Content is important so that there are meaningful things about which to read and write.
3. Students are trusted to want to learn.
4. Students are empowered to make choices and to control much of their time.
5. Curriculum is emerging. When children are involved in making choices about learning, the teacher cannot always predict all of the outcomes.

6. In child-centered thematic teaching, there are multiple rewards for the teacher, including the joy of watching children grow in ability to use reading/writing for problem solving, communication, for pleasure.
7. Learning in school is as much like out-of-school learning as possible. Teachers want to make connections between the outside world and school learning.
8. Children are grouped for tasks, but not by ability levels.

Each of the contributors to this section was asked to write a description of how he or she plans a thematic unit, using a favorite unit as an example. They plan themes that will meet their instructional objectives while allowing for a variety of interesting and meaningful activities.

Climbing the Beanstalk: Kay Stritzel

Meet Miss Stritzel, a kindergarten teacher. As an early childhood educator for more than twenty years, Kay has taught three-, four-, five-, and six-year-olds in a variety of settings. Currently she is teaching a full-day kindergarten in a primary-grade school. This school is a magnet school, meaning that parents from across the school district may elect to enroll their children there. Kay has also taught classes at the college level and is active in the National Association for the Education of Young Children.

Of her educational philosophy, Kay says:

I believe that all children deserve schools that provide for their cognitive, social/emotional, and physical well-being and that are staffed by well-educated individuals. I believe that it is important to work with young children using developmentally appropriate practices.

Here is how Kay Stritzel told us she plans and teaches thematic units.

When I sit down to begin the planning process, whether it is short-term or long-term planning, I want to use developmentally appropriate themes that will be interesting to the children. I look for themes that will fit an integrated curriculum approach because I do not believe in teaching math, social studies, and language arts as isolated and fragmented skills but as an integrated whole. I want a theme that will cover as many of the curriculum areas as possible; if it does not, I will supplement it with other activities.

I also look for a theme I am interested in. I can remember using a theme I was very interested in one year and having it be quite successful. The following year, it wasn't engaging to the children at all, and it was only when I realized my lack of interest in the theme that I understood why the children were not interested.

When I work up a theme, I try to include many more ideas than I can possibly use. I like to know they are there to use should I want to use the theme again, and if one idea does not work I can quickly substitute another activity. I have a large file cabinet and boxes filled with the themes I have developed over the years. I may not teach a theme the same way in subsequent years, but it is there to visit again.

Many of the themes that I have developed in the last few years have revolved around literature as I have become interested in folk tales. It is equally possible to develop an integrated theme starting with any curriculum area. It is easy to emphasize one curriculum area over another by having one area be the cog in the wheel and the other areas be the spokes.

"Jack and the Beanstalk" is a folk tale with a long tradition. The story appears to have originated in Celtic traditions and to have been brought to the United States by the Irish, Welsh, and British settlers. With slightly different characters, it appears as a Southern White mountain tale, and it is found in the Black traditions from the Caribbean. Slightly different versions appear throughout Europe.

This and many other folk tales appeal to children because they help them work through some important issues, such as these:

> independence
> making mistakes
> being afraid of someone large
> outwitting another person
> being a hero.

So I have chosen a theme, and now the specific planning begins. Which activity do I want to do, when do I want to do it, and how long should it last? This theme could be done in one, two, or three weeks. Scheduling decisions depend on what else needs to be done and how much time I have in the year-long schedule. I get busy with my plan book and decide what activities I want to do with the total class and with small groups. This decision is definitely different for each class and depends on how much adult direction the particular group needs and on its ability to work in a large group.

I make sure that I have enough copies of the story on hand. I want the children to be able to listen to the story on their own, so I make a cassette tape of it (if one is not commercially available) to go along with a set of small books or a big book. The tape is often used at a listening center during small-group time, and the children may use it during choosing time. I may even play the story during resting time.

I want some activities that the children can do on their own without adult direction. It is important for them to experience concepts on their own or to repeat an activity as many times as they choose. Following are activities to do with the "Jack and the Beanstalk" theme in language arts, math, science, and the fine arts. Remember that I always plan more activities than I will actually use.

■ Language Arts

1. Reading the Story

Before I read a book to the children for the first time, I ask them some questions like "What do you know about this book?" and "What do you think happens in this book?" The children will respond with a variety of answers about the characters, the story, the pictures, and other pieces of information. I accept all answers.

When reading it for the first time, I like to read the book all the way through without asking questions. I want them to enjoy the story.

I read the story to the children at the beginning of the unit.

With each subsequent reading of the story or a different version of the story, the following activities can be done. They are not listed sequentially.

2. Predicting and/or Recall

If rereading the story, the children can recall what is going to happen next. If reading a different version of the story, the children can predict what will happen.

3. Sequencing Story Events

Talk about what happened first, second, and third in the story. This can be done in a large group, with the teacher acting as facilitator, not director.

Make a set of picture cards that illustrate the main events of the story. If possible, laminate them or cover them with clear Con-Tact® self-adhesive plastic. Lay them out for the children to work with on the floor, chalkrail, or chart pocket.

4. Creating Their Own Books

Provide each child with a blank booklet made of four to six stapled pages. Have the children paginate their books and draw their own illustrations for the story. They can write down their versions of the narrative themselves or dictate them to an adult. These books are read to the class and can be saved for future reading.

I will often write anecdotal records on the children's versions of stories and put them in the children's folders. Since we do many stories, this helps me see their growth in areas such as story interpretation, sequencing, and use of language.

5. "What If?"

In the large group, ask some questions like these:

What would happen if

—Jack did not plant the beans?
—Jack's mother had gone to market?
—the giant had been a midget?
—the giant had been a woman?

6. Big Book

I use a big book version of "Jack and the Beanstalk." If you do not have one, then create your own by having the children draw the different parts of the story on large sheets of paper (18″ × 24″) and write the story at the bottom of the page. Laminate or Con-Tact® this, as it will get a lot of use.

7. Supplying Missing Words

After the story has been read a few times and the children are familiar with it, cover up some of the more predictable words, like *Jack, Beanstalk,* and *giant,* and permit the children to call them out.

8. Words, Words, Words

With the total group, brainstorm words that could be used instead of the ones in the story. For example, find synonyms for *giant, gigantic, ogre, angry, shouted,* and *screech.*

9. "J" Words

Find words that start like Jack and make a list of them. Or you can make a list of names of people that start with *J.*

10. Refrain

"Fee, fi, fo, fum" is a great refrain that the children love to chant. Have them say it each time the story is read. They do not need much encouragement to do this!

Put the refrain on sentence strips (wide pieces of tagboard about 3″ high) so the children can play with them during free-choice time.

After the sentence strips have become familiar, make a set of word cards for the children to use, alone or in conjunction with the sentence strips.

Transform the refrain using different consonants: bee, bi, bo, bum; tee, ti, toe, tum; see, si, so, sum.

11. Refrain
Discuss what "of an Englishman" means. Talk about where England is and ask what else might be substituted.

12. Creating a Class Book
Even if you have the big book copy, you might want to create your own version of the story by having the children write and edit the story, and then draw pictures. Save the book for group or individual reading.

13. Comparing Versions
The children can discuss different versions of the story. The comparison of plots, names, and so on can be done verbally or recorded on chart paper.

■ Math

Many of these activities can easily be adapted for use by large and small groups and by individuals.

1. Story Problems
Make up some situations like these for the children to solve in their heads:

    a. Jack was given four beans. He lost one. How many did he have left?

    b. Jack planted three beans, but two rotted. How many came up?

2. What Comes Next?
Prepare a set of cards. Each card should show a leaf with a numeral written on it (0–10, 0–20). Shuffle the cards, select one, show it to the children, and ask, "What number comes next?"

3. Estimating
Have the children estimate how many beans are in a glass jar. Draw a large picture of the glass jar. Provide pictures of beans on which the children write their estimates and their names. Paste these "beans" on the paper jar. At the end of the unit, count the beans and see who made the closest estimate.

4. Beanstalk Activities

Construct a large beanstalk somewhere in the room where the children will have easy access to it. I usually use the spot where the large measuring tape is kept on the wall.

a. Count backwards. Children are at the castle and must climb down, counting each leaf as they do so.

b. As a group, count the leaves and mark each with a numeral. I alternate the leaves from one side of the stalk to the other. This reinforces the concept of odd and even numbers, but it is left to the children to discover or talk about it. Once the leaves are labeled, you can begin to count from numbers other than 1 so that the counting exercise is not so rote.

5. Activities with Beans

a. How much is a handful? Each child is given a piece of paper that looks like Figure 1. Then the child is asked to predict how many beans are in one handful. After picking up a handful of beans, the child will count and record an answer.

b. Compare quantities using a graph. Each child is given a set of four or five different kinds of beans (limas, pintos, white, black, red, garbanzos, and so on). They separate their sets, compare more and less, and talk about who has how many of what bean. Then they glue their sets of beans on their own individual graphs, as in Figure 2. Next, cook a sample of each kind of bean. When the children have tasted them, they vote for their favorite beans. Tally their responses on a class graph.

6. Calendar

Use the calendar to teach days of the week as the children determine how many days the story takes. The children can vote on which day they wish the story to start so that the days of the week can be added to the storyline. For example, if Jack went to the market on Monday, then he planted the beans on _____, and the beans grew on _____, and so on.

7. Time of Day

Using a large clock with moveable hands, ask the group to answer questions like these:

What time of the day did Jack leave home?
What time of day did he get to the market?

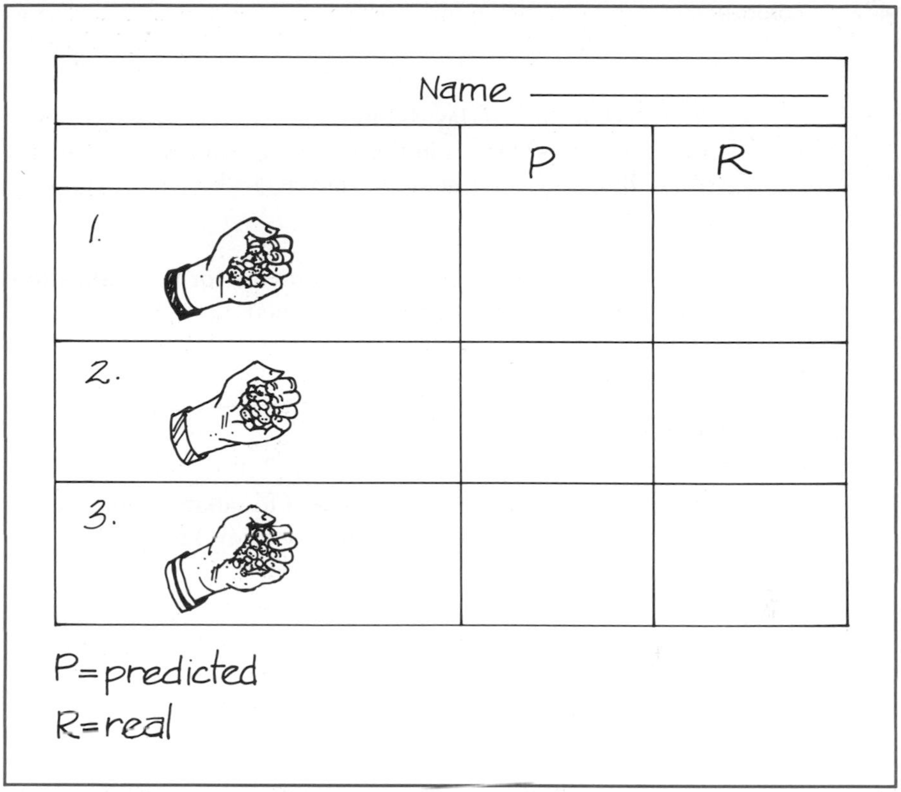

		P	R
1.			
2.			
3.			

P = predicted
R = real

Figure 1   Number of beans per handful.

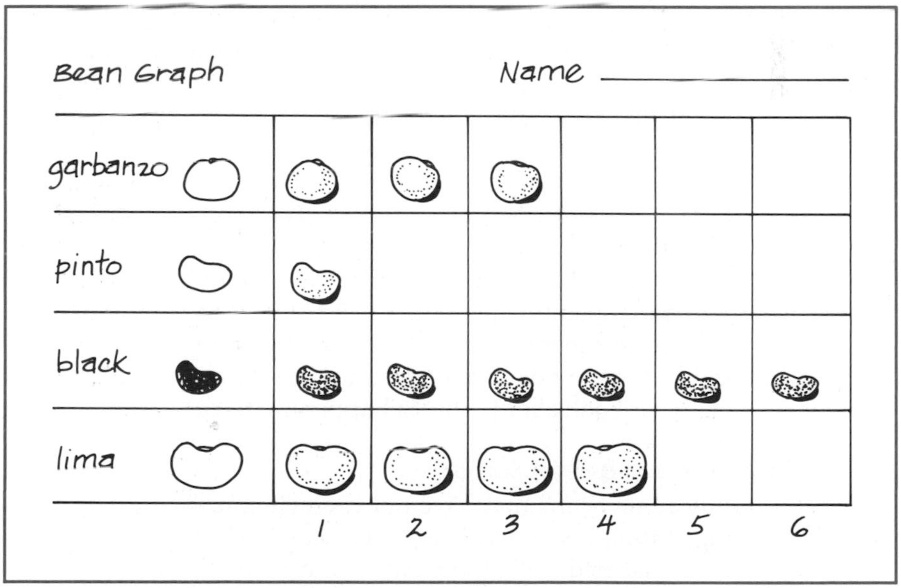

Bean Graph   Name _____

		1	2	3	4	5	6
garbanzo	◯	◯	◯	◯			
pinto	◯	◯					
black	●	●	●	●	●	●	●
lima	◯	◯	◯	◯	◯		

Figure 2   Bean graph.

What time of day did he meet the person who gave him the beans? Was it in the morning, afternoon, or night? Illustrate their answers on the clock.

8. Graphing Story Elements

At large-group time, the children can vote for their favorite versions of the story, their favorite illustrators, or their favorite characters in the story. Create a graph of their responses.

■ Science

1. Animals

Discussing the cow Jack sold can lead to talking about mammals and milk. The children can name other animals they know that give milk, and the teacher can list them on a chart.

2. Activities with Beans

a. Sort the beans. Put a variety of beans on the science table so the children can sort them into different containers. Label the containers.

b. Talk about what will happen if you put a few beans in water and make a chart of the children's predictions. Soak a few beans of each kind overnight; the next morning, discuss and chart the results.

c. Plant some beans (individual activity). Provide a container for each child so they can plant the beans. I usually use clear plastic ones. Place the beans inside the container, against the side, and stuff the container with wet paper towels. This arrangement allows the children to watch the roots growing. After the roots have grown a bit, we transfer them to another container (styrofoam cups or small pots) and put them near a window so they can grow. Each container is labeled with the child's name. A checklist can be used so children can check when they watered their plants.

d. Plant some beans (group activity). On a different day from the individual planting activity, plant some beans in three different containers as an experiment. Water Plant A and put it in the sun. Water Plant B and put it under a box. Put Plant C in the sun and do not water it. Keep a log, chart, or book about what is happening to each plant.

3. Growing Bean Sprouts

Buy some beans that have not been chemically treated and are for sprouting. Mung beans work well. Provide each child with a clear plastic container labeled with their name, ten beans, and a square of cheesecloth. Begin this activity on Monday by soaking the beans in water the first night.

Each day the bean sprouts are rinsed through the cheesecloth. Keep them damp and eat them on Friday.

Each child can chart what is happening to the beans by drawing a picture of the beans each day on a chart like the one in Figure 3.

■ Fine Arts

1. Dramatizing the Story

"Jack and the Beanstalk" is a great story for children to act out, especially after it has been read several times in different versions so that all the children are familiar with it.

Brainstorm what props are needed and make a list. Brainstorm what characters are needed; if there is a dispute over which characters from different versions to include, take a vote. Choose the players and keep track of who plays what part so that the next time the play is acted out, other children can have a part. Run through the play, with the rest of the children acting as the audience.

Do the play again, and again, until you sense that the children are through with it. For me, the fun of this is acting it out for ourselves. Making it a "production" (rehearsed in fixed form and presented before other spectators) is stressful for both the children and the teacher.

2. Mural or TV Program

The children discuss the parts of the story in a large group. There should be enough segments so that each child can draw a scene from the story. These can be drawn on large craft paper, for a mural to be put up in a spacious hallway, or on a roll of paper, which can be put on a "TV" that has been made from a box with a cutout for the screen.

The children can record the story on tape, or the text can be written (by the children or by an adult) and attached to the drawings.

If the TV format is chosen, the children can "play" it over and over as they wish.

Monday	Tuesday	Wednesday	Thursday	Friday

Figure 3   Chart of bean growth.

3. A Magic Place

Using any art medium (paints, crayons, collage), the children create a place they would go if they had magic beans. The pictures can be put into a book or displayed on a large bulletin board with their stories.

4. Castles

After being shown some pictures of castles, children can paint or draw a castle or create a castle with clay, blocks, or boxes. Or the carpentry center could provide wood, and the construction could then be painted. Photographs can preserve a record of their constructions.

5. Role Playing

Either before the play or instead of it, children can act out the roles of Jack, the old man, the giant, the wife, the mother, and the cow. They can play with the many ways to present these characters, with the other children offering help.

6. Musical Accompaniment

Children can decide what rhythm instruments would help create the mood of the story. They can play the instruments while the teacher reads the story. Some ideas include using a drum for the giant's steps, a triangle when Jack throws the beans outside, and bells or the xylophone as Jack climbs the beanstalk.

Make a chart listing the story events, the instruments, and who played the instruments.

7. Creative Movement: The Bean

The children pretend to be the bean. This activity can be done with a small group or with the whole group. The children act out the events in the story of the bean; riding in the old man's bag, bouncing in Jack's hand as he carries them home, being thrown out the window, lying in the ground, growing, having Jack climb on the stalk, and being chopped down.

Finding the Missing Piece: Tom Wrightman

Our spotlight shifts to Mr. Wrightman. Tom is a second-grade teacher in a fairly large school system and taught previously in two small communities. He has ten years of teaching experience at the primary-grade levels.

Tom expresses his philosophy in these terms:

I believe learning occurs through experiences. Experiences that are relevant to development, interests, and needs should be used so we can explore and understand concepts. An environment that allows these experiences should encourage risk taking and accept mistakes as part of the learning process. The respect and love of the learner and of learning itself are essential seeds that first must be planted.

In his own words, Tom explains how his thematic planning grew out of sharing a piece of literature.

The primary goal of using themes is to make the day's study an interconnected whole rather than a collection of pieces that have nothing to do with each other. Themes allow the use of reading and writing in all areas, all day long. The theme is constantly evolving because of new ideas, new materials, and new activities.

The theme I will share with you evolved from a writing lesson. I started by reading *The Missing Piece*, by Shel Silverstein, to the children. After discussing the adventures that the Missing Piece had, the children wrote their own stories. The stories told about the adventures the Missing Piece had as it searched for the whole from which it came.

After editing their stories, the children wrote final drafts and did the illustrations. The next step was having the stories bound into a hardcover book that was called "A Collection of Missing Pieces." Everyone contributed a story to the class book, and then each child was given a copy to keep. A copy was also placed in the school library. I have done this now for many years. Since the first year, the Missing Piece Theme has evolved. Items that relate to things lost or being searched for have been added to the theme.

■ Curriculum Web

Figure 4 illustrates a curriculum web. This device allows you to organize and plan activities that are tied to your central theme. I have indicated the major subject areas in capitals and then filled in activities below them. In the past I have used some of these activities at other times during the year, but now they are part of the Missing Piece Theme. It just makes more sense to do them here. This planning activity is challenging and exciting for me. The ideas sometimes come at 2 A.M., so a pencil and pad are ready and waiting by my bedside. You never know when you will discover that one missing activity you need to make the unit almost perfect!

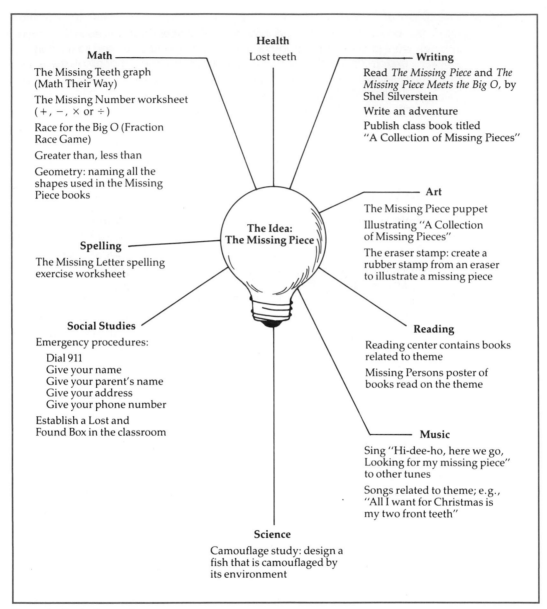

Health
Lost teeth

Math

The Missing Teeth graph
(Math Their Way)

The Missing Number worksheet
($+$, $-$, $\times$ or $\div$)

Race for the Big O (Fraction
Race Game)

Greater than, less than

Geometry: naming all the
shapes used in the Missing
Piece books

Spelling

The Missing Letter spelling
exercise worksheet

Social Studies

Emergency procedures:

Dial 911
Give your name
Give your parent's name
Give your address
Give your phone number

Establish a Lost and
Found Box in the classroom

**The Idea:
The Missing Piece**

Writing

Read *The Missing Piece* and *The
Missing Piece Meets the Big O,* by
Shel Silverstein

Write an adventure

Publish class book titled
"A Collection of Missing Pieces"

Art

The Missing Piece puppet

Illustrating "A Collection
of Missing Pieces"

The eraser stamp: create a
rubber stamp from an eraser
to illustrate a missing piece

Reading

Reading center contains books
related to theme

Missing Persons poster of
books read on the theme

Music

Sing "Hi-dee-ho, here we go,
Looking for my missing piece"
to other tunes

Songs related to theme; e.g.,
"All I want for Christmas is
my two front teeth"

Science

Camouflage study: design a
fish that is camouflaged by
its environment

Figure 4   Curriculum web.

After completing the web, I fit the activities, if possible, into a two-week period of study. I look at my daily and weekly schedule and try to arrange the activities in a natural order of presentation. This may not be perfect the first time you try it, so you may need to make some adjustments the following year. I also try to spread the introduction of new activities throughout the two weeks so I am not introducing them all at once.

These units take time to put together. I was told many years ago that if I would make three or four theme units a year, then in four or five years I would have enough of them to last the whole year long!

■ Related Literature

The literature that I discover is the exciting part. It is gratifying to find a book you can use as a springboard for other teaching opportunities. Once you find something that motivates the children, and you have them on a roll, you can take advantage of their enthusiasm to gain ground in other subject areas that might be a little less stimulating. Tying all these subject areas together simply makes more sense for the kids!

Here is a list of the books I use with the Missing Piece Theme.

Book list: Missing Piece Theme

Allard, Harry. *Miss Nelson Is Missing*. Boston: Houghton Mifflin, 1977.

Cohen, Miriam. *Lost in the Museum*. New York: Greenwillow Books, 1979.

Handford, Martin. *Where's Waldo?* Boston: Little, Brown, 1987.

Handford, Martin. *Where's Waldo Now?* Boston: Little, Brown, 1988.

Jonas, Ann. *Where Can It Be?* New York: Greenwillow Books, 1986.

Kellogg, Steven. *The Mystery of the Missing Mitten*. New York: Dial Press, 1974.

Kroll, Steven. *Is Milton Missing?* New York: Holiday House, 1975.

Lisker, Sonia O. *Lost*. New York: Harcourt Brace Jovanovich, 1975.

Marzollo, Jean. *The Three Little Kittens*. New York: Scholastic, 1985.

Mayer, Mercer. *Liverwurst Is Missing*. New York: Four Winds Press, 1981.

Meyers, Bernice. *A Lost Horse*. New York: Doubleday, 1975.

Meyers, Bernice. *My Mother Is Lost*. New York: Scholastic, 1970.

Nakatani, Chiyoko. *The Day Chiro Was Lost*. Cleveland: World Publishing, 1969.

Nims, Bonnie Larkin. *Where Is the Bear?*. Niles, Ill.: Albert Whitman, 1988.

Nodset, Joan L. *Who Took the Farmer's Hat?* New York: Harper & Row, 1963.

Paul, Anthony. *The Tiger Who Lost His Stripes.* New York: Harcourt Brace Jovanovich, 1980.

Rogers, Jean. *Runaway Mittens.* New York: Greenwillow Books, 1988.

Silverstein, Shel. *A Light in the Attic.* New York: Harper & Row, 1981.

Silverstein, Shel. *The Missing Piece.* New York: Harper & Row, 1976.

Silverstein, Shel. *The Missing Piece Meets the Big O.* New York: Harper & Row, 1981.

Steig, William. *Sylvester and the Magic Pebble.* New York: Scholastic, 1969.

Tafuri, Nancy. *Have You Seen My Ducklings?* New York: Greenwillow Books, 1984.

Vincent, Gabrielle. *Where Are You, Ernest and Celestine?* New York: Greenwillow Books, 1985.

Solving the Mystery: Cheri McLain

We now introduce Mrs. McLain, who has taught for twenty-one years. Cheri has spent most of her career in a self-contained classroom in a university community, but she has had some experience in special education. She is currently teaching fifth grade.

In describing her philosophy, Cheri states:

Using an integrated approach to curriculum, I work at enhancing self-image through skill building. Having been trained in learning styles, I employ a variety of methods to attempt to meet the learning and emotional needs of all the students. Process curriculum is emphasized—the important thing being the journey. Besides language arts, science is one of the tools I use as a catalyst for thinking skills and literacy.

Cheri McLain shares her blueprint for thematic teaching, which grew out of her interest in science.

I am particularly interested in the sciences. I have found that I can use that interest to spark the imagination and inquisitiveness of children, who are almost always drawn to science topics. Science topics make wonderful catalysts for children's reading and writing. One of my favorite themes is the

Mystery Integration Unit. In this unit, which usually lasts two or three weeks, I integrate lessons in science, writing, literature, problem solving, critical thinking, and art.

We begin by having children pretend to be criminologists. The students solve a crime by identifying a set of fingerprints. This activity serves as motivation for reading and creating their own mysteries. Lessons on the elements of mystery writing, math graphing, and the enjoyment of good literature all contribute to the success of this theme. I use these materials:

1. *Fingerprinting* and teacher's guide, Great Explorations in Math and Science (GEMS), Lawrence Hall of Science, University of California, Berkeley, CA 94720
2. Rolls of cellophane tape, paper and pencils, magnifying glasses, overhead transparencies and handouts from *Fingerprinting* teacher's guide, stamp pads, white drawing paper
3. Mystery books from the school library
4. Books to read aloud, including *The Mysteries of Harris Burdick*, by Chris Van Allsburg (Houghton Mifflin); *The Westing Game*, by Ellen Raskin (Dalton); *Mystery and Detective Stories*, by Alfred Hitchcock (Random House); and the Encyclopedia Brown series, by Donald J. Sobol (Thomas Nelson).

Here are some of the instructional activities I have used in the Mystery Theme. You will probably be able to think of others, but this will give you an idea of what we do.

■ Science (Problem Solving/Critical Thinking)

These activities come from the GEMS *Fingerprinting* materials already mentioned. I usually do these over four lessons of about forty-five minutes each.

Lesson 1

Discuss fingerprints and criminologists. Tell the children they are going to become scientists called criminologists or forensic scientists. Teach children how to make fingerprints using lead pencil, cellophane tape, and paper. Let them practice. Make a clean set of fingerprints and look at them with a magnifying glass.

Lesson 2

In teams, children classify a set of ten printed fingerprints using their own systems. Teacher records students' classification systems on board and discusses with class. Teacher defines the three basic fingerprint patterns (overhead transparencies). Students classify ten printed fingerprints into the three basic patterns. Students classify own fingerprints and make own fingerprint formula.

Lesson 3

Teacher tells story of a crime that has been committed and students are given the fingerprint formula found on the safe. Students find fingerprint formulas of suspects and speculate who may have committed the crime. Students given copy of exact prints to match with those of suspects. Hold discussion of reasons this suspect might have had prints on the safe and whether this is conclusive evidence. What other techniques could be used to solve the case?

Lesson 4

Children take notes on teacher's minilectures on fingerprinting facts, including why fingerprints are taken, whether fingerprinting has always been used for identification, what other systems of identification are used, and whether there is something like a fingerprint system for animals.

■ Math

Make a bar graph of fingerprint classifications and show how many of each type occur among your students.

■ Literature

Chris Van Allsburg's short stories are a splendid way to introduce mysteries. Read *The Mysteries of Harris Burdick* and ask the children to write their own ideas of what happened to Burdick or to explain the mysteries in the stories. Share *The Stranger* and ask them to write their ideas of who the stranger was, where he came from, and why changes happened when he was around.

The short mystery stories of Alfred Hitchcock are also a rich source of material for a Mystery Theme. Intermediate classes especially like "The Eyeball." Predicting what will happen next and analyzing clues are excellent thinking/reading strategies to practice.

For a *complicated* mystery to read aloud, especially to fifth- and sixth-graders, an outstanding choice is Ellen Raskin's Newbery Award–winning *Westing Game.*

Select many different kinds of mysteries from the school library and let the children choose one to read. Have them plan ways to share their books that include analyzing elements of character development, clues, suspense, and satisfactory endings.

■ Writing

After the first week of science and literature prewriting activities, brainstorm vocabulary words used by forensic scientists. Display them in a structured overview with *Mystery* in the center. Encourage children to use these words in conversation and writing.

Have children write a mystery story. Pay careful attention in the prewriting stage to the creation of clues, character development, and an ending that relates to the clues. Students could write newspaper articles about solving an invented crime using fingerprints and create stories about the suspects in these fictional crimes.

■ Art

Using Ed Emberley's thumbprint books as a source, do art projects using thumb, full finger, toe, and fist prints. This is a fun way for children to illustrate the stories they have written. Have children use a variety of media to create "Wanted" posters for the suspects in their mysteries.

Hatching the Eggs: Hilary Sumner

We want you to meet Ms. Sumner, a special education teacher who teaches in a resource room. Students identified as having specific learning disabilities in reading, writing, or mathematics leave their regular classrooms to spend some time in the resource room. Hilary's thirteen years of teaching have prepared her for her role as a staff resource in curriculum, philosophy, and instructional strategies for all children.

Of her educational philosophy, Hilary says:

I believe that all people are lifelong learners, that learning happens at all times, and that learning is the continual process of constructing meaning from what is new with what has already been experienced. My charge as a teacher is to orchestrate an environment that invites discovery, risk taking, and challenge. It is my job to encourage, promote, and celebrate my students.

Hilary elaborates views of thematic teaching and tells us how she conducts a unit on embryology.

We work with most of the students in small grade-level groups. Occasionally we group the students across grade levels based on their interests and needs. Our curriculum is varied, and projects frequently develop as we are immersed in specific thematic units. We are bound to some degree to meet district, state, and federal requirements based on our students' Individual Educational Plans, but we are professionals trained to design instruction as we deem necessary for our students.

Our program is based on a holistic philosophy of learning. Empowering students with their learning is the key. In no way does this mean we do not monitor their progress. In fact, careful observation and ongoing evaluation are critical to the success of our classes. But empowering students does allow them to be responsible for and active in their own growth. Children learn through experience. They interact with their environment and actively seek to construct meaning through the process of analyzing, hypothesizing, testing, and reorganizing the information from their experience. They are forming rules about their world and integrating them with previous experience.

In my classroom we center on the child rather than on the curriculum. The child actively controls the learning process through meaningful interaction, exploration, and discovery. I act as facilitator, modeling, clarifying, questioning, supporting, and generally orchestrating the process. I provide an environment that is authentic and enriching—an environment in which students are encouraged to take risks.

We have designed much of our instructional program to include thematic units. These themes can include any topic that is interesting and motivating to the students: the culture of the community, the season, national issues, holidays, and so on. The units are designed in a curriculum web encompassing reading, writing, speaking, and listening and are integrated with most other aspects of the school curriculum. One major intent of thematic teaching is to provide a link between classroom learning, out-of-school learning, and the Special Education Program.

■ Planning a Thematic Unit on Embryology

Our Resource Room has enjoyed greeting the spring for the past four years with an in-depth study of chickens and embryology. Our curriculum developed out of student interest, discovery, and incredible whole-school curiosity. We started with a borrowed, antiquated incubator and twelve questionable eggs. We now have a sophisticated forty-eight-egg incubator purchased by our Parent–Teacher Club. And we have a full-scale curriculum on embryology. This is an excellent example of how a small, entertaining idea can develop into a complex instructional plan by virtue of student interest.

At first we relied on encyclopedias, a feed store manual on fowl production, and the directions to our borrowed incubator for materials.

We now incorporate a wide range of materials, including books, a video, models, and twenty-one actual embryos in glass jars, showing day-by-day development during the three-week incubation period.

We plan each spring to coordinate our chicken unit with the Easter holiday and our spring break. Fertilized chicken eggs can be obtained from a variety of sources. They must be handled very carefully. And you need to decide what you are going to do with the young chicks when the unit is over. For three years I kept the hatchlings myself. Last spring we offered the chicks to the parents of my students. With a carefully worded letter to parents, we offered two chicks each to the first twenty families who wanted them, had facilities to raise them, and knew what it took to care for them. Many children still have the hens and will never forget the incredible experience of it all.

■ Curriculum Web

Figure 5 is a curriculum web for my thematic unit. The curriculum web generally describes the unit and the curriculum areas that can be incorporated.

■ Instructional Plan

This sample instructional plan shows the format and activities I include in my writing component. Each curricular area (reading, speaking, listening, math, social studies, science, and others) can be extended in this manner. For each, an instructional unit can be designed to incorporate important concepts and strategies developed around the theme. It is important to understand that our primary objective in each area is not the content of embryology but the specific strategies of reading, writing, mathematics, and so on, in which each student is weak. The content, however, is the reason for using reading or writing. It is through purposeful reading and writing that learning is natural and relevant.

The following is a sample writing unit within our study of embryology. Because we are a Resource Room, we work with students in grades K–6. Each curricular area and instructional component must be adapted to the developmental level of the students involved.

   A. Project goals
      1. The students will understand the basics of the setup and functioning of an incubator.
      2. The students will become aware of the 21-day gestation of a chicken egg.
      3. The students will observe egg candling to evaluate embryo growth.

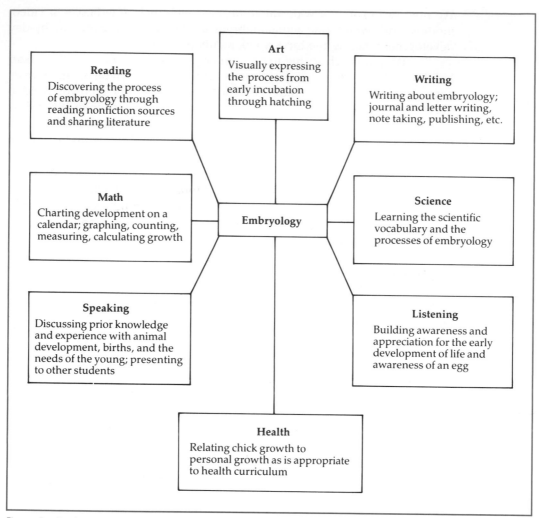

Figure 5   Curriculum web.

4. The students will keep a daily journal recording embryological development, day 7 through day 21, and chick behavior, day 1 through day 5.

B. **Writing goals**
   1. The students will complete a writing piece reflecting on embryology (journal, notes, essay, poem, report, etc.).
   2. The students will use the stages of process writing (pre-writing, drafting, revising, redrafting, editing, and publishing).

C. **Activities**
   The hatching activities can be done with all grade levels. Expectations for student writing should be adjusted accordingly. Children in kindergarten and first grade may need to use drawing and invented spelling.

■ Hatching the Chicks

Incubation: Day 1

1. Student groups observe the eggs newly placed in the incubator. Teacher explains the functioning of the incubator: temperature control, water source for moisture, and egg-turning mechanism. The teacher has numbered the eggs for identification.

2. Each child "adopts" an egg—that is, chooses one egg by number to observe, record notes about, and bond with during the twenty-one day gestation period. More than one child may choose the same egg. Teacher and children discuss how fragile the embryos are and the fact that many of these will not develop into live chicks. Teacher must be prepared to deal with the disappointment of children whose eggs fail to hatch.

Incubation: Days 2–21

3. Each student begins his or her daily written response journal, including date, time, temperature of the incubator, a description of the growth observed during candling, and any predictions, concerns, and feelings.

4. As the twenty-first day approaches, study the hatching process (pipping, air sacs, rotational cracking). Each student records observations in a journal. Writings can be shared in small groups, in pairs, with parents, with homeroom classes, with classroom teachers, with the principal.

5. Throughout the incubation period, students can prepare notes for an oral presentation to visiting classes from the rest of the school. Little is more inspiring than to see first- and second-grade learning-disabled children giving embryology lectures to sixth-grade regular education students!

6.   If you choose to offer the chicks to the students, an excellent writing activity could be the children's writing letters to their parents or to relatives who live in the country. The letters could be both persuasive and descriptive, explaining the need for good homes with the appropriate environment.

Hatchlings: Days 1–5

7.   Once the chicks hatch, each child records observed chick behavior (feeding, socialization, handling).

■ Writing Activities

There are numerous possibilities for writing projects in this unit. These are some I have done:

- ■   Pop-up, shape, flip-up books
- ■   Nonfiction writing depicting the hatching process
- ■   Research reports on related birds
- ■   Student manuals on incubation and chick care
- ■   Plays, poems, songs
- ■   Fiction stories such as "Chicken Licken," "The Little Red Hen," "The Ugly Duckling"

Possibilities in this unit are virtually endless, limited only by the students' and teacher's imaginations. Likewise, each of the other curricular areas is expandable. Your librarian and fellow teachers, as well as district resource persons, will undoubtedly help you discover literature, materials, and references to enrich your thematic units.

Teaching children through thematic units incorporates a belief and trust in the process of learning, the process of moving toward understanding rather than the mere mastery of specific skills in isolation. The developmental path is far more important than the final product. Children deserve to have that path be authentic, interactive, and relevant to their real lives.

And Now for the Teacher You Are Becoming

You have had a glimpse into the planning and teaching processes of four remarkable teachers. We hope that they will serve as models for you as you begin to put into practice the things you have learned, not only from this text and course but from your entire teacher education program. Remember that these four teachers have had years of experience. Each year they get better at their work. Take what you can from them at first, and use it, but do not challenge yourself to do everything they do—at least, not in the beginning.

If we have done our work well, you will have students who view literacy as first-grader Kati Field did in this piece, written in the spring of 1989:

When I grow up, I'm going to be a writer.

I'm going to write those big fat books like the ones in the library.

People will open those books, and there will be all the words that I wrote for them to read.

I like writing a lot.
It makes me feel like magic.
Sometimes it makes me excited, and
Sometimes it makes me peaceful.

I didn't learn my writing,
I came with It.

Appendix A

Instructions for Bookbinding

Instant Minibook

With a few simple folds and a single cut or tear, you can turn a single sheet of paper into an 8-page booklet. If you turn it inside out, you can make a 16-page book. You'll need a rectangular sheet of paper and a pair of scissors.

What to do:

1. Take a rectangular sheet of paper and fold it in half lengthwise.
2. Open it, then fold it in half crosswise.
3. Fold it crosswise again.

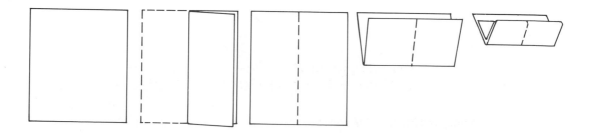

4. Unfold it so that the paper is back as in Step 2. Cut a slit half-way up the middle, like this:

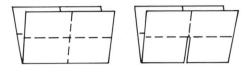

5. Open the paper and fold it lengthwise again as in Step 1, with the slit on the top.

6. Grasp it at either end and push the ends of the slit together like this:

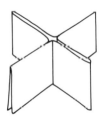

7. Fold it at one edge, like this, to make a book:

8. Punch two holes along the folded edge. Tie string or yarn through the holes to bind the book's pages together.

SOURCE: Jeri Robinson, Activities for *Anyone, Anytime, Anywhere*, Little, Brown.

■ Hardcover Book

1. Fold two pieces of colored construction paper in half and insert typed or blank page papers within.

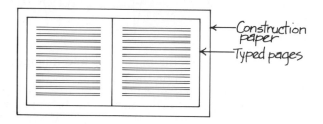

2. Sew page papers together using a bookbinder's stitching pattern down the center fold through the construction paper. Use dental floss or button hole twist (about 20″ long). Beginning at the back of the construction paper at the center, follow the pattern below, leaving 2″ to tie.

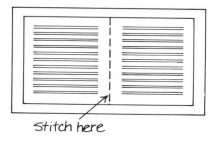

3. Center two pieces of cardboard on wallpaper, fabric, vinyl Con-Tact, or whatever you choose for cover material, leaving about ¼″ in the center between them, and about 1″ of cover material all the way around the cardboard. Draw around the pieces of cardboard so you know where to glue them. Glue them in place with rubber cement.

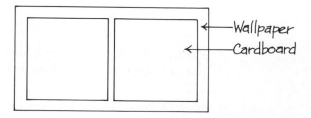

4. Fold each of the four corners of the cover material diagonally. Glue the cover material under the fold to the cardboard.

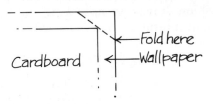

5. Then fold sides of the cover material over the cardboard and glue down. This is your book cover.

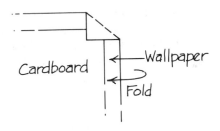

6. Open the book cover so it lies flat, and center the sewn pages inside.
7. Put rubber cement on the back end page (colored construction paper) and press that page onto the cover. Then do the same with the front page.

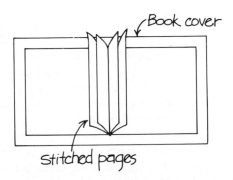

8. Put the book title and your name on the front cover. You might want to add an illustration or design on the end pages. Be sure to put an "About the Author" section on the last page.
9. You have now finished publishing your own book. Hooray!!

▇▇▇ Zig-zag Book

A zig-zag book is one made from a long strip of paper folded in a zig-zag fashion. It requires no sewing, but the folding must be very carefully done if a neat result is to be achieved.

Zig-zag books have many uses:

1. Sequential stories
2. Autobiographies, showing stages of the person's life
3. Life cycles of plants and animals
4. Panels combining picture and description, such as of favorite animals
5. Cyclical events, like seasons
6. And many other possibilities.

Books, of course, can be made in any size. The dimensions used in these directions are included just as an example:

White construction paper: 2 sheets originally 12″ × 18″, cut to 6″ × 18″ with folded panels to 4½″ × 6″
Cardboard covers: 2 pieces 5½″ × 6½″
Cover paper or fabric: 2 pieces 7½″ × 8½″

1. Cut 2 pieces of cardboard for the book covers. These pieces will need to be 1″ larger on all four sides than the inside writing paper.
2. Cut 2 pieces of construction paper or fabric (designed with original artwork) at least 1″ larger on all four sides than the cardboard. Using original artwork as the design on the cover paper or fabric affords the book's creator a much greater sense of pride in authorship.
3. Glue the construction paper or fabric onto the cardboard. Use wallpaper paste for the glue. Wallpaper paste works better than glue because it spreads more easily and smoothly, is less expensive, and is more "forgiving" if a mistake occurs and the paper has to be pulled apart. Spread clean newspaper on a flat work surface. (Plain newsprint is even better, to avoid having black ink come off on the covers.)
   a. Turn construction paper or fabric upside down on a clean piece of newspaper.
   b. Use a wide brush to spread the glue evenly. Wide brushes are best because the glue dries so quickly. Spread the glue evenly over all the paper.

c. Place the cardboard in the center of each glued paper or fabric. Do each cover one at a time because the glue dries so quickly.

d. Turn in each corner and glue onto the cardboard. Don't pull too hard or the corners will puncture because they're wet from the glue and are weak.

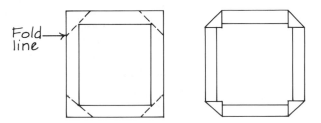

Fold line

e. Lightly glue each turned-down corner, since there has not yet been any glue on these corners.

f. Turn down each side panel onto the cardboard. Use the clean newspaper underneath to press over the paper that is being glued on the cardboard. This will help keep the paper and fingers clean. Remove the newspaper.

g. Repeat Steps a–f with the second piece of cardboard and the cover paper or fabric.

4. Set the paper- or fabric-covered cardboard pieces aside on a flat surface. Place heavy books on top of them so they don't permanently warp.

5. Fold two pieces of 12" × 18" white construction paper into four zig-zag accordion-pleat folds. Refold one piece into a stack. Trim down this rectangular stack so that it is ½" smaller than the three sides of the cardboard. Then trim the other stack of white paper to the same size. The pages, of course, do not have to be white. "White" is used in these directions just to distinguish the writing pages from the other paper of the cover.

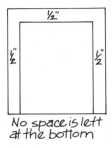

½"

½"   ½"

No space is left at the bottom

6. On a table, stand up the two folded stacks of white pages. Arrange them in an accordion-pleated way. Where the two pieces meet, overlap the two middle panels.

7. Smoothly glue or paste the two middle panels together, being *sure* all the pages are still arranged in an accordion-pleated manner.

8. Cut off and discard *one* end panel. That will leave six panels on each side. This will make the completed book open properly. (The last panel is cut off whenever there is an odd number of writing surfaces so the back opens properly. If three sets of folded papers are used, for example, there are ten writing panels. Since this is an even number, no panel needs to be cut off.)

9. Glue the two end panels of white construction paper onto the insides of the cardboard covers. Place the white pages on the cardboard so the ragged edges of the artwork paper or fabric are neatly covered. However, it is important to have one end *even* with the bottom of the cardboard so the book can stand up open for a display.

10. Place waxed paper or foil between the covers and the dry pages at both ends of the book for the 5 days the book is drying. If the foil or waxed paper is not placed in the book, the dampness from the glue will go through to the other pages and they will permanently wrinkle.

11. Press beneath books. The weight of the books on top doesn't have to be great but it needs to be consistent and as large as or larger than the zig-zag book. Be sure all corners are even before pressing.

Pages fold accordion-style

SOURCE: Dr. Lynda Hatch, Northern Arizona University, Flagstaff, Arizona.

Appendix B

Descriptions of Piagetian Tasks

Task 1

Given a set of red and a set of blue plastic chips, the child will determine if the sets are equal or not equal when chips from one set are rearranged spatially.

The sets should be equal and contain more than five chips, since even very young children can recognize which is more if the sets contain fewer than five. After the sets have been laid out and the agreement reached that they are equal, the administrator moves one of the sets so that it physically takes up more space, then asks the child if the sets are equal. Most preoperational children will answer that the set that is spread apart has more now. Even children who can count will say that the sets are not equal when they occupy different amounts of space. They will often count and make errors, such as counting spaces or counting one chip more than once, in order to prove that their answer is correct. I often stack one of the sets and repeat the questions to check the child's first response. Comparing equivalent sets when one occupies more space is the classic task for determining if the child conserves number.

Task 2

Given a set of red and a larger set of blue plastic chips, the child will determine if there are more blue or more plastic chips.

Use the same chips as in Task 1, but make sure that the child knows the material from which the chips are made. Having determined that all the chips are plastic, ask the child if there are more blue chips or more plastic chips in the set. The usual answer is more blue chips. I usually ask the child, "What did I ask you?" The usual response is, "You asked if there were more red or more blue chips." I say that I asked if there were more blue or more plastic chips. The child's response is nearly always that there are more blue, an answer that reflects the child's difficulty with multiplicative classification in placing the chips in the category of color and material at the same time.

Task 3

Given two pencils that are exactly alike, the child will be asked to compare their lengths when they are held so that their ends are exactly even and when they are held with one extending past the other.

This is an easy check for conservation of length. The preoperational child will point to one of the pencils as being longer when it extends past the end of the other one. I point out that the other pencil extends on the other end, but this does not change their answer. A concrete operational child will look at the administrator as if the question were absolutely the dumbest thing ever asked and respond quite condescendingly that the pencils are still the same length and that moving them around certainly does not change their length.

Task 4

Given a necklace made of a shoelace strung with five large wooden beads and the materials for reproducing the necklace, the child will reconstruct the pattern of the beads on the lace as they would appear if they were in a straight line.

If the child can do this task easily, then he or she could be asked to reproduce a necklace containing eight beads and presented in a figure-8 pattern. The ability to mentally straighten out the circle and reproduce the pattern of beads is an indication of reversibility of thinking. It is very important to observe how the child solves this problem, for often it is not the final result so much as the way the child solves the problem that determines whether or not the child is preoperational in thinking. For example, one child was observed to place a blue bead on the end of the string, then check the original pattern. Upon discovering that the blue bead would be at the opposite end of the string if the string formed a loop, she removed the bead and strung it on the opposite end. An operational strategy would have been to slide the bead down the string or turn the string around. Many children can reproduce the patterns, particularly the figure 8, only if they can touch the beads on the original pattern. This need to physically manipulate the beads indicates their difficulty with mentally rearranging the bead patterns.

Task 5

Given a set of identical paper dolls that are graduated in size from two inches to ten inches tall, the child will be asked to order the dolls from largest to smallest.

The typical preoperational strategy is to pick up two dolls at random, compare their sizes, place the larger of the two first and the smaller second, and then pick up another pair and repeat the procedure. Often preoperational thinkers arrange the dolls so that their heads form a descending line, but with some out of order. A typical response when I have pointed out these out-of-order dolls is to rearrange them so that their feet are ascending. Any ordering task requires that the child hold in mind the object just placed while considering the next object. If the child can order the dolls easily, then he or she is presented with a set of circles of graduated sizes to order. These circles are drawn deliberately to take up more space than the dolls so that they cannot be matched merely by size. The child is asked to order the circles from largest to smallest. If the circles are ordered correctly, then the child is asked which circle "goes with" a doll pointed out by the administrator. A concrete strategy is to count the position of the doll in the first series, count the circles, and find the corresponding item. A preoperational child usually selects the circle by matching the sizes of the circle and the doll as closely as possible or by using some other criterion known only to the child.

Task 6

Given a coin placed inside two containers, the child will determine the location of the coin.

For this task a coin and two small nesting toys (small barrels) are needed. The child is asked to observe carefully as the administrator places the coin inside the smaller of the two barrels, closes it, and places it inside the larger barrel. The child is then asked if the coin is inside the larger barrel. The usual response is that the coin is not inside the larger barrel, but is inside the smaller one. If questioned further, most preoperational children will say that the smaller barrel is inside the larger barrel but the coin is not. If the child is then asked to look for the coin, he or she will immediately open the larger barrel. This inability to describe the coin as being inside the larger barrel is a problem not with language but with the child's inability to think of the coin as being inside both the larger and the smaller barrel at the same time.

Task 7

Given a bottle standing upright and half filled with colored water, the child is asked to draw the position of the water on an outline drawing of the bottle.

After completing the drawing, the child is asked to predict what the water will look like when the bottle is lying flat on the table. The bottle is covered with a small cloth and placed horizontally on the table. The child is then given an outline drawing of the bottle in the horizontal position and asked to draw his or her prediction of the position of the water. The usual response is to draw the water all the way into the neck of the bottle. Only a concrete thinker with a stable concept of the changes that result from the change in spatial position will predict the actual position of the water.

Task 8

Given a set of six identical paper dolls and a circle of paper, the child will be asked to cut an equal piece of the circle for each doll. The dolls are presented in one stack.

     The child will be told that the circle is a cake, that each doll should be given an equal amount, and that all the cake should be used. Make sure that the child knows the meaning of "equal amount" or "same amount" and "all the cake." Provide a crayon and ruler for marking and scissors for cutting the cake. The typical preoperational response is to begin cutting small triangles from around the edge of the circle without any regard for the number of pieces needed. The child may continue cutting small triangles until the circle is completely cut up, or he or she may only cut around the edge. When asked what could be done with the remainder of the cake, a typical response is, "We could eat it!" Some children will then lay out the dolls and place small triangles on them (matching one to one) until they have exhausted the supply of pieces. A concrete thinker would always begin by counting the number of pieces needed and then making some plan to produce that many pieces. Because six is a difficult division to accomplish, the child is considered concrete in his or her thinking if there is a strategy for producing six pieces, even if they are not exactly equal. For example, concrete operational thinkers may fold the paper in half and attempt to cut three pieces from each half, or they may use the ruler to mark the circle into six more or less equal sections.

Task 9

Given a cardboard tube into which three small cars are inserted and which is then rotated 180 degrees in a horizontal plane, the child will be asked to predict which of the cars will emerge from the tube first.

     The task will be repeated, rotating the tube 360 degrees. The administrator will ask the child to observe carefully as the cars are inserted one at a time into the tube. Then the child is asked to observe while the tube is rotated. Preoperational children fail to hold the position of the cars in mind while following the change in position of the cars in space and usually predict that the last car inserted will emerge first. One child who watched this task several times responded, "Do that again. You're magic!"

◼ Task 10

Given a set of blocks, a container, and an egg timer, the child will be asked to state the speed of the flow of the sand in the timer as blocks are placed in the container.

The child will be shown the egg timer, and the administrator will ascertain that he or she knows what it does and how it works. If the child has the concept that it measures time, then the administrator will ask the child to place a collection of small wooden blocks into a container as quickly as possible. Then he or she will be asked what happened to the sand in the timer. The child is then asked to repeat the task but to put the blocks in as slowly as possible. Again the child is asked what happened to the sand in the timer. The typical preoperational answer is that it goes fast if the child was working quickly and that it goes slowly if he or she worked slowly. A concrete answer is that the sand did not change its speed no matter what the child did.

Appendix C

Analytical Rating Guide

Ideas and Content

5 This paper is clear in purpose and conveys ideas in an interesting, original manner that holds the reader's attention. Often, the writing develops as a process of discovery for both reader and writer. Clear, relevant examples, anecdotes or details develop and enrich the central idea or ideas.

- The writer seems to be writing what he or she knows, often from experience.
- The writer shows insight—a good sense of the world, people, situations.
- The writing is often enlivened by spontaneity or a fresh, individual perspective.
- The writer selects supportive, relevant details that keep the main idea(s) in focus.
- Primary and secondary ideas are developed in proportion to their significance; the writing has a sense of balance.
- The writer seems in control of the topic and its development throughout.

3 The writer's purpose is reasonably clear; however, the overall result may not be especially captivating. Support is less than adequate to fully develop the main idea(s).

- The reader may not be convinced of the writer's knowledge of the topic.
- The writer seems to have considered ideas, but not thought things through all the way.
- Ideas, though reasonably clear and comprehensible, may tend toward the mundane; the reader is not sorry to see the paper end.
- Supporting details tend to be skimpy, general, predictable, or repetitive. Some details seem included by chance, not selected through careful discrimination.

- Writing sometimes lacks balance: e.g., too much attention to minor details, insufficient development of main ideas, informational gaps.
- The writer's control of the topic seems inconsistent or uncertain.

1 This paper lacks a central idea or purpose—or the central idea can be inferred by the reader only because he or she knows the topic (question asked).
   - Information is very limited (e.g., restatement of the prompt, heavy reliance on repetition) or simply unclear altogether.
   - Insight is limited or lacking (e.g., details that do not ring true; dependence on platitudes or stereotypes).
   - Paper lacks balance; development of ideas is minimal, or there may be a list of random thoughts from which no central theme emerges.
   - Writing tends to read like a rote response—merely an effort to get something down on paper.
   - The writer does not seem in control of the topic; shorter papers tend to go nowhere, longer papers to wander aimlessly.

Organization

5 The writer organizes material in a way that enhances the reader's understanding, or that helps to develop a central idea or theme. The order may be conventional or not, but the sequence is effective and moves the reader through the paper.
   - Details seem to fit where they're placed, and the reader is not left with the sense that "something is missing."
   - The writer provides a clear sense of beginning and ending, with an inviting introduction and a satisfying conclusion ("satisfying" in the sense that the reader feels the paper has ended at the right spot).
   - Transitions work well; the writing shows unity and cohesion, both within paragraphs and as a whole.
   - Organization flows so smoothly that the reader doesn't have to think about it.

3 The writer attempts to organize ideas and details cohesively, but the resulting pattern may be somewhat unclear, ineffective, or awkward. Although the reader can generally follow what's

being said, the organizational structure may seem at times to be forced, obvious, incomplete or ineffective.

- The writer seems to have a sense of beginning and ending, but the introduction and/or conclusion tend to be less effective than desired.
- The order may not be a graceful fit with the topic (e.g., a forced conventional pattern, or lack of structure).
- The writer may miss some opportunities for transitions, requiring the reader to make assumptions or inferences.
- Placement or relevance of some details may be questionable (e.g., interruptive information; writer gets to the point in roundabout fashion).
- While some portions of the paper may seem unified (e.g., organization within a given paragraph may be acceptable), cohesion of the whole may be weak.

1 Organization is haphazard and disjointed. The writing shows little or no sense of progression or direction. Examples, details, or events seem unrelated to any central idea, or may be strung together helter-skelter with no apparent pattern.

- There is no clear sense of a beginning or ending.
- Transitions are very weak or absent altogether.
- Arrangement of details is confusing or illogical.
- There are noticeable information "gaps"; the reader is left dangling, or cannot readily see how the writer got from one point to another.
- The paper lacks unity and solidarity.

Voice

5 The paper bears the unmistakable stamp of the individual writer. The writer speaks directly to the reader, and seems sincere, candid and committed to the topic. The overall effect is individualistic, expressive and engaging; this paper stands out from the others.

- The reader feels interaction with the writer, and through the writing, gains a sense of what the writer is like.
- The paper is honest. There is a real effort to communicate, even when it means taking a risk (e.g., an unexpected approach or revealing of self).
- The writing is natural and compelling.
- Tone is appropriate and consistently controlled.

■ The writer's own enthusiasm or interest comes through and brings the topic to life.

3 The writer makes an honest effort to deal with the topic, but without a strong sense of personal commitment or involvement. The result is often pleasant or acceptable, yet not striking or compelling in a way that draws the reader in.

■ The reader has only an occasional or limited sense of interaction with the writer.

■ Writer may seem self-conscious or unwilling to take a risk—may seem to be writing what he/she thinks the reader wants.

■ Paper lacks individuality, or the ring of conviction.

■ The writing communicates, but only in a routine, predictable fashion that tends to make it blend in with the efforts of others.

■ Voice may be inconsistent; it may emerge strongly on occasion, only to shift or even disappear altogether.

1 The writer may not have understood the assignment, or may simply have felt indifferent toward the topic. As a result, no clear voice emerges. The result is flat, lifeless, very mechanical and stilted, or possibly inappropriate.

■ The reader has no sense that this writer was "writing to be read," and experiences virtually no writer-reader interaction.

■ The writing has virtually no individual personality or character; there is no identifiable voice behind the words.

■ There is little or no evidence of the writer's involvement in the topic.

Word Choice

5 The writer consistently selects words that convey the intended message in an interesting, precise and natural way. The result is full and rich, yet not overwhelming; every word carries its own weight.

■ Words are specific, accurate, and suited to the subject. Imagery is strong.

■ Lively, powerful verbs give the writing energy, visual appeal, and clarity.

■ Vocabulary may be striking, colorful, or unusual—but the language isn't overdone.

- Expression is fresh and appealing, fun to read. The writer uses cliches or slang sparingly, and only for effect.
- The writer may experiment with uncommon words, or use common words in a delightful way.
- Figurative language, if used, is effective.

3 The writer's word choice is adequate to convey meaning, but the language tends toward the ordinary. The writer doesn't consistently reach for the "best" way to say something, but instead often settles for the first word or phrase that comes to mind. The result is a sort of "generic paper" that sounds familiar, routine, or commonplace.

- Language comunicates quite well, but without a sense of satisfying fullness or power; the reader has the feeling it could have been written better.
- Imagery may be weakened by overuse of abstract, general language.
- Though the reader can interpret the meaning quite readily, some words lack precision or vigor.
- Attempts at the unusual, colorful or difficult are not always successful. The language may seem overdone or calculated to impress rather than natural.
- Though an occasional phrase may catch the reader's eye, cliches, redundancies and hackneyed phrases pop up with disappointing frequency; there are few surprises or enticing twists.

1 The writer is struggling with a limited vocabulary, often groping for words and phrases to convey meaning. Meaning may be difficult to determine (e.g., the writer says one thing but seems to mean another), or else the language is so vague and abstract that only the broadest, most general sorts of messages are conveyed.

- Writing is often characterized by monotonous repetition, overwhelming reliance on worn, threadbare expressions, or heavy reliance on the prompt (topic) itself for key words and phrases.
- Imagery is very weak or absent; the reader lacks sufficient concrete details to construct any mental picture.
- Words tend to be consistently dull, colorless and trite.
- In some instances, word choice may seem careless, imprecise, or just plain wrong.

Sentence Structure

5 The paper is fluid, and reads easily throughout. It has an easy-on-the ear flow and rhythm when read aloud. Sentences have a strong and rhetorically effective structure that makes reading enjoyable.
- Sentence structure clearly conveys meaning, with no ambiguity.
- Writing sounds natural and fluent, with effective phrasing.
- Sentences are appropriately concise.
- Varied sentence structure and length add interest.
- Fragments, if used, are stylistically appropriate. They seem right.

3 Sentences are understandable, but tend to be mechanical rather than fluid. While sentences are usually correct, the paper is not characterized by a natural fluency and grace. Occasional flaws or awkward constructions may necessitate re-reading.
- Sentence structure sometimes clearly conveys meaning—and sometimes not. Structural problems may sometimes create ambiguity.
- Some sentences lack energy, character or effectiveness (e.g., they may be hampered by awkward structure, unnecessary complexity, roundabout expression, wordiness, dangling modifiers, ineffective use of passive voice, or repetitious beginnings—"I did this," "I did that").
- Sentence variety (length or structure) tends to be more the exception than the rule.
- Fragments, if used, may sometimes be ineffective or confusing.

1 The writing is generally awkward and therefore hard to read aloud. It does not sound natural. Sentences tend to be choppy, incomplete, or so rambling and irregular that it may be difficult to tell where one should end and the next begin.
- Because sentence structure frequently does not function to convey meaning, reader may pause several times to question what is meant.
- Sentences lack both fluency and correctness. The writer may not write in conventional sentences at all. Or, sentences may seem stiffly constructed, disjointed, endlessly meandering (e.g., many run-ons), or nonsensical.

- Short, choppy sentences, relentlessly monotonous rhythms or patterns (e.g., subject-verb or subject-verb-object over and over) that produce a jarring or sing-song effect.
- Fragments are confusing or ineffective. Writer seems to have little grasp of how words fit together, or of where one idea logically stops and the next begins.

Writing Conventions

5 The writer's skillful use of standard writing conventions (grammar, capitalization, punctuation, usage, spelling, paragraphing) enhances readability. There are no glaring errors. In fact, while the paper may not be flawless, errors tend to be so minor that the reader can easily overlook them unless searching for them specifically. (Deliberate, controlled deviations from convention—in dialogue, for instance—are acceptable, provided they enhance the overall effect.)
- Grammar (e.g., noun-verb agreement; noun-pronoun agreement; verb tense; forms of nouns, verbs, pronouns and modifiers) is essentially correct.
- Punctuation is smooth and enhances meaning. Informalities, such as dashes or contractions, are allowed.
- Spelling is generally correct, even on more difficult words.
- Usage is generally correct, or acceptable given the purpose of the writing. The writer avoids double negatives (e.g., *couldn't hardly*) and nonstandard usage (e.g., *could of* been, *more better*, she *had ought* to do it, *irregardless, leave me* figure this out). Informalities (e.g., *you will find* rather than the more formal *one will find*) are acceptable.
- Paragraphing (i.e., indenting) works in harmony with the inherent organization of the paper.

3 Errors in writing conventions are noticeable and begin to impair readability. Reader can follow what is being said overall, but may need to pause or re-read on occasion.
- Occasional problems in grammar disrupt the flow of the writing. For example, agreement may be inconsistent; or there may be shifts in tense, improper verb forms (e.g., *lay down* here), improper pronoun forms (*theirselves, me and Jim* will go), use of adjectives for adverbs (he did *good*), and so on.

- Punctuation, capitalization and spelling errors may be sufficiently frequent or serious to momentarily distract the reader.
- Some usage problems (e.g., double negatives, use of non-standard expressions such as *irregardless*) may be evident.
- Paragraphing is attempted, but paragraphs may not always begin at the right places. As a result, paragraph structure (indenting) does not always complement the paper's inherent organization.

1 Numerous errors in usage and grammar, spelling, capitalization and/or punctuation consistently distract the reader, taking attention away from the writer's message and severely impairing readability.
- The student shows very limited understanding of or ability to apply conventions.
- Errors in grammar and usage are frequent and tend to be very noticeable.
- Basic punctuation may be omitted, haphazard, or just plain wrong.
- Capitalization is often incorrect or highly inconsistent.
- Spelling errors tend to be frequent, even on common words.
- Paragraphing is illogical or arbitrary (e.g., paragraphs almost never seem to begin in the right places).

Appendix D

NAEYC Position Statement on Standardized Testing of Young Children 3 through 8 Years of Age*

Statement of the Problem

The practice of administering standardized tests to young children has increased dramatically in recent years. Many school systems now routinely administer some form of standardized developmental screening or readiness test for admittance to kindergarten or standardized achievement test for promotion to first grade. As a result, more and more 5- and 6-year-olds are denied admission to school or are assigned to some form of extra-year tracking such as "developmental kindergarten," retention in kindergarten, or "transitional" first grade (Meisels, 1987; Shepard & Smith, in press). Such practices (often based on inappropriate uses of readiness or screening tests) disregard the potential, documented long-term negative effects of retention on children's self-esteem and the fact that such practices disproportionately affect low-income and minority children; further, these practices have been implemented in the absence of research documenting that they positively affect children's later academic achievement (Gredler, 1984; Shepard & Smith, 1986, 1987; Smith & Shepard, 1987).

A simultaneous trend that has influenced and been influenced by the use of standardized testing is the increasingly academic emphasis of the curriculum imposed on kindergartners. Many kindergartens are now highly structured, "watered-down" first grades, emphasizing workbooks and other paper-and-pencil activities that are developmentally inappropriate for 5-year-olds (Bredekamp, 1987; Durkin, 1987; Katz, Raths, & Torres, undated). The trend further trickles down to preschool and child care programs that feel their mission is to get children "ready" for kindergarten.

---

*Adopted November 1987

508

Too many school systems, expecting children to conform to an inappropriate curriculum and finding large numbers of "unready" children, react to the problem by raising the entrance age for kindergarten and/or labeling the children as failures (Shepard & Smith, 1986, in press).

The negative influence of standardized testing on the curriculum is not limited to kindergarten. Throughout the primary grades, schools assess achievement using tests that frequently do not reflect current theory and research about how children learn. For example, current research on reading instruction stresses a whole language/literacy approach that integrates oral language, writing, reading, and spelling in meaningful context, emphasizing comprehension. However, standardized tests of reading achievement still define reading exclusively as phonics and word recognition and measure isolated skill acquisition (Farr & Carey, 1986; Teale, Hiebert, & Chittenden, 1987; Valencia & Pearson, 1987). Similarly, current theory of mathematics instruction stresses the child's construction of number concepts through firsthand experiences, while achievement tests continue to define mathematics as knowledge of numerals (Kamii, 1985a, 1985b). As a result, too many school systems teach to the test or continue to use outdated instructional methods so that children will perform adequately on standardized tests.

The widespread use of standardized tests also drains resources of time and funds without clear demonstration that the investment is beneficial for children. Days may be devoted to testing (or preparing for it) that could be better spent in valuable instructional time (National Center for Fair and Open Testing, 1987).

Ironically, the calls for excellence in education that have produced widespread reliance on standardized testing may have had the opposite effect—mediocrity. Children are being taught to provide the one "right" answer on the answer sheet, but are not being challenged to think. Rather than producing excellence, the overuse (and misuse) of standardized testing has led to the adoption of inappropriate teaching practices as well as admission and retention policies that are not in the best interests of individual children or the nation as a whole.

Purpose

The purpose of this position statement is to guide the decisions of educators regarding the use of standardized tests. These administrative decisions include whether to use standardized testing, how to critically evaluate existing tests, how to carefully select appropriate and accurate tests to be used with a population and purpose for which the test was designed, and how to use and interpret the results yielded from standardized tests to parents, school personnel, and the media. Such decisions are usually made by school principals, superintendents, or state school officials. Teachers are responsible for admininstering tests and, therefore, have a professional responsibility to be knowledgeable about appropriate testing and to influence, or attempt to influence, the selection and use of tests. It is assumed that responsible and educated decisions by administrators and teachers will influence commercial test developers to produce valid, reliable, and useful tests.

Standardized tests are instruments that are composed of empirically selected items; have definite instructions for use, data on reliability, and validity; and are norm- or criterion-referenced (see definitions on page 45). This position statement addresses *tests*—the instruments themselves, and *testing*—the administration of tests, scoring, and interpretation of scores. This statement concentrates on standardized tests because such tests are most likely to influence policy. Nonstandardized assessments such as systematic observation, anecdotal records, locally or nationally developed checklists, or mastery tests developed by individual teachers (that do not meet the above criteria for standardization) play a vital role in planning and implementing instruction and in making decisions about placement of children. Decisions made on the basis of nonstandardized assessments should take into consideration the guidelines presented in this position statement.

The field of standardized testing is complex. Various types of standardized tests exist for various purposes. These include: achievement/readiness tests; developmental screening tests; diagnostic assessment tests; and intelligence tests (see definitions, page 45). The guidelines in this position statement apply to all forms of standardized testing, but primarily address the uses and abuses of achievement, readiness, and developmental screening tests.

Developmental screening tests are designed to indicate which children should proceed further to a multidisciplinary assessment, only after which a decision regarding special education placement can be made. School readiness tests are designed to assess a child's level of preparedness for a specific academic program (Meisels, 1987). As such, readiness tests should *not* be used to identify children potentially in need of special education services or for placement decisions (Meisels, 1986). Diagnostic assessments are designed to identify children with specific special needs, determine the nature of the problem, suggest the cause of the problem, and propose possible remediation strategies (Meisels, 1985). Intelligence tests are norm- or criterion-referenced measures of cognitive functioning (as defined by a specific criterion or construct) and are often used in diagnostic assessment. No single test can be used for all of these purposes, and rarely will a test be applicable to more than one or two of them. The uses and abuses of diagnostic assessments and intelligence tests have been well documented elsewhere and are beyond the scope of this position statement (Chase, 1977; Goodwin & Driscoll, 1980; Gould, 1981; Hilliard, 1975; Kamin, 1974; Oakland, 1977; Reynolds, 1984).

NAEYC acknowledges and endorses the *Standards for Educational and Psychological Testing* (1985) developed by a joint committee of the American Educational Research Association, American Psychological Association, and National Council on Measurement in Education. Standardized tests used in early childhood programs should comply with the joint committee's technical standards for test construction and evaluation, professional standards for use, and standards for administrative procedures. This means that no standardized test should be used for screening, diagnosis, or assessment unless the test has published statistically acceptable reliability and validity data. Moreover, test producers are strongly encouraged to present data concerning the proportion of at-risk children correctly identified (test sensitivity) and the proportion of those not at-risk who are correctly found to be without major problems (test specificity) (Meisels, 1984). NAEYC's position on standardized testing is intended not to duplicate, but to be used in conjunction with, the *Standards for Educational and Psychological Testing* (1985).

Statement of the Position

NAEYC believes that the most important consideration in evaluating and using standardized tests is the *utility criterion:* The purpose of testing must be to improve services for children and ensure that children benefit from their educational experiences. Decisions about testing and assessment instruments must be based on the usefulness of the assessment procedure for improving services to children and improving outcomes for children. The ritual use even of "good tests" (those that are judged to be valid and reliable measures) is to be discouraged in the absence of documented research showing that children benefit from their use.

Determining the utility of a given testing program is not easy. It requires thorough study of the potential effects, both positive and negative. For example, using a readiness or developmental test to admit children to kindergarten or first grade is often defended by teachers and administrators who point to the fact that the children who are kept back perform better the next year. Such intuitive reports overlook the fact that no comparative information is available about how the individual child would have fared had he or she been permitted to proceed with schooling. In addition, such pronouncements rarely address the possible effects of failure on the admission test on the child's self-esteem, the parents' perceptions, or the educational impact of labeling or mislabeling the child as being behind the peer group (Gredler, 1978; Shepard & Smith, 1986, in press; Smith & Shepard, 1987).

The following guidelines are intended to enhance the utility of standardized tests and guide early childhood professionals in making decisions about the appropriate use of testing.

1. All standardized tests used in early childhood programs must be reliable and valid according to the technical standards of test development (AERA, APA, & NCME, 1985).

Administrators making decisions about standardized testing must recognize that the younger the child, the more difficult it is to obtain reliable and valid results from standardized tests. For example, no available school readiness test (as contrasted to a developmental screening test) is accurate enough to screen children for placement into special programs without a 50% error rate (Shepard & Smith, 1986). Development in young children occurs rapidly; early childhood educators recognize the existence of general stages and sequence of development but also recognize that enormous individual variation occurs in patterns and timing of growth and development that is quite normal and not indicative of pathology. Therefore, the results obtained on a single administration of a test must be confirmed through periodic screening and assessment and corroborated by other sources of information to be considered reliable (Meisels, 1984).

2. Decisions that have a major impact on children such as enrollment, retention, or assignment to remedial or special classes should be based on multiple sources of information and should never be based on a single test score.

Appropriate sources of information *may* include combinations of the following:

- systematic observations, by teachers and other professionals, that are objective, carefully recorded, reliable (produce similar results over time and among different observers), and valid (produce accurate measures of carefully defined, mutually exclusive categories of observable behavior);
- samples of children's work such as drawings, paintings, dictated stories, writing samples, projects, and other activities (not limited to worksheets);

- observations and anecdotes related by parents and other family members; and
- test scores, if and only if appropriate, reliable, and valid tests have been used.

In practice, multiple measures are sometimes used in an attempt to find some supporting evidence for a decision that teachers or administrators are predisposed to make regarding a child's placement. Such practice is an inappropriate application of this guideline. To meet this guideline, the collected set of evidence obtained through multiple sources of information should meet validity standards.

3. It is the professional responsibility of administrators and teachers to critically evaluate, carefully select, and use standardized tests only for the purposes for which they are intended and for which data exists demonstrating the test's validity (the degree to which the test accurately measures what it purports to measure)

Unfortunately, readiness tests (based on age-related normative data) that are designed to measure the skills children have acquired compared to other children in their age range are sometimes used inappropriately. The intended purpose of such instruments is typically to provide teachers with information that will help them improve instruction, by informing them of what children already know and the skills they have acquired. In practice, however, teachers have been found to systematically administer such tests and then proceed to teach all children the same content using the same methods; for example, testing all kindergartners and then instructing the whole group using phonics workbooks (Durkin, 1987). The practice of making placement decisions about children on the basis of the results of readiness tests is becoming more common despite the absence of data that such tests are valid predictors of later achievement (Meisels, 1985, 1987).

4. It is the professional responsibility of administrators and teachers to be knowledgeable about testing and to interpret test results accurately and cautiously to parents, school personnel, and the media.

Accurate interpretation of test results is essential. It is the professional obligation of administrators and teachers to become informed about measurement issues, to use tests responsibly, to exert leadership within early childhood programs and school systems regarding the use of testing, to influence test developers to produce adequate tests and to substantiate claims made in support of tests, and to accurately report and interpret test results without making undue claims about their meaning or implications.

5. Selection of standardized tests to assess achievement and/or evaluate how well a program is meeting its goals should be based on how well a given test matches the locally determined theory, philosophy, and objectives of the specific program.

Standardized tests used in early childhood programs must have content validity; that is, they must accurately measure the content of the curriculum presented to children. If no existing test matches the curriculum, it is better not to use a standardized test or to develop an instrument to measure the program's objectives rather than to change an appropriate program to fit a pre-existing test. Too often the content of a standardized test unduly influences the content of the curriculum. If a test is used, the curriculum should determine its selection; the test should not dictate the content of the curriculum.

Another difficulty related to content validity in measures for young children is that many critically important content areas in early childhood programs such as developing self-esteem, social competence, creativity, or dispositions toward learning (Katz, 1985) are considered "unmeasurable" and are therefore omitted from tests. As a result, tests for young children often address the more easily measured, but no more important, aspects of development and learning.

6. Testing of young children must be conducted by individuals who are knowledgeable about and sensitive to the developmental needs of young children and who are qualified to administer tests.

Young children are not good test takers. The younger the child the more inappropriate paper-and-pencil, large group test administrations become. Standards for the administration of tests require that reasonable comfort be provided to the test taker (AERA, APA, & NCME, 1985). Such a standard must be broadly interpreted when applied to young children. Too often, standardized tests are administered to children in large groups, in unfamiliar environments, by strange people, perhaps during the first few days at a new school or under other stressful conditions. During such test administrations, children are asked to perform unfamiliar tasks, for no reason that they can understand. For test results to be valid, tests are best administered to children individually in familiar, comfortable circumstances by adults whom the child has come to know and trust and who are also qualified to administer the tests.

7. Testing of young children must recognize and be sensitive to individual diversity.

Test developers frequently ignore two important sources of variety in human experiences—cultural variations and variations in the quality of educational experiences provided for different children. It is easier to mass produce tests if one assumes that cultural differences are minimal or meaningless or if one assumes that test subjects are exposed to personal and educational opportunities of equally high quality. These assumptions permit attributing all variances or differences in test scores to differences in individual children's capacities. However, these assumptions are false.

Early childhood educators recognize that children's skills, abilities, and aptitudes are most apparent when they can be demonstrated in familiar cultural contexts. Because standardized tests must use particular cultural material, they may be inappropriate for assessing the skills, abilities, or aptitudes of children whose primary cultures differ from the mainstream. Language is the special feature of culture that creates the greatest problem for test developers. There are many language varieties in the United States, some of which are not apparent to the casual observer or test developer. Although having a common language is definitely desirable, useful, and a major goal of education, testing must be based on reality. For non-native English speakers or speakers of some dialects of English, any test administered in English is primarily a language or literacy test (AERA, APA, & NCME, 1985). Standardized tests should not be used in multicultural/multilingual communities if they are not sensitive to the effects of cultural diversity or bilingualism (Meisels, 1985). If testing is to be done, children should be tested in their native language.

Conclusion

NAEYC's position on standardized testing in early childhood programs restricts the use of tests to situations in which testing provides information that will clearly contribute to improved outcomes for children. Standardized tests have an important role to play in ensuring that children's achievement or special needs are objectively and accurately assessed and that appropriate instructional services are planned and implemented for individual children. However, standardized tests are only one of multiple sources of assessment information that should be used when decisions are made about what is best for young children. Tests may become a burden on the educational system, requiring considerable effort and expense to administer and yielding meager benefits. Given the scarcity of resources, the intrusiveness of testing, and the real potential for measurement error and/or bias, tests should be used only when it is clear that their use represents a meaningful contribution to the improvement of instruction for children and only as one of many sources of information. Rather than to use tests of doubtful validity, it is better not to test, because false labels that come from tests may cause educators or parents to alter inappropriately their treatment of children. The potential for misdiagnosing or mislabeling is particularly great with young children where there is wide variation in what may be considered normal behavior.

Administrators of early childhood programs who consider the use of standardized tests must ask themselves: How will children benefit from testing? Why is testing to be done? Does an appropriate test exist? What other sources of information can be used to make decisions about how best to provide services for an individual child? In answering such questions, administrators should apply the foregoing guidelines.

The burden of proof for the validity and realiability of tests is on the test developers and the advocates for their use. The burden of proof for the utility of tests is on administrators or teachers of early childhood programs who make decisions about the use of tests in individual classrooms. Similarly, the burden of responsibility for choosing, administering, scoring, and interpreting a score from a standardized test rests with the early childhood professional and thus demands that professionals be both skilled and responsible. Ensuring that tests meet scientific standards, reflect the most current scientific knowledge, and are used appropriately requires constant vigilance on the part of educators.

▣ Definitions

Achievement test—a test that measures the extent to which a person has mastery over a certain body of information or possesses a certain skill after instruction has taken place.

Criterion—an indicator of the accepted value of outcome performance or a standard against which a measure is evaluated.

Criterion-referenced—a test for which interpretation of scores is made in relation to a specified performance level, as distinguished from interpretations that compare the test taker's score to the performance of other people (i.e., norm-referenced).

Developmental test—an age-related norm-referenced assessment of skills and behaviors that children have acquired (compared to children of the same chronological age). Sometimes such tests are inaccurately called developmental screening tests.

Diagnostic assessment—identification of a child who has special needs, usually conducted by a multidisciplinary team of professionals; used to identify a child's specific areas of strength and weakness, determine the nature of the problems, and suggest the cause of the problems and possible remediation strategies.

Early childhood—birth through age 8.

Intelligence test—a series of tasks yielding a score indicative of cognitive functioning. Tasks typically require problem solving and/or various intellectual operations such as conceiving, thinking, and reasoning, or they reflect an earlier use of such intellectual functions (e.g., in information questions). Standardized by finding the average performance of individuals who by independent criteria (i.e., other intelligence tests) are of known degrees or levels of intelligence.

Norms—statistics or data that summarize the test performance of specified groups such as test takers of various ages or grades.

Norm-referenced—a test for which interpretation of scores is based on comparing the test taker's performance to the performance of other people in a specified group.

Readiness test—assessment of child's level of preparedness for a specific academic or preacademic program. (See also achievement test and developmental test.)

Reliability—the degree to which test scores are consistent, dependable, or repeatable; that is, the degree to which test scores can be attributed to actual differences in test takers' performance rather than to errors of measurement.

Score—any specific number resulting from the assessment of an individual.

Screening test (also called *developmental screening test*)—a test used to identify children who *may* be in need of special services, as a first step in identifying children in need of further diagnosis; focuses on the child's ability to acquire skills.

Standardized test—an instrument composed of empirically selected items that has definite instructions for use, adequately determined norms, and data on reliability and validity.

Testing—the administration, scoring, and interpretation of scores of a standardized test.

Utility—the relative value or usefulness of an outcome as compared to other possible outcomes.

Validity—the degree to which a test measures what it purports to measure; the degree to which a certain inference from a test is appropriate or meaningful.

    Content validity—evidence that shows the extent to which the content of a test is appropriately related to its intended purpose. For

achievement tests, *content* refers to the content of the curriculum, the actual instruction, or the objectives of the instruction.
Criterion-related validity—evidence that demonstrates that test scores are systematically related to one or more outcome criteria.
Predictive validity—evidence of criterion-related validity in which scores on the criterion are observed at a later date; for example, the score on a test with predictive validity will predict future school performance.

◉ Selected Resources

Cohen, R. (1969). Conceptual styles, culture conflict, and non-verbal tests of intelligence. *American Anthropologist, 71*(5), 828–857.

Cole, M., & Scribner, S. (1974). *Culture and thought: A psychological introduction.* New York: Wiley.

Heath, S. (1983). *Ways with words: Language, life and work in communities and classrooms.* Cambridge, England: Cambridge University Press.

Heller, K. A., Holtzman, W. H., & Messick, S. (Eds.). (1982). *Placing children in special education: A strategy for equity.* Washington, DC: National Academy Press.

◉ References

American Educational Research Association, American Psychological Association, and National Council on Measurement in Education. (1985). *Standards for educational and psychological testing.* Washington, DC: Author.

Bredekamp, S. (Ed.). (1987). *Developmentally appropriate practice in early childhood programs serving children from birth through age 8* (exp. ed.). Washington, DC: NAEYC.

Chase, A. (1977). *The legacy of Malthus: The social cost of scientific racism.* New York: Knopf.

Durkin, D. (1987). Testing in the kindergarten. *The Reading Teacher, 40*(8), 766–770.

Farr, R., & Carey, R. (1986). *Reading: What can be measured?* Newark, DE: International Reading Association.

Goodwin, W., & Driscoll, L. (1980). *Handbook for measurement and evaluation in early childhood education.* San Francisco: Jossey-Bass.

Gould, S. (1981). *The mismeasure of man.* New York: Norton.

Gredler, G. (1978). A look at some important factors for assessing readiness for school. *Journal of Learning Disabilities, 11,* 284–290.

Gredler, G. (1984). Transition classes: A viable alternative for the at-risk child? *Psychology in the Schools, 21,* 463–470.

Hilliard, A. (1975). The strengths and weaknesses of cognitive tests of young children. In J. D. Andrews (Ed.), *One child indivisible.* Washington, DC: NAEYC.

Kamii, C. (1985a). Leading primary education toward excellence: Beyond worksheets and drill. *Young Children, 40*(6), 3–9.

Kamii, C. (1985b). *Young children reinvent arithmetic.* New York: Teachers College Press, Columbia University.

Kamin, L. (1974). *The science and politics of IQ.* New York: Wiley.

Katz, L. (1985). Dispositions in early childhood education. *ERIC/EECE Bulletin, 18*(2), 1, 3.

Katz, L., Raths, J., & Torres, R. (undated). *A place called kindergarten.* Urbana, IL: ERIC Clearinghouse on Elementary and Early Childhood Education.

Meisels, S. J. (1984). Prediction, prevention, and developmental screening in the EPSDT program. In H. W. Stevenson & A. G. Siegel (Eds.), *Child development research and social policy.* Chicago: University of Chicago Press.

Meisels, S. J. (1985). *Developmental screening in early childhood: A guide.* Washington, DC: NAEYC.

Meisels, S. J. (1986). Testing four- and five-year-olds. *Educational Leadership, 44,* 90–92.

Meisels, S. J. (1987). Uses and abuses of developmental screening and school readiness testing. *Young Children, 42*(2), 4–6, 68–73.

National Center for Fair and Open Testing. (1987, Fall). North Carolina legislature drops exams for 1st, 2nd graders. *Fair Test Examiner,* p. 3.

Oakland, T. (Ed.). (1977). *Psychological and educational assessment of minority children.* New York: Brunner/Mazel.

Reynolds, C. (Ed.). (1984). *Perspectives on bias in mental testing.* New York: Plenum.

Shepard, L., & Smith, M. (1986). Synthesis of research on school readiness and kindergarten retention. *Educational Leadership, 44*(3), 78–86.

Shepard, L., & Smith, M. (1987). Effects of kindergarten retention at the end of first grade. *Psychology in the Schools, 24,* 346–357.

Shepard, L., & Smith, M. (in press). Escalating academic demand in kindergarten: Some nonsolutions. *Elementary School Journal.*

Smith, M., & Shepard, L. (1987). What doesn't work: Explaining policies of retention in the early grades. *Educational Leadership, 45*(2), 129–134.

Teale, W., Hiebert, E., & Chittenden, E. (1987). Assessing young children's literacy development. *The Reading Teacher, 40,* 772–776.

Valencia, S., & Pearson, P. (1987). Reading assessment: Time for a change. *The Reading Teacher, 40,* 726–732.

Appendix E

"Why Rabbits Have Long Ears"

Do you think this story about why rabbits have long ears is true? Why? Why not?

Why Rabbits Have Long Ears

by Valery Carrick

Long ago there was a rabbit who made friends with a sheep.
The sheep and the rabbit played together.
They did everything together.
The sheep and the rabbit were very good friends.

One day the sheep said,
"Let's build a house!"

"Yes!" said the rabbit.
"Let's build a house."

So they went into the forest to get
some logs to build a house.
The sheep saw a tall tree.

"I can push this tree down!"
said the sheep.

"You cannot!" said the rabbit.

"Oh, yes I can," said the sheep.
"I'll show you!"

SOURCE: From Valery Carrick, *HBJ Reading Program—Smiles, Pupil Edition* by Margaret Early *et al.*
Copyright © 1987 by Harcourt Brace Jovanovich, Inc. Reprinted by permission of the publisher.

The sheep took a long run.
He hit the tree with his head.
The tree crashed down!
"You did it!" said the rabbit.
"Now I know how to push
down a tree, too."

Soon they saw another tall tree.
"I bet I can make that tree
come crashing down!" said
the rabbit.

"You cannot!" said the sheep.

"Oh, yes I can," said the rabbit.
"I'll show you!"

The rabbit took a long run.
He hit the tree so hard that his
head went into his shoulders.
The tree did not come crashing down.

"Rabbit! Your head went into your
shoulders!" said the sheep.
"I will help you."

The sheep put the rabbit's short
ears into his mouth and started to pull.

He pulled as hard as he could.

"Stop! Stop pulling my short ears!" the rabbit shouted.

But the sheep went on pulling.
At last the rabbit's head came out of his shoulders.

"You just about pulled my ears out of my head!" said the rabbit.

"Look! Look what you did to my short ears.

Now they are very long."

"Yes, your ears are very long," laughed the sheep.

So now you know why rabbits have long ears!

Discuss the Selection

1. Do you think this story about why rabbits have long ears is true? Why?

2. Why did the rabbit's head go down into his shoulders?

3. What made you laugh in this story?

4. When was the first time in the story that you knew that the rabbit would have long ears?

5. Which character in the story did you like best? Tell why.

Appendix F

Patterned Books

Aardema, V. *Bringing the Rain to Kapiti Plain.* New York: Dial Press, 1981.

Adams, P. *This Old Man.* New York: Grossett & Dunlap, 1974.

Alain. *One, Two, Three, Going to Sea.* New York: Scholastic, 1964.

Aliki. *Go Tell Aunt Rhody.* New York: Macmillan, 1974.

Aliki. *Hush Little Baby.* Englewood Cliffs, N.J.: Prentice-Hall, 1968.

Asch, F. *Monkey Face.* New York: Parents' Magazine Press, 1977.

Balian, L. *The Animal.* Nashville: Abingdon Press, 1972.

Balian, L. *Where in the World Is Henry?* Scarsdale, N.Y.: Bradbury Press, 1972.

Barohas, S. *I Was Walking Down the Road.* New York: Scholastic, 1975.

Barrett, J. *Animals Should Definitely Not Wear Clothing.* New York: Atheneum, 1970.

Baum, A., and Baum, J. *One Bright Monday Morning.* New York: Random House, 1962.

Becker, J. *Seven Little Rabbits.* New York: Scholastic, 1973.

Beckman, K. *Lisa Cannot Sleep.* New York: Franklin Watts, 1969.

Bellah, M. *A First Book of Sounds.* Racine: Gordon Press, 1961.

Bonne, R., and Mills, A. *I Know an Old Lady.* New York: Rand McNally, 1961.

Brand, O. *When I First Came to This Land.* New York: Putnam's Sons, 1974.

Brandenburg, F. *I Once Knew a Man.* New York: Macmillan, 1970.

Brown, M. *The Three Billy Goats Gruff.* New York: Harcourt Brace Jovanovich, 1957.

Brown, M. W. *Four Fur Feet.* New York: William R. Scott, 1961.

Brown, M. W. *Goodnight, Moon.* New York: Harper & Row, 1947.

Brown, M. W. *Home for a Bunny.* Racine: Golden Press, 1956.

Brown, M. W. *The Important Book.* New York: Harper & Row, 1949.

Brown, M. W. *The Runaway Bunny.* New York: Harper & Row, 1972.

Brown, R. *A Dark, Dark Tale.* New York: Dial Press, 1981.

Bunting, E. *Scary, Scary Halloween.* New York: Clarion Books, 1986.

Burningham, J. *Would You Rather?* London: William Collins Sons, 1984.

Cameron, P. *I Can't Said the Ant.* New York: McCann, 1961.

Carle, E. *The Grouchy Ladybug.* New York: Thomas Y. Crowell, 1977.

Carle, E. *Have You Seen My Cat?* New York: Franklin Watts, 1973.

Carle, E. *The Mixed Up Chameleon.* New York: Thomas Y. Crowell, 1975.

Carle, E. *The Very Hungry Caterpillar.* Cleveland: Collins World, 1969.

Charlip, R. *Fortunately.* New York: Parents' Magazine Press, 1964.

Charlip, R. *What Good Luck! What Bad Luck!* New York: Scholastic, 1969.

Cook, B. *The Little Fish That Got Away.* Reading, Mass.: Addison-Wesley, 1976.

de Regniers, B. *Catch a Little Fox.* New York: Seabury Press, 1970.

de Regniers, B. *The Day Everybody Cried.* New York: Viking Press, 1967.

de Regniers, B. *How Joe the Mouse and Sam the Bear Got Together.* New York: Parents' Magazine Press, 1965.

de Regniers, B. *The Little Book*. New York: Henry Z. Walck, 1961.

de Regniers, B. *May I Bring a Friend?* New York: Atheneum, 1972.

de Regniers, B. *Willy O'Dwyer Jumped in the Fire*. New York: Atheneum, 1968.

Domanska, J. *If All the Seas Were One Sea*. New York: Macmillan, 1971.

Duff, M. *Jonny and His Drum*. New York: Henry Z. Walck, 1972.

Duff, M. *Rum Pum Pum*. New York: Macmillan, 1978.

Emberley, B. *Drummer Hoff*. Englewood Cliffs, N.J.: Prentice-Hall, 1967.

Emberley, B. *Simon's Song*. Englewood Cliffs, N.J.: Prentice-Hall, 1969.

Emberley, E. *Klippity Klop*. Boston: Little, Brown, 1974.

Ets, M. *Elephant in the Well*. New York: Viking Press, 1955.

Ets, M. *Play with Me*. New York: Viking Press, 1955.

Flack, M. *Ask Mr. Bear*. New York: Macmillan, 1932.

Galdone, P. *Henny Penny*. New York: Scholastic, 1968.

Galdone, P. *The Little Red Hen*. New York: Scholastic, 1973.

Galdone, P. *The Old Woman and Her Pig*. New York: McGraw-Hill, 1961.

Galdone, P. *The Three Bears*. New York: Scholastic, 1972.

Galdone, P. *The Three Billy Goats Gruff*. New York: Seabury Press, 1973.

Galdone, P. *The Three Little Pigs*. New York: Seabury Press, 1970.

Ginsburg, M. *The Chick and the Duckling*. New York: Macmillan, 1972.

Greenberg, P. *Oh Lord, I Wish I Was a Buzzard*. New York: Macmillan, 1968.

Hoberman, A. *A House Is a House for Me*. New York: Puffin Books, 1982.

Hoffman, H. *The Green Grass Grows All Around*. New York: Macmillan, 1968.

Hutchins, P. *Good-Night, Owl*. New York: Macmillan, 1972.

Hutchins, P. *Rosie's Walk*. New York: Macmillan, 1968.

Hutchins, P. *Titch*. New York: Collier Books, 1971.

Kafka, S. *I Need a Friend*. New York: Putnam's, 1971.

Keats, E. *Over in the Meadow*. New York: Scholastic, 1971.

Kent, J. *The Fat Cat*. New York: Scholastic, 1971.

Klein, L. *Brave Daniel*. New York: Scholastic, 1958.

Krauss, Robert. *Big Brother*. New York: Parents' Magazine Press, 1973.

Krauss, Robert. *Whose Mouse Are You?* New York: Collier Books, 1970.

Krauss, Ruth. *Bears*. New York: Harper & Row, 1948.

Langstaff, J. *Frog Went A-Courtin'*. New York: Harcourt Brace Jovanovich, 1955.

Langstaff, J. *Gather My Gold Together: Four Songs for Four Seasons*. Garden City, N.Y.: Doubleday, 1971.

Langstaff, J. *Oh, A-Hunting We Will Go*. New York: Atheneum, 1974.

Langstaff, J. *Over in the Meadow*. New York: Harcourt Brace Jovanovich, 1957.

Larrick, N., compiler. *The Wheels of the Bus Go Round and Round*. San Carlos, Calif.: Golden Gate Jr. Books, 1972.

Laurence, E. *We're Off to Catch a Dragon*. Nashville: Abingdon Press, 1969.

Lear, E. *Whizz: Six Limericks*. New York: Macmillan, 1973.

Lexau, J. *Crocodile and Hen*. New York: Harper & Row, 1969.

Lobel, Anita. *King Rooster, Queen Hen*. New York: Greenwillow, 1975.

Lobel, Arnold. *A Treeful of Pigs*. New York: Greenwillow, 1979.

Lobel, Arnold. *The Rose in My Garden*. New York: Greenwillow, 1984.

MacDonald, G. *Whistle for the Train*. Garden City, N.Y.: Doubleday, 1956.

Mack, S. *Ten Bears in My Bed*. New York: Holt, Rinehart & Winston, 1970.

Mack, S. *Where's My Cheese?* New York: Pantheon Books, 1977.

Mandoza, G. *A Beastly Alphabet.* New York: Grosset & Dunlap, 1969.

Martin, B. *Brown Bear, Brown Bear, What Do You See?* Holt, Rinehart & Winston, 1970.

Martin, B. *Fire! Fire! Said Mrs. McGuire.* New York: Holt, Rinehart & Winston, 1970.

Mayer, M. *If I Had. . . .* New York: Dial Press, 1968.

Mayer, M. *Just for You.* New York: Golden Press, 1975.

McGovern, A. *Too Much Noise.* New York: Scholastic, 1967.

Memling, C. *Ten Little Animals.* Racine: Golden Press, 1961.

Moffett, M. *A Flower Pot Is Not a Hat.* New York: Dutton, 1972.

Morrison, B. *Squeeze a Sneeze.* Boston: Houghton Mifflin, 1977.

Patrick, G. *This Is. . . .* Minneapolis: Carolrhoda, 1970.

Peppe, R. *The House That Jack Built.* New York: Delacorte, 1970.

Polushkin, M. *Mother, Mother, I Want Another.* New York: Crown, 1978.

Preston, E. *One Dark Night.* New York: Penguin Books, 1972.

Preston, E. *Where Did My Mother Go?* New York: Four Winds Press, 1978.

Quackenbush, R. *She'll Be Comin' Round the Mountain.* Philadelphia: Lippincott, 1973.

Quackenbush, R. *Skip to My Lou.* Philadelphia: Lippincott, 1975.

Rokoff, S. *Here Is a Cat.* Singapore: Hallmark Children's Editions, no date.

Rossetti, C. *What Is Pink?* New York: Macmillan, 1971.

Scheer, J., and Bileck, M. *Rain Makes Applesauce.* New York: Holiday House, 1964.

Scheer, J., and Bileck, M. *Upside Down Day.* New York: Holiday House, 1968.

Sendak, M. *Chicken Soup with Rice.* New York: Scholastic, 1962.

Shaw, C. *It Looked Like Spilt Milk.* New York: Harper & Row, 1947.

Shulevitz, U. *One Monday Morning.* New York: Scribner's, 1967.

Simon, N. *I Know What I Like.* Chicago: Whitmand & Co., 1971.

Skaar, G. *What Do the Animals Say?* New York: Scholastic, 1972.

Sonneborn, R. *Someone Is Eating the Sun.* New York: Random House, 1974.

Spier, P. *The Fox Went Out on a Chilly Night.* Garden City, N.Y.: Doubleday, 1961.

Stover, J. *If Everybody Did.* New York: David McKay, 1960.

Sutton, E. *My Cat Likes to Hide in Boxes.* New York: Scholastic Books, 1973.

Taback, S. *Joseph Had a Little Overcoat.* New York: Random House, 1977.

Tolstoy, A. *The Great Big Enormous Turnip.* New York: Franklin Watts, 1972.

Waber, B. *Nobody is Perfick.* Boston: Houghton Mifflin, 1971.

Welber, R. *Goodbye, Hello.* New York: Pantheon, 1974.

Welber, R. *Song of the Seasons.* New York: Pantheon Books, 1973.

Wildsmith, B. *The Twelve Days of Christmas.* New York: Franklin Watts, 1972.

Williams, G. *The Chicken Book.* New York: Delacorte, 1970.

Appendix G

Forty-Five Phonic Generalizations

Generalization (*example*)	Primary (Clymer)	Grades 1–6 (Bailey)	Grades 4–6 (Emans)
	Percentage of utility		
1. When there are two vowels side by side, the long sound of the first vowel is heard and the second vowel is usually silent. (*leader*)	45	34	18
2. When a vowel is in the middle of a one-syllable word, the vowel is short. (*bed*)	62	71	73
3. If the only vowel letter is at the end of a word, the letter usually stands for a long sound. (*go*)	100	100	100
4. When there are two vowels, one of which is final *e*, the first vowel is long and the *e* is silent. (*cradle*)	63	57	63
5. The *r* gives the preceding vowel a sound that is neither long nor short. (*part*)	78	86	82
6. The first vowel is usually long and the second silent in the digraphs *ai, ea, oa,* and *ui*. (*claim, bean, roam, suit*)	66	60	58
ai		71	
ea		56	
oa		95	
ee		87	
ui		10	
7. In the phonogram *ie*, the *i* is silent and the *e* is long. (*grieve*)	17	31	23
8. Words having double *e* usually have the long *e* sound. (*meet*)	98	87	100
9. When words end with silent *e*, the preceding *a* or *i* is long. (*amaze*)	60	50	48
10. In *ay*, the *y* is silent and gives its *a* long sound. (*spray*)	78	88	100
11. When the letter *i* is followed by the letters *gh*, the *i* usually stands for its long sound and the *gh* is silent. (*light*)	71	71	100

Generalization (example)	Percentage of utility		
	Primary (Clymer)	Grades 1–6 (Bailey)	Grades 4–6 (Emans)
12. When *a* follows *w* in a word, it usually has the sound *a* as in *was*. (*wand*)	32	22	28
13. When *e* is followed by *w*, the vowel sound is the same as represented by *oo*. (*shrewd*)	35	40	14
14. The two letters *ow* make the long *o* sound. (*row*)	59	55	50
15. *W* is sometimes a vowel and follows the vowel digraph rule. (*arrow*)	40	33	31
16. When *y* is the final letter in a word, it usually has a vowel sound. (*lady*)	84	89	98
17. When *y* is used as a vowel in words, it sometimes has the sound of long *i*. (*ally*)	15	11	4
18. The letter *a* has the same sound (*o*) when followed by *l*, *w*, and *u*. (*raw*)	48	34	24
19. When *a* is followed by *r* and final *e*, we expect to hear the sound heard in *care*. (*flare*)	90	96	100
20. When *c* and *h* are next to each other, they make only one sound. (*charge*)	100	100	100
21. *Ch* is usually pronounced as it is in *kitchen*, *catch*, and *chair*.	95	87	67
22. When *c* is followed by *e* or *i*, the sound of *s* is likely to be heard. (*glance*)	96	92	90
23. When the letter *c* is followed by *o* or *a*, the sound of *k* is likely to be heard. (*canal*)	100	100	100
24. The letter *g* is often sounded similar to the *j* in *jump* when it precedes the letter *i* or *e*. (*gem*)	100	100	100
25. When *ght* is seen in a word, *gh* is silent. (*tight*)	100	100	100
26. When the word begins with *kn*, the *k* is silent. (*knit*)	100	100	100
27. When a word begins with *wr*, the *w* is silent. (*wrap*)	100	100	100
28. When two of the same consonants are side by side, only one is heard. (*dollar*)	100	100	100
29. When a word ends in *ck*, it has the same last sound as in *look*. (*neck*)	100	100	100
30. In most two-syllable words, the first syllable is accented. (*bottom*)	85	81	75
31. If *a*, *in*, *re*, *ex*, *de*, or *be* is the first syllable in a word, it is usually unaccented. (*reply*)	87	84	83

Generalization (*example*)	Percentage of utility		
	Primary (Clymer)	Grades 1–6 (Bailey)	Grades 4–6 (Emans)
32. In most two-syllable words that end in a consonant followed by *y*, the first syllable is accented and the last is unaccented. (*highly*)	96	97	100
33. One vowel letter in an accented syllable has a short sound. (*banish*)	61	65	64
34. When *y* or *ey* is seen in the last syllable that is not accented, the long sound of *e* is heard. (*turkey*)	0	0	1
35. When *ture* is the final syllable in a word, it is unaccented. (*future*)	100	100	100
36. When *tion* is the final syllable in a word, it is unaccented. (*nation*)	100	100	100
37. In many two- and three-syllable words, the final *e* lengthens the vowel in the last syllable. (*costume*)	46	46	42
38. If the first vowel sound in a word is followed by two consonants, the first syllable usually ends with the first of the two consonants. (*dinner*)	72	78	80
39. If the first vowel sound in a word is followed by a single consonant, that consonant usually begins the second syllable. (*china*)	57	48	37
40. If the last syllable of a word ends in *le*, the consonant preceding the *le* usually begins the last syllable. (*gable*)	97	93	78
41. When the first vowel element in a word is followed by *th*, *ch*, or *sh*, these symbols are not broken when the word is divided into syllables and may go with either the first or second syllable. (*fashion*)	100	100	100
42. In a word of more than one syllable, the letter *v* usually goes with the preceding vowel to form a syllable. (*travel*)	73	65	40
43. When a word has only one vowel letter, the vowel sound is likely to be short. (*crib*)	57	69	70
44. When there is one *e* in a word that ends in a consonant, the *e* usually has a short sound. (*held*)	75	92	83
45. When the last syllable is the sound *r*, it is unaccented. (*ever*)	95	79	96

Appendix H

Picture Song Books

Abisch, R. and Kaplan, B. *Sweet Betsy from Pike.* New York: McCall, 1970.

Adams, P., illus. *There Was an Old Lady Who Swallowed a Fly.* New York: Grosset & Dunlap, 1975.

Adams, P., illus. *This Old Man.* New York: Grosset & Dunlap, 1975.

Aliki. *Go Tell Aunt Rhody.* New York: Macmillan, 1974.

Aliki. *Hush Little Baby.* Englewood Cliffs, N.J.: Prentice-Hall, 1974.

Bangs, E. *Steven Kellogg's Yankee Doodle.* Illustrated by S. Kellogg. New York: Parent's Magazine Press, 1976.

Bonne, R. *I Know an Old Lady.* New York: Rand McNally, 1976.

Brand, O. *When I First Came to This Land.* Illustrated by D. Burn. New York: McGraw-Hill, 1965.

Broomfield, R., illus. *The Twelve Days of Christmas.* New York: McGraw-Hill, 1965.

Chase, R. *Billy Boy.* Illustrated by G. Rounds. Chicago: Golden Gate, 1966.

Child, L. *Over the River and through the Wood.* Illustrated by B. Turkle. New York: Coward, McCann and Geoghegan, 1974. Paperback: Scholastic Book Services, 1975.

Conover, C., illus. *Six Little Ducks.* New York: T. Crowell, 1976.

de Regniers, B. S. *Catch a Little Fox.* Illustrated by B. Turkle. New York: Seabury Press, 1970.

Emberley, B. *One Wide River to Cross.* Illustrated by E. Emberley. Englewood Cliffs, N.J.: Prentice-Hall, 1966.

Emberley, E., illus. *London Bridge Is Falling Down.* Boston: Little, Brown, 1967.

Freschet, B. *The Ants Go Marching.* Illustrated by S. Martin. New York: Scribner's, 1973.

Galdone, R., illus. *The Star Spangled Banner.* New York: Thomas Y. Crowell, 1966.

Glazer, Tom. *On Top of Spaghetti.* Garden City, New York: Doubleday, 1982.

Goudge, E. *I Saw Three Ships.* Illustrated by M. Tomes. New York: Coward McCann, 1969.

Graboff, A., illus. *Old MacDonald Had a Farm.* New York: Scholastic Book Services, 1973.

Green, C. *The Thirteen Days of Halloween.* Children's Press, 1983.

Hazen, B. *Frere Jacques.* Illustrated by L. Obligado. New York: Lippincott, 1973.

Ipcar, D., illus. *The Cat Came Back.* New York: Knopf, 1971.

Johnson, J. W., and Johnson, J. R. *Lift Every Voice and Sing.* Illustrated by M. Thompson. New York: Hawthorn Books, 1970.

Karasz, T., illus. *The Twelve Days of Christmas.* New York: Harper & Row, 1949.

Keats, E. J., illus. *The Little Drummer Boy.* Words and music by K. Davis, H. Onorati, and H. Simeone. New York: Macmillan Paperback, 1972.

Keats, E. J., illus. *Over in the Meadow*. Words by O. A. Wadsworth. New York: Scholastic Book Services, 1972.

Keller, L. *Glory, Glory, How Peculiar*. Englewood Cliffs, N.J.: Prentice-Hall, 1976.

Kellogg, S., illus. *There Was an Old Woman*. New York: Parent's Magazine Press, 1974.

Kent, J., illus. *Jack Kent's Twelve Days of Christmas*. New York: Scholastic Book Services, 1973.

Knight, Hilary. *Hilary Knight's The Twelve Days of Christmas*. New York: Macmillan, 1981.

Langstaff, J. *Frog Went A-Courtin'*. Illustrated by F. Rojankovsky. New York: Harcourt Brace Jovanovich, 1955. Paperback: Scholastic Book Services, 1973.

Langstaff, J. *Oh, A-Hunting We Will Go*. Illustrated by N. W. Parker. New York: Atheneum, 1974.

Langstaff, J. *Ol' Dan Tucker*. Illustrated by J. Krush. New York: Harcourt Brace Jovanovich, 1963.

Langstaff, J. *Over in the Meadow*. Illustrated by F. Rojankovsky. New York: Harcourt Brace Jovanovich, 1957. Harcourt Paperback, 1973.

Langstaff, J. *The Swapping Boy*. Illustrated by B. Krush and J. Krush. New York: Harcourt Brace Jovanovich, 1960.

Miles, A. *Over the Rolling Sea*. New York: Scholastic, 1977.

Nic Leodhas, S. *Always Room for One More*. Illustrated by N. Hogrogian. New York: Holt, Rinehart & Winston, 1965. Owlet Paperback, 1965.

Nic Leodhas, S. *Kellyburn Braes*. Illustrated by E. Ness. New York: Holt, Rinehart & Winston, 1968.

Parker, R., illus. *Sweet Betsy from Pike*. New York: Viking, 1978.

Paterson, A. B., illus. *Waltzing Matilda*. New York: Holt, Rinehart & Winston, 1972.

Peek, M. *Mary Wore Her Red Dress and Henry Wore His Green Sneakers*. New York: Clarion Books, 1985.

Peek, M. *Roll Over. A Counting Song*. New York: Houghton Mifflin, 1981.

Quackenbush, R. *Clementine*. New York: Lippincott, 1974.

Quackenbush, R. *Go Tell Aunt Rhody*. New York: Lippincott, 1973.

Quackenbush, R. *Old MacDonald Had a Farm*. New York: Lippincott, 1972.

Quackenbush, R. *Pop Goes the Weasel and Yankee Doodle*. New York: Lippincott, 1976.

Quackenbush, R. *She'll Be Comin' Round the Mountain*. New York: Lippincott, 1973.

Quackenbush, R. *Skip to My Lou*. New York: Lippincott, 1975.

Quackenbush, R. *The Man on the Flying Trapeze*. New York: Lippincott, 1975.

Quackenbush, R. *There'll Be a Hot Time in the Old Town Tonight*. New York: Lippincott, 1974.

Rounds, G., illus. *Casey Jones*. Chicago: Golden Gate/Children's Press, 1968.

Rounds, G., illus. *The Strawberry Roan*. Chicago: Golden Gate, 1970.

Rounds, G., illus. *Sweet Betsy from Pike*. Chicago: Children's Press, 1973.

Rourke, C. *Davy Crockett*. Illustrated by J. McDonald. New York: Harcourt Brace Jovanovich, 1955.

Sanders, S. *Hear the Wind Blow*. Bradbury, 1985.

Sawyer, R. *Joy to the World.* Illustrated by T. S. Hyman. Boston: Little, Brown, 1966.

Schackburg, R. *Yankee Doodle.* Illustrated by E. Emberley. Englewood Cliffs, N.J.: Prentice-Hall, 1965.

Seeger, P., and Seeger, C. *The Foolish Frog.* Illustrated by M. Jage. New York: Macmillan, 1973.

Spier, P., illus. *The Erie Canal.* Garden City, N.Y.: Doubleday, 1970. Paperback: Zepher, 1970.

Spier, P., illus. *The Fox Went Out on a Chilly Night.* Music by B. Ives. Garden City, N.Y.: Doubleday, 1961. Paperback: Zepher, 1961.

Spier, P., illus. *London Bridge Is Falling Down!* Garden City, N.Y.: Doubleday, 1967. Paperback: Doubleday, 1985.

Spier, P., illus. *The Star Spangled Banner.* Garden City, N.Y.: Doubleday, 1973.

Watson, W. *Fisherman Lullabies.* Music by S. Watson. Cleveland: World Publishing Company, 1968.

Wildsmith, B. *Twelve Days of Christmas.* Franklin Watts, 1972.

Yulya. *Bears Are Sleeping.* Illustrated by N. Hogrogian. New York: Scribner's, 1967.

Zemach, M., illus. *Hush Little Baby.* New York: Dutton, 1976.

Zemach, H. *Mommy Buy Me a China Doll.* Illustrated by M. Zemach. New York: Farrar, Straus & Giroux, 1975.

Zuromskis, D., illus. *The Farmer in the Dell.* Boston: Little, Brown, 1978.

Index